THE *DIANSHIZHAI PICTORIAL*

點石齋畫報

問淳館主人署

THE *DIANSHIZHAI PICTORIAL*

Shanghai Urban Life, 1884–1898

Ye Xiaoqing

Center for Chinese Studies
The University of Michigan
Ann Arbor

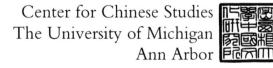

MICHIGAN MONOGRAPHS IN CHINESE STUDIES
ISSN 1081-9053
SERIES ESTABLISHED 1968
VOLUME 98

Published by
Center for Chinese Studies
The University of Michigan
Ann Arbor, Michigan 48104-1608

© 2003 The Regents of the University of Michigan
All rights reserved

Library of Congress Cataloging-in-Publication Data

Ye, Xiaoqing
    The Dianshizhai Pictorial : Shanghai urban life, 1884-1898 / Ye Xiaoqing.
      p. cm. − (Michigan monographs in Chinese studies ; 98)
    Includes bibliographical references and index.
    ISBN 0-89264-162-2 (alk. paper)
    1. Illustrated periodicals—China. 2. China—History—Guangxu, 1875-1908—Pictorial works. 3. Shanghai (China)—Social life and customs—Pictorial works. I. Title: Shanghai urban life, 1884-1898. II. Title. III. Series.

PN5367.P4 Y4 2003
951'.132035'0222—dc21

2002074134

To the memory of my parents

CONTENTS

Acknowledgments *viii*

Introduction *1*

Part One: A Brief History of the *Dianshizhai Pictorial*
  1. The *Shenbao* and the *Dianshizhai* *4*
  2. The Shanghai literati *12*
  3. The nature of the *Dianshizhai* *20*

Part Two: Shanghai: Old City, New City
  1. Roads and transportation *43*
  2. Water supply and hygiene *47*
  3. Gas and electricity for public lighting *53*
  4. Urban life in the settlements *57*
  5. Immigrants to Shanghai *76*
  6. Conflicting legal systems *85*
  7. Law enforcements in the settlements *98*

Part Three: A New Urban Culture
  1. The Shanghai attitude towards things foreign *117*
  2. Concepts of health and the human body *132*
  3. Changes in the pattern of human relations *145*
  4. Relations between the sexes *153*
  5. Challenges to the traditional social order *161*
  6. Vagrants and criminals *165*

Part Four: Religious Practices
  1. Official attitudes *188*
  2. Attitude of the literati *194*
  3. Organizers of religious activities *197*
  4. Social environment and its effect *205*

Afterword *225*

Key to Illustrations *227*
Bibliography *230*
Index *246*

Acknowledgments

When sitting down to write these lines, again I had the opportunity to reflect on the kindness and support of a large number of people over the years. Here I can only mention those directly connected with the formation of this book.

I became fascinated with China's past as a result of the Cultural Revolution, when I was living in a small village in Anhui. I did not imagine fate would lead to the study of Chinese history becoming my 'career.' After nine years in the village, I returned to Shanghai, and began publishing in academic journals. At that time, Shen Yixing and Tang Zhenchang headed the Institute of History in the Shanghai Academy of Social Sciences, and appointed me to a full-time research position, battling tirelessly with the bureaucracy to do so. Shortly after I joined the Institute, I was offered a scholarship to study for my doctorate at the Australian National University. My supervisor, Lo Hui-min, and his family, in particular Helen and Ping, gave me the greatest help and support in adjusting to life in Australia. That was all more than a decade ago. Shen Yixing and Tang Zhenchang have passed away, and Lo Hui-min is seriously ill. I am deeply indebted to them, and it saddens me that I was never able to express my gratitude properly.

During my studies in Australia, I enjoyed the friendship, support and intellectual inspiration of many fellow historians: Warren Sun, Brian Martin, Esta Unger, Terry Narramore, Brian Moloughney, Tim Wright, John Fitzgerald, Antonia Finnane, Gloria Davies, Linda Jaivin, Christian Henriot, Bryna Goodman and Geremie Barmé. Bill Jenner, Mark Elvin, Harold Kahn, Frederic Wakeman and Nathan Sivin offered valuable suggestions at various stages. The Shanghai Library allowed me to use their original copies of the *Dianshizhai,* and arranged for copies of over one hundred illustrations to be made specifically for this book. In this regard I would particularly like to thank Sun Jilin, whose never-failing help made everything possible.

The Australian National University provided the scholarship that enabled this project to be started, and Macquarie University provided me with generous research grants which have enabled me to complete it. To both I am deeply grateful. It is a great privilege to be published by the University of Michigan's Center for Chinese Studies. The efficiency and approachability of Noriko Kamachi and Philip Ivanhoe made life much easier. Terre Fisher's sharp eye and questioning mind helped me to regain much commonsense I had lost through becoming overly familiar with the *Dianshizhai* and taking much for granted.

I would also like to thank my husband Daniel and my son Ian, but whatever words I might choose would be inadequate.

Ye Xiaoqing
Sydney
March 2003

INTRODUCTION

Fundamental economic and social change in its foreign concessions during the nineteenth century transformed Shanghai from a relatively unpopulated area contiguous to a minor county seat to the glittering "ten *li* of foreign territory"[1]—the "nightless city." In the settlements, new surroundings brought new attitudes and new values. The construction of broad roads enabled the introduction of the rickshaw and the horse-drawn carriage. As these began to replace the sedan chair, certain social distinctions became blurred: While the sedan chair implied status, a carriage could be hired by anyone with money to pay the fare. Symbols of social hierarchy, such as types of clothing, dwellings, and courtesy titles began to lose their significance in a society dominated by commerce and the tastes of the nouveau riche.

Traditional activities took on new forms and meanings. The largest teahouses, for example, could seat more than a thousand people and offered various forms of entertainment. They provided opportunities for people of different backgrounds to mix socially, though at the expense of the intimacy of the traditional teahouse. The longstanding moral and legal prohibition against eating beef was challenged by the new menus in Western restaurants, and the increased use of the printed word in the modern press, journals, and on stationery used in commercial activities challenged the traditional "reverence for lettered paper."

The introduction of running water not only improved sanitary conditions, it allowed the introduction of the concept "hygiene" and the notion of public health. It also provided the necessary infrastructure for the development of Western hospitals, where treatments offered sometimes clashed with traditional Chinese concepts of the human body and health. Surgery was an obvious challenge to the traditional holistic view of the body, and that challenge extended to questions of legal procedures for autopsies carried out in coroners' enquiries.

Many of these developments can be followed in the pages of the *Dianshizhai Pictorial*, published between 1884 and 1898.[2] The *Dianshizhai*, the first successful pictorial in China, took its material from a variety of contemporary sources, illustrated them with sketches, and added commentary. Among the *Dianshizhai*'s 4,500-odd sketches and commentaries we find descriptions of festivals, religious processions, human relations, living conditions, and leisure activities recorded over a period of fourteen years. The material in the *Dianshizhai* can be supplemented by the newspaper *Shenbao*, other newspapers, and novels set in Shanghai, Shanghai Municipal Council records, and orders issued by both Chinese and Western authorities, all of which provide much valuable information about the daily life of the time. The *Shenbao* and the *Dianshizhai* were the most popular and widely read newspapers of the day, and they played a profound role in influencing popular tastes.

The crucial question about the *Dianshizhai* is its reliability as a source for understanding the culture of the time. How typical are its stories of everyday life in Shanghai in the late nineteenth century? To what extent do its commentaries reflect the prejudices of its authors?

Both the *Shenbao* and the *Dianshizhai* were modern commercial newspapers. The basic aim of their founder, Ernest Major, was to provide a vehicle for the accurate provision of news of the day. Most sketches in the *Dianshizhai* were based on local stories. Some were based on news from overseas, and these are often inaccurate. The experience of the *Dianshizhai* staff was limited to what they were truly familiar with—everyday life in Shanghai. Their attention was attracted by anything that differed from the past, or from other areas of China—precisely the areas of *change* in a transitional society.

Commentaries in the *Dianshizhai* highlight notable aspects of urban life in Shanghai, even though the facts of a particular story may not be verifiable It is clear from the content, style, language, and calligraphy of the commentaries that their authors were well educated. They themselves may not have believed stories about the supernatural, for example, but included such stories for their entertainment value, or to draw a moral from them. Details of an incident at a brothel may or may not be accurate, but the accompanying sketch still gives a useful idea of the material surroundings one might encounter there, such as clocks on the wall and gas lighting. A story about a fight during the Festival of the Hungry Ghosts may not be verifiable, but we learn from it that such celebrations did occur in Shanghai at the time. Praise for Western hospitals in the *Dianshizhai* is paralleled elsewhere by hospital statistics showing growth in the number of Chinese patients. The statistics by themselves cannot reveal why people went to Western hospitals, or how their attitudes toward them changed. The *Dianshizhai*'s detailed stories are thus a useful supplement. Some of the stories may have been sensationalized, either out of a desire to attract readers or to educate them, but for local matters they could not depart too far from reality.

Most stories were chosen because they exemplified common social phenomena which the writers of the *Dianshizhai* felt worthy of special notice. Commentaries around particularly important themes might appear several times. These themes and issues also turn up frequently in other contemporary sources—novels, memoirs, and official reports.

Major's policy was to allow his Chinese editors to produce a journal which would appeal to a Chinese readership. His editors admired and were fascinated by those aspects of Western culture they became familiar with in the settlements. When commenting on major disputes between China and the foreign powers, however, the *Dianshizhai* adopted a Chinese viewpoint. From time to time the commentators even published views which differed from those of the Chinese authorities. This suggests that they enjoyed a degree of personal security living in the settlements and working for a foreign enterprise, which allowed them to express their own opinions. There is no evidence that news in the *Dianshizhai* was slanted to reflect the views of the foreign proprietor.

The literati were relatively open minded and receptive to "new learning" and other aspects of Western culture, but they were distressed at many of the social changes in the settlements. The Western presence there introduced a new set of values backed by Western legal and political power. This situation may have had its positive aspects, but its negative side, as far as the literati were concerned, was the disintegration of traditional norms and mores.

Material from the *Dianshizhai* has been used by Western and Chinese scholars in numerous works on Chinese history. Collections of sketches from the *Dianshizhai* and reproductions of the whole series have appeared over the last few decades. Three specialist studies of the *Dianshizhai* were published in recent years in English, Japanese, and German.[1] They are mainly translations of certain commentaries and reproductions of some of the illustrations. To date there has been no systematic study of this publication as a source of Shanghai social history. This book will consider material in the *Dianshizhai* in light of the fascinating picture it presents of a society undergoing dramatic change.

Notes

[1] This name derived from the fact that the main roads in the settlement stretched out for about ten *li* away from the Yangjingbang Creek. It is referred to as such in Ding 58; Zhu 40; Shu 48; Yu 72; Xin 88. The term strictly refers only to the British Settlement, because the American Settlement in Hongkou was not in the most prosperous area of Shanghai. On the origins, extensions and land regulations of the foreign settlements, see Ching-lin Hsia, *The Status of Shanghai* (Shanghai: Kelly and Walsh Limited, 1929), 1–40; Richard Feetham (The Hon. Mr. Justice Feetham, C.M.G.), *Report to the Shanghai Municipal Council*, vol. 1 (Shanghai: North China Daily News and Herald Ltd., 1931–1932), 346–59. Cf. also Hanchao Lu: "The walled county town, in spite of its prosperity before the mid-nineteenth century, formed only a small proportion of modern Shanghai, about one-twentieth of Shanghai proper in the Republican period. In that sense, the modern city of Shanghai did spring from obscure rural origins." Hanchao Lu, *Beyond the Neon Lights: Everyday Shanghai in the Early Twentieth Century* (Berkeley: University of California Press, 1999), 26.

[2] The *Dianshizhai Pictorial* was republished in 1983 in by the Guangdong renmin chubanshe, but this edition omitted the advertisements and the supplementary materials. The forty-four volumes in this edition are designated in the following order: Jia, Yi, Bing, Ding, Wu, Ji, Geng, Xin, Ren, Gui, Zi, Chou, Yin, Mao, Chen, Yi★, Wu★, Wei, Shen, You, Xu, Hai, Jin, Shi, Si, Zhu, Pao, Tu, Ge, Mu, Li, Yue, She, Yu, Shu, Shu★, Wen, Xing, Zhong, Xin★, Yuan, Heng, Li★, Zhen. Asterisks are used to distinguish characters which would otherwise be the same in romanization. Sketches in the *Dianshizhai* in this book are referred to by the volume, followed by the page number.

[3] Fritz van Briessen, *Shanghai-Bildzeitung 1884–1898, Eine Illustrierte aus dem China des ausgehenden 19. Jahrhunderts* (Zürich: Atlantis Verlag AG, 1977); Don J. Cohn, ed. and trans., *Vignettes from the Chinese: Lithographs from Shanghai in the Late Nineteenth Century* (Hong Kong: The Chinese University of Hong Kong, 1987); Nakano Miyoko and Takeda Masaya, *Seikimatsu Chūgoku no Kawara-ban: E-iri Shinbun Tensekisai Gahō no Sekai* (Tokyo: Fukutake Books, 1989); Rudolf G. Wagner, "The Shanghai Illustrated Newspapers *Dianshizhai huabao* and *Feiyingge huabao*: An Introductory Survey," paper presented at the Association for Asian Studies Annual Convention, April 1991; Wang Ermin, "Zhongguo jindai zhishi pujihua chuanbo zhi tushuo xingshi: *Dianshizhai huabao li*" (Pictorial representations of the dissemination and popularization of knowledge in nineteenth century China: Examples from the Dianshizhai Pictorial), in *Zhongyang yanjiuyuan jindaishi yanjiusuo jikan*, no. 19 (June 1990): 135–72.

PART ONE

A Brief History of the *Dianshizhai Pictorial*

1. The *Shenbao* and the *Dianshizhai*

The brothers Ernest and Frederick Major arrived in China in the early 1860s to set up business in the tea industry. In 1871 Ernest Major and three friends, C. Woodward, W. B. Pryor and John Mackillop, each contributed four hundred taels of silver to establish a Chinese language newspaper, the *Shenbao*.[1] The specific rights and obligations of each of the shareholders were set out in detail in the contract. Major was to be responsible for management of the newspaper; any profits or losses were to be split into three shares, of which Major would get two, and the other three one-third between them. Major hired Jiang Zhixiang as editor-in-chief, and He Guisheng and Qian Xinbo as assistant editors. Major sent Qian Xinbo to Hong Kong to seek the assistance of Wang Tao, an experienced journalist, who agreed to help.[2] Some time later Jiang Zhixiang was awarded the *jinshi* degree, and He Guisheng became editor-in-chief. The first issue of the *Shenbao* was published on the 30th of April, 1872.[3] It was highly successful, and after only eight months forced the closure of its main competitor, the *Shanghai Xinbao*.[4]

The Dianshizhai Printing Company

From the 1860s to the 1890s, the Major brothers controlled six different enterprises in China, including the *Shenbao* and the Dianshizhai Printing Company.[5] In 1876 when Major established the "Tien Shih Chai Photolithographic Publishing Works," he introduced a type of new technology into China, the lithograph.[6] Slightly earlier, in 1874, a French missionary produced a number of religious tracts by the lithographic method at the Tushanwan Printing Company in Xujiahui, but the first use of lithography for mass printing was undertaken by the Dianshizhai Printing Company. Major hired a Chinese printer from the Tushanwan Printing Company, Qiu Zi'ang,[7] and employed altogether about two hundred people.[8] The first major achievement of the press was its 1882 edition of the Kangxi Dictionary. It produced forty thousand copies, which were distributed by the Shenchang Painting and Calligraphy Shop and sold out in a few short months. The second printing was sixty thousand copies and happened to coincide with the imperial examinations in the capital. Many examination candidates bought five or six copies, for themselves or for friends, and the second printing also sold out in a matter of months. The success of the Dianshizhai Printing Company caused no little envy among other businessmen, and before long a merchant from Ningbo had established a printing house called Baishishanfang, and another from Guangdong had set up the Tongwen Bookstore, to compete in the growing print market.[9]

The Dianshizhai Printing Company specialized in reprinting classical works, producing facsimiles of rubbings of famous calligraphy and the like. In May 1887 Major placed a number of advertisements in the *Shenbao*, in which he announced his intention to reprint the Kangxi Encyclopedia (*Gujin tushu jicheng*). Between the years 1885 and 1888, Major's publishing company printed 1,628 volumes in this series. Major also spent much time collecting a number of premodern Chinese works and published more than one hundred and sixty volumes in a series entitled *Juzhenban congshu*, in imitation of the Chinese series of the same title from the Qianlong period.[10] Major's enthusiasm for collecting old books, especially valuable ones, at one stage involved him in a book-theft scandal.[11]

The *Dianshizhai Pictorial*

Soon after the success of the *Shenbao*, Major published the *Yinghuan Pictorial*, but it closed down after only five issues.[12] Its contents were taken directly from English magazines, with a Chinese commentary by Cai Erkang. Major again took up the idea of a Chinese pictorial after successfully publishing works by a number of Chinese artists, including Wu Youru's woodblock prints depicting the defeat of the French general Henri L. Rivière by Liu Yongfu in Hanoi. Major approached the artists with a proposal that they contribute their work for publication to the Dianshizhai Lithographic Printing Company, and thus the *Dianshizhai Pictorial* was born, in 1884.[13] Wu Youru was its principal artist for nine years, and it was sometimes called the *Wu Youru Pictorial*. Published three times a month, the journal featured eight sketches, with commentaries, in each issue.[14]

The first issue of the *Dianshizhai Pictorial* appeared on the 8th of May, 1884. Major had placed advertisements on the front page of the *Shenbao* every day for over a month announcing:

> This company is publishing a new pictorial; we have specially invited famous artists to chose items from the daily news to surprise and entertain you, and to provide illustrations and commentaries. It will be printed by the Dianshizhai Printing Company, and will be published at regular intervals each month. Each issue . . . will be sold together with this newspaper by those who now deliver it; for each issue we will charge five cash to cover the costs. The sketches are done with meticulous care and the calligraphy is the finest. They are traditional Chinese realistic paintings characterized by fine brushwork and close attention to detail. We are sure that you, the purchasers, will see this for yourselves."[15]

Once the *Dianshizhai* began appearing, Major continued to advertise it on the front page of the *Shenbao* until December 30, 1887, its 136th issue.

Not long after the *Dianshizhai* entered circulation, the publishers began to sell bound-volume editions of it, each volume containing twelve issues. These bound volumes were issued continuously until the magazine ceased publication.[16] In all there were 4,509 sketches in forty-four volumes.[17] Each sketch is signed by the artist, and each has a title and a commentary. The commentary sometimes provides background to the news story—when and where it happened—but usually does not make its sources specific. Commentaries also contain observations and criticisms, and each accompanying text ends with a pithy remark in the form of a seal. In 1885, for example, the *Dianshizhai* featured a picture of the French Parliament investigating the culpability of a French army commander for the loss of the Battle of Liangshan during the Sino-French War. The title of the sketch is "Trial of a French Official" and the seal reads, "Listening to the Words of the Devil."[18] Another sketch describes an accident in Singapore in which a spectator was injured during a cock-fighting match. There are two seals, one of which comments, "Such Entertainment!", the other "Cruel Killing."[19] Still another sketch refers to Li Hongzhang's romantic involvement with an American girl on a visit to New York. Here the seal chides, "Excessive

Affection."[20] Typically one or two seals appear on each picture; sometimes their characters are cut in relief, sometimes in intaglio.

Editorial policy

Major's editorial policy was based on his understanding of the market. He believed "new" and "sensational" would sell, but news too unfamiliar to Chinese readers would hardly be interesting for them. He also felt the manner of the illustrations should not be too different from what his readers were used to. Major stressed that purpose of the illustrated news stories was "to surprise and entertain."[21] He relied on his Chinese editors and artists to select appropriate items and illustrate them as they saw fit.

The Chinese New Year Festival of February 1885 was the first big event after the inception of the *Dianshizhai*. To mark the occasion, the publisher announced that anyone who bought nine copies of the pictorial could claim, free of charge, a painting produced by the Dianshizhai Printing Company.[22] In accordance with the spirit of the festival, the *Dianshizhai* carried no items about wars or accidents, but produced nine sketches illustrating New Year's stories and customs taken from historical records or other sources.[23] From then on, it regularly published reproductions of paintings by famous artists like Ren Bonian and Sha Shanchun,[24] and every Chinese New Year the *Dianshizhai* presented its readers with traditional *nianhua*, drawings of children, peaches, fish, and other auspicious symbols.[25]

Major believed news had to be both timely and accurate. He sent journalists to make on-the-spot reports and occasionally got involved in news gathering himself. The *Dianshizhai*'s first year (1884) coincided with the outbreak of the Sino-French War. Major hired a Russian to accompany the French troops, and the reports in the *Shenbao* were detailed and accurate. The first two sketches in the first issue of the *Dianshizhai* cover that conflict.[26] Major also sent Wu Youru himself to inspect war preparations at Wusong.[27] A German friend passing through Shanghai gave Major an eyewitness account of the situation at the front; Major immediately passed on this information to one of his artists, Zhang Zhiying, who illustrated the sketch "Detailed News of French Defeat."[28]

In 1885 the French fleet attacked Ningbo, and again Major dispatched journalists to the front. Their reporting was immediate and detailed, and the *Hu Bao*, another foreign-owned Chinese language newspaper, could not keep up with them.[29] The French attack was illustrated in the sketch "The Battle of Yongjiang,"[30] which clearly shows the deployment of the French ships, and the positions of the cannon. After initial suspicions about the motives of the *Shenbao*,[31] Chinese came to regard it as the most authoritative source of information about the war, and its circulation increased dramatically.[32]

The Chinese point of view

Since Major's policy was to attract Chinese readers, the *Shenbao* and the *Dianshizhai* generally reflected the Chinese point of view.[33] The tone of the commentaries, and even the titles, is often vivid and emotional. There are twenty-six pictures about the Sino-French War throughout the first four volumes (see for example Figs. 1 and 2).[34] Terms such as "tigers, wolves, evil beasts" and "jumping, howling, wild, biting" are used to describe the French.[35] The advertisement for issue No. 10, which contained a news item about the sinking of a French ship, remarks, "The number

1. A Chinese military map used during the Sino-French War (1885). It was acquired by Wu Youru from an officer in Taiwan.

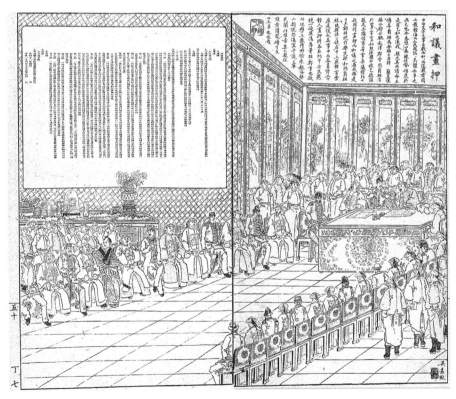

2. The treaty-signing ceremony at the conclusion of the Sino-French War (1885). The complete text of the treaty is given on the upper-left part of the sketch.

of people killed or wounded is a punishment from Heaven. This is such good news; readers will be happy to read about it."[36] The advertisement for issue No. 18 commented, "The news of the Chinese army's great victory in Taiwan, in which innumerable French were killed or wounded, makes people shout with joy." The *Dianshizhai* went to the trouble of obtaining a photograph of Liu Yongfu, the commander of the Chinese troops, and reproduced it lithographically "for the admiration of the Chinese people."[37]

The *Dianshizhai* showed no inclination to support the English in disputes between China and Great Britain. In 1885 a steamship owned by Jardines collided with and sank a small Chinese steamboat in the Huangpu River. The English made no attempt to rescue anyone, and out of more than one hundred people on board the Chinese boat, only twenty survived. The *Dianshizhai* reported this case under the title "Many Lves Cruelly Llost" (Fig. 3),[38] and commented, "[the English] regard Chinese lives less valuable than dogs or chickens; their pernicious ways and disregard of principles have descended to this . . . they are not of the same race, and their hearts are different. We Chinese should carefully remember this." When another accident occurred between two steamers in 1887, the *Dianshizhai* adopted a similar attitude.[39]

3. A British steamship belonging to Jardines collides with a Chinese boat (1885).

As far as I can ascertain, only once was the news slanted in order not to offend Major personally. On June 1, 1888, a serious fire broke out at the Sui Chong Match Factory, one of the Major brothers' enterprises. The phosphorus plant caught fire and six two-story buildings and nineteen single-story buildings were destroyed. Five people lost their lives, and damage was estimated at five to six thousand taels of silver.[40] This type of news was regularly reported in the *Dianshizhai*, but the journal is silent about this incident.[41]

Major's "Chinese" image

From the very beginning Major sought to create for himself a Chinese image. In the editorial for the *Dianshizhai*'s inaugural issue, he chose the sobriquet "Master of the Pavilion of Respect for the News," after the manner of the Chinese literati. The editorial is completely Chinese in style and content, and Major's seal is affixed to it. In the editorial, Major states that the journal's contents are suitable for after-dinner conversation, and the news stories are selected for their entertainment value.[42] By the sixth issue, when the *Dianshizhai* had become well established, Major adopted the moral stance of a Chinese scholar:

> This company publishes the *Pictorial* not only to provide amusement for people through the medium of pen and ink, but also to introduce the principles of retribution in the sketches, so as to admonish and warn by means of these illustrations.[43]

Not surprisingly, Major was close to a number of literati, particularly those associated with his papers—Wang Tao, Cai Erkang, He Guisheng, Qian Xinbo, Shen Gongzhi,[44] and Wu Youru.[45]

In December 1884, an attempted coup d'état occurred in Korea, and the Chinese and Japanese governments became involved. The following year, the *Dianshizhai* published a special issue, *Turmoil in Korea*, containing a commentary signed by Major condemning those involved in the coup (Fig. 4).[46] It is impossible to know if this article was really written by Major himself. Although he was known to have a good command of Chinese, it is doubtful that he would have been able to compose an article so typical of the Chinese scholarly class in both language and attitude.[47] Whether the article was touched up by a Chinese scholar, or even written entirely by someone else on Major's instructions, Major himself signed it and agreed to publish it.

Distribution

In Shanghai the *Dianshizhai* was distributed by *Shenbao* agencies, and by the Shenchang Painting and Calligraphy Shop, owned by Major Brothers, Limited.[48] The pictorial could also be obtained in at least twenty-four other places across China. It was distributed by individuals, companies, foreign firms, and private postal services. In Beijing two bookshops carried it; in Tianjin, Nanjing, and Anqing it was distributed by private individuals; in Niuzhuang, Jiangxi, Baoding, Jiujiang, Guangdong, Guangxi, Chongqing, Changsha, and Qingsha by private post; in Yantai, Wuchang, Yangzhou, Suzhou, Ningbo, and Wenzhou by various companies; in Fuzhou by a foreign firm, and in Hong Kong through the office of *Xunhuan Ribao*.[49] In Hankou, Hangzhou, and Jiaxing it was distributed by local branches of the Shenchang Painting and Calligraphy Shop.[50] By 1889 the Dianshizhai Printing Company had branches in twenty-one locations in China, and the *Dianshizhai* was available directly from all of them.[51]

Although the *Dianshizhai* was distributed in all major Chinese cities, it is difficult to obtain accurate circulation figures. According to Chinese sources, only 600 copies of the *Shenbao* were printed for the earlier issues, but the number rose to 5,000 by 1877 and 7,000 in 1912.[52] These figures, however, are very different from those given by Patrick J. Hughes in his 1887 report on trade in Shanghai. He claimed that the daily circulation of the *Shenbao* was 12,000 to 13,000, and this increased to 18,000 during the Sino-French War.[53] According to the same source, copies of the *Shenbao* actually changed hands several times in the course of a day, and when they were no

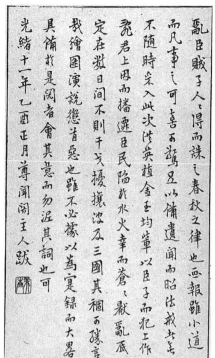

4. Major's editorial statement on the Kapsin coup in Korea (1885). It is signed "Master of the Pavilion of Respect for the News," and the seal reads *Meicha* (Major). The statement says: "Disloyal and traitorous officials—everyone has a responsibility to kill them. This was established in the *Spring and Autumn Annals*. This pictorial, although it adopts no high moral tone and merely reports matters to surprise and entertain, still has a responsibility to report such events, to make the consequences very clear to those people who might violate the law. On this occasion, Hong Yong-sik, Kim Ok-kyun, and the rest were officials, but they rebelled against their sovereign. We have drawn a number of sketches to illustrate this story of evil being punished. Although they may not be correct in every detail, in general terms they are accurate. The reader will get the general idea, and need not be concerned about the details."

longer needed in Shanghai they would be given to the staff of the China Postal Service to be sent inland to areas not accessible by boat. According to Li Boyuan, Shanghai also had a newspaper rental service; the cost of renting a newspaper was about one tenth of the purchase price.[54] We can conclude that the actual readership of the *Shenbao* was much higher than the print run suggests. The advertisement for the second issue of the *Dianshizhai* claims that its inaugural issue "was sold out within three to five days . . . we printed several thousand more, so those gentlemen who had missed out can still purchase a copy."[55]

Even if we do not take this claim literally, it is reasonable to believe that the *Dianshizhai* was an immediate success. The advertisement for issue No. 4 claims that several thousand additional copies had been printed.[56] That issue included an announcement inviting advertisements, "The *Pictorial* published and sold by this company has the unanimous approval of readers all over China, and those who want to buy and read it crowd together, jostling one another. We find it difficult to keep up with demand."[57] The advertisement for issue No. 6 also stated, "From the time we starting this publication, its circulation has been growing day by day."[58] In 1884 the *Shenbao* ran an article under the pseudonym "Master of the Hall of That Which Has Been Seen" entitled "After Reading the *Pictorial*." It related, "During the last month or more, there have been just so many readers. By the time the latest issue arrives, the previous one has already sold out. The printers, working with stone and ink, change shifts several times a day, but they still cannot keep up with demand. The next issue of the *Pictorial* will appear in ten days. It will doubtless have hundreds and thousands of readers."[59] Despite possible exaggerations and vague statistics, the fact that issues of the *Dianshizhai* were reprinted and bound in single volume editions is clearly an indication of its popularity.

Reaching out to a wide audience

Major believed that illustrations would attract a much wider readership than plain text. We read in an announcement in 1886: "There might be people who do not like to read newspapers, but there is no one under Heaven who does not like to enjoy pictorials."[60] Major made sure to keep the price as low as possible. Each issue had at least eight pages, and after the sixth issue the size increased to ten pages. The price remained five cash, half the price of the *Yinghuan Pictorial* or the *Shenbao*.[61]

It is not possible to obtain accurate figures for the literacy rate in Shanghai at that time, and only scattered information on the educational and social background of the *Dianshizhai*'s readership survives. Wu Jianren's novel *Bizarre Happenings Eyewitnessed Over Two Decades* mentions housewives reading the *Dianshizhai*.[62] In his memoirs, Bao Tianxiao recalls,

> When I was twelve or thirteen, a magazine called the *Dianshizhai Pictorial* appeared in Shanghai. I enjoyed reading it very much. Children, of course, liked to look at the pictures, but this pictorial was also enjoyed by adults. Every time it arrived in Suzhou, I would use my pocket money to buy a copy. It appeared every ten days, and ten issues were bound together in a single volume. At that time I had quite a few bound volumes. Although the artists did not have any broad learning, one could pick up quite a lot of general knowledge from their drawings. Shanghai was a very open-minded place, and all sorts of new inventions and new things from foreign countries would appear there first.[63]

In 1895, after Major had left China, the *Shenbao* published an editorial, "The Educational Value of Pictorials." It stated,

> After Shanghai became an open port, daily newspapers also made an appearance, as is the case in the West. Their aim was that everyone under Heaven would know about the affairs of the world. This was an excellent intention. But the literate in China are few, and the illiterate many. Not everyone could completely understand the newspapers, or conceptualize the things referred to in them. So the pictorials were produced, several issues each month. Some of them took their material from ancient themes, describing them in pictures, and some took recent events from the newspapers and illustrated them to expand people's experience and knowledge. Since we have begun to engage in international trade and the world has become one, there is no lack of strange things from all corners of the globe. Some people, although they may live in small villages, know about world affairs. . . . The reason pictorials have such a high circulation is because whether people are literate or not, they can all increase their knowledge and open their minds [while enjoying the illustrations]. Not only can scholars read them, but there is no reason why merchants should not do so, too; not only can simple villagers read them, but there is no reason why women should not look at them also. We might add that they are also useful for small children.[64]

The *Shenbao* claimed that the *Dianshizhai* was read by both the educated and the working classes. It indubitably had a wide readership, but it is doubtful it included many of the working class. It was not just a question of affordability—its "middle-brow" concerns and taste were far from the interests of workers. The "labor aristocrats" of the twentieth century did not exist, as a group, in the Shanghai of the nineteenth century.[65]

2. The Shanghai literati

Sketches in the *Dianshizhai* are usually signed by an artist. It is not clear from the illustrations, however, whether the artists themselves wrote the commentaries. The commentaries are written in the literary Chinese used by educated people of the late imperial period, with its classical syntax and literary allusions. A careful examination of the commentaries and original sketches confirms that the commentaries were in fact written by Shanghai literati associated with the *Shenbao*. We may conclude that the attitudes and messages in the commentaries reflect the values of this group.[66]

The artists of the *Dianshizhai*

Wu Youru was the most important artist at the *Dianshizhai*, but he did not achieve any scholarly honors or official rank.[67] From the signatures on the illustrations we learn that the other *Dianshizhai* artists included Zhang Zhiying (Zhang Qi), Ma Ziming, Jin Chanxiang (Jin Gui), Tian Zilin (Tian Ying), Fu Genxin (Fu Jie), Zhou Muqiao (Zhou Quan), He Yuanjun (He Mingfu), Jia Xingqing and Zhu Ruxian. There are also unfamiliar names which appear once or twice, such as Wang Zhao and Shen Meipo. These draftsmen-painters were apparently quite well known in Shanghai at the time,[68] but none of them, apart from Wu Youru, is listed in modern reference works on the artistic history of the period.[69]

The biography of Wu Youru in the standard *History of Painting in the Qing Dynasty*[70] reads as follows:

> Wu You, also named Jiayou, with the style Youru, was a native of Yuanhe. He liked painting, and was especially good at traditional fine line drawing. People, beautiful women, mountains, rivers, flowers, plants, birds, beasts, insects, fish—he excelled in all of these. Zeng Zhongxiang Gong [Zeng Guoquan] commissioned him to paint a scroll entitled *A Portrait of Meritorious Officials Victorious at Jinling*. The Emperor heard about this at Court, and from then on his fame grew day by day. In the year *jiashen* [1884] he was invited to draw for the pictorial of the Dianshizhai Printing Company. Afterwards he himself established the *Feiyingge Pictorial*. His genre paintings and sketches of current affairs are drawn in fine detail and are very realistic. He could be considered a modern Qiu Ying.[71] His paintings of beautiful women are especially refined. He was given the epithet 'Master Craftsman.'

According to his biography, Wu Youru's greatest achievements were his traditional paintings of beautiful women. The modern art historian Huang Mengtian disagrees: "Connoisseurs of traditional paintings of beautiful women regard Wu Youru's drawings in *One Hundred Classical Beauties* as his most outstanding achievement. They know that he also produced a large number of genre paintings in the *Dianshizhai*, but they do not regard them as being among his most important work. In fact, however, the reason Wu has a place in the history of Chinese art is mainly because of his genre paintings, which are so full of realistic significance."[72]

In 1909, the Wenruilou Publishing Company in Shanghai published Wu Youru's collected works in thirteen volumes, under the title *A Treasury of Wu Youru's Illustrations*. This was reprinted in 1983 by the Shanghai Shudian, with a preface by Zheng Yimei, in which we read about Wu's humble background and painting career:

> He was young when the Taiping Rebellion occurred, and he took refuge in Shanghai. It was there that he took up painting. Whenever he saw original works by famous painters, he would gaze at them intently and copy them; he would be so absorbed as to forget food and sleep. However, he could not stay long in Shanghai. He returned to his native town of Suzhou. On the introduction of a relative, he became an apprentice in the Yunlange Studio on West Street in the Changmenchengnei district, which specialized in mounting traditional Chinese paintings. That shop also sold calligraphy and painting of a hackneyed and vulgar sort; everyone called it "lowbrow stuff." Wu Youru already had mastered basic skills in painting when he began studying with an experienced painter, Zhang Zhiying. He started by copying models, and his talent was outstanding, especially for figure painting and traditional paintings of beautiful women. Because of this, the variety of paintings in the Yunlange Studio became more extensive than that in other shops, and his career advanced day by day. Gradually the gentry began to notice him, and commissioned paintings and paid substantial sums for them. They compared him to a modern Qiu Shizhou (Qiu Ying). Wu Youru's reputation as an artist spread from North to South. Even the governor-general of Liang-Jiang, Zeng Guoquan, commissioned him to paint a scroll entitled *A Portrait of Meritorious Officials Victorious at Jinling*, which was submitted to the Emperor for inspection. There was a degree of compulsion in this project; it was not a painting he wanted to do. After finishing it, he returned home as if relieved of a heavy burden. On the way home he passed through Shanghai. An Englishman, Major, who had established the *Shenbao*, and in addition wanted to publish the *Dianshizhai Pictorial*, invited Wu Youru to be the chief illustrator. Wu Youru expanded the themes of the illustrations and introduced all manner of things from foreign countries—high buildings and large mansions, locomotives and steamships, acoustics, optics, electronics, chemistry and so on. All of them were included in his paintings.[73]

It is clear from this biography that Wu was primarily an artisan; he did not have a classical education or scholarly background.

We have only a few pieces of scattered information about the other artists. From Wu Youru's biography, we learn that Zhang Zhiying also came from Suzhou. From an article about Shanghai's tabloid newspapers, we learn that Zhou Muqiao provided illustrations for a newspaper called *Jin'gangzuan*, so we can presume that after the *Dianshizhai* ceased publication, Zhou remained in Shanghai to work for that publication.[74]

The settlement literati—a new lifestyle

Choosing to abandon a traditional career path to make a living in the foreign settlements required the Shanghai literati to make major adjustments, both mentally and practically. They were now employees of foreign enterprises, and no longer part of the Chinese elite. As Yao Gonghe put it,

> In previous times, being the editor of a newspaper was not considered respectable. The person in question would not dare reveal his occupation to other people. A man from my home town, Mr. Shen Renquan, was employed by a certain newspaper in Shanghai at the beginning of the Guangxu period, and from then on worked at various newspapers continuously until the end of that reign period. When asked, however, he would only hem and haw and did not dare tell anyone about it.[75]

Li Pingshu, who held the degree of senior licentiate and was a county magistrate, did write a few lead articles for the *North-China Herald*. This was, however, during a period of mourning following the death of his grandmother in 1882. In 1884, the period of mourning had been completed. The moral code did not permit him to pursue his official career during the period of mourning, but there was no restriction on engaging in relatively trivial matters. As soon as the period of mourning was over, Li took the advice of his teachers, left the service of the newspaper, and immediately resumed the serious business of preparing for the imperial examinations.[76]

The low status of literati-turned-journalists was pointedly noted by Zuo Zongtang, who tried to borrow money from foreign bankers in Shanghai to finance his military expenditure in Xinjiang. When his scheme met with opposition in the local press, Zuo furiously denounced the journalists as "scoundrel literati from Jiangsu and Zhejiang who have ended up working for newspapers as a last resort."[77]

The settlement literati had lost their traditional privileges and were now little more than clerks in the International Settlement. The social circles in which the settlement literati moved were small. This group included Wang Tao, the mathematician Li Shanlan, the famous translator Lin Shu, and writers associated with the *Shenbao*—Cai Erkang, He Guisheng, Qian Xinbo, and Li Boyuan. There were also a few younger members—Zhang Chunfan, author of *The Nine-tailed Turtle*; Sun Yusheng, author of *Dreams of Prosperity in Shanghai*; and Zeng Mengpu, author of *Flowers on the Sea of Sin*. These literati would meet each other in the upper-class courtesan establishments, or at banquets accompanied by courtesans. Occasionally they recommended a particular courtesan to a friend, or a friend to a courtesan. The famous relationship between Cai E and Xiao Fengxian, for example, was initiated by Zeng Mengpu.[78]

Some literati who made their living in the settlements had come from well-known scholar-official families. Gong Cheng (Gong Xiaogong) was a son of Gong Zizhen; Yuan Xiangpu, a grandson of Yuan Mei. Most of them had abandoned any hope of an official career, having failed the examinations at one point or another, some several times. Cai Erkang took the provincial level examinations several times without success before seeking employment with the *Shenbao*.[79] The newspaper editor and novelist Sun Yusheng adopted the sobriquet *Haishang shushisheng*, "The Scholar Who Rinses His Mouth with Rocks," that is, he had assumed a hermit's lifestyle.[80] This hermit had taken refuge in the foreign settlements, as far removed from the strictures of traditional society as the mountains. When he was twenty-five he changed the name of his study to *Tuixinglu* (The Hut of Withdrawal and Awakening), symbolizing his having abandoned dreams of an official career.[81]

We now see them as pioneers: Wang Tao is usually considered a reformist thinker, who contributed greatly to the early modern newspaper industry in China. Li Shanlan was the most outstanding mathematician of his time, a master of both traditional Chinese and Western mathematics, and founder of the discipline of modern mathematics in China. These men were open-minded and progressive, but the modern concept of the "progressive intellectual" did not exist at that time. Shanghai literati were relatively open-minded, but not politically radical, and by the turn of the century, the younger generation regarded them as conservatives.[82]

Self-indulgence and self-destruction

Living in the prosperous surroundings of the settlements, the Shanghai literati consoled themselves with wine and women. Almost all of Shanghai's literati in the nineteenth century came from the Jiangnan area. Jiangnan literati had been known since the Ming dynasty for their distinctive lifestyle; with a particular taste for poetry, music, and wine, "their style of living became part of the environment."[83] Jiangnan culture was regarded by the Manchu rulers of the Qing as rich, learned, and artistically refined, but also decadent. As the Qianlong emperor put it, "Luxurious and corrupt, lower Yangtze society erodes virtue as sugar erodes teeth."[84]

The literati were proud of their relationships with courtesans—that is to say, upper-class courtesans.[85] Qian Xinbo, who was short-sighted, chose the sobriquet "The Guest Who Admires Flowers through the Mist." Li Shanlan could only write poetry if the ink was prepared by the courtesan Cai Yunqing.[86] Wang Tao said of himself, "From the end of the Daoguang period to the present day, I have passed forty years among clusters of flowers." One famous courtesan, preferring the company of Wang Tao, would decline all invitations, even those to attend banquets with rich patrons. Wang was also delighted that another had kept the gift he had given her on their first meeting for four years.[87] Li Boyuan, who chose the sobriquet "Master of Entertainment in Shanghai," had no qualms about writing on the subject of his lifestyle and interests.

The settlement literati even published their poems in praise of various courtesans in the newspapers. The *Shenbao* often carried such poems and articles, some on the front page. For example, in 1872 it published a *Letter to Lady Academician Zhuqing* next to its editorial.[88] There are too many such poems to list here; but we can give a few titles for their flavor: *Recollections of a Dream Shadow*,[89] *In Praise of Ten Beauties of Shanghai*,[90] *To Lady Academician Chen Yuqing*,[91] and so on. Some of Shanghai's courtesans became quite famous due to the public praise heaped on them by the settlement literati. Li Shanshan was highly appreciated by the chief editors of the *Shenbao*, Qian Xinbo and He Guisheng.[92] Qian Xinbo was also full of praise for two others, Wang Keqing and Huang Xiaojun.[93] Zhu Zhuqing's admirer was "The Scholar of the Land of Dreams," Huang Shiquan.[94] Wang Tao's adventures with prostitutes and his praise of them are chronicled in *Bizarre Happenings Eyewitnessed Over Two Decades*.[95] Three other books by Wang Tao, *Tales of Trivia from the Banks of the Wusong*, *A Guide to the Brothels of Shanghai*, and *Episodes from the Land of the Flowers* are detailed works on Shanghai prostitution.[96]

The literati also initiated beauty contests among the courtesans. Popular during the 1870s, they were known as "flower appreciations," and their results were published in the *Shenbao*.[97] In 1877 twenty-eight courtesans were chosen, each represented by the name of a flower.[98] Similar contests were held annually. The literati would extol the loveliness of each new beauty queen. In 1896 Li Boyuan founded the first of what came to be known as the "mosquito press," the *Entertainment News*. The following year the newspaper announced a competition to nominate the "four temple gods" of the Shanghai demi-monde. In 1898 they nominated the "top prize winner in the land of flowers," followed by the second and third prize winners, using the terms *zhuangyuan*, *bangyan*, and *tanhua*, as in the imperial examinations.[99] On the day the results were announced, readers would rush to buy the *Entertainment News* and enthusiastically discuss their views on the judges' choices. Again mimicking the imperial examinations, the newspaper would send messengers with gongs and drums to the residence of the top prize winner to announce the good news. These "flower name lists" increased the newspaper's circulation, and it was not long before Shanghai saw more "mosquito press" publications specializing in news about prostitutes.[100] By this stage the competitions involved much serious preparation and strategy by both the commercial world and the prostitutes.[101]

The lifestyle of the Shanghai literati, including their overindulgence in wine, women, and opium, led to many of them dying young. Han Ziyun died at the age of thirty-nine.[102] Zhou Bingyuan was addicted to opium and alcohol; he died at the age of forty-two. Gao Taichi died at a similar age.[103] Li Boyuan frequented prostitutes to the end of his days (he died at forty); his close friend and assistant, Ouyang Juyuan, contracted venereal disease from a prostitute and died in a small roadside inn at the age of twenty-five.[104] Wang Tao lived to seventy, but he had lost most of his teeth by age thirty-five, and his eyesight was severely weakened.[105]

Others deliberately flaunted conventional morality in their attempts to compensate for their loss of social status and the non-recognition of their abilities. Gong Xiaogong, for example, had studied Manchu, Mongol, and Sanskrit while living in Beijing, and was regarded by his contemporaries as an extremely erudite scholar. His private library was among the best in Zhejiang and Jiangsu. He moved from Beijing to Shanghai in 1850, and in 1860 was engaged as a secretary to Thomas Wade, an influential British diplomat. His overindulgence in wine and neglect of his appearance led to acquaintances shunning him. He rejected the "five relationships," calling himself Gong Banlun ("half a moral relationship"), a reference to his concubine. He did not see his wife (the daughter of the Hanlin academician Chen Xianzeng) for ten years, and when his sons came to Shanghai to visit him, he drove them from his house. He also refused to see his brother, a magistrate. After his death, neither his children nor his friends felt any obligation to collect and publish his works, and as a result none of his writings were issued. Thirteen volumes of his unpublished manuscripts on etymology, phonetics, and epigraphy survive in Hangzhou.[106]

Gong Xiaogong became something of a legend. He appears as a character in *Flowers on the Sea of Sin*, which depicts him as approving of burning the Yuanmingyuan on the grounds that it was preferable to give the empire to the foreigners than to leave it in the hands of the Qing. It was said that when he was editing Gong Zizhen's works for publication he would work with his late father's spirit tablet by his side and would occasionally beat it with a wooden ruler. He explained that when he was a child his father had beaten him when he made mistakes in his essays, and now he was returning the favor.[107] Whether or not these stories are true, what we know of Gong Xiaogong, from comments made by Wang Tao, suggests they were pretty much in character.

Nostalgia

Settlement literati were drawn to the traditional image of the "talented courtesan," a well-educated, beautiful, and charming companion who could entertain the scholarly class with poetry, music, dance, and other accomplishments. The "talented courtesans" in China were very few, and they were even rarer in the foreign settlements. Hua Xiangyun could be considered one, and when she died of consumption at an early age in 1887, the literati contributed to her funeral expenses.

> Hua Xiangyun was a woman of outstanding ability amongst the courtesans of Shanghai. Gentle by nature, she loved literature and entertained the resident literati of Shanghai, who wrote poems praising her. Beneath the lamps, with wine at their side, she was tireless in her conversation with them. She would not even glance at the "fellows in silk breeches," even if they offered a large amount of money. The sisters in her profession regarded her as a bookworm. Xiangyun pitied herself because she had fallen and had not met a person with whom she might share her soul. She often knitted her eyebrows in distress. From morning to night horses and carriages would gather at her door, but her spiritless and unenthusiastic manner made rich merchants unhappy, and they left. In autumn of the year *dinghai* [1887] she died of consumption. Before she died, she smiled at her foster mother and said, "Amah, the money tree has fallen." The following year, all the poets collected money to bury her in an unoccupied piece of land at the western side of the Jing'an Temple. They erected a stone pavilion and

inscribed a memorial stone: "Here lies the buried fragrance of Hua Xiangyun, Imperial Attendant." They planted a dozen or so trees around it: plum, apricot, crab-apple and pear. On a fine day in spring or autumn, crowds would pass by, and scholars would write a few words of condolence on the pillars of the pavilion (Fig. 5).[108]

Wang Tao wrote of her,

I pitied no one more than Xiangyun. She had just reached the age at which she would lose her virginity. Her complexion was like jade, her waist was so slender one could grasp it. Charming eyes like waves, fine bones and slender body, her step was so light she did not leave a footprint in the dust. The Scholar of the Late Evening Clouds loved her to distraction. He often used to grasp her in his arms, and lift her body into the air. He could almost make her dance in the palm of his hand—she was like a fairy rising to the clouds. When she began to cough blood, she refused to call a doctor or take medicine; she simply said, "This is my fate." She wanted to offer her pure body to the highest of the heavens. After she died they lifted her corpse into her coffin and placed it in a deserted place. The Scholar of the Late Evening Clouds wanted to buy land on which to bury her, but he was not able to do so.[109]

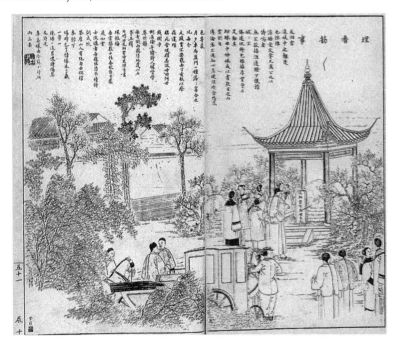

5. Shanghai literati at the grave of courtesan Hua Xiangyun (1889).

The image of the "talented courtesan" is often to be found among Wang Tao's biographical sketches. Chen Yue'e was a daughter of a well-off family who had fallen into prostitution after the death of her father. She could compose verse and "liked to discuss poetry with scholars . . . she was proper, dignified, and careful in her speech and laughter." The madam, however, forced her to entertain the rich. Her favorite client was a man who had given up literature for business. He was not successful, however, and remained poor. The madam would not tolerate him, and eventually he was forced to stay away.[110]

A BRIEF HISTORY   17

These women fit the image of the traditional "talented courtesans," but we might question the degree of accuracy of the accounts. As far as the literati were concerned, such images provided them a certain consolation. They had lost their traditional status and privileges when they took up residence in the settlements. The prostitutes there were not in the same class as traditional courtesans, and the settlement literati did not constitute their major clientele. For love affairs, the courtesans generally preferred more virile types, such as young actors and carriage drivers. Financially—or when considering marriage—they preferred rich merchants. Most of the merchants and compradors in Shanghai were typical *nouveau riche*—wealthy but uneducated. This was even more galling for the literati.

The ambivalent attitude of the settlement literati to the "new" can be detected in their attitude towards prostitutes. While they considered themselves "avant-garde" and were happy to enjoy the material benefits of living in the settlements, they were dissatisfied with losing their traditional privileges, including the privilege of associating with high-class courtesans. The world represented by Hua Xiangyun was a world they had irrevocably lost.

Self-pity of the literati

The income of the literati was usually insufficient to support their lifestyles, and their poverty was a constant source of distress. Most had not inherited wealth, nor did they have wealthy relatives. They had to support their families with no outside help, and they often could not meet their expenses.[111] Those who did have a degree of wealth soon squandered it. Han Ziyun came from a prominent family, but he spent his inheritance in brothels. It was said that his inheritance provided him with the raw material for his novel *Flowers on the Sea*.[112] Gong Xiaogong came from an even wealthier family. When his famous library was destroyed by fire, however, he could no longer continue to sell rare books to cover his living expenses and died in poverty.[113]

Visiting high-class brothels was expensive. Settlement literati were merely wage earners, and they could not get involved too deeply. As mentioned above, Wang Tao observed that The Scholar of the Late Evening Clouds wanted to contribute towards Hua Xiangyun's burial expenses, but was unable to do so, presumably for financial reasons. Hua's coffin had to remain unburied until the literati of Shanghai could put together enough money to make funeral arrangements. Each man had his favorite courtesan, but generally did not have enough money to monopolize her company, or to redeem and marry her.[114] In an article on the famous courtesan Lin Daiyu, Qian Xinbo lamented, "Those who become prostitutes have only two things in mind: one is the wallet of her guest, the other is his looks. If he is good looking but has little money, she can tolerate him. If his wallet is full but his face ugly, she can cope, for the sake of the money. But those who can write beautiful poetry—even if Li Bai came back to life, he would not be appreciated in the least."[115] Again, it was clearly hard for the literati to accept their change of status.

In 1884, the *Dianshizhai* carried a story about a dispute in the Diyilou Teahouse. A scholar began to flirt with a maid-servant of one of the prostitutes. The servant laughed at him, suggesting this was a case of "a toad lusting after swan flesh." The scholar could not tolerate this affront and beat her (Fig. 6).[116] In this case, the swan was not even the prostitute, but her servant. Wang Tao commented, "Shanghai is the land of many beautiful women. Extravagance and profligacy are the rule. Wealth is power. Overpowering dandies and bullying merchants know how to display their wealth, but they are illiterate."[117]

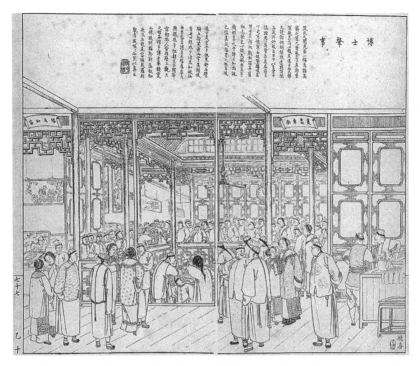

6. A scholar is insulted by a prostitute's servant (1884). A Confucian scholar attempts to flirt with the prostitute's maid-servant, who rebukes him as a "toad lusting after swan's flesh." The incident occurred in the Diyilou Teahouse.

Such views were also printed from time to time in the *Shenbao*. In 1875 an article complained that courtesans were once the exclusive property of the scholar-official class, but nowadays any ruffian who could "crow like a cock and snatch like a dog" could enjoy this pleasure.[118] Other articles gave more detail: "Those in the Green Bowers like rich merchants. We impoverished scholars can only gaze at them from a distance. When they meet their clients, they are sure to ask what business they are in. The world is turned upside-down; the Way of the Gentleman is lost. Whenever I think of this, I want to weep like Ruan Ji."[119] The article went on to describe these people as "so unprepossessing in their appearance, their speech so vulgar . . . . If you ask them their profession, they are either compradors or interpreters. They do not have a decent bone in their bodies, from the top of the head to their heels. But still they put great effort into trying to be elegant."[120]

General feelings of unrecognized talent, poverty, and dissipation were not unusual among the literati in traditional China. The Shanghai literati felt these particularly keenly. Their new careers did not compensate them for the loss of their traditional identity in either social status or financial advantage. They were significant participants in the creation of a new urban culture, yet showed a deep sense of nostalgia for a world they had lost, and a sense of anomie about their rapidly changing society. The alienation that traditional scholars across China would suffer with the abolition of the imperial examination system had already gripped the literati in Shanghai half a century earlier.

3. The nature of the *Dianshizhai*

One adjustment the Shanghai literati had to make was to learn to write for a new purpose and readership. The Chinese educated elite traditionally wrote for serious purposes or for self-expression. As journalists, they now had to learn to write for consumers.

Major gave his writers enough latitude to accommodate both commercial principles and their own personal attitudes. "New" was the main attraction of the *Dianshizhai*, and "new learning" occupied an important position in it. Generally speaking, the Shanghai literati welcomed aspects of material Western civilization such as wide streets and running water. Many of the sketches in the *Dianshizhai* addressed local news—about the theatres, restaurants, brothels and various types of new entertainment—aspects of life in Shanghai familiar to both the writers and their readers. Yet the attitudes expressed in the commentaries remain those of traditional literati and reveal a deep-seated discontent with the new urban culture developing in the settlements.

The challenge and excitement of "the new"

Introduction of knowledge about the West was a major aim of the *Dianshizhai*. The authors paid particular attention to new discoveries in the fields of science and technology. The advertisement for issue No. 6 states, "Whenever a new invention appears in the West, whenever they create something new, we will introduce and illustrate all those things which are useful to the country and the people. These can be used by officials and merchants, not only to expand their knowledge, but also to be of practical use."[121] The authors expressed their admiration for the "strange skills and excessive ingenuity" of Westerners.[122] When introducing the hot-air balloon they note, "Science and technology in the West are becoming more and more developed . . . Westerners are curious by nature and feel ashamed to follow the same old ways, so they are able to come up with new ideas (Fig. 7)."[123] An article on a submarine comments, "There is no end to Western ingenuity. Hot-air balloons that can fly, and steamships that can travel so quickly—such things we have already seen or heard about. Now we have heard a story about a boat that can travel under water . . . (Fig. 8)."[124] Introducing X-rays and their medical use, the commentary reads,

> The skill of Western science and technology is applied to the use of lenses. The telescope can reach into the furthest distances, and the microscope can analyze the awn of wheat. This is far removed from 'ancient mirrors reflect an image, neither the beautiful nor the ugly can escape,' is it not? It just becomes more and more amazing. Now there is a ray of light which can penetrate the darkest and most hidden places. . . . If you want to be good at something you must first sharpen your tools. Western doctors are constantly improving their skills and certainly do not rest on their laurels. So their skills continue to improve."[125]

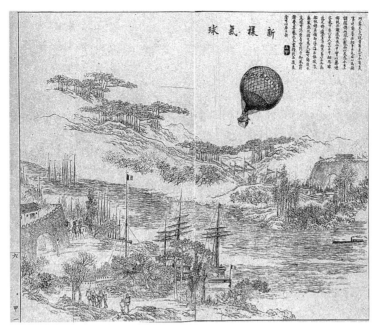

7. A hot air balloon (1884). This sketch is from the first issue of the *Dianshizhai*. The commentary notes the balloon was used in the Franco-Prussian War for gathering military intelligence.

8. A submarine (1884). This sketch is also from the first issue of the *Dianshizhai*. The text says it was three hundred feet (*chi*) long and traveled along the seabed as if it were dry land.

The artists had not traveled overseas, and the amount of information they could acquire through photographs or drawings was limited. In many cases, their imaginations became the main means by which events in foreign countries were depicted. It was inevitable that this led to mistakes and misunderstandings. One drawing shows an American skyscraper structured like a Chinese pagoda;[126] another dresses Eskimos (living in a thickly forested environment) in European costumes[127] and another dresses Tibetans like Arabs.[128]

Sometimes the stories exaggerated the achievements of Western science. One story concerned a man from Australia who possessed rainmaking magic and could make rain fall in any district he wanted.[129] Another related how Westerners could shrink corpses chemically and put them in a wooden box so they could be carried around,[130] yet another how they turn human corpses into fertilizer. The accompanying sketch looks like a slaughterhouse (Fig. 9).[131] The following year the *Dianshizhai* published a retraction of these two stories (Fig. 10), but not so much because of their incredibility—the *Dianshizhai* was full of stories of ghosts and sensational oddities. These two stories impinged on a Chinese cultural taboo, the integrity of the human body, including corpses, and offended public sentiment (see also pages 134–36).[132]

The *Dianshizhai* also introduced items of general interest, such as an earthquake in Britain,[133] a fire in a New York skyscraper,[134] a bicycle race in London,[135] the 1890 World Fair in Paris,[136] discoveries in the Gobi desert by a Swedish archaeological expedition,[137] eucalyptus trees,[138] and ways of exterminating wild rabbits in Australia.[139] It covered the coronation of the Russian czar, with envoys of the various countries of the world, including Li Hongzhang, participating in the ceremonies,[140] and reported injuries among the spectators due to overcrowding.[141] In 1896 it dedicated five sketches to an expedition to the North Pole, describing the welcome extended to the Norwegian explorer on his return home and the lifestyle of the Eskimos.[142] It also introduced customs of other lands, such as bullfighting in Spain,[143] and Hindu respect for the cow.[144] In informing its readers that Westerners sometimes kiss each other on parting, the *Dianshizhai* noted,

> Different countries have different customs. Some people salute with the hands raised together, some kneel, some make a low bow with the hands in front. Each is a way of expressing politeness. Shaking hands, pecking the cheeks, kissing the mouth, are also ways of expressing politeness. This makes their bodies close to each other. This is considered an expression of feelings . . . Westerners stress feelings the same way Chinese stress politeness. The manner of expression may be different, but the intention is the same.[145]

The Western approach to marriage was also of interest to the *Dianshizhai*. "According to Western customs, when a man and woman want to marry, they must first become betrothed, so that they can observe each other's natures and personalities. If there are no conflicts between them, they exchange letters. In this way they develop their relationship. If both sides are willing, they agree to become husband and wife."[146] The writers even noted the concept of equality between men and women:

> In China, the difference in status between men and women is emphasized. The difference is like that between Heaven and Earth. People are used to this and do not have any particular feelings on the matter. Western countries are different. Both men and women enter school when they are young, so there are many Western women who understand mathematics.[147]

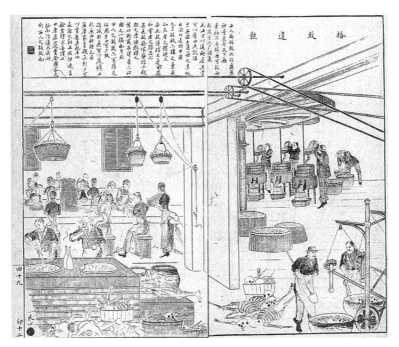

9. Westerners transform corpses into fertilizer (1888). "Westerners value science. They can transform the corruptible into the miraculous." The commentary goes on to say that corpses can be transformed into fertilizer, so the poor are spared funeral expenses and make some money as well.

10. An editorial correction (1889). "For some time, this studio has published a pictorial in the Western style. All the news is from newspapers of various countries. In the eighth month of last year we printed an item about a magical method of shrinking corpses. In the tenth month we published items on the investigation of human remains and the mutilation of corpses. We had a source for each item, but having thoroughly investigated the matter, we now know these items were fictitious. The studio here announces a correction. Not long ago we received official notice from the Shanghai daotai instructing us to immediately publish an announcement in the newspaper recognizing these mistakes, in order to dispel public doubt."

Their understanding of gender issues may surprise modern readers:

> The Chinese custom is to discriminate in favor of men over women. Where there are capable women, people laugh at them and say are they are like hens crowing at dawn; *yin and yang* must not be inverted. In the West, it is different. They value women highly, much more than men. So women of talent are often to be seen. So now there are women doctors, women lawyers and women ship captains.[148]

Some Western political concepts were also introduced through descriptions of the democratic process. In a story about the United States president Ulysses S. Grant, who was reported to be living in relative poverty after his retirement, the *Dianshizhai* introduced the idea of an elected president.[149] Describing the public libraries of England, the *Dianshizhai* criticized the Chinese tradition of personal libraries: "Chinese traditional academies also have well-stocked libraries for their scholars to read, but there is no such a thing as a public library. Du Fu wrote: 'If we could build a mansion of ten thousand rooms, and all poor scholars under Heaven could take refuge there, such joy would be on their faces.' When we recite these words . . . alas, alas!"[150]

A new artistic style

The unconventional style and content of the sketches in the *Dianshizhai* led to some criticism of its artists, especially Wu Youru. Wu Youru countered that "Painting should change with the times. Whatever is present in a certain period can be used as subject matter. When we look at Song and Yuan paintings, we regard them as ancient, elegant, and far from vulgarity. But surely we know that the Song and Yuan artists were doing no more than painting scenes which were in front of their eyes. So, since now we are in contact with new things, why should we reject them?"[151]

Art historians recognize that the *Dianshizhai* developed a style that mixed Western elements with traditional Chinese painting. As Yu Yueting put it,

> After the lead given by Wu Youru and the *Dianshizhai*, painting new things became all the rage for some time . . . he [Wu] absorbed some of the techniques of European artists, such as perspective and so on. This gave new life to traditional Chinese art. . . . The *Dianshizhai* was widely distributed, and its influence on later artistic developments was greater than that of anything similar. The reason why New Year prints and illustrated storybooks nowadays are quite different in appearance is not unconnected to the influence of the *Dianshizhai*.[152]

Major also had some influence in the introduction of new painting techniques for his pictorial. In an article attached to the first issue he commented,

> Chinese prefer to learn things through the written word, and there is no need to rely on the appearance of things in order to know them. I have often thought about the reasons for this. Probably it is because the drawings of the West are different from those of China. Western illustrations are realistic—nine out of ten are photographs, developed in a chemical solution. Things as fine as a hair, or depths of dimension, are all included. Huge lenses can enlarge small things, and can show everything near, far, deep, or shallow. They can catch everything so wonderfully, even the shadow of clouds on the ripples of the water; the difference between the light of a candle and the aura of the moon, the difference between clear skies and rain, between night and day all can be clearly shown. Even for those things which, to normal vision, are

blurred and cannot be distinguished, through this instrument, it is as if you yourself had entered the scene. People are so vividly depicted they seem to be alive. Chinese painters are restricted to traditional techniques. They have to follow certain rules. First they have to work out the appropriate positions, then fill in the details . . . . In short, Western illustrations of good or average quality are expected to be lifelike . . . . However, this has not been used before in illustrating the news. The world has developed to the present stage, and society is more open minded. For example, nowadays many Chinese understand Western languages. With long familiarity, customs will also change.[153]

The mixed artistic styles in the *Dianshizhai* sketches must have impressed the reader as one which was both fresh and new, but not too unfamiliar. The areas touched up in the original sketches were those involving perspective—the new technique characteristic of the *Dianshizhai*. It is clear that the Chinese painters had not yet completely mastered it.

The relatively superficial understanding of the West represented in the *Dianshizhai* became an object of ridicule among twentieth-century elites. Lu Xun's comments are well known:

> Prior to this had appeared the *Tien-shih-chai Pictorial* edited by Wu Yu-ju [Wu Youru], with pictures of men and immortals, domestic and foreign news. But since Wu was rather hazy about foreign affairs, he depicted a battleship as a cargo boat with cannon on the deck, and "A duel" as two uniformed soldiers fighting with swords in a sitting-room till all the vases were broken. Still, his "Bawd beats a strumpet and hooligan assaults a girl" were excellent drawings, doubtless because he had seen so many cases in real life. Even today in Shanghai, we can see many faces just like those he painted. This pictorial was extremely influential in its time, selling in every province, and considered required reading for all who wished to understand 'current events'— the equivalent of present-day 'new learning.' Some years ago it was reprinted under the title *Wu Yu-ju's Album*, and the extent of its influence was fantastic. We need not mention illustrations in novels; even textbook illustrations often have children with caps askew, slant eyes, fleshy jowls and the look of hooligans.[154]

Reinforcing traditional moral values

In order to "surprise and entertain," a large number of the items in the *Dianshizhai* are ghost stories and oddities (Fig. 11). There are stories about a walking corpse chasing people in Ningbo, a Daoist priest who met a ghost on the road at night, and a destitute man contemplating suicide when he heard a conversation between ghosts.[155] Oddities included a chicken with the face of a man, discovered in America;[156] a huge stone which turned into a goblin, also in America;[157] deformed fetuses in Japan,[158] a man in England who discovered an underground water source by magic;[159] the discovery of a fish in London that had leaves growing on its body,[160] and so on. Strange tales from China include a woman in Beijing who gave birth to a tortoise,[161] a woman in Hankou who gave birth to a snake;[162] a donkey that laid an egg;[163] a six-legged ox in Zhejiang,[164] and many others of this type.

From issue No. 6 on, the *Dianshizhai* distributed, free of charge, a collection of tales of the strange and supernatural by Wang Tao, entitled *Random Jottings of a Wusong Recluse*.[165] In his preface, Wang Tao states that Major had repeatedly urged him to write such a book, so he collected a number of strange tales from the past thirty years; Major had also asked Wu Youru to provide illustrations.[166] In the advertisement for issue No. 5 Major wrote, "This company cultivates the literary and the elegant; we spare no expense in pursuit of the excellent. . . . This book is so wonderful that the reader will strike the table and shout 'Bravo!' and will continue to marvel all the way through it."[167] In his advertisement for issue No. 6, Major was also full of praise for Wang Tao: "There is no book he has not read and is thoroughly familiar with, and this is the reason his writing is so marvelous." He adds, "*Strange Tales from a Chinese Studio* has stories but no pictures; but there is a picture for every story in Wang Tao's book, so in this way it surpasses the *Strange Tales*, and in every other way matches its standard."[168] The publication of this title in serial form continued for more than a year, up to issue No. 61 of December 21, 1885.

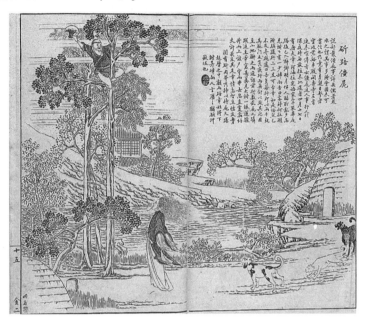

11. A drunk encounters a walking corpse (1891). He escapes only by climbing a tree and striking the corpse's head with his axe.

The literati as educated Confucians would not have believed such stories themselves. For Major, ghosts and demons were perennial Chinese concerns, and their bizarreness would attract more readers. Given the basic editorial policy of the *Dianshizhai* "to surprise and entertain," the literati could not really object to the publication of such stories. Moreover the stories provided them an opportunity to reinforce aspects of Confucian morality. The dual purpose of such stories is made clear by a note usually appended to them pointing out that "Confucian scholars will probably deny this sort of story and say they are far-fetched and not to be believed. There are, however, people who have witnessed these things for themselves."[169]

Many of the stories concern filial piety, either the praising behavior that properly exhibited it, or condemning behavior that did not. They include a story about a filial daughter who cut flesh from her arm as a cure for her father's illness (Fig. 12);[170] and another about at young child who, having seen his mother fall into a well, jumped in to save her but was himself drowned. This spirit of self-sacrifice moved Heaven, and the child was brought back to life.[171] Even stranger is the tale of the filial daughter who moved Heaven and was turned into a man, to gladden the hearts of her parents, who had no sons.[172]

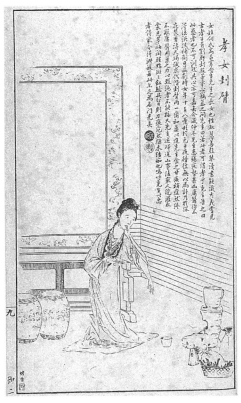

12. The filial daughter of a *Shenbao* editor (1895). The daughter of He Guisheng cuts flesh from her arm to make a medicinal broth for her ailing father. The *Dianshizhai* did not approve of self-mutilation, but praised her filial piety. Both the writer and illustrator must have known He Guisheng personally. The daughter's dress in the sketch is pre-Qing—presumably the illustrator thought it made her appear more traditional. "This woman is surnamed He. She is the eldest daughter of the Cold Food Scholar of Gaochang, He Guisheng. She is intelligent and kind-hearted by nature, and skillful at playing the zither. Her reading ability is such that she can grasp the general meaning.

She had often read of filial children in ancient times, who did such things as cut out their livers and gorge out the flesh from their thighs. In her heart she admired such acts. She once asked her father if these acts should be considered filial piety. Her father told her that such acts were misguided filial piety and should not be imitated. Their intentions were good, however, and should be praised.

This year during the winter, her father developed ulcers. His condition became very serious, and the doctors, incompetent as they were, could not come up with an effective cure and erroneously prescribed tonics. His health deteriorated daily. His daughter at this time was eighteen years old, and worry was written on her face. She paced to and fro, day and night. She didn't know what to do. One night she lit incense and prayed to Heaven, begging that she might suffer in her father's place. Hiding herself away, she cut a slice of flesh from her arm and mixed it with medicine and presented it [to her father]. It was sweet to her father's lips, and he felt slightly better. However, it was no match for the harmful effects of the tonics prescribed by the charlatans.

This pure act of filial piety could not change the predestination of Heaven, and her father entered paradise—alas, alas! The father handed down the principles of filial piety, and now his kind and gentle daughter has brought glory to her family."

Filial piety was followed by feminine chastity. Most of these stories tell of widows who maintained chaste lives after the death of their husbands, and were rewarded for this (Fig. 13). When one old woman who had remained chaste for many years fell ill, a strange monk happened to pass by her door, and her illness was cured without treatment.[173] A chaste woman was killed in a fire, but since her face remained unscarred, people said she had been protected by Heaven.[174] When a widow grew whiskers and almost became a man [in appearance]; this was Heaven determining that she should not remarry.[175]

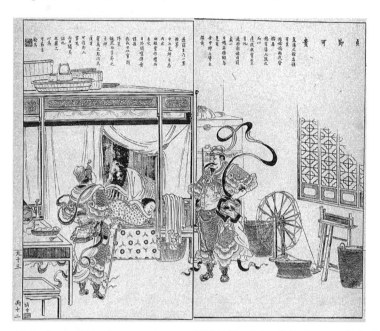

13. A chaste widow becomes pregnant (1885). She claimed this happened after being visited by a spirit in a dream. The commentary says the story is ridiculous, but takes the opportunity to praise the virtue of chastity in widows.

Stories of retribution abound—criticizing corrupt officials who stole money intended for victims of natural disasters,[176] and praising those who financially helped victims of such disasters.[177] Others praise honesty and incorruptibility.[178] There are stories in which people who perform some act of kindness to animals and fish are rewarded,[179] and others relating how those who kill animals and eat their meat are punished.[180] Some stories praise the kind-hearted nature displayed by certain animals, such as the cat that killed a snake to save its owner's child,[181] the horse that died soon after its master,[182] and the dog of Deng Shichang, captain of a Chinese warship in the Sino-Japanese War of 1894, which loyally followed its master to his death.[183]

Commercial and enlightened, but not politically radical

The *Shenbao* and the *Dianshizhai* were commercial enterprises, and Major did not want them to become highly political. In 1872 when the *Shenbao* was inaugurated, Major published an editorial titled "*The Peking Gazette* and a Newspaper are Different," explaining that the *Shenbao* was a new-style newspaper, such as had never existed in China before. He declared that it had no intention of offending the Court.[184] In 1885 Major, speaking as the proprietor of the *Shenbao*, again articulated this policy in another editorial: "Our purpose is to publish a newspaper. We are careful not to comment on current affairs, nor to criticize individuals, which might invoke the anger of the present government and run the risk and the shame of being banned. Thus each is concerned only with his own affairs, and this is beneficial to all."[185] Major had good reasons for this policy. During the 1870s, two clashes erupted between the *Shenbao* and Chinese officialdom. The first involved the Shanghai magistrate Ye Tingjuan over the case of a Peking opera performer, Yang Yuelou. The second concerned publication of an article which offended Guo Songtao, the first Chinese minister to Great Britain. The *Shenbao* was able to deal with the first problem easily enough, but the incident with Guo Songtao caused Major a good deal of trouble. The *Shenbao* had no choice but to publish an apology.[186] The *Dianshizhai* itself did not make any such statements, but in the editorial to the inaugural issue Major stated its purpose clearly—it was to be light reading, amusing, interesting. Its aim was to introduce new knowledge, and to open up new horizons—not to criticize the government.

This policy suited the literati. Writers for the *Shenbao* and the *Dianshizhai* were not political radicals, but rather individuals who supported the Self-strengthening Movement, and were interested in Western science and technology. In their story on the observatory at the Interpreters College in Beijing, they noted, "All Western science is based on mathematics, so mathematics is the origin of all the sciences. Astronomers also rely on mathematics to make their predictions."[187] Another story described an envoy who had been sent to the West and returned with more than two hundred volumes on science and technology. The commentary reveals the attitude of the *Dianshizhai* writers to the old examination system: "The present dynasty continues the old system of the Ming, relying on eight-legged essays to choose officials. Scholars with the ambition to advance must exhaust all their energies and abilities to master this style. Since we have begun communication with Western countries the situation has changed, and those who hold power in the country are making the best use of it. They have established the Interpreters College and recruit intelligent young people; they have invited Westerners to supervise and teach in every field. It has gradually become quite impressive."[188]

The settlement literati enjoyed a certain degree of immunity from official censorship by virtue of their residence and employment. The *Dianshizhai* did not generally adopt a critical attitude, nor did it incite clashes with Chinese officialdom. If any official of note visited Shanghai, the *Dianshizhai* would be sure to report the occasion. When Zeng Guoquan visited Shanghai in 1884, Major sent Wu Youru to the pier to observe the scene, and later published Wu's sketch of the welcoming ceremonies.[189] In 1896, Li Hongzhang passed through Shanghai, and the *Dianshizhai* reported this as a visit of great importance.[190] In the same year the *Dianshizhai* published two portraits of Li Hongzhang, one of them on the occasion of his seventieth birthday.[191] There was continuous military strife between China, France, and Japan, and the *Dianshizhai* was full of praise for Liu Yongfu, the commander of the Chinese troops. In 1888 and 1895, it published two identical portraits of him.[192] It also gave accounts of officials such as Zuo Zongtang in a series of sketches that showed their various meritorious deeds.[193] Other officials mentioned in the *Dianshizhai* include Zhang Zhidong[194] and Feng Zicai.[195] In his advertisement for issue No. 9, Major announced, "As soon as it receives any portraits of high officials of the dynasty, this company immediately commissions artists to make copies of them and also lists their recent deeds in the *Pictorial*. In issue No. 3, we printed portraits of Li Hongzhang and Zeng

Guofan, and in issue No. 9 we are printing portraits of His Highness (*Qinwang dachen*) and Zuo Zongtang...."[196] In 1884, on the occasion of the birthday of the Guangxu emperor, the *Dianshizhai* published a picture entitled "Grand ceremony in honor of the birthday of the emperor.[197] In 1894, on the occasion of the Empress Dowager's sixtieth birthday, the *Dianshizhai* also commissioned a picture in her honor.[198] Wang Tao would also occasionally contribute a few lines of calligraphy to accompany the portraits of officials reproduced in the *Dianshizhai*.[199]

The *Dianshizhai* adhered strictly to this policy, even after Major left China. In 1895, after the Sino-Japanese War, Kang Youwei led more than 1,200 provincial graduates in submitting a memorial protesting against the Treaty of Shimonoseki. This was a remarkable event, but the *Dianshizhai* only mentioned it once, reporting the protest against the treaty which ceded Taiwan to Japan; it did not mention that the memorial went on to demand reform (Fig. 14).[200]

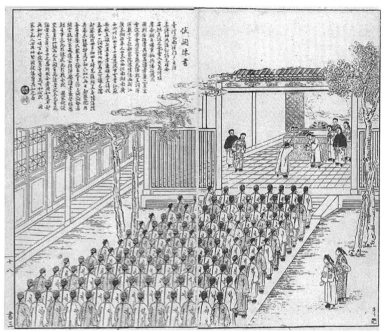

14. Provincial examination candidates present a petition in the capital (1895). After China's defeat in the Sino-Japanese War of 1895, one thousand candidates for the *jinshi* degree examination in Beijing presented a petition to the Censorate. The commentary does not mention Kang Youwei, nor that the petition demanded reform.

The *Dianshizhai* also reported the establishment of the Republic of Taiwan as an attempt to resist the Japanese annexation. The Treaty of Shimonoseki was signed on April 17 and ratified on May 8. Zhang Zhidong and the acting governor of Taiwan, Tang Jingsong, suggested the establishment of an independent republic on Taiwan to thwart the provisions of the treaty. This plan was condemned by the Qing court, Li Hongzhang, and the Western powers. There was strong support for this plan in Taiwan, however, and Tang declared the establishment of the Republic of Taiwan with himself as president. The *Dianshizhai* published a sketch and commentary praising Tang's actions, and only hinted at public anger against Li Hongzhang, who had criticized Zhang Zhidong and Tang Jingsong for "inciting rebellion" (Fig. 15).[201]

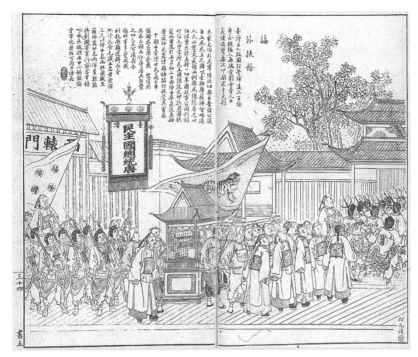

15. The "Republic of Taiwan" (1895). Fuyu was the name of an ancient state in the area of the Sungari which had close relations with the central plains during the Eastern Han period. Here it refers to Taiwan: "Taiwan has been registered on our maps, it has been managed and built up for more than two hundred years. Now the Japanese dwarves have snatched it for no reason. Righteous anger fills the breasts of all the people of Taiwan. They have repeatedly entreated the court to spare them this separation, but their requests have not been approved. The mood of the people has become urgent.

    Having aroused themselves, they decided through public discussion to establish a republic. The governor of Taiwan, Tang Weishuai [Tang Jingsong], being extraordinarily intelligent and beloved by the people, in accordance with Western precedent, has been made president. The seal of Boli and the seal of Tiande have been bestowed on him, and he has been put in charge of all military and state affairs. The inscription reads: 'Seal of the President of the Republic of Taiwan.' They have adopted a national flag—a yellow tiger on a blue background. When on the second day of the fifth month the gentry led the people to present the seals and the flag at the Governor's Residence, Tang Jingsong realized it would not be easy to dismiss the feelings of the people and reluctantly accepted them. Then he sent a telegram to the Court: 'The people of Taiwan are determined not to be the subjects of the Japanese dwarves. They want their island to remain under the Qing forever, to observe its calendar, and to be its protective screen.'

    Their efforts in coping with the situation cannot be denied. The situation is constantly changing. Success or failure, profit or loss are difficult to predict. The gentry and people of Taiwan, eating the emperor's grain and occupying the emperor's land, have expressed their loyalty to the throne and their love of country. This has lead to heightened morale and great national prestige. Tang Jingsong faced a crisis, and each step was fraught with difficulties. Together with Liu Yongfu, he has brought matters under control with great grace. They are as firm as the Great Wall. They cannot be spoken of in the same breath with certain people who fawn on the enemy and bend their heads to serve the foe."

According to Wu Micha, when the petitioners arrived at the governor's residence, Tang Jingsong, "wearing his official robes, turned in the direction of the imperial capital and kowtowed nine times. Then, facing the north, he accepted this commission, burst into tears, and withdrew." The banner in the sketch reads: "President Tang of the Republic of Taiwan". The smaller banner reads: "Expel the Japanese bandits." The middle banner is the Taiwan national flag, a yellow tiger on a blue ground. At the center of the picture is a shrine in which the presidential seals have been placed.

During the ensuing Reform Movement, politically committed Chinese language newspapers appeared in Shanghai,[202] but the *Dianshizhai* maintained its neutrality as before. Even during the Hundred Days Reform, the *Dianshizhai* published only one picture that even hinted at the political situation. When the Guangxu emperor issued an edict on the examination system in 1898, several thousand Guangxi scholars educated under the old system objected. The *Dianshizhai* criticized them as out of touch with the times and commented, "Chinese scholars persist in their bad habits—how ridiculous!" (Fig. 16).[203]

16. Eight-legged ghosts (1898). The term *shiwen* (current writings) was a derogatory name for the eight-legged essay during the Hundred Days Reform. This is one of the illustrations in the last issue of the Dianshizhai. The commentary here ridicules those scholars who opposed reform.

The *Dianshizhai* advocated the study of Western science and supported the new education system. Its contributors supported the reform of the examination system, and this was the theme of a sketch and commentary in the final issue of August 8–16, 1898. One month later, the Hundred Days Reform was suppressed. The *Shenbao* was silent for three months and had no choice but to issue a statement in support of the conservatives, including the reinstitution of the examination system.[214] By that time, the *Dianshizhai Pictorial* had ceased publication.

Notes

[1] The idea of establishing a newspaper seems to have originated with a comprador, Chen Huageng. Sources differ as to the name of this man. See Zhang Jinglu, *Zhongguo jindai chuban shiliao chubian* (Historical sources on publishing in Modern China, Part I)(Shanghai: Qunyi chubanshe, 1953), 270; Yu Yueting, *Woguo huabao de shizu* (The ancestor of the pictorial in China) (Beijing: Xinhua chubanshe, 1981), 150; Zheng Yimei, *Shu bao hua jiu* (Talks about the old days of books and newspapers) (Shanghai: Xuelin chubanshe, 1983), 84; Roswell S. Britton, *The Chinese Periodical Press 1800-1912* (Shanghai, 1933; reprinted Taipei: Ch'eng-wen Publishing Company, 1966), 64; Xu Zaiping, "*Shenbao* shi ruhe jikua *Shanghai Xinbao* de?" (How did the *Shenbao* gain ascendancy over the *Shanghai Xinbao*), in *Xinwen yanjiu ziliao* (Beijing: Zhongguo zhanwang chubanshe, 1982), vol. 15, 209.

[2] This story is given in many sources, sometimes word for word. See Zhang Jinglu, *Chuban shiliao chubian*, 270; Yu Yueting, *Huabao de shizu*, *passim*; Xiang Dicong, "Shanghai *Dianshizhai* shiyin shu bao ji qi jiqizhe" (Lithographic printing of books and newspapers at the *Dianshizhai* in Shanghai, and their successors), in *Shanghai difangzhi ziliao* (Shanghai: Shanghai shehui kexue chubanshe, 1986), vol. 4, 245; Zheng Yimei, *Shu bao hua jiu*, 84; Cohn, *Vignettes from the Chinese*, 1; Britton, *Chinese Periodical Press*, 64; *Shenbao* shiliao bianxiezu, "Chuangban chuqi de *Shenbao*," in *Xinwen yanjiu ziliao* (Beijing: Xinhua chubanshe, 1979), vol. 1, 138. Wang Tao was the father-in-law of Qian Xinbo (Qian Zheng). See Paul A. Cohen, *Between Tradition and Modernity: Wang T'ao and Reform in Late Ch'ing China*, (Cambridge, Mass.: Harvard University Press, 1974), 77, 82, 292 n. 51.

[3] *Shenbao* shiliao bianxiezu, "Chuangban chuqi," 134.

[4] The *Shanghai Xinbao* was the first Chinese language newspaper in Shanghai. It was established in 1861; most of its news items were translated from the *North-China Daily News*. It was initially a weekly, and was later published every second day. It was managed by John Allen Young and others. It could not compete with the *Shenbao*, and ceased publication of the 31st of December, 1872. See Xu Zaiping, "*Shenbao*," 208–213. According to Liang Jialu, (*Zhongguo xinwenye shi* [A history of the press in China], Guangxi renmin chubanshe, 1984, 37), Major convinced the proprietor of the *Shanghai Xinbao*, Henry Shearman, to withdraw that newspaper from competition with the *Shenbao*, since Shearman already owned the *North-China Herald* and the *North-China Daily News*.

[5] These were: (i) The *Jiangsu Yaoshuichang*, known in English as Major's Acid Works or the Kiangsu Chemical Works; (ii) the *Shenbao* Office, founded in 1872; (iii) the Shen Chang Bookshop (Shenchang Painting and Calligraphy Shop); (iv) the *Dianshizhai* Printing Company, known at that time in English as the Tien Shih Chai Photolithographic Publishing Works, founded in 1876; (v) Major's Soap Factory, founded during the 1870s and (vi) the Sui Chong Match Factory, founded during the 1880s. In 1889 the two brothers amalgamated all these companies into one, Major Brothers Limited, with a capital value of three hundred thousand taels of silver. See Sun Yutang, *Zhongguo jindai gongye shi ziliao, diyi bian*, 111, 125, 236–40. The Major brothers also had interests in Singapore, including forty thousand *mu* of land on which rubber, tobacco, and sugar were produced. See Fang Hanqi, *Zhongguo jindai baokan shi* (A history of the press in modern China), vol. 1 (Taiyuan: Shanxi renmin chubanshe, 1981), 42. On the Jiangsu Chemical Works, Pott notes, "Among the first industrial establishments founded in Shanghai was the Kiangsu Chemical Works, started by the Major Brothers in the early 'sixties, near the old stone bridge which crossed the Soochow Creek." See F. L. Hawks Pott, *A Short History of Shanghai* (Hong Kong and Singapore: Kelly and Walsh), 1928, 135.

[6] Zhang Jinglu, *Zhongguo jindai chuban shiliao, erbian* (Historical sources on publishing in modern China, part 2) (Shanghai: Qunyi chubanshe, 1954), 356. Cohn has pointed out that *Dianshizhai* literally means "The Studio of Touching the Stone," and refers to both the process of lithography (stone-printing) and the phrase *dianshi chengjin*, "touching a stone and turning it into gold," meaning to improve the quality of a literary composition. Cohn, *Vignettes from the Chinese*, 1 n. 1.

[7] Zhang Jinglu, *Zhongguo xiandai chuban shiliao, yibian* (Historical sources on publishing in contemporary China, part 1) (Beijing: Zhonghua shuju, 1959), 269–70, n. 7.

[8] Sun Yutang, *Zhongguo jindai gongye shi ziliao*, 238.

[9] Yao Gonghe, *Shanghai xianhua* (Chats on Shanghai) (Shanghai: Shangwu yinshuguan, 1917), 16; Zheng Yimei, *Shu bao hua jiu*, 84–85; Xu Ke, *Qing bai lei chao* (A collection of Qing anecdotal material), vol. 5 (Shanghai: Shangwu yinshuguan, 1920; reprinted Beijing: Zhonghua shuju 1984), 2316.

[10] *Shenbao* shiliao bianxiezu, "Chuangban chuqi," 136. See also Britton, *Chinese Periodical Press*, 69: "In 1884 Major took over and completed one of its outstanding projects, a reproduction of the K'ang-hsi Imperial Encyclopaedia, the *T'u-shu chi-ch'eng*. This, known as the Major Bro's edition, was printed with metal type in 1,628 volumes, 1885–1888, though the title page is dated 1884."

[11] *North-China Herald*, October 29, 1884.

[12] Xu Renhan, "*Shenbao* qishiqi nian da shiji" (Major events over seventy-seven years of the *Shenbao*), in *Shanghai difangzhi ziliao*, vol. 5, 24; Yu Yueting, *Huabao de shizu, passim*; Fang Hanqi, *Jindai baokan shi*, vol. 1, 54.

[13] See the introduction to the edition of the *Dianshizhai* published by the Guangjiaojing Publishing Company, Hong Kong, 1983, and Major's introduction to the inaugural issue of the *Dianshizhai*. Its English subtitle was "The Illustrated Lithographer," but contemporary usage prefers to call it the *Dianshizhai Pictorial*.

[14] Britton, *Chinese Periodical Press*, 70.

[15] *Shenbao*, April 14–May 16.

[16] Sources differ as to the actual year the *Dianshizhai* ceased publication. Some, such as Yu Yueting (*Huabao de shizu*, 151) give 1896; Nakano and Takeda (*Tensekisai Gahō no Sekai*, 12) also give this date. Others, such as Xiang Dicong ("Shanghai *Dianshizhai*," 247) have concluded the date cannot be determined. Cohn (*Vignettes from the Chinese*, 3) and van Briessen (*Shanghai-Bildzeitung*, 11) both give the date as 1898. The last volume of the *Dianshizhai* mentions the Hundred Days Reform, which proves that the *Dianshizhai* could not have ceased publication in 1896.

[17] The *Dianshizhai Pictorial* was republished in 1983 by the Guangdong renmin chubanshe in forty-four volumes. Cohn (*Vignettes from the Chinese*, 3) mentions 45 volumes, but this is not correct.

[18] Yi 50.

[19] Tu 45.

[20] Yuan 34.

[21] *Shenbao* May 8, 1884; June 4, 1884; Jia 2.

[22] *Shenbao*, February 12, 1885.

[23] Bing 41–48.

[24] See the advertisement for Issue No. 49 (*Shenbao*, August 25, 1885): a painting by Ren Bonian; advertisement for Issue No. 54 (*Shenbao*, October 13, 1885): a painting of elephant and pine tree, by Ren Bonian; advertisement for Issue No. 55 (*Shenbao*, October 23, 1885): a painting of donkey and unicorn, by Ren Bonian; advertisement for Issue No. 56 (*Shenbao*, November 2, 1885) and Issue No. 58 (*Shenbao*, November 22, 1885): a painting of Buddhist saints (*lohan*) by Ren Bonian; advertisement for Issue No. 59 (*Shenbao*, December 3, 1885): a painting by Sha Shanchun; advertisement for Issue No. 60 (*Shenbao*, December 11, 1885): a painting of classical beauties by Guan Qu'an; advertisement for Issue No. 61 (*Shenbao*, December 21, 1885): another painting by Sha Shanchun.

[25] A Ying, "Mantan chuqi baokan de nianhua he rili" (On new year pictures and calendars in the early period of newspapers and magazines), in *A Ying sanwen xuan* (Collected essays of A Ying), ed. Qian Xiaoyun and Wu Taichang (Tianjin: Baihua wenyi chubanshe, 1981), 280–81.

[26] Jia 1; Jia 2.

[27] Jia 91.

[28] Jia 93.

[29] Huang Xiexun, "Ben bao zuichu shidai zhi jingguo" (Development of this newspaper in its earliest period), in *Zuijin wushi nian, di erbian* (The most recent fifty years, volume 2), ed. Shenbao Guan (Shanghai: Shenbao Guan), 1922.

[30] Bing 67.

[31] Huang Xiexun, "Zuichu shidai," 26. See also the Introduction to the Taiwan reproduction of the *Shenbao*, vol. 1 (Taipei: Xuesheng shuju, 1965), 2.

[32] Huang Xiexun, "Zuichu shidai," *passim*. See also Bao Tianxiao, *Chuanyinglou huiyilu* (Memoirs of the Bracelet Shadow Chamber) (reprinted Hong Kong: Dahua chubanshe, 1971), *shang ce*, 106: "We were very hard pressed for news of victory in the war. As soon as the *Shenbao* arrived, we would always ask Father to read us news and stories about the war." At that time Bao Tianxiao and his family were living in Suzhou, more than one hundred kilometers from Shanghai.

[33] The *Hu Bao*, mentioned above, was another Chinese language newspaper in Shanghai. It was foreign owned, and, like the *Shenbao* and the *Dianshizhai*, the foreign manager has no control over the Chinese editor. See also Bryna Goodman, "Improvisations on a Semi-Colonial Theme, or How to Read a Celebration of Transnational Urban Community," *Journal of Asian Studies*, vol. 54, no. 4 (November 2000): 902.

[34] Jia 3, 4, 19, 51, 77, 83, 91, 92; Yi 3, 12, 21, 26, 35, 42, 50, 58, 79; Bing 67, 71, 76, 92; Ding 10,18, 49, 50, Yi* 15.

[35] Jia 3; Jia 4.

[36] *Shenbao*, August 5–14, 1888; Jia 77. The advertisement for the next issue (*Shenbao*, August 15–25, 1884) for Jia 83 is similar.

[37] *Shenbao*, October 24–November 1, 1884.

[38] Ding 6.

[39] Ren 82.

[40] *North-China Herald*, June 9, 1888.

[41] A brief notice was printed in the *Shenbao* on June 2, 1888.

[42] Jia 2.

[43] *Shenbao*, June 26–July 5, 1884.

[44] Shen Gongzhi, who used the sobriquet "Master of the Hall of Knowing the Tide" (Wenchaoguan zhuren), contributed the seal script title of the *Dianshizhai*.

[45] Hu Daojing, "Shanghai xinwen shiye zhi shi de fazhan" (The development of the history of the press in Shanghai), *Shanghai tongzhiguan qikan* (December 1934) (reprinted Hong Kong: Longmen shudian, 1965), *juan* 2, no. 3, 952. Wu Youru left the *Dianshizhai* in 1890; some scholars claim that this was because he had fallen out with Major. See Zheng Yimei, "Wu Youru yu *Dianshizhai huabao*" (Wu Youru and the *Dianshizhai Pictorial*), *Xinmin Wanbao* (Shanghai), November 4, 1956. In his later study, *Shu bao hua jiu*, Zheng again puts forward this view. This has been accepted by some others, for example, Yu Yueting in his work *Huabao de shizu*. However, Major left China in 1889, the year before Wu Youru left the *Dianshizhai*, so it seems less likely that Wu left because of some disagreement with Major.

[46] Bing 57.

[47] The *Shenbao* obituary on Major (March 29, 1908) stated that "he knew both spoken and written Chinese." See also Rudolf G. Wagner, "The Role of the Foreign Community in the Chinese Public Sphere," *China Quarterly* (1995): 432 n 25; Ge Yuanxu, *Huyou zaji* (Miscellaneous notes on travels in Shanghai) (Shanghai, 1876; reprinted Shanghai: Shanghai guji chubanshe, 1989), *juan* 1, 12.

[48] Advertisement for the first issue of the *Dianshizhai*, in *Shenbao*, April 14, 1884.

[49] The *Xunhuan ribao* (*Tsun Wan Yat Pao*) was a Chinese language newspaper founded in 1873 in Hong Kong by Wang Tao and Huang Sheng. See Lai Guanglin, *Zhongguo jindai bao ren yu bao ye* (Newspapermen and the press in modern China), vol. 1 (Taiwan: Shangwu yinshuguan, 1980), 94–95; and F. H. H. King and Prescott Clarke, eds., *A Research Guide to China-Coast Newspapers 1822–1911* (Cambridge, Mass.: East Asian Research Center, Harvard University, 1965), 27–28.

⁵⁰ *Shenbao*, May 28, 1884.

⁵¹ In 1889 the *Dianshizhai* published an *Announcement Concerning the Availability of the Dianshizhai Pictorial in Provincial Branches*: "The lithographic reproduction of books originated with this Publishing House. It is expanding and flourishing gradually day by day. During the past ten years or so we have been lithographically reproducing books. If you check the names of all commonly used reference books in your study, you will find that we have all of them in stock. So during the years of 1888 and 1889 we have established branches in the provinces, for the convenience of scholars and merchants wishing to purchase them. A list of these branches follows below: Liulichang, Jingdu (Beijing); Dongpailou, Jinling (Nanjing); Yuanmiaoguan, Suzhou; Qingyunjie, Hangzhou; Sandaojie, Hubei; Huangpijie, Hankou; Fuzhengjie, Hunan Province; Hongying'anjie, Henan Provincial Capital; Gulouqian, Fujian; Shuangmendi, Guangdong; Shaanxijie, Chongqingfu, Sichuan Province; Shengxuedaojie, Chengdu; and attached to the Examination Hall (Gongyuan) in Jiangxi, Shandong, Shanxi, Guizhou, Shaanxi, Yunnan, Guangxi and Gansu." Wu★ 17.

⁵² Hu Daojing, "*Shenbao* liushiliu nian shi" (A history of sixty six years of the *Shenbao*), in *Xinwen shi shang de xin shidai* (A new era in the history of journalism) (Shanghai: Shijie shuju, 1946), 103; Rudolf G. Wagner, "The *Shenbao* in Crisis: The International Environment and the Conflict Between Guo Songtao and the *Shenbao*," *Late Imperial China*, vol. 20, no. 1 (June 1999): 108.

⁵³ Li Bingzhang, ed. and trans., *Shanghai jindai maoyi jingji fazhan gaikuang 1854–1898—Yingguo zhu Shanghai lingshi maoyi baogao huibian* (General outline of the development of trade and economics in modern Shanghai, 1854–1898; trade report of the British Consulate in Shanghai) (Shanghai: Shanghai shehui kexueyuan, 1993), 728.

⁵⁴ Li Boyuan, *Wenming xiaoshi* (A short history of civilization) (Shanghai: Shanghai guji shudian, 1982), 100.

⁵⁵ *Shenbao*, May 17–24, 1884.

⁵⁶ *Shenbao*, 7 June 1884.

⁵⁷ Jia announcements.

⁵⁸ *Shenbao*, June 26–July 5, 1884.

⁵⁹ *Shenbao*, June 19, 1884.

⁶⁰ Advertisement for the *Xin* volume (1886).

⁶¹ Advertisement for the first issue of the *Dianshizhai*, in the *Shenbao*, May 8, 1884. Cf. Cohn, *Vignettes from the Chinese*, 2: "It came free of charge with the *Shen Pao*, but was also sold separately for five cash." In fact, the *Dianshizhai* was not distributed free of charge with the *Shenbao*. The mistake probably derives from Zhang Jinglu, *Chuban shiliao, erbian*, 298, where it is implied that the *Dianshizhai* was distributed free of charge, but could be bought separately for five cash. Some sources give other figures for the price of a copy of the *Dianshizhai*. Ge Gongzhen, *Zhongguo baoxue shi* (A history of the press in China) (Taipei: Xuesheng shuju, 1982), 109, gives the price as eight cash. Xu Renhan, "*Shenbao*" gives the figure of three cash.

⁶² Wu Jianren (Wu Woyao), *Ershi nian mudu zhi guai xianzhuang* (Bizarre happenings eye-witnessed over two decades) (reprinted Taipei: Guangya youxian gongsi, 1984), 184.

⁶³ Bao Tianxiao, *Chuanyinglou huiyilu, shang ce*, 83; Xiang Dicong, "Shanghai *Dianshizhai*," 249.

⁶⁴ *Shenbao*, August 29, 1895.

⁶⁵ The term "labor aristocrats" refers to a group in twentieth century Shanghai who had at least an elementary education, worked at companies which provided generous wages, free clinics, libraries, night schools and recreation facilities. See Elizabeth J. Perry, "Strikes among Shanghai Silk-weavers," in Frederic Wakeman and Wen-hsin Yeh, *Shanghai Sojourners* (Berkeley: University of California Press, 1992), 305–8.

⁶⁶ A considerable number of the original sketches of the *Dianshizhai* have been preserved in the Shanghai History Museum. The original drawings do not have commentaries, nor are they signed with the artist's name. The commentaries and the signatures were added later, and are in the same handwriting. On some of the original sketches, there was insufficient room left for the commentaries, and they had to be altered. The sketches were drawn on special paper 47.5 cm long and 28 cm wide, provided by the *Dianshizhai*. The originals are 2.5 times larger than the published versions, and many details can be seen much more clearly. On some, the artist has added his own signature, such as Jin Chanxiang on Jia 23, but his characters are quite clumsy, and very different from the elegant script of the commentary. Perhaps the artists were not necessarily calligraphers, and the task of writing the commentaries on the sketches was left for copyists. On one occasion

(Yi★ 82) the text clearly reveals that the commentary and the illustration were done by different people. The illustrations were first sketched in pencil, then copied using a Chinese writing brush. Several places have been corrected, using a sort of white paste. These were not the paintings of the traditional scholar-artist; they were the sketches of artisans. This is probably why their names are not included amongst the lists of notable artists of the time. A close examination of the original sketches has led me to the conclusion that the artists were not the same people as those who wrote the commentaries. The commentaries were probably written first by the literati associated with the *Shenbao*, and the sketches drawn to illustrate them. There may also have been some cases of an illustration coming first, in the case of a scene eye witnessed by one of the artists, but these would be a small proportion of the total number.

[67] Gong Chanxiang, "Wu Youru jianlüe" (Wu Youru: A brief introduction), *Meishu yanjiu*, (1990, no. 3): 31–38.

[68] Zhang Jinglu, *Chuban shiliao, yibian*, 408; Britton, *Chinese Periodical Press*, 70.

[69] Zhu Hongjun, ed., *Gujin huashi* (History of ancient and modern painting) (Shanghai: Guangyi shuju, 1917), contains biographies of 198 artists of the Qing period. The only artist associated with the *Dianshizhai* listed in this book was Wu Youru.

[70] Di Pingzi, ed., *Qingdai huashi* (History of painting in the Qing dynasty) (Shanghai: Youzheng shuju, 1927), *juan* 5, 13. This biography was taken from Yang Yi, *Haishang molin* (Painting and calligraphy in Shanghai) (Shanghai, 1920; reprinted Shanghai: Shanghai guji chubanshe, 1989).

[71] Qiu Ying (1493–1560), also known as Qiu Shizhou, was one of the four great painters of the Ming dynasty.

[72] Summarized and paraphrased from Huang Mengtian, *Tan yi lu* (A record of discussions on art) (Hong Kong: Shanghai shuju, 1973), 81.

[73] Preface to the Shanghai shuju reprint of *Wu Youru huabao* (1983). The same book contains an inscription written in honor of Wu Youru by Xie Guozhen in 1981. Zheng Yimei (*Shu bao hua jiu*, 85–87), gives almost the same information. This book mentions that Wu Youru lost his father when he was young, and that his family was very poor. There is also a short biography of Wu Youru by Hua Rende in the preface to *Wu Youru shinü baitu* (One hundred classical beauties of Wu Youru) (Shanghai: Shuhua chubanshe, 1988). See also Gong Chanxing, "Wu Youru jianlüe". Gong interviewed many old artists, and visited Wu Youru's grand-daughter. This paper indicates that the stories about Wu losing his parents while very young, his impoverished family background and so on have no basis in fact. It confirms, however, that Wu took up painting only after he came to Shanghai during the Taiping Rebellion.

[74] Yao Jiguang and Yu Yifen, "Shanghai de xiao bao" (Tabloid newspapers in Shanghai), in *Xinwen yanjiu ziliao*, vol. 3 (Beijing, Xinhua chubanshe, 1981), 234.

[75] Yao Gonghe, *Shanghai xianhua*, 181

[76] Li Pingshu, *Qiewan laoren qishi zixu* (Autobiography of Old Man Stubborn at Seventy) (Shanghai, 1923; reprinted Shanghai: Shanghai guji chubanshe, 1989), 17.

[77] Hu Daojing, "Shanghai xinwen shiye zhi shi de fazhan," 952.

[78] Zheng Yimei, *Zheng Yimei xuanji* (Selected writings of Zheng Yimei) (Haerbin: Heilongjiang renmin chubanshe, 1991), vol. 2, 177–78.

[79] Hu Daojing, "Shanghai xinwen shiye zhi shi de fazhan," 952.

[80] The reference is to the Western Jin scholar Sun Chu (Sun Jing). Cf. Liu Ts'un-yan, ed., *Chinese Middlebrow Fiction—From the Ch'ing and the Early Republican Eras*, Hong Kong: Chinese University of Hong Kong Press, 1984), 12; Richard B. Mather, trans., *Shih-shuo Hsin-yü, A New Account of Tales of the World, by Liu I-ch'ing, with commentary by Liu Chün* (Minneapolis: University of Minnesota Press, 1976), 402 n. 6.

[81] Haishang shushisheng, *Haishang fanhuameng* (Dreams of prosperity in Shanghai) (Shanghai, 1896; reprinted Shanghai: Shanghai guji chubanshe, 1991), 13.

[82] Mary Backus Rankin, *Elite Activism and Political Transformation in China: Zhejiang Province, 1895–1911* (Stanford: Stanford University Press, 1986), 142.

[83] John Meskill, *Gentlemanly Interests and Wealth on the Yangtze Delta*, (Ann Arbor, Mich.: Association for Asian Studies, 1994), 8.

[84] Philip A. Kuhn, *Soulstealers—The Chinese Sorcery Scare of 1768*, (Cambridge, Mass.: Harvard University Press, 1990), 71.

[85] See Christian Henriot, "Chinese courtesans in the Late Qing and Early Republican Shanghai (1849–1925)," *East Asian History*, no. 8 (December 1994): 33–52; Christian Henriot, *Prostitution and Sexuality in Shanghai—A Social History, 1849–1949* (Cambridge: Cambridge University Press, 2001), 21–46; Gail Hershatter, *Dangerous Pleasures: Prostitution and Modernity in Twentieth Century Shanghai*, (Berkeley: University of California Press, 1997), 42–43; Ye Xiaoqing, "Commercialization and Prostitution in Nineteenth Century Shanghai," in *Dress, Sex and Text in Chinese Culture*, ed. Antonia Finnane and Anne McLaren (Melbourne: Monash Asia Institute, 1999), 37–57.

[86] Wang Tao, *Yingruan zazhi* (Maritime and littoral miscellany) (Shanghai, 1875; reprinted Shanghai: Shanghai guji chubanshe, 1989), *juan* 5, 97–98.

[87] Wang Tao, *Songbin suohua* (Tales of trivia from the banks of the Wusong) (Shanghai, 1893; reprinted Hunan, Yuelu chubanshe, 1987), *juan* 7, 1, 20.

[88] *Shenbao*, October 3, 1872. The term *nüjiaoshu* "female collator" originally referred to Xie Tao, but was later used generally of an erudite courtesan.

[89] *Shenbao*, December 29, 1875.

[90] *Shenbao*, June 29, 1878.

[91] *Shenbao*, August 30, 1873.

[92] Xiaoxiangguan shizhe, *Haishang huatianjiudi zhuan* (Dissipation and debauchery in Shanghai) (Shanghai, 1884), *juan* 1, 6; Gu Wu-Yue shike (Observer of the Old World of the Wu Area), *Haishang fanhua tu* (Illustrations of the prosperity of Shanghai) (Shanghai, 1884), 4.

[93] Xiaoxiangguan shizhe, *Haishang huatianjiudi zhuan*, *juan* 1, 13; *juan* 2, 29.

[94] Xiaoxiangguan shizhe, *Haishang huatianjiudi zhuan*, *juan* 1, 18.

[95] Wu Jianren, *Guai xianzhuang*, vol. 1, 307.

[96] Ye Xiaoqing, *Shanghai yangchang wenren de gediao* (Lifestyles of the literati in the Shanghai foreign settlements), *Ershiyishiji* (February 1992): 134–36.

[97] Songbei yushensheng (Wang Tao), *Haizou yeyoulu* (A guide to the brothels of Shanghai) (Shanghai, 1879), *juan xia*, 23.

[98] *Shenbao*, August 22, 1877.

[99] Chen Boxi, *Lao Shanghai* (Old Shanghai) (Shanghai: Taidong shuju, 1919), *xia ce*, 91–92; Lu Dafang, *Shanghaitan yijiulu* (Memories of the Shanghai Bund) (Taipei: Shijie shuju, 1980), 23. On Li Boyuan and the *Youxi bao*, see Li Boyuan, *Nanting si hua* (Four talks from the South Pavilion) (reprinted Shanghai: Shanghai shudian, 1985), 1; Zheng Yimei, *Shu bao hua jiu*, 109; Zhang Junliang, "Haishang xiaobao fanlun" (A general discussion on the mosquito press of Shanghai), *Shinian* (The Decade) (Shenshi dianxunshe, 1934), 173.

[100] *The Chuckler* (1898); *Flowers and Moon on the Spring River* (1901), *The Express* (1902), *Flower Sky Daily* (1902), *The World of Flowers* (1903), *Leisure Daily* (1905) and so on. These papers also ran flower competitions, on the model of the *Entertainment News*, and even took the opportunity to extort money from prostitutes for the honor to appear on their lists. See Haishang shushisheng, *Haishang fanhuameng*, vol. 2, 609–17 and Haishang shuomengren, *Xiepuchao* (Quiet tides on the Huangpu River), vol. 1 (Shanghai: Shanghai guji chubanshe, 1991), 79 give examples of such financial arrangements between the literati and prostitutes.

[101] Haishang chuanzhusheng (The Pearl-attired Scholar of Shanghai), *Shanghai funü huo xianxing* (True to life descriptions of Shanghai women), vol. 3 (Shanghai: Xinxing shuju, 1928), 72.

[102] Hu Shi, "Haishanghua liezhuan xu" (Preface to *Flowers on the sea*), in *Haishanghua*, translated and annotated by Zhang Ailing (Taipei: Huangguan zazhi chubanshe, 1983), 9. Zhang Ailing's work translates *Haishanghua liezhuan* (Life stories of flowers on the sea), by Huayeliannong (Han Ziyun), from Shanghai dialect into standard Chinese.

[103] Haishang shushisheng, *Haishang fanhuameng*, 18–19.

[104] Wei Shaochang, *Li Boyuan yanjiu ziliao* (Research material on Li Boyuan) (Shanghai: Shanghai guji shudian, 1980), 30, 494.

[105] Zhang Hailin, *Wang Tao pingzhuan* (A critical biography of Wang Tao) (Nanjing: Nanjing Daxue chubanshe, 1993), 47.

[106] Wang Tao, *Songbin suohua*, juan 5, 16–17; Wang Tao, *Yingruan zazhi*, juan 5, 90; Yu Xingmin, *Shanghai 1862 nian* (Shanghai in the year 1862) (Shanghai: Shanghai renmin chubanshe, 1991), 408–9; Shanghai tongshe, ed., *Shanghai yanjiu ziliao xuji* (Continued collection of historical materials for research on Shanghai) (Shanghai: Zhonghua shuju, 1939; reprinted Shanghai: Shanghai shudian, 1984), 650; Arthur W. Hummel, ed. *Eminent Chinese of the Ch'ing Period* (reprinted Taipei: Ch'eng-wen Publishing, 1970), 433.

[107] Zeng Pu, *Niehaihua* (Flowers on a sinful sea) (reprinted Shanghai: Shanghai guji chubanshe, 1985), 8, 19–20.

[108] Chen 5.

[109] Wang Tao, *Songbin suohua*, juan 9, 2b, 3; Jiaochuan zizhu shanfang zhuren (Master of the Purple Bamboo Mountain Hut on Dragon River), *Hua Xiangyun zhuan* (Biography of Hua Xiangyun), in *Xinji Haishang qinglou tushuo* (New illustrated edition of green bowers in Shanghai), 1895, juan 2, 20.

[110] Songbei yushensheng, *Haizou yeyoulu*, Appendix 4.

[111] Yu Xingmin, *Shanghai 1862 nian*, 419.

[112] Zhang Ailing's concluding remarks to her translation of *Haishanghua liezhuan*, 630.

[113] Wang Tao, *Songbin suohua*, juan 5, 16–17.

[114] An exception was Jiang Jianren, a *Shenbao* editor, who took a courtesan as concubine. See Yu Xingmin and Tang Jiwu, *Jindaihua de zaochan er—Shanghai* (Shanghai: A premature child of early modernization) (Taipei: Taiwan Jiuda wenhua gufen youxian gongsi, 1992), 254.

[115] Wei Shaochang, *Li Boyuan yanjiu ziliao*, 519.

[116] Yi 77.

[117] Songbei yushensheng, *Haizou yeyoulu*, juan xia, 19.

[118] *Shenbao* October 18, 1875.

[119] The "green bowers" (an elegant term for brothel) was so called "because the woodwork was lacquered green, as that of opulent mansions." See R. H. van Gulik, *Sexual Life in Ancient China* (Leiden, 1974), 175–76. Ruan Ji (219–263), one of the Seven Sages of the Bamboo Grove, was noted for his melancholy poetry.

[120] Xiaoxiangguan shizhe, *Haishang huatianjiudi zhuan*, juan 2, 10, 18.

[121] *Shenbao*, June 26–July 5, 1884.

[122] This might be compared to the time of the Self-strengthening Movement, and the attacks of the conservatives against the "strange skills and excessive ingenuity" of the West. See Ye Xiaoqing, "Jindai Xifang keji de yinjin ji qi yingxiang" (The introduction of Western science and technology and its influence), *Lishi Yanjiu*, no. 1 (1982): 13–14.

[123] Yu 21.

[124] Tu 46.

[125] Li 19, Xin 39.

[126] Chen 40.

[127] Hai 71.

[128] Li 99.

[129] Jin 73.

[130] Mao 32.

[131] Mao 49.

[132] The Chinese attitude toward autopsies and dissections is discussed further in Part Three.

[133] Jia 27.

[134] Jia 72.

[135] Zhen 10.

[136] Heng 90.

[137] Zhong 90.

[138] Mu 86.

[139] Yin 15.

[140] Xing 42.

[141] Xing 57.

[142] Wen 91; Zhong 44; Zhong 75; Xin 34, Xin 62.

[143] Bing 61

[144] Yu 75.

[145] Wu★ 60.

[146] Shi 81.

[147] Xin 80.

[148] Ge 30.

[149] Ding 34.

[150] Tu 90.

[151] Zheng Yimei, *Shu bao hua jiu*, 86; Yu Yueting, *Huabao de shizu*, 177–78.

[152] Yu Yueting, *Huabao de shizu*, 178. Huang Mengtian has similar comments: "Wu Youru excelled at line drawings of human figures. The sketches in the *Dianshizhai*, although not all by Wu, are much the same in style. He basically inherited the traditional technique of Chinese painters, but, in order to make them suitable for printing, he did not use ink, but simply lines. He generally used many lines to demonstrate the weight of an object, even the degree of brightness of an object, and was very particular about perspective. This already shows a degree of integration with one aspect of Western technique. This integration makes Wu Youru's type of drawing much more expressive. This sort of expressiveness was particularly influential on later illustrated story books." See Huang Mengtian, *Tan yi lu*, 82–83.

[153] Jia 1.

[154] Lu Xun, "A Glance at Shanghai Literature," in *Selected Works of Lu Hsün*, vol. 3 (Beijing: Foreign Languages Press, 1959), 116. Later Lu Xun also wrote: "However, Wu's influence was deplorable. You will find that in the illustrations of many recent novels or children's books all the women are drawn like prostitutes, all the children like young hooligans, and this is very largely the result of the artists seeing too many of his illustrations." Lu Xun, *Dawn Blossoms Plucked at Dusk* (Beijing: Foreign Languages Press, 1976), 107–8. Wang Ermin calls Lu Xun's comments "A load of nonsense to fool the masses and insult the readers." See Wang Ermin, "Dianshizhai huabao li," 170.

[155] Jin 15, Jin 4, Shu 63. Similar stories concern the ghost of a suicide searching for a body to inhabit (Yue 56), the ghost of a drowned man terrifying a boatman (Shu★ 7), and a corpse in an unburied coffin which became a wandering ghost (Gong 19).

[156] Zhong 47.

[157] Heng 60.

[158] Mu 21, Yu 31.

[159] Heng 81.

[160] Wen 65.

[161] Jin 72 *xia*.

[162] Zhu 57.

[163] Jin 33.

[164] Ge 30.

[165] Wang Tao, *Songyin manlu* (Random jottings of a Wusong recluse) (Shanghai, 1887; reprinted Beijing: Renmin wenxue chubanshe, 1983). This book was also called *Hou Liaozhai zhiyi tushuo* or *Huitu Hou Liaozhai zhiyi* (Illustrated sequel to the *Strange Stories from a Chinese Studio*). Some sources (such as Chen Dingshan, *Chunshen jiuwen* [Old tales of Shanghai] [Taipei: Chenguang yuekan she, 1964], 113) claims that this book was distributed with the *Feiyingge Huabao*, a later publication edited by Wu Youru, but this is not so.

[166] Wang Tao, *Songyin manlu*, 2–3.

[167] *Shenbao*, June 17–25, 1884.

[168] *Shenbao*, July 6–16, 1884.

[169] Jin 15, Li 81, Zhong 20. Similar comments are: "Although the concept of *karma* is not discussed by Confucian scholars, retribution will always be realized" (Li 89); "the concept of retribution is not discussed by Confucian scholars, but it cannot be said that such things do not exist" (Xing 88); and "the concept of *samsara* originated in the Buddhist classics, and Confucian scholars do not speak of it, but it can be definitely proven" (Zhong 42).

[170] Yu 9.

[171] Li 77.

[172] Ge 25; Yi★ 30. Other examples are Wen 75: "The filial daughter-in-law who moved the gods"; Si 42: "The Court commends a filial daughter"; Yuan 61: "A fox shows respect to a filial daughter"; Wen 95: "The filial beggar"; and Mu 17: "The tiger avoids a filial son." There are all sorts of retributions to those who are lacking filial piety, such as Shu 40: "Heaven executes an unfilial son"; Zhu 33: "An unfilial son falls into a well"; Mu 52: "The spirits execute an unfilial child"; Zhen 38: "Lightning buries an unfilial woman"; Yu 15: "An unfilial woman becomes a tortoise"; Shu★ 60: "Begging Heaven to forgive a crime"; Jin 46: "A plot to kill by poison punished by Heaven," and many others.

[173] Pao 92.

[174] She 28.

[175] Zhen 35. Other examples are Shi 5: "Heaven Protects a chaste woman"; Pao 25: "Loyal servant dies after the death of his master"; Pao 65: "Preserver of chastity receives good fortune"; Mu 66: "The chaste and filial should be praised." There are also some examples of unchaste women and retribution, such as Xing 93: "Heaven warns a lascivious old woman."

[176] Mu 67; Geng 75; Zi 81.

[177] Pao 37: "Charitable contributions exorcise ghosts"; Shen 66: "Organizing relief brings a reward."

[178] Xing★ 29: "Money returned and child saved"; Shu 49: "Money returned and sickness cured."

[179] Pao 50: "Those who release living things receive a reward."

[180] Xing 40: "Butcher killed by a pig"; Jin 88: "Wife of pigeon eater gives birth to a pigeon"; Yu 78: "Life taken by tortoise spirit."

[181] Xing 11.

[182] Shi 16.

[183] Shu★ 27.

[184] *Shenbao*, July 13, 1872.

[185] *Shenbao*, August 4, 1875.

[186] On the Yang Yuelou case, see Ye Xiaoqing, "Unacceptable Marriage and the Qing Code: The Case of Yang Yuelou," *Journal of the Oriental Society of Australia*, vol. 27–28 (1995–1996): 195–212. On the Guo Songtao case, see Ma Guangren, ed., *Shanghai xinwen shi: 1850-1949* (A history of the press in Shanghai: 1859–1949) (Shanghai: Fudan Daxue chubanshe, 1996), 66–67. See also Rudolf G. Wagner, "The *Shenbao* in Crisis," 107–43.

[187] Ren 11.

[188] Wu 59.

[189] Jia 75.

[190] When Li Hongzhang passed through Shanghai in 1896, he was entertained on two occasions, by the Shanghai officials and gentry, and by the Hong Kong and Shanghai Banking Corporation. The *Dianshizhai* published two sketches detailing the festivities: Wen 90 and Zhong 51.

[191] Xing 1; Wen 51.

[192] Yin 60; Shu★ 1; this portrait is also mentioned in Shu★ 10.

[193] Pao 89–91.

[194] Tu 57.

[195] Ji 81.

[196] *Shenbao*, July 17–25, 1884.

[197] Yi 2. See the advertisement for issue No. 13 in *Shenbao*, September 5–14, 1884: "The twenty-eighth day of the sixth month (August 18) was the Emperor's birthday. We have specially commissioned a picture 'Court Officials Extend Congratulations' showing how people both inside and outside the Court joined together in celebrating this event."

[198] She 74–75.

[199] See Wang Tao's calligraphy accompanying the portrait of Liu Yongfu in Bing 60.

[200] Shu 18.

[201] The Republic lasted only a few days, and was regarded as a farce by people like Liang Qichao. The episode was noted in the late Qing novel *Flowers on the Sinful Sea*, in which some details are historically accurate. (Zeng Pu, *Neihaihua*, 321–23). See also Harry J. Lamley, "The 1895 Taiwan Republic: A Significant Episode in Modern Chinese History," *Journal of Asian Studies*, vol. 27, no. 4 (1968): 739–62; Wu Micha, *Taiwan jindaishi yanjiu* (Research on modern Taiwan history) (Taipei: Daoxiang chubanshe, 1990), 1–51.

[202] Such as the *Qiangxue Bao* established by Kang Youwei on January 12, 1896, and the *Shiwu Bao* founded by Huang Zunxian, Liang Qichao, and Wang Kangnian on August 9 of the same year.

[203] Zhen 94.

[204] Xu Renhan, "*Shenbao* qishiqi nian da shiji," 26. By that stage, many people thought the main writers of the *Shenbao* were conservatives. See Ma Guangren, *Shanghai xinwen shi*, 186–87.

PART TWO

Shanghai: Old City, New City

1. Roads and transportation

By the 1880s, the wide, clean streets of Shanghai's settlements immediately impressed the visitor. In 1887 the *Dianshizhai* reminded its readers of how the roads had been built. The sketch shows more than twenty Chinese, bound to each other by ropes, pulling a huge stone roller along the road. They are supervised by a policeman. The commentary explains that these people were petty criminals who had been sentenced to a period of hard labor, since they had no one to pay their fines. The commentary goes on to say that the level roads in the International Settlement were "filled with the blood and tears of Chinese. Visitors from other parts of China should not envy [Shanghai's roads] (Fig. 17)."[1] A contemporary photograph presents a scene very similar to the sketch in the *Dianshizhai*; it is from a private collection and gives no indication of a specific date.[2]

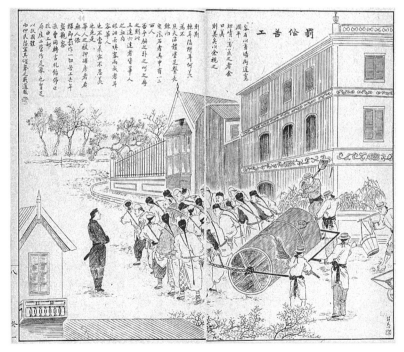

17. Chinese convicts employed in road building (1887).

Settlement authorities claimed that the reason they used criminals for road building was a lack of funds to hire laborers.[3] In 1886 a well-known resident, Cao Xiang, wrote a letter of complaint to the Shanghai magistrate, who in turn raised the matter with the settlement authorities. As a result of the official protest they agreed to use hired laborers rather than prisoners. In his letter Cao Xiang pointed out, "The Shanghai Mixed Court sentences criminals to hard labor; twenty or thirty are chained together, and under the supervision of a policeman they are forced to pull a stone roller to crush stones and rocks. They are treated like dogs or sheep and driven like oxen or horses . . . hard labor is a Western punishment and only suitable for Western criminals. If the police catch a Western criminal, he is handed over to his own consulate to be dealt with. I have never seen one of them being sentenced to hard labor on the roads."[4] Cao's complaints practically constitute a commentary on the *Dianshizhai* sketch.

Specialized transportation

The construction of modern roads made it possible to introduce Western-style horse-drawn carriages into the International Settlement, and the sketches in the *Dianshizhai* indicate that these were a very common means of transport at the time.[5] The first rickshaw was imported into Shanghai on March 24, 1874.[6] The commentary to one of the sketches mentions that in the past the rich in Shanghai used sedan chairs, and the poor single-wheeled carts pushed by men or pulled by men or mules.[7] A photograph taken in Shanghai "about 1900" shows a woman in a single-wheeled cart.[8] By the early twentieth century, the sedan chair had "practically dropped out of Shanghai street life."[9]

A highly specialized transport system began to develop, and traffic in the International Settlement increased. The commentary to a sketch in the *Dianshizhai* dated 1889 noted,

> There is a diversity unparalleled elsewhere of types of carriages in the Foreign Settlement. Apart from horse-drawn carriages, single-wheeled carts, and rickshaws, the carriages of the artisans are the most numerous. Those who deliver wood have their carts, as do those who deliver stones; those who deliver doors, windows, bricks, and cement all have their own carts. These are followed by the colliers' carts, which deliver coal and firewood. Then there are the launderers' carts and the milk deliverers' carts. There are carts which deliver Western delicacies to Western people and carts which transport stones to build the roads. Carts collect rubbish twice a day, and water sprinklers wash the roads every few days. Many carts are not allowed on roads the Westerners use. The way the roads intersect, vertically and horizontally, four or five meeting in one place, dazzles the eyes and makes the heart quake, so those who walk around the foreign settlements are full of fear and trepidation.[10]

The Municipal Council in 1872 promulgated a list of traffic regulations,[11] but accidents continued to increase. At least ten sketches in the *Dianshizhai* show traffic accidents, particularly those involving horse-drawn carriages, but the accident rate did not diminish the general enthusiasm for this form of transport (Fig. 18).[12]

> Since horse-drawn carriages reached this city, they have become extremely numerous and popular. Covered carriages have been in use a long time; some are fitted with two wheels, some with four wheels. Those with four wheels used to be made of wood; now some have steel spokes, but these cost twice as much, and not many of them are in use, so it cannot be said that the wooden variety has become obsolete. It does not matter whether a few people or many sit in such a carriage, nor does it matter if the weather is rainy or clear. . . . Officials, merchants, ordinary people—men, women, old, young—all without exception

take great joy in riding in them. So the carriage companies are becoming more numerous, and their business is flourishing."[13]

Sedan chairs were strictly divided into many classes, but there were only four types of horse-drawn carriages: those with four wheels, two wheels, wooden wheels, and metal wheels.[14] Fares were fairly cheap, and one did not have to be rich to afford them.[15] They were popular for people in a hurry or people who simply wanted to enjoy the scenery.[16] Prostitutes on the way to an assignation, or in the company of their guests or lovers, could comfortably go by carriage.

Both Chinese and foreign officials made constant use of the horse-drawn carriage. In 1885, when the newly appointed French consul-general Emile Desiré Kraetzer arrived in Shanghai, he took a carriage from the pier to his hotel.[17] In 1883 when Li Hongzhang was invited by the United States consul-general to inspect foreign factories in the settlements, he also traveled by horse-drawn carriage.[18]

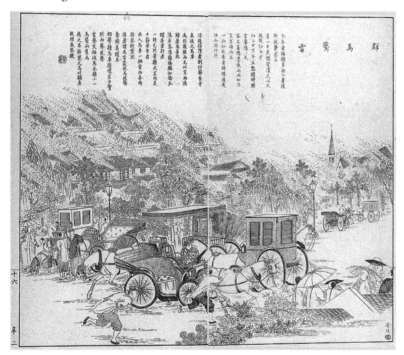

18. Horse-drawn carriages cause road congestion and traffic accidents (1886).

Sanitary regulations

It took some time for the rules and regulations relating to traffic and public sanitation to be understood by the general public. In 1890 the *Dianshizhai* mentioned that throwing rubbish into the streets in the settlements was forbidden. Rubbish was carted away twice a day by special garbage carts, and every second day a water cart would wash the streets down.[19] In the 1870s, however, the *Shenbao* recorded cases of Chinese being fined for not respecting basic principles of public hygiene, and in quite a few cases the fines were severe. An 1874 news item in the *Shenbao* reports policemen escorting a group of fifteen Chinese men and women who had violated public health regulations to court, where they were found guilty and fined.[20] In 1875 the *Shenbao* reported a foreign firm suing a number of boatmen who had deposited a pile of rubbish at their front door. The court ordered that the boatmen wear the wooden collar and be put on public display as punishment.[21] A commentary in the *Dianshizhai* (1887) notes, "Westerners are so particular about cleanliness that even horse dung dropped on the roads is collected immediately. Recently the weather has been very hot, and the Municipal Council issued regulations forbidding livestock on the roads. A village swineherd, who was not aware of the regulations, drove his pigs through the streets of the French Concession and was arrested by the police . . ." (Fig. 19).[22] The settlement authorities implemented regulations about hygiene with such force that, although most Chinese had nothing in principle against them, a certain degree of resistance developed. The *Dianshizhai* commentary called the regulations "tyrannical." These coercive measures, however, did ensure that the streets of Shanghai were immeasurably cleaner and more orderly than those of any other Chinese city. A short report in the *Shenbao* in 1874 noted that travelers from Beijing complained at how dirty their streets were, and what bad repair their roads were in, compared to Shanghai.[23]

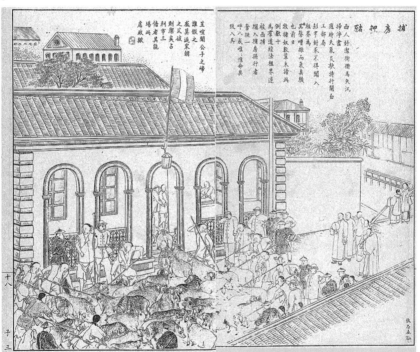

19. Sanitary regulations in the settlements (1887). The Municipal Council imposed a regulation that animals could not be brought into the settlement during hot weather. A villager, ignorant of this, is caught by the police. The commentary does not indicate his punishment.

Unfortunately few sketches in the *Dianshizhai* depict the streets of the Chinese city. There is only one sketch in which we can see the city wall, and glimpse beyond it the shops and the narrow streets crammed with people, rickshaws, sedan chairs and single-wheeled barrows transporting goods.[24]

By this time, sedan chairs were rarely seen in the streets of the foreign settlements. Rickshaws, small and inexpensive, started to appear in the settlements in the 1880s.[25] Since horse-drawn carriages could barely make their way through the streets of the Chinese city, one could only travel from the settlements to the Chinese city (other than on foot) by sedan chair. Two sketches in the *Dianshizhai* show foreigners in sedan chairs going to the Chinese city to view Chinese court proceedings.[26]

Contemporary descriptions of the Chinese city in the 1860s and 1870s mention the narrowness and dirtiness of the streets. Mine Genzō, a Japanese visitor, wrote, "Ships of all countries gather along the Huangpu River; we do not know how many of them belong to China. The sails and the masts are like a forest—it is truly a prosperous place. Inside the Chinese city, apart from official residences and temples, there are small shops and houses. The streets in the Chinese city are extremely narrow, at most six *chi* [two meters] across. People moving to and fro are crowded and disorderly. Rubbish and excrement piles up along the streets; mud and dust bury one's feet. The stench attacks the nostrils and the filth is indescribable."[27]

In 1875 the *Shenbao* carried a news item entitled "Answers to Questions from a Western Visitor about the Chinese City." A foreigner arrived in Shanghai and inspected the foreign settlements. He then visited the Chinese city and was shocked at the narrowness and dirtiness of its streets, and asked a Chinese why it was so. The Chinese answered that Shanghai (the settlements) was an important port for trade between Chinese and the West, whereas Shanghai (county) was only one of China's 1,297 counties, merely a rather small county on the coast. It was not surprising that it should be an unprepossessing place. The foreigner then asked, "Whether it is an important place or not, why should the streets be so dirty and crowded—why don't the officials do something about it?" The Chinese replied, "When the officials go through the streets, everyone gives way to them, so they don't find the streets crowded. In any case, they're busy with their duties. They have no time to concern themselves with such matters. You could say that they look but they do not see."[28]

The inhabitants of the Chinese city began to feel the dirtiness of their streets was unbearable, and repeatedly demanded that the International Settlement regulations be adopted in the Chinese city as well.[29] The first modern road in the area controlled by Chinese authorities was finally started in 1896 and completed the following year.[30] Only then could carriages and rickshaws penetrate beyond the settlements. There is a reference in *The Human Tide* to a visitor to Shanghai who finds it difficult to determine the border of the International Settlement. A local tells him that even Shanghai's blind beggars can tell the difference: the roads in the settlements are smooth and flat; in the Chinese territory the opposite is the case.[31]

2. Water supply and hygiene

According to the picture provided by the *Dianshizhai*, fire hydrants were quite common in the streets of Shanghai, and running water was readily available.[32] This utility was first provided in 1883; before that

> the principal source of water supply had been the Whampoo River or the Soochow Creek. The water from wells was brackish and unfit for drinking purposes, and the water carried from the river or creek in buckets to the various houses was muddy and subject to contamination from

sewers or refuse. It was poured into large kongs or jars and settled by the use of alum. Then it was boiled, but even so there was considerable danger connected with using it for drinking purposes. In many cases it was probably the cause of typhoid fever and cholera."

Advantages and objections

According to Western doctors in Shanghai, "Of the five chief causes of disease in the settlements, three are related to water."[34] The bad quality of the drinking water became a public health issue in Shanghai after an epidemic of cholera and dysentery in 1862. Ge Yuanxu wrote that the people of Shanghai "would wait until the tide came in to collect water to drink. When the tide went out, there was a terrible stench, and people who drank the water would easily contract diseases. People who had just arrived particularly disliked it. Wells were dug to provide drinkable water, but it could hardly be considered sweet."[35]

The need for an ample supply of water for firefighting also necessitated improvement in the water provision system. As the Reverend F. L. Hawks Pott, a long term resident of Shanghai noted, "The waterworks were of great value not only for the health of the community but also in increasing the facilities for extinguishing fires, the firemen previously being dependent entirely on the fire wells sunk into various localities."[36]

The possibility of establishing a company to provide running water in Shanghai was considered during the 1870s, but why no sustained advocacy for a safe water supply developed until that time is unclear. The proposal went through many twists and turns, including disputes over a variety of technical issues, but eventually the company was formally established in 1881, and shares issued.[37] During those years, the *Shenbao* published many editorials on the unhygienic character of the drinking water in Shanghai and the advantages of installing running water.[38] When the water company put its shares on the market, a "large number of shares [were] applied for by the native bankers and merchants of Shanghai."[39] This led to a misunderstanding that the Chinese population would welcome running water.[40] The "native bankers" and merchants who had bought shares in the company were, however, by no means representative of the people of Shanghai. Opposition to the plan came from three sides.

First were the professional water carriers—at least three thousand of whom operated in the International Settlement.[41] Water cost ten cash a load, regardless of the distance it had to be carried.[42] Water carriers are mentioned three times in the *Dianshizhai*,[43] and also in a *Shenbao* editorial. "They are vagrants without a proper trade, but there is no lack of people who make a living at [water carrying]."[44] The water company was clearly a threat to their livelihood, as noted in a *Shenbao* article supporting the introduction of running water.[45]

The second objection concerned the high cost of the water plan.[46] The third was the suspicion that running water was poisonous. According to Pott, "There were rumors that the water was poisonous, or spoiled by lightning, or that people had been drowned in the water tower."[47] Chen Boxi also commented on this: "The availability of running water in the Shanghai settlements began in the ninth year of the Guangxu period [1883]. At that time society was still rather narrow-minded, and few Chinese made use of it. They even said that it had some poisonous substance in it, and that anyone who drank it would be harmed. They warned each other not to use it."[48] On February 15, 1884, the *Shenbao* published an official notice from the Huang Chengyi, deputy of the magistrate of Shanghai at the Mixed Court.[49] Huang announced that Shanghai local officials had received a formal note from the United States consul-general, observing that some people had been spreading rumors about running water. These rumors "have made some Chinese people not dare to drink it," and the note asked officials to "put the people's minds at ease." Huang obligingly concluded, "It is true that running water did not exist before. But now we already have it, and nothing untoward has happened." He also pointed out that running water was hygienic and useful for putting out fires.

Uses of running water

According to statistics in Huang Chengyi's announcement, "There are one hundred and seventy-six water taps in the British Settlement, ninety-seven in the French Concession and sixty-four in the American Settlement."[50] The same year Li Guangdan, the magistrate of Shanghai, also published an official notice urging people who lived in the Chinese city to purchase running water from the taps.[51] The *Dianshizhai* did not mention the objections to running water, presumably because its editorial policy supported the introduction of technology from the West.

A sketch dated 1885 recommends the "sweet and beautiful" taste of running water and its immediate availability: "From ancient times, there has never been such a beneficial public utility."[52] A few sketches from that same year show the practice drills of the Shanghai Municipal Council Fire Brigade.[53] According to statistics of the Shanghai Waterworks Company, even in 1885 there were few Chinese customers in the International Settlement, and the water carriers' business still flourished. This posed a problem for the company.[54] To dispel the rumors and attract more users, the company ran water lines to several teahouses free of charge.[55] As early as 1884 homes owned by the Western firm Iveson and Company in Little Langhuan Lane installed running water, and the rent on each room was increased. This seems to be the first time rooms rented to Chinese in the settlements were supplied with running water.[56] Company records show that Chinese users in the British Settlement began to increase in 1886, and some residents even requested installation of running water in private homes.[57] In 1888 the *Shenbao* reported the case of the Changchunyuan Tiger Stove,[58] whose owner got into a fight over the whether a running water tap should be installed in his shop. A "tiger stove" (*laohu zao*) was a single-room shop where hot water, and occasionally tea, was sold. Only the poorest people would drink tea there.[59] By 1889 one third of the Chinese inhabitants of the settlements were using running water.[60]

In 1887 the *Dianshizhai* carried a series of pictures showing the International Settlement celebrations of the Fiftieth Anniversary of the Accession of Queen Victoria. One of the drawings shows a fountain on Nanjing Road, near the Bund, with a large crowd of Chinese onlookers (Fig. 20).[61] In 1889 and 1890 sketches appeared of police and the fire brigade dousing fires with the aid of running water (Fig. 21).[62] In 1896 the *Dianshizhai* noted, "There are now fire hydrants in all districts of Shanghai. First they attach a rubber hose, then spray out the water to put out the fire; this method is extremely effective."[63] One can also find many comments in the writings of the literati of the time praising Shanghai's water system.[64]

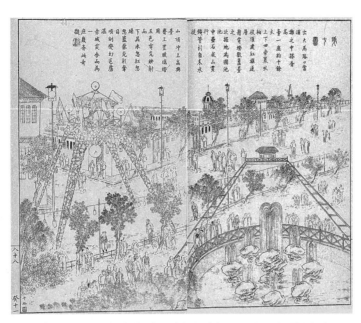

20. A public fountain built for the jubilee celebrations (1887). This is the seventh in a series of sketches covering the Fiftieth Anniversary of the Accession of Queen Victoria. Colored electric lights decorate Nanjing Road near the Bund. In the lower left-hand corner of the sketch, a group of Chinese can be seen admiring the fountain.

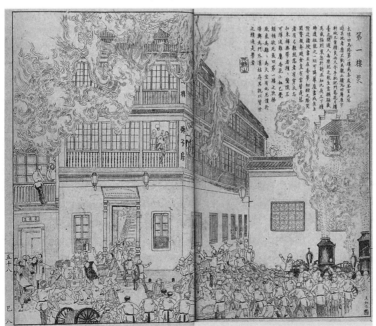

21. The Diyilou Teahouse (1889). This is was the biggest teahouse in Shanghai, accommodating more than one thousand people. The time is 3:00 a.m., but in the "nightless city" the teahouse is still packed. A fire has broken out, and people are pouring into the streets—including prostitutes from a nearby upper-class brothel.

In 1897 the *Dianshizhai* carried a sketch depicting a blaze in the Forbidden City. Sometime after midnight on the 5th of September, a room at the side of the Imperial Apothecary caught fire. In the sketch we can clearly see the members of the water teams, their queues hanging down their backs, trying to extinguish the fire with water delivered in carts. The fire was not brought under control until 4:00 a.m. More than twenty rooms had been gutted, including the room Prince Gong used to change into court robes before entering the palace. The Imperial Apothecary survived, but the clothing of the princes and high officials stored in adjoining rooms was destroyed.[65] This was in marked contrast to the firefighting facilities in Shanghai.

A sketch published in the *Dianshizhai* in 1896 shows the degree to which even the poorest people of Shanghai had become dependent on running water. When a dispute occurred in the French Concession over access to running water, the ensuing fight claimed a life. "In the French Concession, running water falls under the administration of the Conseil Municipal. Anyone can draw water from the hydrants without paying, and there are no restrictions. Now so many people come to collect water, there is no respite day or night. So the Conseil Municipal determined the times beyond which water could not be collected. With so many people wanting water and so few to administer, incidents could easily happen (Fig. 22).".[66] Free municipal water could be obtained only in the French Concession.[67]

22. Free water supply in the French Concession (1896). A fight breaks out in a crowd of people trying to get water, and one person is killed. The commentary urges the authorities to improve management of the water supply.

The Chinese who collected their water from these hydrants were too poor to have running water in their homes. Company policy forbade connecting water lines to substandard housing, such as simple rooms or shacks.[68] The population of the settlements had grown to such a degree that the provision of public hydrants "placed in all the streets at convenient distances" gave rise to the sort of incident mentioned above. Even more pressing was the need of the residents of the Chinese city, who came to envy the modern facilities of the settlements.

Urgent need in the Chinese city

The concept of hygiene followed from the introduction of running water, and the link between dirty water and disease had convincingly been made. A "bamboo branch rhyme" of the time ran, "Everyone in Shanghai is keen on hygiene. Running water is just so clean!"[69] The advantages of this new utility in fire fighting and public hygiene, not to mention its convenience, were obvious, and residents of the Chinese city began to press for the installation of running water there. In 1874 the *Shenbao* editorialized:

> In the Chinese city, traveling merchants are as numerous as clouds, and it is densely populated by local people. Those who need water can obtain it only twice a day, when the tide comes in, and must hire water carriers to collect it. The entrances and exits to the city are muddy, sticky, wet, and slippery. Even inside the city, in areas along the river, the streets large and small become sticky and slippery when the tide comes in, and the water carriers struggle to collect water . . . I have been living in the settlements for some years now, but I know [the Chinese city] is like this, so I am afraid to go there. Yesterday I had no choice; I simply had to go. On a street inside the New North Gate I met an old man who looked like a local and seemed to be more than sixty years old. The road was wet and slippery, and his legs could not support him. Suddenly he lost his footing, and bystanders had to help him to his feet. He had fainted and was unaware of what was going on about him. How tragic, how pitiable![70]

In 1883 the water company entered into negotiations with authorities in the Chinese city to discuss laying water pipes.[71] By 1886, however, nothing had been decided.[72] The *Dianshizhai* described the situation in the Chinese city in 1886 in the following terms: "The river is blocked, so the tides are irregular. If an accident [fire] starts, it will destroy tens, even hundreds of dwellings. Concerned people have discussed establishing a plant that would supply running water. This matter has been raised many times and blocked many times."[73]

Li Pingshu and his close friend Yao Zirang, both leading members of the Shanghai gentry, devoted much effort to local administration and modernizing the Chinese city. According to Li Pingshu's memoirs, when the water company was established in the settlements in 1883, he and Yao Zirang proposed that the people of the Chinese city should also have running water, the main reason being its use in fire fighting and "hygiene." They decided to set up a bureau to purchase water for the Chinese city and hired water-carriers to transport the water and advertised its availability. People in the Chinese city initially showed little interest, and they sold less than one hundred loads a day. By 1884 the market had gradually improved, and Li and other members of the Shanghai gentry petitioned for a running-water plant to be established in the southern part of the Chinese city. The proposal was opposed, however, by the Tongren Fuyuantang, the organization responsible for public works.[74]

Even at the turn of the century, a foreign resident of Shanghai noted that

> Shanghai Chinatown enjoys the reputation of being very dirty and disgusting . . . the water between us and the houses looked foul and sluggish, like a canal rather than a river, and a canal badly used, with everything flung into it. It is all these poor people have for washing, cooking, drinking. And yet just at hand there is the foreign Concession, with its abundant supply of

wholesome pure water, and an enterprising company doubtless thirsting to prolong its mains into the Chinatown whenever the Taotai will allow it. Meanwhile the poor people die of cholera, and who can wonder looking at that water, which must also be far more objectionable when the tide is out.[75]

3. Gas and electricity for public lighting

The Shanghai Gas Company, Ltd. was founded in the 1860s, and gaslight became common in Shanghai after 1865. Before that, "the streets were lit at night with oil lamps, and were nearly as dark as those within the [Chinese] city wall."[76] The Municipal Council introduced kerosene lamps in the 1850s,[77] but their use was not widespread. By the 1870s, however, the introduction of gas and electricity for public lighting made Shanghai famous as "the nightless city."[78]

Gas lights and "earth fire"

By the era of the *Dianshizhai*, gaslight was fairly common.[79] Since gas pipes ran underground, Chinese sometimes called gaslight "earth fire" (*di huo*).[80] In the writings of the literati praising Shanghai innovations, "earth fire" figured prominently.[81] Wang Tao, for instance commented,

> Westerners install lamps along the streets at regular intervals. The lamps are hexagonal and made of glass; seen from a distance, they shine like stars. The light comes from gas and is brilliant white. The gas is collected from coal mines and blazes brightly. Even from a distance it shines brilliantly. There is a gas company, and if anyone wants to have a gas lamp, they apply to the company, which installs it [a technical description follows]. . . . Every user has a meter installed on the iron pipes, by which the amount of gas used can be calculated. Employees of the company examine the meters once a month to determine the cost. All this is meticulously constructed—one can barely imagine it.[82]

Although some difficulties had to be resolved before gas was generally accepted,[83] by the time of the *Dianshizhai* it was largely taken for granted. The hexagonal gas lamps described by Wang Tao were part of the street scene in the Shanghai of the *Dianshizhai*. Gas lamps, for example, lined the Racecourse (1884)[84]; they illuminated the bridge over the Yangjingbang Creek (1884)[85]; the street in front of the Mixed Court (1885)[86]; the Baida Bridge over the Huangpu River (1885)[87]; the Jing'an Temple and Hongkou Road (1886)[88]; and Yangshupu Garden (1890).[89] Gas lighting was also noted along various roads, the names of which were not indicated.[90]

It was not long before Chinese also began using gas lamps. "At first, there were only gaslights in the streets. Then they appeared in inns, shops, teahouses, wine shops, and theaters, and then in private houses—there was no place they were not used."[91] The *Dianshizhai* features quite a few examples of brothels proudly displaying gas lamps over their front doors or in the windows.[92] Teahouses[93] and opium dens, including the famous Nanchengxin Opium Hall,[94] also featured gas lighting.

Electricity

The Shanghai Electric Company was established in 1882. The aim of its founder, R. W. Little, was to replace the gas lamps with electric lighting. The Shanghai Municipal Council agreed to install ten electric lamps along the Bund.[95] According to Pott, "The Company entered into a contract with the council in 1883 for the lighting of the Bund, Nanking Road, and Broadway."[96] In *Dianshizhai* sketches of the Bund dated 1884, one can already see telegraph poles and wires and electric lights.[97] But the adoption of electricity did not proceed unopposed. Pott notes, "Electric lighting, like all other modern improvements, met with serious obstacles. In the first place, the Taotai objected on the grounds that it was not safe, inasmuch as the current could kill a man, burn up a home, or destroy a whole city. In this letter to the Council he stated: 'This electric disaster will happen, if you do not put an end to electricity.'"[98]

Similar observations are to be found in Chinese sources:

"Self-coming fire" (*zilai huo*) [i.e., gas] was introduced to Shanghai in the last years of the Tongzhi period and the beginning of the Guangxu period. Gas companies were formally established; iron pipes were buried everywhere, silver flowers [gas lamps] bloomed in profusion. Before electricity was introduced, these gas lamps gave rise to the name "the nightless city." When the gas company was first established, there were rumors in abundance. Chinese believed that the places through which the fire was transported must become scorched and unbearably hot. Some people walked along the streets wearing thick soles to protect themselves; others, such as barefooted laborers, rushed along the road fearing the poisonous heat would attack their hearts, and this would result in death. The company was located at the northern end of Xizang Road, and people believed that the earth there would be extremely hot and warned each other to avoid that area. When, after a few years, the Westerner Little wanted to introduce electric lighting, the people of Shanghai became even more suspicious and fearful than before. They believed that electricity was violent, and contact with it could be life threatening. These rumors led the daotai of Shanghai to ask the foreign consulates to prohibit its use. In response the Westerners set up demonstrations in which they repeatedly used electrical lighting and yet came to no harm, so in the end [local authorities] allowed them to install it.[99]

At first electric lighting did not prove as satisfactory as anticipated. It was more expensive than gas and less dependable; the generating equipment frequently broke down.[100] This was probably because the first type of electric lamp used was the arc lamp. Nonetheless, drawings in the *Dianshizhai* show that electric lamps were installed along several main roads before 1890. A drawing dated 1887 shows that the electric lamps had already replaced gas lighting along Fuzhou Road.[101]

Electric lighting played an important role in several festivals. In the 1887 sketches depicting celebrations in honor of the Fiftieth Anniversary of the Accession of Queen Victoria, electric lighting can be seen along all of Shanghai's main roads.[102] A water tower illuminated with multicolored electric lights was built along the riverfront in front of the Shanghai Waterworks Company (Fig. 23).[103] Colored electric lights festooned a large platform erected off Nanjing Road near the Bund.[104] Another sketch depicting the visit of the Prince of Wales, for whom the settlements organized a huge welcoming ceremony, shows the Prince and his consort riding through the city in a horse-drawn carriage the shape of a ship, to inspect the colored lights along the Huangpu River and the Bund. This display was designed to be the major spectacle of the welcoming ceremony.[105]

Foreign banks and other modern buildings adopted electric lighting very quickly. The Chartered Mercantile Bank of India had done so by 1886.[106] In 1885 the Shanghai Polytechnic Institute used electricity to show color slides.[107] In a sketch dated 1889 telegraph poles and electric wires can be seen outside the Gengshangyicenglou Teahouse.[108]

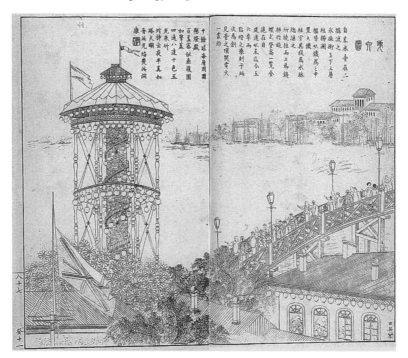

23. A water tower on the Huangpu River (1887). The tower decorated with multi-colored electric lights for the celebration of the Fiftieth Anniversary of the Accession of Queen Victoria.

Electricity supported the development of nightlife in Shanghai.

After the lights go on, workers' carts stop, and transport vehicles also come to a rest. The horse-drawn carriages and the single-wheeled carriages are fewer than during the daytime. Only the rickshaws, which run day and night, still ply the roads and the lanes. The areas around the theaters are unimaginably crowded.[109]

Places of entertainment frequented by Westerners also installed electric lighting fairly early. Electric lights illuminated performances of foreign circus troupes visiting Shanghai in 1886 and 1889,[110] as well as a roller coaster installed in 1890.[111]

As far as it is possible to ascertain from the *Dianshizhai*, the first Chinese establishments to use electric lighting were the Diyilou Teahouse, the largest on Fuzhou Road, in 1884,[112] followed by a brothel,[113] a teahouse,[114] the Chinese-style Western restaurant Haitianchun,[115] and the Tianxian Teahouse.[116] The Tianxian Teahouse was in fact a theater, but changed its name due to restrictions in force against entertainment immediately following the death of the Tongzhi emperor.[117]

The incandescent lamp made its appearance in Shanghai in 1890. Electric lighting became more reliable, especially after the Shanghai Municipal Council incorporated the Shanghai Electric

OLD CITY, NEW CITY 55

Company in 1893. That year, there were 6,325 electric lamps in Shanghai, and the number continued to grow.[118] From the *Dianshizhai* it is clear that many Chinese buildings had electric lighting. A 1894 sketch of the Nanchengxin Opium Hall shows the use of electric lights,[119] while an earlier sketch of the same establishment shows that in 1886 they were using gas.[120] In 1894 the Pinyulou Sing-song Hall installed electricity,[121] as did a small brothel in Tongan Lane.[122] By 1897 the *Dianshizhai* shows that two Western-style restaurants run by Chinese, the Yipinxiang and the Wanjiachun, had also installed electric lights.[123]

The electric street lights in the *Dianshizhai* are round, quite different from the hexagonal gas lamps. Tan Yingke also noted: "Along the Bund and all the main roads—such as Nanjing Road, Fuzhou Road, Guangdong Road, and all such flourishing areas—every intersection has a tall pole, topped by an electric lamp. They shine brightly, like the full moon."[124]

In 1894 the *Dianshizhai* reported an accident in which a man died from an electric shock. The man, a thirty-year-old employee of the Shanghai Electric Company, was responsible for looking after the lamps along Broadway Road. The accident occurred when he climbed one lamp's pole to make repairs (Fig. 24).[125] This incident tells us two things: that electric street lights were common enough to require men specially employed to repair them; it also suggests that in spite of the accident, there was no public outcry against the use of electricity. How different from the objections of the daotai to the Shanghai Municipal Council only a few years earlier!

24. Death caused by an electric shock (1894). An employee of an electricity company is accidentally electrocuted while checking street lamps.

In contrast to the "nightless city" of the settlements, the Chinese city had neither gas nor electric light. The gates to the city were closed about 9:00 p.m. When the gentry of the city celebrated a wedding or conducted a funeral, they had to ask the authorities to postpone the closing of the gates, so their guests could come and go. For a small bribe, one could also arrange for the gates to be opened after hours, but this was still inconvenient and contrasted strikingly with the foreign settlement. In the words of one writer, "A comprehensive survey of the situation in Shanghai shows that it certainly had an atmosphere of modernity. . . . Life inside the Chinese city, however, including the customs and habits of the officials and the people, was the same as it had been for quite a few centuries."[126]

4. Urban life in the settlements

Shanghai's new physical environment provided the setting for a new urban lifestyle and new forms of entertainment. Even traditional activities took on new forms and new meanings.

A ride through the streets

From the *Dianshizhai* sketches, it is obvious that the carriage was not merely a means of transportation. Taking a carriage ride became a new source of enjoyment. People would invite a few friends, hire a carriage near the Huangpu River or on Nanjing Road, and go for a ride, just for the pleasure of the experience.[127] During the summertime young lovers would hire a carriage in the middle of the night and revel until dawn. Along the way they might stop at a teahouse, or a similar establishment, for some diversion.[128] Picking up prostitutes and riding around with them was the height of fashion for Shanghai's "dandies" (*huahuagongzi*). Many of the horse-drawn carriages were Hansom cabs, which the Chinese thought was derived from the English word "handsome."[129]

A ride through the streets in a horse-drawn carriage was one of the major activities for visitors, others attractions being theaters, restaurants, teahouses, opium dens, sing-song halls and brothels.[130] Most of these establishments were grouped along Fuzhou Road:

> The area of Fuzhou Road in Shanghai's International Settlement is prosperous and lively. Sing-song halls and dance halls are scattered there like stars in the sky or men on a chessboard. Those who stroll through this area feel they have entered a 'chamber of enchanting fragrance' or the 'nightless city.'[131]

Tea drinking in the "Crystal Palace"

Tea drinking in small, intimate teahouses had long been a part of traditional life in the Chinese city. From the 1860s on, however, several large new-style teahouses along Fuzhou Road took pains to create quite a different an atmosphere.[132] The Diyilou Teahouse, for example, was housed in a three-story Western-style building, with wide glass windows opening out on all sides. It was so bright inside that the Chinese called it the "Crystal Palace." With billiard rooms on the ground floor, more than one thousand tea drinkers could be accommodated on the first and second floors. It was a major Shanghai attraction.[133]

Teahouses mentioned in the *Dianshizhai* included the Diyilou,[134] the Wucenglou Teahouse,[135] the Huazhonghui Teahouse,[136] and several others. The Diyilou Teahouse had special facilities for opium smoking, and guests could take turns at sipping tea and smoking opium. From noon till well after midnight there was not an empty seat to be found.[137] *Dianshizhai* drawings unvaryingly show teahouses to be extremely crowded flourishing businesses. The Gengshangyicenglou, a combined teahouse and opium den run by British merchants, was also on Fuzhou Road.[138] The *Dianshizhai* describes its patrons as young and old, men and women. One of the sketches (Fig. 25) shows the chaos provoked by a false fire alarm in a sing-song hall opposite. As the teahouse guests rushed out, the volume of people was such that the stairs broke under their weight.[139] We can see from the *Dianshizhai* that Shanghai's teahouses and opium dens were meticulously designed and constructed, often "richly furnished with carved blackwood from the south."[140]

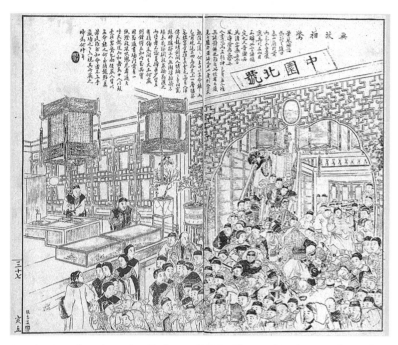

25. The Gengshangyicenglou Teahouse (1891). This combined opium den and teahouse was run by British merchants and located on Fuzhou Road. In this sketch, a false fire alarm causes chaos.

Tea was served in the opium dens, and opium-smoking facilities were provided in teahouses; some teahouses were also set up in conjunction with sing-song halls. Similar to ordinary teahouses, these establishments also featured a stage. The *Dianshizhai* mentions by name the Pinyulou and the Yeshilou sing-song halls on Fuzhou Road. These were fairly large and similar in design. The Yipinlou staged performances of over a dozen sing-song girls every day, and tea-drinking clients could request a particular song.[141]

Shanghai's growing prosperity also attracted a large number of prostitutes. Fuzhou Road, famous for its teahouses and restaurants, was also renowned for its brothels, particularly in the area around Hujiazhai.[142] When "the electric lights go on, the sounds of the *pipa* begin to stir," and Fuzhou Road became very lively. Men would start visiting the brothels, or otherwise find a woman for the night. Courtesans who had been hired for an evening's company or to provide singing entertainment at a banquet would move from one address to another (Fig. 26).[143] In some of the sketches one can see "wandering prostitutes" (*liuji*) soliciting customers off the streets (Fig. 27).[144]

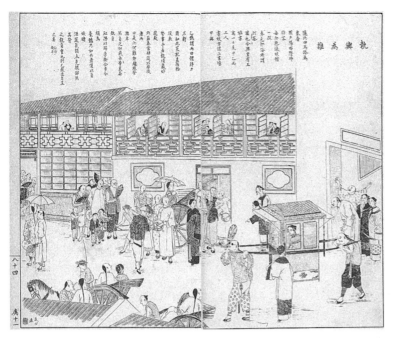

26. Fuzhou Road at night (1886). Prostitutes hurry to visit their clients. The sketch features a dandy (in sunglasses), who carries the sedan chair of a particular courtesan in the hope of gaining her favors.

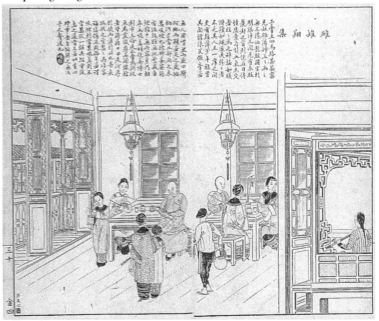

27. Street prostitutes in a teahouse (1891). The author noticed a group of garishly made-up women in a teahouse on Fuzhou Road. Called "wandering prostitutes," they were on the lookout for clients. The author disapproved and called for the Municipal Council to ban this practice.

These sorts of prostitutes were also known as "wild chickens" (*yeji*), and one section of Fuzhou Road was known as "Wild Chicken Corner" (Yejitun).¹⁴⁵ "[On] Fuzhou Road in the International Settlement . . . the goings-on are so bad, one can only heave a sigh on seeing them."¹⁴⁶ Western descriptions are similar: "[It] is a narrow street with nothing at first sight to arrest the attention, but men shake their heads at the mention of it and women avoid it if possible."¹⁴⁷

Early performances in the sing-song halls were mainly traditional storytelling done by prostitutes. By the 1880s, however, most performances were various types of Chinese opera.¹⁴⁸ There was no lack of "indecent operas" in this repertoire. An amazing spectacle occurred in the Yeshilou Sing-song Hall in 1887, when a Western prostitute was employed to sing a Chinese folksong, *The Eighteen Caresses* (Fig. 28). She sits at center stage playing a *pipa*, with six Chinese prostitutes around her, also holding *pipas*. Two male musicians sit behind them. The hall is packed; the audience is dressed respectably and appears fascinated.

> For the past few years, both sides of Fuzhou Road have been packed with storytellers and singers, as far the eye can see. People passing through that area are annoyed by the noise. Now the owner of the Yeshilou has invited a Western prostitute to perform every few days, so as to be different from everyone else. All she can sing is one indecent Chinese song. . . . Those who have heard of this do not approve and think it is extremely silly.¹⁴⁹

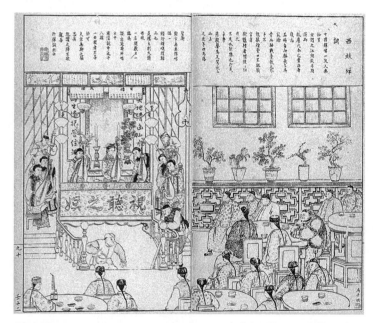

28. A Western prostitute on stage in a sing-song hall (1887). Two billboards posted above the stage indicate the daytime and evening programs of that particular day.

Western-style restaurants

Shanghai residents of the late nineteenth century did not exactly change their eating habits, but quite a few of them acquired a taste for Western food. Chinese entrepreneurs accommodated this by opening Western restaurants along Fuzhou Road.¹⁵⁰

In the beginning few people showed any interest, but over the past few years many Chinese have developed a taste for Western food, so other restaurants, such as the Haitianchun and the Yijiachun, were opened. . . . All these restaurants have seats in separate compartments; their furnishings are elegant and clean, and on Saturdays and Sundays the seats are usually full. The cost is one *yuan* per person; to sit and take tea costs seven *jiao* and snacks cost five *jiao*. They also provide opium, wine, and tidbits, as well all types of Chinese and foreign wine. One can also engage prostitutes to accompany one's wine drinking.[151]

Chinese operated as many as nine Western-style restaurants on Fuzhou Road at that time, the most famous of which, the Yipinxiang, boasted more than thirty private rooms on two levels.

The Yipinxiang menu included fried pork chops, steak, beef broth, pudding, champagne and beer.[152] "An eating house, just like in the West . . . most famous is the Yipinxiang. The knives and forks are bright as snow. The rooms are elegant and cool, the cups and plates so fine and bright. Foreign flowers and foreign fruits are all so new. After the meal, a cup of coffee to pour down your innards twists and turns."[153] In the *Dianshizhai* sketches men with queues and women with bound feet eat with knives and forks. Contemporary sources indicate that eating Western food in a Chinese-run Western restaurant was by no means unusual, but few Chinese ate in restaurants run by foreigners. The prices in the Chinese-run restaurants ran ten or fifteen cash for each dish; in Western-run restaurants the price was one *yuan* per person for a full nine-course meal (Fig. 29).[154]

Some Chinese-style teahouses also served Western meals. In 1883 the Huazhonghui Teahouse placed the following advertisement in the *Shenbao*: "From the twenty-third of the eighth month, this establishment will offer English and French banquets. Famous chefs have been specially invited to prepare them. We also serve all sorts of Western delicacies, and you can sit in spacious comfort. Special price, day or night: five cash per person."[155]

Gradually certain Western foods not traditionally part of the Chinese diet came to be accepted. In 1888 the chief editor of the *Shenbao*, He Guisheng, tasted imported salmon for the first time at the Huazhonghui Teahouse. He found it so delicious he wrote a poem about it in the *Shenbao*.[156] Even beef, which in the past had been morally unacceptable to eat, began to be more common fare.[157]

Restaurants also occasionally came up with other attractions. China did not have anything like a Western zoo at that time, but the Yipinxiang purchased a boa constrictor and a leopard, and exhibited them by the main door of the restaurant (Fig. 30).[158]

Public gardens

Another important innovation in Shanghai was the appearance of "public space." Shanghai had gardens attached to the City Temple, but these were open to the public only on special occasions, such as for festivals or flower displays.[159] The most famous of the new public gardens was the Zhangyuan.[160] It is mentioned three times in the *Dianshizhai*, and one commentary gives a little of the history of the place.

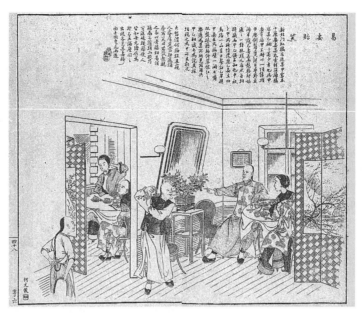

29. Chinese in a Western restaurant (1897). The Yipinxiang Restaurant was a Western establishment run by Chinese. Men with queues and women with bound feet can be seen eating with knives and forks. They seem to be fairly well off. The commentary refers to a husband who went to the Yipinxiang with his lover, and his wife who happened to be at the restaurant with her lover at the same time.

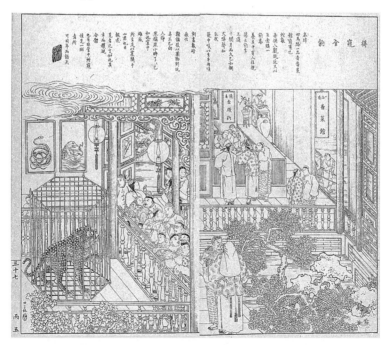

30. Display of a leopard in front of a restaurant (1885). A popular attraction before Shanghai had a zoo. Guests can be seen buying tickets to have a look.

To the north of Shanghai, outside the earthen walls, is a place called the Zhangyuan. Pavilions and halls there tower to the heavens. Until recently few people had heard of it. But now the owner manages it with great care. There are tea pavilions and opium couches, facilities for wine banquets and "kitten plays" (*mao'er xi*), all perfectly presented. So guests flock to this place like ants, like flies around mutton, and gradually the smell of the place attaches itself to them.[161]

The *mao'er xi* was a sort of banquet accompanied by operatic performances by prostitutes. The term is said to have originated with Li Mao'er, a Peking opera performer who trained young girls in Shanghai to sing and perform. Another explanation suggests that their singing sounded like the mewing of kittens, thus the name.[162]

In the nineteenth century public spaces such as teahouses and meeting halls in the Zhangyuan were used by locals merely as places of entertainment. By the twentieth century, with the raising of locals' political consciousness, the Zhangyuan acquired a new function. Revolutionaries and men of letters held meetings or made speeches there, and the venue played a critical role in the development of Shanghai's political life.[163]

In sketches of the Zhangyuan one can see Chinese-style pavilions and halls, pools and lotus ponds, alongside Western furniture and a large Western-style hall (Figs. 31 and 32). Shanghai residents were also attracted to the Yangshupu Garden, about twenty *li* from the settlements. Apart from the usual Chinese halls and pavilions, the Yangshupu also featured animals, the likes of which could not be seen elsewhere in China.[164]

> The Garden is about six hundred *mu* in area. It contains a wide river, large enough for small paddle boats to travel to and fro. It has all sorts of animals, such as lions, elephants, and leopards. There are also all sorts of fish, prawns, mussels, and clams in an enclosure with a glass wall, which contains sea water [i.e., an aquarium]. There are bird cages twenty *zhang* high, several times wider, and about half a *li* in length. Five or six large trees grow inside, and a larger number of smaller ones. Birds can fly around as they like. It is really a marvel to behold.[165]

On the banks of the Huangpu River another "public garden" had been laid out. Chinese occasionally frequented it, but it had only trees, plants, and flowers, and none of the special attractions of the other gardens. This place was mentioned by Chi Zhicheng on the same page as the Yangshupu Garden, but no details are given. There seems to have been less early interest in this garden than in the Yangshupu or the Zhangyuan, although it was to become notorious in the twentieth century.[166]

Such places provided men and women with opportunities to meet. For many the real pleasure of spending time in a teahouse or an opium den was the chance to rendezvous.

> On summer nights, the horse-drawn carriages in Shanghai do a brisk business. They go out in the middle of the night and do not return until dawn. In the area around Yuyuan, outside the Nicheng Bridge, some people stop to take tea, while others do not even descend from the carriages, but turn out the lamps and stop under the shade of the trees, while philandering and troublesome types dart under the wheels of the carriage and between the feet of the horses, hoping to get a glance at the women.[167]

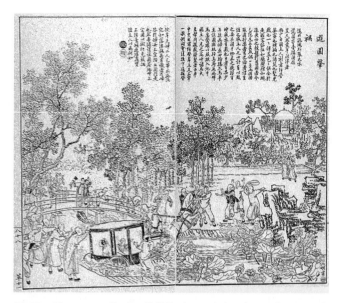

31. The Zhangyuan Garden (1893). A couple in a horse-drawn carriage falls into a lotus pond. Onlookers comment that women should think twice before venturing out of their chambers. The commentator agrees, but adds that a fence should be constructed around the pond to prevent accidents.

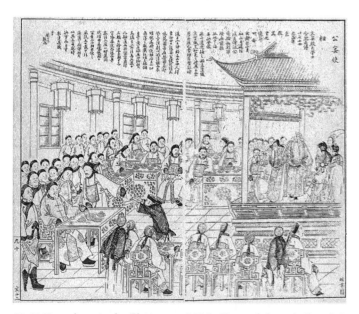

32. Li Hongzhang in the Zhangyuan (1896). Li passed through Shanghai on his way to Russia as special envoy to the coronation of the Russian czar. Twenty-four Shanghai officials and local gentry have arranged a banquet on an auspicious day in his honor. It is held in the Zhangyuan, a luxurious place of entertainment; and a Peking opera troupe is performing on the stage. Li Hongzhang is attired in full court costume. The commentary notes that Li arrived in a four-wheeled carriage drawn by two horses but is not accompanied by his official escort.

The contemporary expression "to flirt" was *diao bangzi*, literally "to hang on the [other person's] arm." One day an employee of a foreign firm, smartly dressed and smoking a cigarette, was standing by the carriage of a certain prostitute, staring fixedly at her. Suddenly the carriage driver raised his whip and the horses galloped off. The young man could not get out of the way in time, and his sleeve got caught in the carriage. He was not seriously hurt, but the *Dianshizhai* could not resist punning that young man really did have to hang onto his arm (Fig. 33).[168]

33. An outing on a summer evening (1897). This was an occasion for men and women to flirt in public.

Sports

Various sporting activities introduced by Westerners also attracted the enthusiasm of Shanghai residents. Horse racing was the most important. "A Britisher in Shanghai once made the remark, 'There are two things an Englishman must have: a King and a racecourse.'"[169] Horse racing made its appearance not long after the foreign settlements were established—a race course is mentioned in Shanghai as early as 1850.[170] The first issue of the *Shenbao*, published on April 30, 1872, carried racing news, and the second issue of the *Dianshizhai* included a sketch and commentary explaining the sport in some detail.

> Westerners organize Spring and Autumn racing carnivals, each of three days duration. They offer a large sum of money as a prize, which the fastest horse wins. The course is circled by three concentric fences. During the race, the jockeys wear clothes of satin, and the horses have reins of gold. On the corners stand pavilions, which the Westerners mount to observe [the race]. People on all sides applaud the winner. To the participants, this is one of the joys of their lives. The onlookers [i.e., Chinese], who surround the place like a wall, are indifferent to who wins and who loses, but their joy is even greater than that of the participants.[171] (Fig. 34)

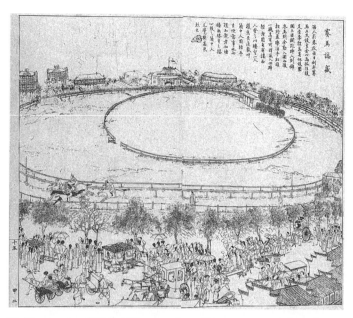

34. Horse racing (1884). This event drew Chinese spectators from all social backgrounds—officials, poor peddlers, prostitutes, women and children. Chinese were not permitted to take part in the actual horse racing, but they did not seem to object, since they could enjoy the occasion more as spectators.

Shortly afterwards, another sketch described in detail equestrian competitions on the third day of the racing carnival.[172] Here we can see men and women, young and old, hurrying to the scene in all sorts of vehicles—horse-drawn carriages, rickshaws, even sedan chairs. Peddlers can be seen among the crowd, carrying their goods on bamboo poles. Everyone is obviously treating the occasion as a social outing. *Dreams of Prosperity in Shanghai* tells of a prostitute who demanded that her client buy her a new set of clothing and ornaments so that she could accompany him to the races.[173]

> Horse racing is so popular in the International Settlement that all offices are closed for three days. In the afternoon crowds gather to watch. Precious horses, scented carts, silks and satins without end.[174] . . . With crowds of people coming to the races, traffic accidents also increased.[175] . . . Amongst the spectators are high officials and poor peddlers. They rub shoulders and knock heels; those who arrive late have nowhere to get a foot in. [One can even see] glossy jade-green "fragrant carriages" with attendants and delicate ladies covered in gold, powder, and rouge.[176]

Boat racing on the Suzhou Creek was also a sport enjoyed by both Chinese and foreigners. "Rowing made its appearance in 1863 . . . it became very popular and an international cup was keenly competed for. . . . The races were rowed on the Soochow Creek. In later years as Shanghai developed, the congested traffic on the waterways near Shanghai made it necessary to hold the annual regatta out in the country at Henli."[177] Boat racing was mentioned in the *Dianshizhai* in 1884: "During the Spring and Autumn holidays Westerners organize boat races. They offer a large amount of money in prizes. Those that come first win, and those who come in later lose. The participants are extremely excited, and onlookers applaud on all sides. The whole city is crazy about it."[178] In these two drawings we can see many Chinese, young and old on both banks of the river. There are also women arriving by horse-drawn carriage.

Charles M. Dyce, a resident of Shanghai at the time, noted in his memoirs, "Shanghai was an absolutely ideal place of residence for a young man who loved sport because he could get plenty of it, easily and cheaply.... Every kind of sport was available, and almost at our doors...."[179]

Paper hunting was another popular sport. "This involves at least ten horses—sometimes fifty or sixty—there is no precise limit. One man carries a bag full of pieces of colored paper. He throws them into the wind, and the others chase them" (Fig. 35).[180] According to Pott, paper hunting was introduced by military officers who had been familiar with it elsewhere.[181]

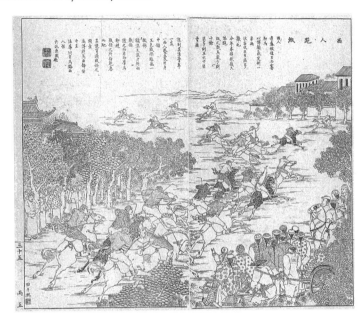

35. Paper hunting (1885). This event was held in Shanghai every spring and autumn, each time for three days. It was similar to horse racing, and attracted many onlookers. The sport is no longer practiced.

Another foreign sport introduced in the pages of the *Dianshizhai* was cricket. "Throwing a ball is also a common skill in Western countries. There are many varieties ... Westerners use this to help the circulation of the blood and *qi*, and to exercise the muscles and sinews" (Fig. 36).[182] The term "cricket pitch" (*paoqiuchang*) even became the name of one of Shanghai's streets.[183] According to Pott, "Cricket, as already noted, was one of the chief forms of sport. The first recorded cricket match was played somewhere in Hongkew, and on this ground a match between a team of officers from H.M.S. *Highflyer* and a Shanghai eleven was played on April 22nd, 1858. The first interport match with Hong Kong took place in 1866."[184]

The Chinese people of the nineteenth century never took part in these sports themselves, but they were certainly enthusiastic spectators. All *Dianshizhai* sketches about various sports show numerous Chinese among the spectators. Reports in the *Shenbao* on horse and boat racing frequently included such expressions as "Chinese and Western spectators were packed together like a wall, and the crowding was extraordinary."[185] In 1873 the *Shenbao* carried a report to the effect that the prize for a track and field competition was awarded by a local Chinese native bank, and noted that "this is meant to extend the friendship between Chinese and Westerners."[186]

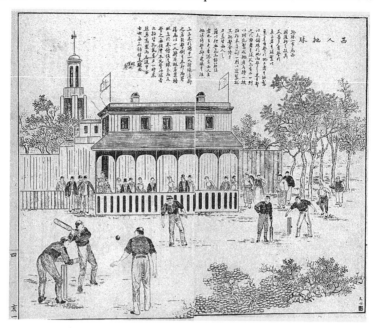

36. Cricket in Shanghai (1891). The commentary describes the game of cricket and introduces its basic rules. "Men who play this sport are very strong and brave. [The onlookers] become excited and are so happy they forget to go home. Both Western and Chinese men and women arrange with their friends to come and watch the matches."

For the Westerners, of course, such activities came under the rubric of "sport." For the Chinese such occasions became a new type of social festival. Every year at a particular time or season, men and women would dress in their best clothes to observe these activities with great interest. They were never actually permitted to take part in them (nor would they have wanted to), but that did not diminish their enthusiasm for going to enjoy the spectacle.

Celebrations in the settlements

Various celebrations in the settlements came to be viewed primarily as spectacle. They may have had political or patriotic significance to the Westerners, but to Chinese they were simply the occasion for the lively, energetic display of color, enthusiasm, and excitement.

According to the *Dianshizhai*, the whole settlement turned out to celebrate such events, and the streets were invariably packed.[187] The greatest celebration of the period under discussion occurred in 1893, to mark the Fiftieth Anniversary of the Founding of the Foreign Settlements. The *Dianshizhai* dedicated an entire issue to the celebrations.[188] On the morning of the November 19, 1893, the Reverend Dr. William Muirhead gave an address on the Bund; this marked the official start of the celebrations.

On the tenth day of this month, Western officials and merchants celebrated the fiftieth anniversary of the establishment of the open port. In the area between the Bund and Nanjing Road, policemen set up poles, joined together by rope, on which hung all sorts of flags and colored paper lanterns. Colored lanterns, vying with each other, hung outside the shops along the route. This was to strengthen the friendship between Chinese and foreigners. On that day, early in the morning, the Shanghai Volunteer Corps and English, German, and American sailors, carrying their rifles and pushing their cannon, performed all sorts of military maneuvers under the leadership of their officers. Afterwards they returned to the Harry Smith Parkes statue on the Bund, where a missionary, Mr. William Muirhead, dressed in formal coat and tails, and standing on a leather stool, praised the outstanding achievements in trade over the past fifty years. He related these one by one, as if they were family treasures. Soldiers and sailors, Chinese and Westerners, listened in quiet fascination.[189]

The Reverend Muirhead ended by summarizing the progress made in Shanghai:

Shanghai is the center of our higher civilization and Christian influence for all of China. We are here in the midst of a people proud and prejudiced in favor of the ancient line of things, and what have we introduced amongst them, for their benefit as well as our own . . . houses and streets lit with gas and electricity, streams of pellucid water flowing in all directions, and sanitary arrangements according to the best medical advice. We have steamers, telegraphs, and telephones in communication with all the world; there are cotton and paper mills and silk filatures of foreign invention.[190]

After his speech, the procession started. The foreign settlements blazed with color and light; the Fire Brigade joined the procession with its firefighting equipment, followed by a band of more than thirty people.[191] Chinese guilds followed, beating gongs and drums (Fig. 37).[192] Foreign banks along the route, such as the Chartered Bank of India, Australia, and China, and the Hong Kong and Shanghai Banking Corporation had gas lamps arranged in such a way as to spell out the names of their companies.[193] These activities were unprecedented. From the nine sketches describing the celebrations we can see that even the windows and balconies of the houses facing the main streets were packed. Chinese and foreign policemen are present, doing their best to maintain order. The Chinese were by no means all from Shanghai—many had come in for the day from outlying districts. The fares on the rickshaws and the carriages increased by a factor of ten, and all the hotels and other lodgings were booked up.[194]

Two other major occasions recorded by the *Dianshizhai* include the jubilee of 1887—the Fiftieth Anniversary of the Accession of Queen Victoria to the throne (and her 68th birthday)—and the Queen's Diamond Jubilee in 1897, to mark the sixtieth anniversary of her accession. In 1887 the *Dianshizhai* dedicated seven sketches to the celebrations. From these we learn that ships on the Huangpu sounded their horns as a gesture of congratulations, and the settlement shone bright with illuminated decorations. There was a procession, with the Fire Brigade participating. The Bund featured a fountain and a platform illuminated with multicolored electric lights.[195] The celebrations in 1897 followed the same pattern but added a bicycle race and a children's horse race.[196]

Masses of people also turned out to witness any sort of celebration organized by the French Concession. On Bastille Day 1885, the main streets from the Huangpu River to the French Concession were decorated with lamps and red, white, and blue bunting (Fig. 38).

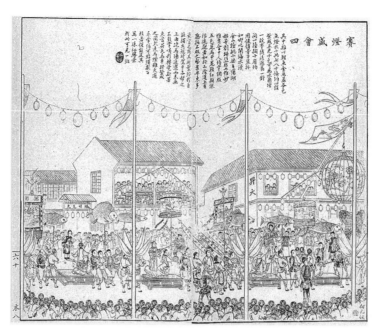

37. Lanterns displayed for the anniversary celebrations (1893). This sketch, one of a series on the Jubilee, shows a lantern display sponsored by Cantonese merchants. "There are many rich merchants who hail from Canton. Their lanterns are far better than those of any other group. They set off from the racecourse to applause and shouts of approval."

38. French National Day celebrations (1885). "The third day of the current month is the fourteenth of July in the Western calendar. This was the day when France became a democracy."

The commercialization of leisure

Western investment in leisure activities contributed to the growing "commercialization of leisure." A sketch dated 1889 shows a Western female acrobat balancing on a plank supported by a rubber ball. Westerners and Chinese alike stand in the audience, but it is the Chinese who are the most enthralled.[197]

We learn from the *Dianshizhai* that the same circus visited Shanghai three times—in 1880, 1886 and 1889 (Fig. 39). In 1886 the *Dianshizhai* noted, "From the very first performance, people have been bringing their friends and relatives. When they talk about it their eyebrows fly and their faces become animated."[198] When the circus returned in 1889, large numbers of people flocked to watch its arrival. So many people filled the roads along the wharves that one man was even knocked into the water.[199] The *Dianshizhai* devoted five sketches to circus performances that year, showing acrobats and magicians. One depicts a female performer doing a horse riding act that allegedly originated in ancient Rome. The commentary notes that such performances "can broaden the experience of the Chinese."[200] Wang Tao also provided a detailed description of the Western circus and conjurers in his *Maritime and Littoral Miscellany*.[201]

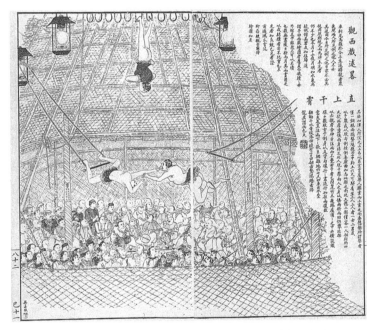

39. The circus (1889). Wu Youru and one of the editors of the *Shenbao* go to the circus. The editor suggested a story be written about the circus to accompany a sketch done some time earlier. The signs on the pillars holding up the tent read: 'Best seats (*guanzuo*)—nine *yuan* each box. Stall seats—one *yuan* each place.' The term *guanzuo* in Beijing at the time referred to seats reserved for officials responsible for monitoring the content of local drama. In Shanghai it meant the most expensive seats.

Even more astonishing was the appearance in 1890 of a roller coaster. One sketch shows the ride packed with Chinese and a long line of people waiting their turn. The picture also shows men, women, and children hurrying to the scene in their rickshaws and carriages, with Chinese and Sikh policemen doing their best to maintain order (Fig. 40).[202]

Other novelties were not meant to be forms of amusement, but they became such for the people of Shanghai. Crowds of curious Chinese gathered to watch the drills of the Shanghai Fire Brigade.[203] One might contrast this situation with Shanghai before its establishment as a commercial port, when the only sources of entertainment were the festivals and temple fairs associated with the Temple of the City God,[204] or theatrical performances organized by the guild halls to collect money for some purpose or to express gratitude towards a particular patron deity. These were quite different in nature from the public performances staged in the settlements.

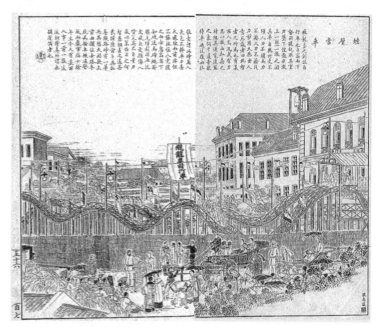

40. A roller coaster (1890). This sketch shows men, women and children queuing up for a ride, and more people outside waiting their turn. Sikh and Chinese policemen maintain order.

A new concept of time

The import of the accurate measurement of time also took root in Shanghai. Before the arrival of clocks, Chinese used the twelve branches to denote twelve two-hour periods making up the day. During the night, a watchman would beat the watch every two hours. The Chinese living in the settlements, however, soon abandoned this way of denoting time. In 1884 the *Dianshizhai* carried a sketch, entitled "The Sun at Noon," which has often been used in books and articles on Chinese history. It shows a wind-flag and a time-ball set up on the Bund in the French Concession. Every day, at 10:00 a.m. precisely, the wind-flag was raised; different flags were raised depending on the direction of the wind. At 11:45 a.m. the ball was raised halfway up its mast; at 11:55 a.m. it was lifted to the top, and at 12:00 noon precisely it was let drop. This procedure enabled the inhabitants of the Concession to determine the precise time (Fig. 41).[205]

41. "The Sun at Noon" (1884). The sketch shows the "wind flag" and the "time ball" on the Bund in the French Concession. At the stroke of noon, the time ball was released. A large public clock shows the time to be 11:45 a.m.

In 1893 the *Dianshizhai* carried a sketch on the installation of a new clock on the Customs Building, which needed to be wound only once every eight days (Fig. 42). The commentary mentions that chiming clocks already had been installed at various places in the French Concession and the International Settlement, at the Catholic churches in Xujiahui and Hongkou, as well as at the Racing Pavilion. These, however, were not very loud, and could not be heard very far away. At night the Customs Building clock face was lit by electric lights, and people could see it from quite a distance.[206] "The [likes of this] huge chiming clock is not to be found in Beijing. High in the sky, its hands can be so clearly seen. People come to it and hurry to adjust their vest pocket watches. They do not notice the other people leisurely walking by."[207]

Personal watches and clocks were highly prized by merchants and others who could afford them. They were considered items of value, and thus were often stolen.[208] Whether rich or poor, everyone who lived in Shanghai had a very clear concept of time. The Shanghai lifestyle characterized by the expression "When the tide comes in they go fishing, when the tide goes out they go to sleep"[209] had passed forever. In 1874 the *Shenbao* carried an article about a Westerner who had gone to Beijing from Shanghai, and found the absence of Shanghai-style public clocks a great inconvenience, since he had no way of checking the time.[210] This common use of clocks and watches changed the concept of time, and made people more aware of punctuality for meetings, theatrical performances, and the like. The concept of punctuality for appointments is also clear from novels like *Dreams of Prosperity in Shanghai*.[211] In the rapidly commercializing atmosphere of Shanghai, the use of clocks and watches brought a change in the rhythm of everyday life, and introduced the idea that "time is money."

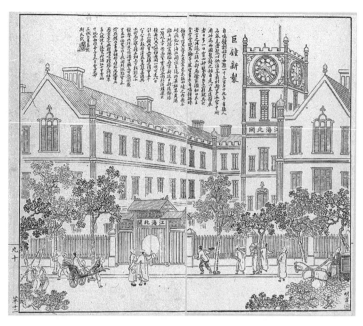

42. The newly installed chiming clock at the Chinese Customs House (1893). This was the only building on the Bund owned by the Chinese.

"Shanghai is not China"

By this stage the Shanghai settlements had become one of China's largest urban areas. As the *Dianshizhai* put it, "Now merchants regard Shanghai as the biggest of the trading cities. Visitors come and go like sand in the river."[212] Foreigners who had previously regarded Shanghai as a place of exile began to regard it as home. "By the early 1880s, the word 'settlement' implied fewer distinctions than had formerly existed between the disparate foreign nationalities; and 'Settlements' began to be capitalized in the press and in private correspondence in the same sense that 'Home' was."[213] In 1893 the *Dianshizhai* commented, "Shanghai has now become a trading center, and many Westerners bring their sons and daughters here."[214] Chinese migrants continued to flood into Shanghai. The city also attracted many travelers and visitors. The *Dianshizhai* mentions the visit of a Brazilian nobleman (1889),[215] the visit of the Prince of Wales on his way back to England from India (1890),[216] and the visit of a French envoy to the county administration in 1895.[217] Even a three-man bicycling team on a round-the-world trip rode through the streets of Shanghai in 1898.[218]

Many people came to Shanghai for a short visit, merely to have a look at the place,[219] or specifically to buy something.[220] Sometimes people from villages in the district also came to the city to participate in some celebration, such as those mentioned above.[221]

Naturally, Chinese and foreign traders flocked to Shanghai—in the words of the *Dianshizhai*, "Shanghai—hundreds of goods like stars in the sky; tens of thousands of merchants crowd together like clouds."[222] By this stage trade in the city was so established that each area had its own particular type of merchandise.[223] All sorts of curious imported items from the West could be found in certain areas.[224] One of the *Dianshizhai* sketches shows a shop run by Westerners, with Chinese customers inside and curious onlookers crowding the door. A variety of desk clocks and pendant lamps can be seen. The commentary informs us that Chinese sales assistants could explain these gadgets in great detail, and that the variety of goods in the shop was such that "it was like being on the road to Shanyin; there were so many things to see that the eyes could not take them all in" (Fig. 43).[225]

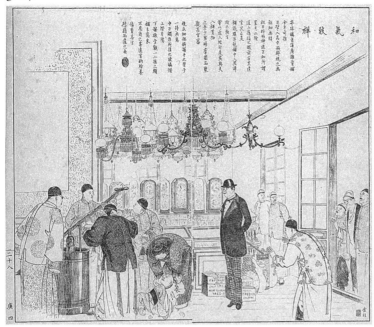

43. A shop specializing in imported goods (1886). A number of Chinese are admiring the strange and unusual objects, which the amiable Western proprietor is explaining. An onlooker breaks one of the lamps, and some broken glass injures a child. The proprietor is sympathetic and offers compensation. The title reads: "Geniality leads to Prosperity."

More than one thousand Chinese hotels had opened in the settlements by the beginning of the 1880s. The largest, such as the Wan'anlou, the Jixinggong, and the Changfa, were imposing Western-style buildings with luxurious furnishings; they could accommodate more than a thousand guests.[226] A detailed description of the Changfa Hotel in *Dreams of Prosperity in Shanghai* informs us that each room had two beds, gaslight, and food provided; guests had to hand in their room keys to the reception desk when they went out, and so on.[227]

The luxury of the Shanghai settlements of the time is described in a short poem quoted by Wang Tao: "Ten *li* of foreign territory really opens the eyes: one almost suspects one is actually traveling in foreign lands."[228] In 1888 the *Shenbao* published an article "An Eyewitness Account of the Foreign Territory" under the pseudonym "A Man on First Opening His Eyes." The author says he used to live in a small town and had never traveled. He had read in the *Shenbao* that Shanghai had telegraph, telephones, and electric light, but could not believe it. It was only after he had actually visited the city that he could bring himself to believe these things.[229] Shanghai's glamorous image even drew the curiosity of the Imperial Court, including the Empress Dowager. In 1893 a Peking opera troupe was invited to the Palace to perform "Visiting Shanghai in a Dream" (*Meng you Shanghai*). It was later invited for a repeat performance.[230] A Republican-period source informs us that the artistic level of this opera was very low, but it was nonetheless very popular in the late nineteenth century. Clearly the attraction was the Shanghai theme, even for the Imperial Court.[231]

There was nothing approaching the Shanghai lifestyle anywhere in the rest of China. As a later Western resident noted, "[What strikes] the inquiring tourist who visits the metropolis on the Whangpoo" is that "Shanghai is not China."[232]

5. Immigrants to Shanghai

Before 1853 the Chinese population in the International Settlement numbered no more than five hundred people, and the resident foreign population was about three hundred. After the Small Sword Society uprising, many Chinese fled into the International Settlement, and by the next year the Chinese population had swelled to twenty thousand.[233] During the Taiping army attacks in Jiangsu and Zhejiang in the next decade, even more Chinese took refuge in the International Settlement. By 1865 the Chinese population there had reached 90,587, and the foreign population 2,297. After the Taipings were defeated, many Chinese returned to their home villages, and by 1870 the Chinese population had decreased to 75,047. This had a negative impact on Shanghai's economic and industrial development. Four of the six foreign banks on the Bund closed their doors, and it was at this time, too, that the Major brothers' businesses registered a loss, and Ernest Major decided to establish a newspaper.[234]

By 1876, however, the population had again risen—to 95,662, and by 1890 to 168,122. In 1895, the Chinese population in the International Settlement stood at 240,995, and the foreign population at 4,684. In 1900 the figures were 345,276 and 6,774, respectively. The Chinese came from all over China—Jiangsu, Zhejiang, Guangdong, Anhui, Shandong, Hubei, Hebei, Hunan, Jiangxi, Fujian, Henan, Sichuan, Guangxi, Shanxi, Yunnan, Shaanxi, Guizhou, but most of them were from Jiangsu, Zhejiang, Guangdong and Anhui. The foreigners in Shanghai hailed from more than twenty different countries. Most were English, Japanese, Americans, and Portuguese.[235]

The situation in the French Concession was similar. According to population statistics compiled by the Conseil Municipal in 1865, there were 55,465 Chinese residents and the foreigner resident population was 460. Most of the Chinese at that time were taking refuge from the Taiping Rebellion. In 1879, when the French authorities conducted their second census, the total population of the French Concession was 33,660, of whom 33,353 were Chinese. In 1890 the Chinese population increased to 40,722, with 444 Westerners. In 1895, there were 51,758 Chinese and 430 Westerners; in 1890 the corresponding figures were 91,646 and 622.[236]

The immigrants after the 1870s were quite different from the earlier refugees from various wars and uprisings. Shanghai was now an expanding city, a place of opportunity.[237] While the statistics cannot give information on the backgrounds of the migrants or their motives or expectations, the *Dianshizhai* provides much interesting material to supplement the numbers.

From the analysis of relevant examples from the *Dianshizhai*, we can classify the Chinese migrants into the following six groups.

Refugees fleeing the effects of natural disasters

Refugees were not normally individually newsworthy, and only three examples in the *Dianshizhai* specifically concern people who had arrived in Shanghai after some natural disaster. One featured a man from Jiangxi, who had come to Shanghai in the wake of floods in his locality. He set up a transport business, ferrying porcelain wares between Shanghai and Jiangxi, and, after some years, accumulated a handsome profit.[238] This story dates from 1896, and relates that the man had been in Shanghai for more than twenty years. Records confirm flooding in Jiangxi in 1869 and 1876,[239] so this man must have fled the floods in 1869. The second example is a story dating from 1890, of a grandfather and grandson begging in the streets of Shanghai. They claimed they were from Jiangbei, and had left due to floods in that region.[240] These people had just arrived in Shanghai, and this too corresponds with contemporary records that report continuous flooding in the Jiangbei area during the years 1888 and 1889.[241] The third story, dating from 1897, tells of a family which had left Jiangbei some years earlier because of floods. The father became a peddler in the city, and one day the mother recognized their daughter with whom they had lost contact for many years walking past in the street.[242]

Those looking for economic opportunities

This category includes people of both the greatest ambitions and the most humble aspirations. The latter constituted the working class, whose main concern was to be able to earn enough money through physical labor to eat and keep themselves warm. Many of the most influential entrepreneurs of late nineteenth and early twentieth century China came from impoverished backgrounds. They had come to Shanghai as children or young adults and had struggled their way to success. Rong Zongjing, Ye Chengzhong, Zeng Zhu, Zhu Dachun, Zhu Baosan, and Xu Run are examples.[243] The following types are commonly featured in the *Dianshizhai*:

(a) Merchants who had already achieved a certain degree of success often came to Shanghai in search of greater opportunities. Examples include a rich merchant from Guangdong,[244] a merchant from Xiamen whose business was buying and selling land,[245] and a jeweler from Nanjing who set up shop on the busy Nanjing Road in the International Settlement.[246] There is also a story about a Fujianese merchant who traveled between Taiwan and Shanghai, transporting sugar and cotton. This type of business was very profitable at the time.[247] Chen Zhuping, who arrived in Shanghai in 1850 and traded in silk, had become one of the richest men in Shanghai by 1860.[248] He involved himself in various public works, especially fundraising for victims of natural disasters.[249] When Chen died in 1889, the *Dianshizhai* covered his funeral (Fig. 44).[250] Chen's funeral made a tremendous impression on the local Chinese residents, who still talked about it decades later.[251]

(b) Small-time peddlers and handy men wandering through the streets of Shanghai offered their services: The *Dianshizhai* features a peddler from Taizhou in Zhejiang,[252] a rice peddler from Shanxi,[253] a man from Anhui who opened a shop to sell socks and stockings,[254] a chicken vendor from Fujian,[255] a man from Qingpu who came to Shanghai in search of business,[256] carpenters from Nanjing and Ningbo,[257] and a tailor from Chongming who employed five people.[258] There were also Muslim peddlers[259] selling beef, who came to Shanghai towards the end of the nineteenth century from Nanjing, Suzhou, and Yangzhou.[260] Muslim residents of Shanghai are mentioned several times[261] in the *Dianshizhai*, which explained the significance of Muslim fasting during Ramadan[262] and gave details of the Muslim quarter in Nanjing.[263]

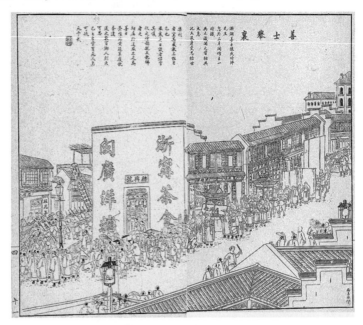

44. The funeral of Chen Zhuping (1889). Chen was known as the "Good Man of Zhe-Hu" and was famous for his charitable works.

(c) Peasants and others were attracted to Shanghai in search of work or other opportunities. There are at least ten examples in the *Dianshizhai* of peasants, particularly women, coming to Shanghai to find work in the newly established factories (Fig. 45).[264] Some people left their villages to become shop attendants or waiters in restaurants, such as the peasant who became an attendant in a perfume shop,[265] the woman who was employed as a domestic servant,[266] and the family from Chongming—the husband worked as a water-carrier for the Tongwen Bookstore,[267] the daughter was employed in the same bookstore, and the wife earned money as a washerwoman.[268] Itinerant entertainers had an even harder life. Four *Dianshizhai* stories featured such people—the entertainer from Shanxi (Fig. 46),[269] the circus performers from Shandong (Fig. 47),[270] and the monkey trainer from Jiangbei.[271] These people commonly performed dangerous acts, and serious accidents sometimes occurred.[272]

(d) Unscrupulous types in search of easy money. In 1886 of a band of porters from Xuzhou and Shandong, who made a living transporting fruit, decided it was a pity not to get rich in a place like Shanghai. They managed to get hold of a few guns and held up the Chartered Mercantile Bank of India (Fig. 48).[273] All of them were eventually apprehended and taken into custody. All sorts of shady businessmen thrived in Shanghai, such as the Hunanese who opened an opium den,[274] and the Cantonese who ran both opium dens and brothels.[275]

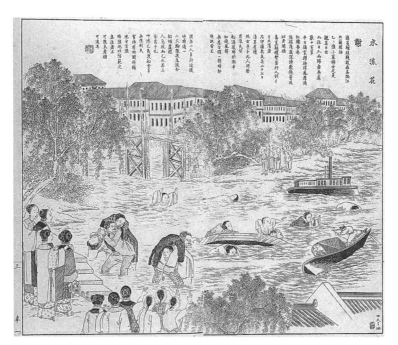

45. Village girls drown in a boating accident (1886). Hurrying in an overloaded boat to their work at the Keechong Silk Filature in Shanghai, three young women drowned when the boat capsized. The commentary expresses the hope that local officials will implement safety measures to prevent such accidents from happening in the future.

46. Girl performing on a tightrope (1889). Cai Lianxi and his family, from Datong, Shanxi, were itinerant entertainers in Shanghai. It is his daughter depicted performing here.

OLD CITY, NEW CITY

47. Circus bear kills a child (1895). Dong Zhengming, an itinerant entertainer from Shandong, had a performing bear in his act. The commentary relates how the bear broke free from its chains and attacked a member of the audience, a young girl, who died soon afterward. Dong provided forty *yuan* compensation to the girl's family, and the bear was put down. Although the text has the victim a young girl, the sketch clearly shows a baby boy at the bear's mouth.

48. Armed bank robbery (1886). The bank is the Chartered Mercantile Bank of India. The text says that the robbers had guns, but the sketch only shows broadswords.

Opium dens run by the Cantonese were particularly famous. Even if the surroundings were plain and simple, their preparation of the opium was done with the greatest care.²⁷⁶ We also read of an old woman from the countryside who opened a *maison de rendezvous* (*taiji*)—a discreet place for those engaged in illicit affairs to meet.²⁷⁷ Sorceresses,²⁷⁸ Daoist priests,²⁷⁹ bogus Buddhist monks and nuns, and adherents of other religions and sects²⁸⁰ also made their way to Shanghai. Stories in the *Dianshizhai* mainly describe how such people used various schemes to cheat money from people (Fig. 49). Examples include a witch from Nanjing,²⁸¹ a sorcerer from Guangdong,²⁸² a Daoist priest from Hubei²⁸³ and so on.

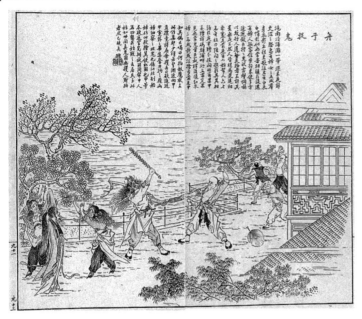

49. Robbery by Jiangbei women (1897). The area around the Huangpu River in the southern part of Shanghai was believed to be haunted. It turned out that Jiangbei boat women had dressed up as ghosts to rob passers-by.

(e). Those with other motives. "A certain woman from Ningjun [Nanjing] had a daughter with jade like skin smooth as ice; she was a real beauty. She had reached marriageable age, and [her mother] went in search of a son-in-law who would be a good spouse for her. She decided that only in a prosperous place like Shanghai were men of talent to be found, so she conceived the idea of taking her daughter there."²⁸⁴ Another case involved a man who had a fight with his wife and in a fit of rage fled to Shanghai, where he eventually found work as a shop assistant.²⁸⁵

Criminals on the run

Criminals often took refuge in the International Settlement. In a city with a constantly shifting population, where the origins of individuals and their backgrounds was not always clear, it was easy enough to blend in. "The area to the north of Shanghai [the foreign settlements] is a mishmash from everywhere; bandits and the like can hide themselves there."²⁸⁶ We read of the rich man from Suzhou, an opium addict and illegal gambler for whom a warrant had been issued by the local authorities. He had no choice but to flee to the International Settlement.²⁸⁷ Another case involved a hoodlum from Hubei who had broken some law there and was wanted by the authorities. He fled to Shanghai, where he opened a brothel.[288] There is also the case of the prostitute from Jiangbei. The *Dianshizhai* does not specify why she was wanted, but authorities in Yancheng sent their men to Shanghai and caught up with her in a brothel (Fig. 50).[289] These three cases were deemed newsworthy because previous crimes had caught up with the perpetrators. One can imagine that such examples were in the minority, however.

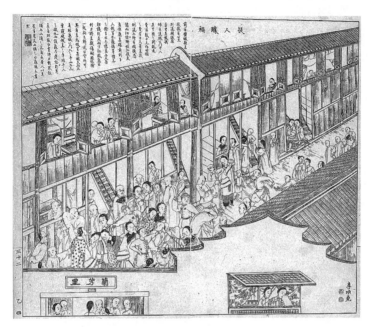

50. A "flower and opium" den (1884). This was the lowest class of brothel. The sign at the bottom of the sketch reads Lanfang Lane, which was where most such brothels were congregated. Here the Yancheng yamen has sent runners to reclaim a girl who had run away. When they arrive, they discover that another group of people, also claiming to be runners from Yancheng, had already been there the day before and accepted a ten *yuan* bribe from the brothel to go away. The brothel owner is furious, and starts a fight with the runners, in the course of which several people are wounded. The case was referred to the Mixed Court.

Shanghai was not only a refuge for Chinese criminals; foreign criminals found safe haven there as well. As Pott put it, "The need of a gaol was soon realized, for Shanghai from the start had to cope with a criminal class, sailors on shore who often gave serious trouble, and the influx of Chinese into the Settlement brought many of the undesirable class."[290] The *Dianshizhai* does not give details about foreigners with shady pasts—of course, such information would not have been available to them. But it does carry stories about disorderly sailors, for example an American and two Englishmen who, after causing trouble in the International Settlement, were arrested by the police (Fig. 51),[291] or the two Americans who got into a gunfight in the Hongkou district and were arrested and escorted to the United States Consulate.[292] There was also the case of the second mate on a steamship who arranged for a Cantonese prostitute to visit him onboard. He got drunk and becoming violent, ended up stabbing the girl and wounding her seriously.[293]

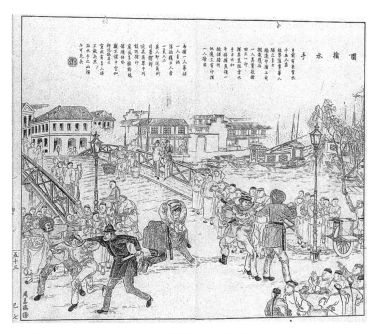

51. Three foreign sailors arrested (1889). Two British and one American are arrested in the settlement and escorted to the police station.

People who had transgressed the moral boundaries of their own localities

These people were not criminals, but found it more comfortable to live in the morally relaxed atmosphere of Shanghai. Most were illicit lovers. A migrant himself, who had spent all his working life in Shanghai, Yao Gonghe noted in 1917,

> For people who suffered the disapproval of public opinion, Shanghai was the only place in the world to which they could escape. Unaccepted elsewhere, only in Shanghai were such relationships not unusual, and so they felt secure . . . whenever something happened to offend public morality, public opinion would generally have it that it was lucky such a thing occurred in Shanghai. If it were to occur inside China proper, even if the perpetrators were to escape the net of the law, they could not avoid the scorn of society.[294]

A widow from Pudong traveled to Shanghai to be able to live with her lover. Her son and some of his fellow villagers tracked her down and forced her to go home (Fig. 52).[295] A prostitute from Ningbo eloped with her benefactor to Shanghai.[296] A married woman from Chuansha eloped with her lover to Shanghai; she, too, was forced home by her husband's family and fellow villagers.[297] A woman from Jiangsu despised her husband because he was too short and ugly, and went to Shanghai where she took a lover.[298] Her husband followed her to Shanghai and reported the matter to the police, saying that he had already discovered where she and her lover were staying.[299] These examples of unsuccessful fugitives suggest the public interest in such stories; the successful ones simply disappeared and became indistinguishable from any ordinary person.

52. Women flee to Shanghai to be with their lovers (1886). This sketch shows a widow being discovered by her son, who forces her to return home. Another sketch (Ren 64 *xia*) tells a similar story, about a married woman from Chuansha.

Those kidnapped or otherwise deceived into coming to Shanghai

Among the population of Shanghai engaged in less respectable occupations such as prostitution, a large number had been kidnapped or deceived into leaving their home villages. One story relates how a woman from Guangdong kidnapped five or six children, so that in a few years time she could sell the girls into brothels and the boys into coolie labor.[100] We also read of a former prostitute who had been kidnapped from her home in Jiangbei and sold into a brothel,[101] or of a migrant to Shanghai who bought a young girl as a servant only to discover that the girl was from his home village. Her parents had died, and she had been kidnapped to be sold in the city.[102]

Refugees from military strife

The *Dianshizhai* was founded long after the Taiping Rebellion, and the people who had fled from that fighting had already been settled in Shanghai for two or three decades. There was no reason to mention why they had originally come to Shanghai. When it came to military conflict, only the Sino-Japanese War of 1894 and the consequences of the Treaty of Shimonoseki figured in the pages of the *Dianshizhai*. After China's defeat, Fujianese fled from Taiwan to Shanghai, taking their money with them. For example, one merchant who fled to Shanghai started a small business there; he later met up with a son, with whom he had lost contact; it turned out that both father and son had decided to leave Taiwan for Shanghai, but neither knew the other's intentions.[103] Another story tells of people whose boat overturned on the way from Taiwan; they were saved, but all their possessions were lost.[104]

Foreigners

The *Dianshizhai* had little interest in the background of various foreigners, and often even their nationalities and professions were not made explicit; they were simply referred to as "a certain Westerner." Still, the material in the *Dianshizhai* indicates several sorts of foreigners resident or active in Shanghai:

(a) Foreign diplomats and their families;[305]
(b) Missionaries;[306]
(c) Doctors and lawyers;[307]
(d) Employees in foreign firms;[308]
(e) Soldiers, for example French,[309] German,[310] English,[311] and Japanese troops;[312]
(f) Sailors;[313]
(g) Policemen, including Sikhs;[314]
(h) Hoodlums and swindlers.[315]

Among the foreigners, too, one can clearly distinguish respected members of Western society, such as diplomats, missionaries, doctors and lawyers, from the sailors, soldiers, hoodlums and swindlers. The social and cultural mosaic in Shanghai was thus very complex, with different social groups representing various social strata, both Chinese and Western.

The future course of Shanghai—its atmosphere and its character, and in particular the degree to which it would accept Western culture and develop its own characteristic urban culture—had its basis in the heterogeneous nature of its denizens.

6. Conflicting legal systems

When Chinese flooded into the settlements during the Taiping Rebellion, the foreign authorities were not keen for them to stay there, and had no interest in exercising any jurisdiction over them—except in matters of taxation or public order.[316] The Chinese police could enter the settlements at any time, and take those arrested to the Chinese city for trial and punishment. Very soon, however, the foreign authorities realized that this state of affairs was inappropriate, and in 1864 a Mixed Court was established in the International Settlement.[317]

Once the Mixed Court had been instituted, Chinese authorities had to go through it if they wished to impose any regulations. The Mixed Court was not simply a court where criminal or civil cases were judged; it was practically the only channel through which the Chinese authorities could try to impose their values on the resident Chinese population. Foreign authorities were not particularly interested in the moral issues dear to the Chinese officials, but if the Chinese were adamant, the settlement authorities were inclined to bend to their wishes. However, with few exceptions, the foreign court was lukewarm about enforcing the regulations and prohibitions requested by the Chinese authorities.

Conflict and compromise in the Mixed Court

The Mixed Court was established on the understanding that there would have to be mutual compromises. If the abolition of severe torture can be considered a concession from the Chinese side, retention of the wooden collar and the bamboo cane can be seen as a concession from the Western side. In *Dreams of Prosperity in Shanghai* the author notes, "The practice of the New Yamen [the Mixed Court] is as follows: the morning session is conducted together with a Western official, and torture is not employed. In the afternoon session a Chinese official presides alone, and the procedure is the same as in the county court."[318] If Western interests were involved, the Western judge could be particularly uncompromising and demand that the principles of Western law be employed in determining the outcome of the case. In such cases, objections from the Chinese side fell on deaf ears.

Many sketches in the *Dianshizhai* show Chinese and Western officials jointly hearing evidence on a case.[319] There are also sketches which show that sometimes the Western side was not represented, and these cases were judged by the Chinese side alone—especially cases that did not concern foreigners.[320] The court was, by its very nature and name, a compromise between China and the West, and could not have functioned without a certain amount of give and take. Torture was still used, but modified: a light bamboo instead of a heavy one, a reduction in the weight of the wooden collars and so on.[321]

The *Dianshizhai* records how the accused often wore the wooden collar, or cangue.[322] One can see the Chinese and Western assessors sitting solemnly before the court, the accused on his knees, and a number of constables lined up at the side, with strips of bamboo in their hands, ready to inflict punishment (Fig. 53).[323] Compulsion to wear the wooden collar in public was a possible sentence, as was the penalty of having to wear it for part of a prison sentence. In one case three policemen were sentenced to jail, and they were also obliged to wear the cangue for one month each year.[324] In most cases the requirement to wear the wooden collar was more a mark of shame rather than of physical pain, especially if the criminal was compelled to walk through the streets wearing it, sometimes with foot shackles or fetters.[325] This was a common punishment for people reported on in the *Dianshizhai*, such as the illegal opium den hostess, the proprietor of a *maison de rendezvous*, swindlers of various sorts, common criminals, and corrupt police.

The differences between the Mixed Court and the Chinese yamen were substantial and significant. A variety of instruments of torture in common use in the Chinese yamen, and shown in the pages of the *Dianshizhai* (see for example Fig 54),[326] were never used in the Mixed Court. In 1889 in a report on the trial of a famous robber, Yang Hanqing, the commentator noted, not without a tinge of regret, that "the Mixed Court never uses heavy torture, so those types never fear it. A photograph in the files is not so obvious as a brand on the face."[327] Sometimes when the Chinese deputy wanted to use torture, the Western assessor would object, or insist on the mildest possible degree. They would also refuse to witness such torture.[328]

The disparity between Chinese and Western law soon drew public attention. As early as 1876 the *Shenbao* carried an editorial, "On the differences between Chinese and Western law."[329] And as the *Dianshizhai* noted, "Chinese and Western laws have long been different. The Westerners say that in their country, apart from imprisonment, the most severe punishment is execution. There is no torture. . . . Even though there are Chinese deputies in the International Settlement and the French Concession, they are not allowed to use heavy torture."[330] It did happen, however,

53. Female opium den attendants punished (1884). Female attendants were discovered in four opium dens in the French Concession. The sketch shows the punishment decreed by the deputy magistrate of the Mixed Court: whipping and wearing the wooden collar.

54. A thief on trial in the Shanghai yamen (1884). Note the instruments of torture: the trestle and the squeezers.

OLD CITY, NEW CITY 87

that both Western and Chinese police inflicted torture on criminals, in violation of the law.[331] There was also a degree of arbitrariness in the use of torture.

An 1892 story in the *Dianshizhai* told of Wang Asan, of Ningbo, a hermaphrodite who habitually dressed in women's clothing. Chinese policemen in the French Concession heard of this, and one day had him arraigned before the Mixed Court. The court ordered him to submit to a physical examination at the Renji Hospital. He was expelled from Shanghai, on the grounds of being "an offence against public morality." The *Dianshizhai* commentators noted that this was a case of the police interfering in matters that were none of their concern; they contended that the court should not have heard this case.[332] The court record does not reveal the views of the Western assessor, but it is clear that Chinese moral standards were fully upheld. In other cases, the Chinese side had to compromise. As Kotenev put it, "The Taotai tried to establish a certain analogy between the Chinese custom and British Law and based his decision on both of them."[333]

Occasionally the Western assessor would take an interest in purely Chinese matters. In 1887 the manager of the Liuchun Theater got into a fight with one of his employees over an unpaid debt. The matter was referred to the Mixed Court. The case had nothing to do with the repertoire of the theater, but the British assessor, through the Chinese deputy, took the occasion to ask if indecent operas were being performed there. The manager denied it, but the court stressed that, if the theater was to be discovered staging such performances in the future, the owners would be severely punished.[334] This was an unusual case, and was mentioned in the regular column "Notes from the Mixed Court" published in the *Shenbao*. The paper also published an editorial, "On the solicitous attitude of Western officials in the prohibition of indecent operas," which drew the editors' strong approval:

> Western people in the International Settlement never go to see Chinese operas. Even if some should occasionally go, they would not necessarily understand the plot. As for the dialogue, the feeling, and meaning of the lyrics, they would understand even less. So if Western people were to see an indecent opera, it would be as if they had not seen it at all. What is more, only one or two in a hundred or a thousand would [go to a Chinese opera], so it would them no harm ... Even if Western officials did not forbid them, they could not be reprimanded for not banning something harmful. The fact that the Western officials took the advice of the Chinese official and cooperated in forbidding them means that they treat us equally."[335]

On occasion the yamen in the Chinese city would ask the Mixed Court of the settlements for assistance in technical matters. In 1889 the *Dianshizhai* reported a series of deaths as a result of some sort of throat infection in the Chinese city. Someone suspected that the victims had been poisoned after using cottonseed oil. The Chinese authorities asked the Mixed Courts of the International Settlement and the French Concession to join them in the investigation. It turned out that a merchant had laced his cottonseed oil with quicklime.[336]

Westerners' curiosity about Chinese torture

To foreigners, the torture regularly employed by the yamen was something out of a museum.[337] Both the *Shenbao* and the *Dianshizhai* carried reports of foreigners visiting Chinese yamens to witness the proceedings, which had gained almost tourist attraction status in Shanghai. In 1874 the American consul visited the Mixed Court and brought with him a certain "Doctor of Philosophy" who was visiting China. This scholar wished to see how the Chinese courts applied torture. The Chinese side obliged and chose the most serious criminal case on the docket. After sentencing, the criminal was immediately flogged three hundred strokes in the court and then paraded through the streets wearing a wooden collar.[338] Whenever a foreigner expressed an interest in witnessing criminal proceedings, Chinese officials were happy to arrange for someone accused of a serious crime to be interrogated and proudly demonstrated the instruments of torture. The Chinese authorities did not understand the combination of curiosity, disgust, and moral superiority on the part of foreigners interested in the more gruesome aspects of the Chinese legal system. Occasionally the Mixed Court would arrange such a demonstration, but more usually anyone wanting to see instruments of torture in use had to visit the yamen in the Chinese city. The *Dianshizhai* gave details of an 1889 visit by a Brazilian aristocrat to a local yamen.

> The grandson of the emperor of Brazil included Shanghai on his travels. He said he would like to see how Chinese courts try various types of criminal cases. So his consulate made a formal request to the magistrate of Shanghai, Pei Dazhong, to arrange a suitable time. On the first day of the eighth month, the emperor's grandson, accompanied by the consul and an interpreter, made the trip to the yamen by sedan chair. The magistrate received them according to protocol. After tea and snacks, he struck his gavel on the bench, and the proceedings began. There were four cases heard on that day. The most serious was that of the bandit Li Chunjiang, the second was that of an unfilial son, Jiang Bosen. Li was whipped one thousand times, and Jiang five hundred times, after which they were placed in wooden cages. One was an outlaw, the other a rebel against filial piety, so the punishment was appropriate to the gravity of the crimes. After the trials, the emperor's grandson took his leave, and the magistrate respectfully bade them farewell.[339]

The *Dianshizhai* also reported a similar visit of a French official to a yamen in 1895 (Fig. 55).[340]

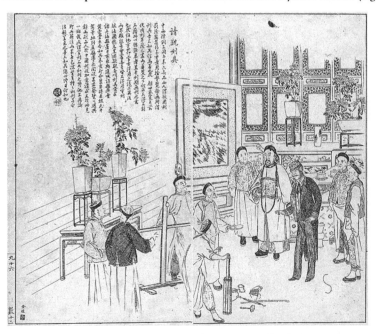

55. Torture instruments on display for foreign visitors (1895). The sketch shows the visit of a French official to the Chinese yamen. "There are deputies of the magistrate of Shanghai [in the Mixed Court] in both the French Concession and the British Settlement, but they are not allowed use heavy torture. So when a

certain French envoy wanted to see various implements of torture, they had to ask the Shanghai yamen. A few days ago, the envoy, traveling by sedan chair, paid a courtesy call on Magistrate Huang Aitang. The magistrate knew the purpose of the visit, so he ordered the yamen constables to display the squeezers and the trestle in his residence, and took the visitor to inspect them. The envoy examined them all and was very satisfied. He then took his leave. From this small incident it can be seen how eager Westerners are to understand Chinese criminal law and process."

The Mixed Court as a "New Yamen"

Educated Chinese were not happy with the *laissez-faire* attitude of foreigners with regard to moral matters. After describing settlement regulations on hygiene and public order, Huang Shiquan noted, "What foreigners are most concerned about, what they spend the most time and energy on, are really minor matters. Things that are important, such as gambling dens, brothels, flower-drum songs, and other such evils, do not particularly worry the foreign authorities. They concern themselves with the unimportant, and do not pay attention to urgent problems. All the Chinese can do is laugh at them."[341]

Despite their best efforts, Chinese authorities did not succeed in using the Mixed Court to exert control over the Chinese population.[342] On the contrary, the Mixed Court became an agent for the introduction of certain basic Western concepts. Details of its cases and decisions were reported in the *Shenbao* and the *Dianshizhai*, and through these we can trace how ordinary Chinese gradually came to know something of the Western concept of the law.

In principle, prisoners in the settlement were entitled to humane treatment. But they did not always get it. In 1898 the *Dianshizhai* reported that prisoners in the International Settlement jail were being mistreated, and this generated a good deal of discussion. The Western inspector of police visited the jail on the 23rd of May, accompanied by a lawyer and an interpreter. He found the prisoners unkempt and living in conditions of abject poverty. Many claimed that they had been unjustly accused and imprisoned. Criminals from well-off families were provided with their own food, but those less well off got only two meals a day provided by the prison authorities. The inspector was moved by what he saw and immediately took four pieces of silver from his pocket to buy food for those prisoners whose families could not afford to provide it themselves. Six or seven prisoners had been dying every day, and the prison was responsible for providing coffins and burying them. Those who were ill were escorted to the Refuge for the Homeless (Qiliu Gongsuo)[343] for treatment. By 1898, however, the Mixed Court had ceased sending fines it collected to the Refuge, so sick prisoners were refused, and the jail had to accommodate them. The *Dianshizhai* wondered if anything would result from this tour of inspection (Fig. 56),[344] but the fact that such an inspection even took place shows that, in theory at least, Western law did not allow prisoners to be mistreated.

In one case reported in the *Dianshizhai* in 1885, a maid-servant in a foreign company fell out with her husband. The husband demanded that his wife return, but she refused, and her employer supported her. The husband brought the matter to the Mixed Court. The Chinese judge argued that although the husband was a ne'er-do-well, the principle "a wife follows her husband" still demanded that she return to him. The Western judge, however, felt that the woman herself had the right to determine where she wanted to live, and this was the eventual decision of the court.

56. The Inspector of Police assesses jail conditions (1898). Accompanied by his deputy and a lawyer, the inspector interviews prisoners about living conditions in the settlement prison.

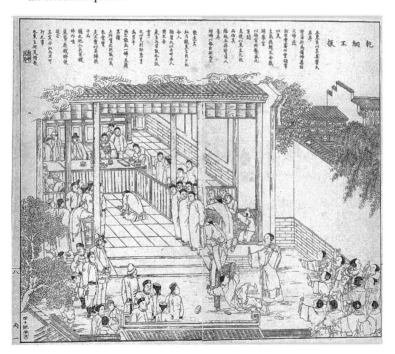

57. A husband is beaten by his wife's employer (1885). The husband of a runaway wife refuses to accept the decision of the Mixed Court and is beaten up by the wife's Western employer. Women onlookers are clearly delighted. The Mixed Court has already moved on to another case.

When the decision was handed down, the husband refused to accept it. He argued with his wife and her employer in front of the court, and was beaten up by the wife's employer. In the view of the *Dianshizhai* commentators, the wife was not behaving as a wife should; the husband, however, was supposed to act like a man, and by sending his wife out to work as a servant, he had only himself to blame for her wanting to leave him (Fig 57).[145]

In theory, only minor cases involving Chinese were dealt with by the Mixed Court, and more serious cases were handed over to the yamen. However, no precise criteria had been agreed to by the Western and Chinese authorities on the one hand, and the Western assessor and the Chinese police on the other, so the question of just what constituted a crime, or which crimes were minor and which more serious, remained open to negotiation.

In 1895 a carpenter from Ningbo was accused of mistreating his wife, forcing her to wear wooden fetters around her feet so that she could not walk. The neighbors reported the case to the police. The Mixed Court could see that the wife had been severely beaten all over her body, and considered the case serious enough to refer to the yamen. The yamen, however, considered this a minor matter, and merely gave the husband a verbal reprimand before releasing him (Fig. 58).[146] In another case a teacher at a private school in the International Settlement assaulted a former student. The student's father took the matter to the Mixed Court, which decided that this was a serious matter and referred it to the Shanghai yamen. The yamen felt there was nothing wrong with a teacher beating a student, but he should not have beaten a *former* student. His behavior was improper, and he was sentenced to be beaten on the palms of the hands one hundred times, then released.[147]

58. A runaway wife is put in the stocks (1895). "A carpenter from Ningbo, Li Dunfu, lived in Xihua Lane in the American Settlement. He married Mme. Xiao, who had just reached the age of twenty-four. She was really quite graceful and charming and worked as a servant in the house of a neighbor. Recently for some unknown reason she was suddenly summoned back to her own house. Her husband's widowed sister-in-law, Mme. Zhuo-Li, bullied and abused her in a hundred ways. A Western-style timber plank was

sawn into two pieces, two holes were cut into it, and Mme. Xiao's feet were placed between them. Iron nails were driven into the two sides to fasten them. The result was that Mme. Xiao could not even move an inch. Her cries of pain could be heard far away, outside the house. She was not released for a period of three days and the neighbors finally informed the local police. The matter was referred to the Mixed Court for trial. Mme. Xiao was still in the stocks, and covered in bruises from head to toe. A jail matron examined her wounds. The investigation showed that the planks were excessively tight, causing her feet to swell. Bruises, caused by beating with coarse bamboo, covered her body. Her back had been lacerated by a foreign knife. Full of compassion, the assessor immediately called a carpenter to pry the stocks apart. The nails were hammered in so tightly they could hardly be moved. The assessor found that Li Dunfu had used extraordinary torture to mistreat his wife. The crime was unforgivable. The case was transferred to the county court, where Li would receive severe punishment. The case was brought before Shanghai County Magistrate Huang. According to Li Dunfu's testimony, his wife often ran away. That is why he used the stocks to fasten her feet. It seemed that the treatment was not without reason. The magistrate reprimanded him for disciplining his wife in such a cruel manner and ordered him to guarantee that he would not use private punishment again. Huang then leniently dismissed the case."

The compromising attitude of the court and the behavior of the Chinese police led to many foreigners to the conclusion that the Mixed Court was no mixed court at all, but a purely Chinese institution.[348] For the Chinese, however, the Mixed Court was Western enough for them to recognize how different it was from a traditional Chinese yamen, and their term for it was the "New Yamen."[349] The practices of the New Yamen introduced a new range of issues and questions to the Chinese public regarding just what constituted a crime, the scope and limits of the law, and appropriate methods of punishment. It became clear that traditional Chinese practice was not the only standard. Once people realized this, it became possible to exploit the differences between Western and Chinese law to protect oneself and one's "rights."

Chinese officials as moral police

Chinese officials in the Chinese city also fulfilled the role of moral policemen. They often interfered in matters which had nothing to do with the law or any criminal activity. In 1888 the *Dianshizhai* reported how the magistrate of Shanghai, Pei Dazhong, was traveling through the streets of the Chinese city in his sedan chair, when he saw a girl combing her hair in front of a curtain shop at the Huajin Memorial Arch. He felt disgusted at what he considered the girl's "inelegance," and on returning to the yamen he issued an order for the girl's father to appear in court, where he berated him, accusing him of not bringing up his daughter properly, and advised how he should supervise her in future (Fig. 59).[350]

That same year the *Dianshizhai* also carried a sketch "On Keeping Puppies." Thirty years earlier, during the Small Swords Uprising, the Shanghai magistrate, Yuan Youcun [Yuan Zude], had been killed. His four dogs kept guard over his coffin and refused to eat; eventually they starved to death. They had, however, offspring, and by 1888 the number of their descendants had grown to more than eighty. Pei Dazhong issued an order that all the local constables should take care of one each.[351] This was entirely within Pei's area of responsibility, and no matter how much the local constables may have resented the order, none of them would have dared protest. On another occasion, Pei also ordered a woman who had become a nun because she hated her husband to return to secular life.³⁵² He also ordered a monk with an allegedly evil physiognomy to return to secular life, on the grounds that his appearance was not appropriate for a monk.³⁵³ Pei Dazhong clearly regarded his actions as appropriate and setting a good moral tone.

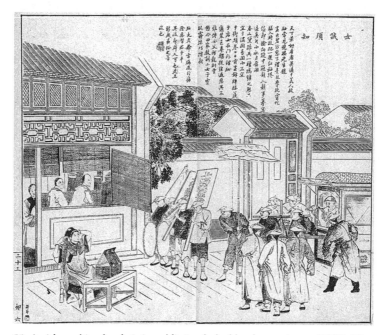

59. A girl combing her hair in public is rebuked by the magistrate (1888). The magistrate summoned her father to admonish him at his daughter's unbecoming behavior.

It was the same Magistrate Pei, who in 1890 was traveling in his sedan chair when he spied a beggar carrying an old woman on his back (Fig. 60). The beggar's clothing was tattered, and the old woman was wearing even less. Pei stopped his sedan chair and asked the beggar for his story. It turned out he was a refugee from a natural disaster in Jiangbei. Pei accused him of lacking filial piety, since he was wearing clothes, tattered though they were, while his grandmother was barely covered. The beggar was taken to the yamen for interrogation, and was forced to take off his clothes, so that he would know what it was like to feel cold. He was also beaten ten times with a large stick. Pei then gave the grandmother a set of clothing and sent them on their way. The *Dianshizhai* commentary thoroughly approved of Pei's solicitous attitude towards the welfare of his people.³⁵⁴

In the yamen, the crime of lacking in filial piety was second only to that of rebellion. After repeated whippings, a culprit was placed in a wooden cage and exposed to public ridicule as a warning to others (Fig. 61).³⁵⁵ In the settlements, however, there was no way for the law to deal

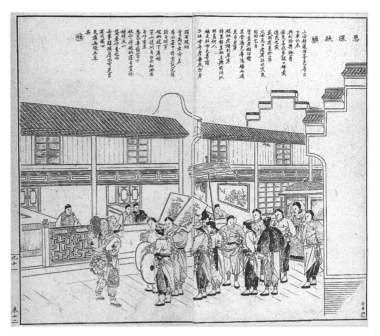

60. The magistrate punishes an unfilial grandson (1890). The Shanghai magistrate notices two beggars in the street. The young man has warmer clothing than his grandmother, a breach of filial piety, and the magistrate orders that he be punished.

61. Unfilial sons sentenced to stand in a wooden cage (1889). The commentary quotes Confucius: "Few who are filial and fraternal are likely to offend their superiors. Those who do not offend their superiors are not likely to cause disorder." The sketch shows three unfilial sons who must take turns standing in a wooden cage. This punishment was ordered by the magistrate as an example to the masses.

with infringements of this moral code. A foreign policeman saw a mentally ill old man on the streets and escorted him to the police station. He told a Chinese police officer to accompany the old man home. When they arrived the old man's son rushed out and punched him, and cursed and swore at him; the Chinese officer could do no more than verbally reprimand him (Fig. 62).[356]

62. A son beats his father (1885). A policeman escorts a mentally ill old man home, where the angry son beats his father even with the policeman still present. Such a scene could only happen in the settlements.

Occasionally young women would be found intoxicated in the streets of the settlements. The police could only take them to the police station and send them home the next day (Fig. 63).[357] Lying drunk in the street is much more disgraceful than the case of the young girl in the Chinese city, whose combing of her hair in public so upset the local magistrate. But this was not a matter for the Mixed Court.

The matter of selling aphrodisiacs points to other differences in police and legal thinking. While aphrodisiacs were widely advertised and sold openly in the settlements (Fig. 64),[358] they were banned in the Chinese city. The *Dianshizhai* tells of Wang Yide of Shaoxing, who owned a pharmacy in the Chinese city known as the Hall of Unusual Inheritance. It specialized in eye medicines, which were in fact aphrodisiacs. The Chinese magistrate at the Mixed Court,[359] Ge Fanfu, came to hear of this, and sent his personal servant to buy some. Having determined that it was, in fact, an aphrodisiac, he reported the matter to the authorities in the Chinese city. Wang Yide was arrested. In his defense he claimed that he had inherited the pharmacy from his father and had no idea there were aphrodisiacs among the merchandise. Business was bad, and he was in very difficult circumstances. The yamen found that he was indeed ignorant of the true nature of the medicines, and had made no profit from selling them. His punishment was relatively light: one hundred strokes of the bamboo, and wearing the wooden collar in public for one month.

63. Women lying drunk in the streets of Shanghai (1891). A drunken middle-aged woman collapses in the International Settlement. The police tease her: "Do you think you're Yang Guifei in *The Tipsy Concubine*?" She was sent to the Mixed Court, and her family was asked to collect her when she sobered up. Another story (Yi★ 49) reported that a young woman about seventeen or eighteen years old had fallen drunk in the street and was taken to the police station. Neither story mentions whether the women were charged.

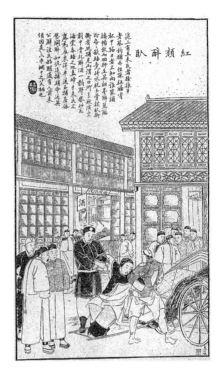

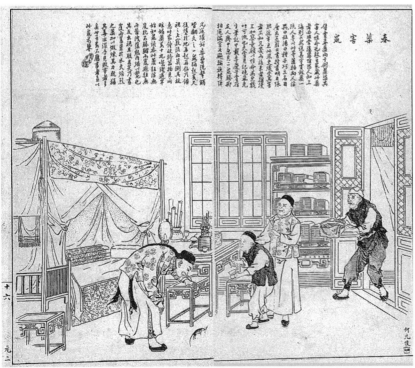

64. Selling aphrodisiacs (1897). "Selling aphrodisiacs has always been prohibited, for fear that the drugs would be harmful to life and health. Families who had a

OLD CITY, NEW CITY   97

supply of this medicine had to be extremely secretive, for fear that people would find out. In Shanghai this was not the case. People selling false medicines under the guise of a true prescription would use them to help increase sexual desire. They had names like 'Robust Virility' and 'Numerous Progeny.' Sellers would concoct all sorts of names—there was no end to the varieties. They would make extravagant claims, utterly brazen and flagrant. In recent years this practice has become even worse. It is impossible to know how many people have been harmed. But even now people are still casual and careless, and they treat their lives in a trifling manner." The commentary goes to tell a story by Ji Xiaolan of how a rat died after taking aphrodisiacs; that story is illustrated here.

7. Law enforcement in the settlements

Chinese residents of the International Settlement were theoretically subject to the jurisdiction of the Chinese authorities. However, as the British minister at Beijing, Sir Frederick Bruce noted, "The Chinese residents in the settlement were not under effective control either by the municipal authorities or by their own authorities outside."[360] This observation was made before the establishment of the Mixed Court, but remained an accurate description of the situation even afterwards. This led to policemen becoming very powerful in their implementation of the law. As far as Chinese residents were concerned, the people with the most immediate jurisdiction, and direct power, over them were the police, especially the Chinese police.

Western, Indian, and Chinese police

Three types of policemen worked in the International Settlement: Westerners, Indians (Sikhs) and Chinese police.[361] The reputation of the Western police was good, although there was occasionally criminal behavior among them, as when a French policeman beat a Chinese to death,[362] or the case of the drunken officer who burst into a brothel and raped a prostitute.[363] This sort of behavior was not often reported, however, and the news report on the latter case was preceded by a comment: "The police station has been established in the International Settlement to investigate and arrest criminals. They are not supposed to rely on their power to lord it over others, to bully the good and the weak, nor are they allowed to harass women or beat people at will. There are, however, such people amongst the Chinese and the Indian police. The British police are most conscientious in the performance of their duties, so people respect them highly. We have never heard of them causing any trouble."

The reputation of the Indian police, the Sikhs, was not so good. There were two stories in the *Dianshizhai* about Sikh policemen using their authority to break the law. The first of these was in 1888, when a Sikh policeman tried to steal a gold ring from a monk in the Yangshupu district. The monk immediately swallowed the ring, but the policeman would still not let him go, and demanded money to allow him to pass freely. Eventually the monk gave the policeman two *yuan*, and the Sikh let him go.[364] On another occasion two Sikh officers noticed a Chinese with a silver watch pacing to and fro in front of a theater. They moved forward and snatched his watch, then immediately made their escape. They were eventually arrested and punished (Fig. 65).[365]

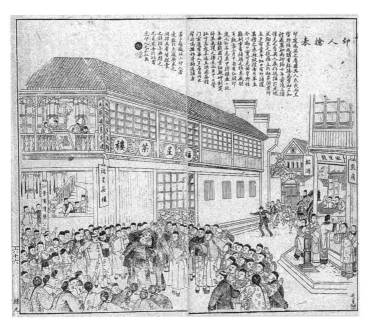

65. Sikh policemen steal a silver watch (1892). The Chinese chase them to the Hongyuan Teahouse where a crowd of onlookers has by this time gathered. The thieves are arrested and escorted to the police station. In the far right of the sketch one can see a shop selling pickled vegetables and Shaoxing wine. There is a fire hydrant in front of the shop.

The reasons for the Sikhs' bad reputation may stem from more than their behavior. In Chinese eyes these Indians were *wangguonu*—slaves who had lost their country and therefore their dignity. The Chinese were loath to take orders from anyone lower in status than themselves. In 1892 the *Dianshizhai* described the Sikhs in the following terms: "Tall and black, they are savage by nature and have the habits of wild beasts. They know nothing of propriety, morality, modesty, and shame. Ten years ago they were seldom seen in Shanghai. Then the English hired them as policemen, and these swarthy ruffians appeared all over the International Settlement."[366] A certain degree of resentment against the Indian police was still noticeable in the twentieth century.[367]

Most resentment, however, was directed against the Chinese police whose power and abuse of power was widespread.[368] In the settlements, of course, Western authorities were not so familiar with the area and its people, and the power of especially Chinese police employed by those authorities, led to a certain brutality against local residents.

Notoriety of the Chinese police

There are at least eleven stories in the *Dianshizhai* about objectionable behavior of the part of the Chinese police, and complaints from the general public against them.[369] The Chinese police were subdivided into policemen "on the beat" and plainclothes detectives. Detectives were chosen from among the regular officers and were responsible for the collection of information. Their salary was slightly higher than that of ordinary policemen.[370]

Ge Yuanxu's *Travels in Shanghai* was a popular guidebook first published in 1876. It described the police in these terms:

> In the police station established by the Municipal Council, half the police are Westerners and half are Chinese. Chinese [seeking employment there] have to provide references from people with property. Their uniforms display their numbers in both Chinese and English, so that people can identify them easily. Day and night they patrol the streets, which are divided into various precincts. At night, they have a torch hanging from their waist. The Western police carry knives and the Chinese truncheons. They patrol throughout the whole night, and so there are few thieves and robbers in the foreign settlements; the city is quite safe. If they do catch a thief, the matter is referred the next day to the Mixed Court for investigation . . . Detectives are the eyes and ears of the police. They are employed by the Municipal Council to collect information on all manner of things. For example, they are sent to look into cases of theft or purse cutting. Their job is to investigate. They dress quite splendidly, because their salaries are very generous.[171]

Both uniformed policemen and plainclothes detectives can be seen in the pages of the *Dianshizhai*. One of the commentaries gives us a clue to their social origins: "In origin, they [Chinese police] derive from rogues and ruffians."[172] This was still the situation in the twentieth century.[173]

The Chinese police had no understanding of Western law[174] and were hardly models of traditional Chinese morality, either. The Western police had no choice but to rely on them to a great extent, because of language difficulties. This was particularly true in the case of the detectives. Their power led Chinese police to commit various outrages in the settlements. They most often got away with this conduct unless the ensuing uproar was so great they had to be punished or dismissed. In 1898 the *Dianshizhai* devoted three pages to the case of policemen from the Hongkou area who had beaten suspects so savagely that they had been crippled (Fig. 66). The suspects complained to the Inspector of Police, who referred the matter to the Municipal Council (Fig. 67). The Mixed Court was convened and immediately dealt out punishment (Fig. 68).[175]

66. Chinese detectives beat a suspect (1898). Zhang Ayou, Ren Guisheng and Fu Ajin, three plainclothes Chinese detectives in Hongkou, are beating a suspect, who confesses under duress.

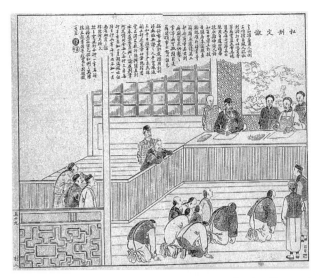

67. Detectives on trial (1898). The suspect beaten by the Chinese detectives complained to the sergeant, who referred the matter to the Mixed Court. The Mixed Court sentenced the two detectives to three years in jail. Every six months they had to wear the wooden collar for one month. Another was sentenced to two years in jail, and to wear the wooden collar one month every year. Yet another two were sentenced to one year in jail, and then deported to their original hometown.

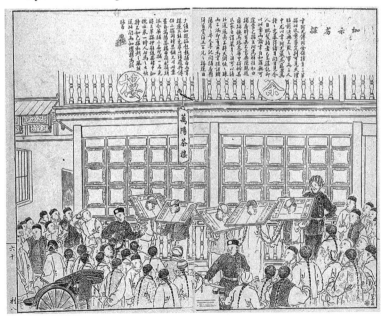

68. Detectives sentenced (1898). After the sentencing, the detectives were escorted to the police station in Hongkou. On the way, one escaped and took refuge with his lover. One of their victims, a Cantonese, offered a reward of five hundred *yuan* for his capture. Eventually he was brought to justice. The sketch shows the five culprits wearing the wooden collar in front of the Wanyang Teahouse.

Three other instances of policemen facing punishment for infringements of the law are recorded in the *Dianshizhai*. Reporting on one case in 1892, the *Dianshizhai* noted:

> The Chinese police in the International Settlement use their authority to bully others. They grasp any excuse to carry out such activities. We hear about this sort of thing all the time. They regard the police station as their protective talisman. Once they get to the station, they know the police inspector will only listen to their side of the story. So they confuse right and wrong, and juggle black and white. They can sell their stories even in the Mixed Court, and no one exposes them. Nowadays the situation is even worse. Even if they are sometimes discovered, they are never punished. No wonder they become more audacious and brazen. During the ninth lunar month in the International Settlement a Chinese policeman, Number 305, by the name of Shi Tujin, was trying to catch a dog with a collar around its neck belonging to one Weng Ada. He alleged that Weng had contravened a regulation. When Weng tried to stop him, he beat Weng viciously. In the process he tore his uniform and crushed his helmet. He filed a false report to deceive people. He had no idea that he was about to be brought to judgement for countless misdeeds. His conduct was investigated by Deputy Cai Eryuan, who reported to the Inspector of Police. The policeman was immediately dismissed, and also served one month in prison. This was a warning to those who know the law but break it. We hope that after this, the arrogance of the police may be somewhat lessened.[376]

The sketch shows a dogcatcher trying to get the dog into an enclosed cart, like a kennel on wheels. The text does not specifically indicate what regulation was violated, but it is clear that Shanghai had such regulations, a registration system and a dog pound for unregistered dogs.

In 1897 the *Dianshizhai* reported a similar story:

> Chinese police in the International Settlement use their authority to lord it over others. Ordinary people suffer from their viciousness, and there is no one to whom they can appeal to redress the injustices done to them. This has led to the police become more audacious and blustering. A few days ago an off-duty policeman, Wang Xinhai, at the break of day was buying soybean milk in the bean curd shop run by Zhang Heshang in Hujiazhai in the International Settlement. He felt that [service] was too slow, so he started shouting and cursing. The shop assistant, Qian Shunyuan, tried to calm him down, but Wang was so angry he bristled with rage. Suddenly he rushed into the middle of the street and called a Chinese police on duty, Gu Chunyuan, to accompany him back to Zhang's shop. They beat Zhang and Qian with clubs, seriously wounding Zhang on the head and the forehead; his blood covered the ground. Even so, the two policemen still did not release him. Neighbors who witnessed this treatment were outraged by the injustice and shouted for them to stop. The policemen then turned on the neighbors, not realizing in the heat of the moment that they could not afford to incur public wrath. Just at that moment a detective, Huang Cifu, passed by and also became an eyewitness to the scene. After making enquiries he discovered it was the two policemen who were at fault, so he immediately came forward, arrested them, and escorted them to the police station, where he explained what had happened. . . . Each officer was sentenced to two hundred strokes, and required to wear the wooden collar for three weeks. . . . Had it not been for Detective Huang, Zhang would have been accused of beating the policemen.[377]

Another case in 1888 concerned a Chinese policeman in the French Concession, Hou A'er. He was found guilty of gambling, sentenced to wear the wooden collar and be paraded through the streets.[378]

Public anger towards the Chinese police

Policemen who were actually punished were a small minority. For the most part the general public had no choice but to suffer in silence. Occasionally they would get so angry that a group would form to beat up a few policemen. Such an incident occurred in 1888 to a Chinese policeman in the French Concession. The *Dianshizhai* notes:

> Chinese and Western policemen carry clubs and beat people at will. The weak fear their overbearing behavior and when they see them run away like rats; even the strong can only show anger in their eyes and dare not utter a word. We all know that when accumulated grievances under heaven have reached a critical mass, a crevice must appear to provide some release. He who flaunts his power must realize that there is no good fortune without misfortune; for every voyage there is a return. It is a natural principle that this should be so. Some time ago in the French Concession a Chinese policeman, Number 37, was on patrol near the moat along the wall outside the Old North Gate. There he was set upon by a group of men, who forced him inside the city walls, and then raised the drawbridge. It was the policeman who got the worst of it this time. So people say that those who rely on other people's power are like the fox relying on the tiger's prestige. This policeman's mishap was entirely his own doing.[379] (Fig. 69)

69. Chinese detective beaten (1888). A Chinese detective in the French Concession is lured into the Chinese city, where he is beaten up by an angry crowd. Chinese detectives were "the ears of the foreigners," and as such often unpopular among their fellow Chinese.

Another incident witnessed by one of the artists of the *Dianshizhai*, Ma Ziming, involved the rickshaw-puller he had hired. A Chinese policeman ordered the puller to stop, but he had done nothing wrong and so did not comply. When the policeman caught up with them, he beat the puller with his baton. The puller demanded to know what he had done wrong, but the policeman was unable to name any specific infraction. As the policeman left, the rickshaw puller said, "Just wait until you take off your uniform—I'll still recognize you!"[380] These examples strongly suggest that police officers habitually used violence in their dealings with the public. Detectives enjoyed a different sort of power: they could arrest anyone at will and have them incarcerated. In daily life, the power of the Chinese police was, in effect, greater than that of the officials. "Chinese officials were not to be entitled to make arrests in the settlements on warrants issued by the Chinese authority outside, or by the Mixed Court magistrate himself, except after notice to the Municipal Police Authority, and by their agency or with their assistance."[381]

Chinese police as moral guardians

The Chinese police also interfered in other people's business, on the pretext of upholding moral standards.

In 1891, two male actors who played female roles in operas at the Dangui Theater, Xiao Guilin and Xiao Jinbao, were dressed in female attire while traveling by rickshaw through Fuzhou Road, when they were recognized by a Chinese plainclothes detective (Fig. 70). He arrested them and took them to the Western inspector. The inspector judged that it was the custom of actors to dress in this way, and there was no reason to harass them. He ordered them to be released.[382]

Another case involved a Chinese sculptor who had carved a nude statue on commission from a foreigner; he was discovered by a detective and brought before the court.[383] The story of the hermaphrodite who was arrested and forced to undergo a medical examination has already been mentioned.[384] Yet another example is a prostitute who went out wearing men's clothing; she was recognized by a detective from the International Settlement, Gu Aliu, and brought before the court (Fig. 71). Such behavior did not contravene any of the laws or regulations of the International Settlement or the French Concession; the police, however, regarded these things as "offences against public morality" or "harmful to the public good" and pursued them on their own initiative.

Some Sikh policemen followed suit. One day the famous courtesan, Lin Daiyu, and the equally famous actor, Zhao Xiaolian, were discovered under the shade of the trees around the Jing'an Temple in their carriage engaged in sexual intercourse. A Sikh policeman escorted them to the police station, where the inspector just laughed and let them go.[385]

From the accounts in the *Dianshizhai*, it seems that two detectives in the International Settlement were particularly active. One was Gu Aliu, whose beat was the area around Hujiazhai. He was also among the detectives involved in a raid on a brothel in that area.[386] His name often appeared in the column "News from the Mixed Court" in the *Shenbao*.[387] The other was Qin Shaoqing. He appeared in the 1884 *Dianshizhai* story about a robbery,[388] and again in 1886, when he arrested two suspicious looking travelers, who turned out to be members of a Hubei secret society.[389] His name also appeared frequently in "News from the Mixed Court."[390]

It is clear from the language used in the news reports that these detectives were powerful men. A report from a detective was enough to have someone arrested and taken to the police station.

If anyone commanded the power to uphold traditional Chinese morality in the settlements, it would not have been the gentry or the Chinese officials, but rather the Chinese police. They had the power to control and supervise the general population, but in the end were no substitute for the gentry in providing moral leadership and example.

70. Transvestites arrested by a Chinese detective (1891). These transvestites were Peking opera female impersonators. The sketch shows the detective lifting the skirt of one of the actors, revealing his large feet. They were later released at the insistence of the Western police sergeant.

71. A transvestite prostitute arrested (1894). She was arrested by a Chinese detective and brought to court.

Notes

[1] Gui 8. On the same day, March 20, 1887, the *Shenbao* published an editorial, "On the use of prisoners to perform hard labor." As early as June 20, 1876 the *Shenbao* carried a news item "Criminals forced to work" reporting how more than ten criminals were chained together and forced to build a road.

[2] Burton F. Beers, *China in Old Photographs 1860–1910* (New York: Charles Scribener's Sons, 1978), 129.

[3] Pott, *History of Shanghai*, 75.

[4] Cao Xiang began studying in a Western-style school when he was eight, and began working in the Municipal Council as an interpreter around 1862, during which time he compiled an English-Chinese dictionary. In 1874 he was employed as an interpreter by the magistrate of Shanghai, Mo Xiangzhi, and was later involved in various civic affairs. Cao Xiang's letter and this case are discussed in detail in *Minguo Shanghai xian zhi* (Taipei: Chengwen chubanshe, 1975), vol. 3, *juan* 14, 25–26, 29. Cf. Michel Foucault, *Discipline and Punish: The Birth of the Prison* (London: Peregrine Books, 1979), 8: "The use of prisoners in public works, cleaning city streets or repairing the highways, was practiced in Austria, Switzerland and certain of the United States, such as Pennsylvania . . . This practice was abolished practically everywhere at the end of the eighteenth or the beginning of the nineteenth century."

[5] According to Xiaoxiangguan shizhe, *Haishang*, *juan* 1, 4–5, there were more than two thousand rickshaws in Shanghai at that time. The fare was about 14 cash per *li*.

[6] Shanghai shi shizhengfu gongcheng guanliju, ed., *Shanghai gonglu shi*, (Beijing: Renmin jiaotong chubanshe, 1989), vol. 1, 26.

[7] Shu★ 56.

[8] J. V. Davidson-Houston, *Yellow Creek, the Story of Shanghai* (London: Pitnam and Company Limited, 1962), 129.

[9] Mary Ninde Gamewell, *The Gateway to China: Pictures of Shanghai*, (Shanghai: Fleming H. Revell & Company, 1916; reprinted Taipei: Ch'eng-wen Publishing, 1972), 91.

[10] Wu 79.

[11] *Shenbao*, May 21, 1872.

[12] Geng 36; Geng 72; Xin 16; Wu 96; Ding 55; Mu 15; Bing 6; Wu 78; Yu 72; Ge 88; Zi 58.

[13] Wu 78. According to Xia Lin'gen, *Jiu Shanghai sanbai liushi hang* (Three hundred and sixty trades in Old Shanghai) (Shanghai: Huadong shifan daxue chubanshe, 1989), 98, there were carriages drawn by mules in northern China before that time, and in the capital there were also carriages drawn by four horses, but these were for the exclusive use of the Emperor. In Shanghai, anyone with the money could hire a carriage drawn by four horses.

[14] Wu 78.

[15] Geng 72.

[16] Geng 36; Geng 72.

[17] Wu 55.

[18] *North-China Herald*, 6 July 1883.

[19] Wu 79. Cf. the second chapter of Huayeliannong, *Haishang hua liezhuan*, vol. 1, 9, in which the author describes the garbage carts and the workmen sweeping the streets.

[20] *Shenbao*, May 12, 1874.

[21] *Shenbao*, November 22, 1875.

[22] Zi 18.

[23] *Shenbao*, March 3, 1874.

[24] Jia 41.

[25] See Zhang Ailing, *Haishanghua*, 61. According to Zhang, "The horse drawn carriages and the rickshaws (*renliche*), also known at that time as *dongyangche*, imported by the foreigners into the settlements, were not permitted to enter the Chinese city." From the sketch in the *Dianshizhai*, however, we can see that Zhang's comment is not accurate. The rickshaw was invented in Japan in 1869, and "within the next few years there were as many as fifty thousand in the city." Edward Seidensticker, *Low City, High City: Tokyo from Edo to the Earthquake: How the Shogun's Ancient Capital Became a Great Modern City, 1867–1923* (San Francisco: Donald S. Ellis, 1983), 42.

[26] Wu★ 86; Shu★ 96.

[27] Quoted in Kuai Shixun, *Shanghai gonggong zujie shigao* (A draft history of the Shanghai settlements) (Shanghai: Shanghai renmin chubanshe, 1980), 622–23.

[28] "Xi ke yue Hucheng wenda" *Shenbao*, January 29, 1875.

²⁹ *Shenbao*, May 15, 1874; April 19, 1879.
³⁰ The name of this road was Nanshiwai Malu. See Shanghai shi shizhengfu gongcheng guanliju, *Shanghai gonglu shi* (A history of public roads in Shanghai) (Beijing: Renmin jiaotong chubanshe, 1989), vol. 1, 43–44.
³¹ Wangzhusheng (The Spiderweb Scholar), *Renhaichao* (The human tide) (Shanghai: Zhongyang shudian, 1926; reprinted Shanghai: Shanghai guji chubanshe, 1991), *shang ce*, 306.
³² Bing 19, Si 66.
³³ Pott, *History of Shanghai*, 109.
³⁴ Kerrie L. Macpherson, *A Wilderness of Marshes: The Origins of Public Health in Shanghai, 1843–1893* (Oxford: Oxford University Press, 1987), 87.
³⁵ Ge Yuanxu, *Huyou zaji, juan* 2, 40.
³⁶ Pott, *History of Shanghai*, 110.
³⁷ Macpherson, *Public Health*, 83–105.
³⁸ *Shenbao* editorial, February 28, 1873, "Shanghai yinshui huihai ji yi qingjie lun" (On the dirtiness of Shanghai drinking water and why it ought be purified); January 22, 1874, "Quan chengnei shendong juban zilaishui shuo" (Urging gentry-managers in the Chinese city to arrange for the provision of running water); September 12, 1878, "Qing yong zilaishui shuo" (A request to use running water); February 15, 1880, "Yi chuang zilaishui" (Suggestion to provide running water); February 18, 1880, "Lun zilaishui zhi li" (On the advantages of running water) etc.
³⁹ *North-China Herald*, April 19, 1881.
⁴⁰ *North-China Herald*, June 9, 1882.
⁴¹ Macpherson, *Public Health*, 120: "Resistance to extension of the company water service was also mounted by the water carriers' guild whose vested interest lay with the status quo. Approximately 3,000 of these workers laboured in Shanghai in the 1880s."
⁴² Huang Shiquan, *Songnan mengyinglu* (Record of dream shadows of Songnan) (Shanghai, 1883; reprinted Shanghai: Shanghai guji chubanshe, 1989), *juan* 4, 10 *xia*.
⁴³ You 71; Geng 1, Tu 32.
⁴⁴ *Shenbao*, February 18, 1880, editorial.
⁴⁵ *Shenbao*, January 22, 1874.
⁴⁶ Macpherson, *Public Health*, 120.
⁴⁷ Pott, *History of Shanghai*, 110.
⁴⁸ Chen Boxi, *Lao Shanghai, shang ce*, 144.
⁴⁹ The official representative *(huishenyuan)* of Chinese officialdom at the Mixed Court. His position was higher than a judge; he was the Chinese authority on all matters concerning Chinese or China.
⁵⁰ It is not clear if these figures include private water taps, or if they refer to public taps on the main roads. *Shenbao*, February 15, 1884.
⁵¹ *Shenbao*, June 1, 1884.
⁵² Bing 19.
⁵³ Wu 49; Bing 18.
⁵⁴ *North-China Herald*, May 27, 1887.
⁵⁵ Chen Boxi, *Lao Shanghai, shang ce*, 177.
⁵⁶ *Shenbao*, May 5, 1885.
⁵⁷ *North-China Herald*, May 27, 1887.
⁵⁸ *Shenbao*, June 23, 1888.
⁵⁹ *Shanghai cidian* (Dictionary of Shanghai), ed. Shanghai shi difangzhi bangongshi (Shanghai: Shehui kexueyuan chubanshe, 1989), 320–21.
⁶⁰ *North-China Herald*, March 15, 1889.
⁶¹ Gui 88.
⁶² Mao 30, Xu 13.
⁶³ Wen 12.
⁶⁴ Sun Baoxuan, *Wangshanlu riji* (Diary of the master of Wangshan Studio) (Shanghai: Shanghai guji chubanshe, 1983), 163–64; Tan Yingke, *Shenjiang shixia shengjing tushuo* (Illustrated guide to beautiful scenery in contemporary Shanghai) (Shanghai, 1894), *shang juan*, 10.
⁶⁵ Heng 58.
⁶⁶ Xing 95.
⁶⁷ Macpherson, *Public Health*, 118.

[68] Xiang Hua, *Shanghai shi hua* (Talks on the history of Shanghai) (Hong Kong: Muwen shuju, 1971), 111.
[69] Zhu Wenbing, *Haishang zhuzhici* (Bamboo branch rhymes of Shanghai) (Shanghai: Jicheng tushu gongsi, 1908), 38.
[70] *Shenbao*, January 22, 1874.
[71] *North-China Herald*, April 4, 1883.
[72] *North-China Herald*, June 25, 1886.
[73] Geng 34.
[74] Li Pingshu, *Zixu*, 17. Mark Elvin, "The Administration of Shanghai, 1905–1914," in *The Chinese City between Two Worlds*, ed. Mark Elvin and G. William Skinner (Stanford: Stanford University Press, 1974), 241, suggests the English translation "Hall of Impartial Altruism and Support for the Fundamental" for the *Tongren Fuyuantang*. This hall was a combination of two earlier halls, thus the double name.
[75] Mrs. Archibald Little, *The Land of the Blue Gown* (New York: Brentano's, 1902), 43.
[76] Pott, *History of Shanghai*, 74.
[77] Jerome Ch'en, *China and the West* (London: Hutchinson and Co., 1979), 209–10.
[78] Xu 13; Shen 42. The term is also often encountered in other material, e.g. Ge Yuanxu, *Huyou zaji*, *juan* 2, 38–39; Ranli laoren et al. ed., *Shanghai yangchang*, manuscript, Shanghai Library.
[79] Xu 13, Gui 29.
[80] Ge Yuanxu, *Huyou zaji*, *juan* 3, 49.
[81] Apart from the references in Ge Yuanxu, see also "Yangchang yongwu ci si shou" (Four poems in praise of things in the foreign settlements) in Ranli laoren, *Shanghai yangchang*.
[82] Wang Tao, *Yingruan zazhi*, *juan* 6, 124–25.
[83] Pott, *History of Shanghai*, 74.
[84] Jia 15.
[85] Jia 37.
[86] Bing 19.
[87] Bing 82.
[88] Xin 16; Geng 36.
[89] Wei 18.
[90] Geng 57; Yi 9; Wu 63; Zhu 39; Yi★ 53.
[91] Ge Yuanxu, *Huyou zaji*, *juan* 2, 38.
[92] Ding 6; Jia 16; Jia 17; Yin 18; Wu 39; Shu★ 23.
[93] Jin 30.
[94] Yi★ 83; Geng 17.
[95] *North-China Herald*, September 15, 1882.
[96] Pott, *History of Shanghai*, 111; Yao Gonghe, *Shanghai xianhua*, 22.
[97] Yi 75.
[98] Pott, *History of Shanghai*, 111.
[99] Chen Boxi, *Lao Shanghai*, *shang ce*, 183.
[100] Pott, *History of Shanghai*, 111. See also *North-China Herald*, August 7, 1885.
[101] Zi 21.
[102] Gui 84; Gui 86.
[103] Gui 87.
[104] Gui 88.
[105] Shen 42.
[106] Xin 84.
[107] Ji 47.
[108] Chen 49.
[109] Wu 79.
[110] Geng 42; Yi★ 82; Yi★ 83; Yi★ 90; Yi★ 91.
[111] You 56.
[112] Yi 77.
[113] Wu 23.
[114] Zi 3.
[115] Zi 21.
[116] Chen 22.

[117] He Ma, *Shanghai xianhua (1)* (Chats on Shanghai) (Shanghai: Wenhua chubanshe, 1956), 1–4
[118] Sun Yutang, *Zhongguo jindai gongye shi ziliao* (Materials on the history of modern industry in Shanghai) (Beijing: Kexue chubanshe, 1957), vol. 1, 198–99.
[119] Li 64.
[120] Geng 17.
[121] Li 48.
[122] Wei 15.
[123] Heng 48; Xin 79.
[124] Tan Yingke, *Shenjiang shixia shengjing tushuo, juan shang*, 16.
[125] Yue 40.
[126] Shanghai tongshe, *Shanghai yanjiu ziliao* (Historical materials for research on Shanghai) (Shanghai: Zhonghua shuju, 1936, reprinted Shanghai shudian, 1984), 548.
[127] Geng 72.
[128] Yuan 79.
[129] Heng 16; Yi 9. Liu Yanong, *Shanghai xianhua* (Chats on Shanghai) (Taiwan: Shijie shuju, 1960), 125; Li Boyuan, *Nanting si hua*, 482; Zhiwuyashi zhuren (Master of the Hall of Knowledge Without Boundaries), *Ru ci Shanghai* (Such is Shanghai), vol. 1 (Shanghai: Dadong shuju, n.d.), 8
[130] Tan Yingke, *Shenjiang shixia shengjing tushuo, juan shang*, 2.
[131] Xu 13.
[132] Geng 40.
[133] Huang Shiquan, *Songnan mengyinglu*, 109.
[134] Yi 77.
[135] Zhu 40.
[136] Yin 74.
[137] Yi 77.
[138] Yi* 32; Hai 37.
[139] Hai 37.
[140] Gamewell, *The Gateway to China*, 47–48.
[141] Li 48.
[142] Shu 48.
[143] Geng 48.
[144] Ren 74.
[145] Li 61.
[146] Gui 29.
[147] Gamewell, *The Gateway to China*, 47.
[148] *Shenbao*, July 6, 1888.
[149] Ren 90. It is by no means certain whether the Western woman referred to was really a prostitute, or if the commentator presumed that any woman performing in a sing-song hall must have been.
[150] Heng 48; Xin 79.
[151] Hushang youxi zhuren (Master of Entertainment in Shanghai), *Haishang youxi tushuo* (Illustrated guide to entertainment in Shanghai) (Shanghai, 1898), *juan* 4, 24. According to Chen Dingshan (*Chunshen jiuwen*, 190–91), the Wanjiachun was the first Western-style restaurant to be run by a Chinese. The Yipinxiang came later, but its Western-style cooking was better and thus became more popular.
[152] Haishang shushisheng, *Haishang fanhuameng*, vol. 1, 24–25.
[153] Hushang youxi zhuren, *Haishang youxi tushuo*, *juan* 2, 15. The most famous of the genuine Western restaurants was the Hôtel des Colonies, but Chinese seldom went there. It is mentioned once in the *Dianshizhai*, in connection with the newly arrived French consul-general Emile Desiré Kraetzer, who went there for a meal immediately after his arrival in Shanghai. Wu 55.
[154] Haishang shushisheng, *Haishang fanhuameng*, vol. 1, 24–25.
[155] *Shenbao*, October 9, 1883.
[156] *Shenbao*, October 9, 1883.
[157] Geng 72 xia.
[158] Bing 37. See Wu Shenyuan, *Shanghai zuizao de zhongzhong* (First appearance of various things in Shanghai) (Shanghai: Huadong shifan daxue chubanshe, 1989), 108.

[159] Chi Zhichen, *Huyou mengying* (Dream shadows of travels in Shanghai) (Shanghai, 1893, reprinted Shanghai: Shanghai guji chubanshe, 1989), 161.
[160] Shanghai tongshe, *Shanghai yanjiu ziliao*, 569–73.
[161] Ge 88. Also mentioned in Ge 48 and Li* 39.
[162] Hu Xianghan, *Shanghai xiao zhi* (Concise gazetteer of Shanghai) (Shanghai: Chuanjingtang shudian, 1930, reprinted Shanghai: Shanghai guji chubanshe, 1989), 33–34.
[163] Tang Zhenchang, *Shanghai shi* (History of Shanghai) (Shanghai: Shanghai renmin chubanshe, 1989), 750; Jia You, "Zhangyuan yu Xinhai Geming" (The Zhangyuan and the 1911 Revolution), in *Shanghai yishi* (Anecdotes about Shanghai), ed. Tang Weikang et al. (Shanghai: Wenhua chubanshe, 1987), 166–68; Liu Yazi, *Nanshe jilue* (An outline record of the Southern Society), in the series *Liu Yazi Wenji* (Collected Works of Liu Yazi), ed. Liu Wuji (Shanghai: Shanghai renmin chubanshe, 1983).
[164] Wei 18; Wu 13.
[165] Chi Zhichen, *Huyou mengying*, 163.
[166] This matter will be discussed in Part Three.
[167] Tan Yingke, *Shenjiang shixia shengjing tushuo, juan shang*, 2.
[168] Yuan 79.
[169] Gamewell, *Gateway to China*, 46.
[170] Pott, *History of Shanghai*, 83.
[171] Jia 15.
[172] Wu 74.
[173] Haishang shushisheng, *Haishang fanhuameng*, vol. 1, 61.
[174] Wu 73.
[175] Geng 36.
[176] Tan Yingke, *Shenjiang shixia shengjing tushuo, juan shang*, 12.
[177] Pott, *History of Shanghai*, 87–88.
[178] Wu 65.
[179] Charles M. Dyce, *The Model Settlement: Shanghai 1870–1900* (London: Chapman & Hall Ltd., 1906), 99.
[180] Bing 35.
[181] Pott, *History of Shanghai*, 87. Christopher Cook (*The Lion and the Dragon: British Voices from the China Coast* [London: Elm Tree Books/Hamish Hamilton Ltd., 1985], 60–61) notes that the "Paper-Hunters Annual Ball" was still being held in Shanghai in 1935 and 1936.
[182] Hai 4.
[183] She 20; Shi 87.
[184] Pott, *History of Shanghai*, 87.
[185] *Shenbao*, October 29, 1872; November 5, 1873; October 24, 1874; May 5, 1875.
[186] *Shenbao*, May 19, 1873.
[187] Ding 80.
[188] Mu 57–65. For a comprehensive study of this celebration, see Bryna Goodman, "Improvisations on a Semicolonial Theme," 889–926.
[189] Mu 57.
[190] Rhoads Murphey, *Shanghai, Key to Modern China*, (Cambridge, Mass.: Harvard University Press, 1953), 6.
[191] Mu 58.
[192] Mu 59–63.
[193] Mu 62.
[194] Mu 64. Pott, *History of Shanghai*, 126–27.
[195] Gui 82–88. Pott, *History of Shanghai*, 130.
[196] Yuan 59–60.
[197] Wu 2.
[198] Geng 42.
[199] Yi* 76.
[200] Yi* 90, 91.
[201] Wang Tao, *Yingruan zazhi, juan* 6, 126–30.
[202] You 56.
[203] Wu 49; Wu 52.
[204] Shanghai tongshe, *Shanghai yanjiu ziliao*, 511.

[205] Yi 75.
[206] Ge 90.
[207] Hushang youxi zhuren, *Haishang youxi tushuo*, juan 3, 15; Ge Yuanxu, *Huyou zaji*, juan 3, 56.
[208] Zi 89, Si 676, Ding 11, Bing 2, Mao 22; *Shenbao*, July 26, 1885.
[209] Wang Tao, *Yingruan zazhi*, juan 5, 107.
[210] *Shenbao*, March 9, 1874.
[211] Haishang shushisheng, *Haishang fanhuameng*, vol. 1, 19.
[212] Ren 74.
[213] MacPherson, *Public Health*, 103.
[214] Ge 82.
[215] Wu★ 86.
[216] Shen 42.
[217] Shu★ 96.
[218] Li★ 40.
[219] Shen 21; Shen 93.
[220] Yi★ 43.
[221] Mu 65.
[222] Yin 62.
[223] Ge Yuanxu, *Huyou zaji*, juan 2, 26–27 gives a description of the type of merchandise each area specialized in and was famous for.
[224] Wang Tao, *Yingruan zazhi*, juan 2, 22.
[225] Geng 28. Shanyin is an old name for the area to the south-east of Shaoxing.
[226] Huang Shiquan, *Songnan mengyinglu*, 143.
[227] Haishang shushisheng, *Haishang fanhuameng*, vol. 1, 12–13.
[228] Wang Tao, *Yingruan zazhi*, juan 6, 111–12.
[229] *Shenbao*, March 31, 1888.
[230] Chinese First Historical Archives, Beijing. The documents are in the file *Shengpingshu, No. 450: Guangxu 19 nian: Yue-xi-dang* (Monthly records of theatrical performances).
[231] Qi Rushan, *Jingju zhi bianqian* (Changes in Peking opera) (Beiping: Guoju xuehui 1935), 65.
[232] William Crane Johnstone, *The Shanghai Problem* (Stanford: Stanford University Press, 1937; reprinted Connecticut: Hyperion Press, 1973), vii.
[233] Pott, *History of Shanghai*, 37; cf. Kuai Shixun, *Shanghai gonggong zujie shi gao*, 347.
[234] *Shenbao* shiliao bianxiezu, "Chuangban chuqi," 136. Refugees returning to their home villages accounted for an increase of 68.78 percent in the average population growth rate in Zhejiang during the years 1866–1874. After 1875, the rate of population growth returned to normal. See Zhao Wenlin and Xie Shujun, *Zhongguo renkou shi* (History of China's population) (Beijing: Renmin chubanshe, 1988), 425. On the influence of the Taiping Rebellion on Jiangsu, and the consequent influence on the population of Shanghai, see Benjamin A. Elman, *From Philosophy to Philology* (Cambridge, Mass.: Harvard University Press, 1984), 248–49.
[235] For details see Luo Zhiru, *Tongjibiao zhong zhi Shanghai* (Shanghai in statistical tables) (Nanjing: Guoli zhongyang yanjiuyuan, 1932), 22, 25, 27. These statistics do not include the large numbers of workers in the Shanghai factories who still lived in the villages around Shanghai.
[236] Shanghai shi wenxian weiyuanhui, *Shanghai renkou zhi liie* (Outline if the population of Shanghai) (Shanghai, 1948), 23–24.
[237] Xu Ke, *Qing bai lei chao*, vol. 4, 1848.
[238] Zhong 48.
[239] Chen Gaoyong et al., *Zhongguo tianzai renhuo biao* (Tables of natural and man-made disasters in China) (Shanghai: Shanghai shudian, 1986), 1655, 1660.
[240] Wei 91.
[241] Chen Gaoyong, *Tianzai renhuo biao*, 1668.
[242] Heng 56.
[243] Sun Yutang, *Zhongguo jindai gongye shi ziliao*, vol. 1, 948–952; 954–956; 958–959; 965–967.
[244] Xin 68.
[245] Xin 85.

[246] She 46. Xu Xuejun et al., trans., *Shanghai jindai shehui jingji fazhan gaikuang 1882–1931*, "Haiguan shinian baogao 1892–1931 (Shanghai: Shekeyuan chubanshe, 1985), 21. This is a translation of "Decennial Reports on the Ports Open to Foreign Commerce in China and Korea, and on the Condition and Development of the Treaty Port Provinces," prepared by the Chinese Customs Service; it also mentions the merchants from Nanjing in Shanghai, selling silk, jade, watches and diamonds.

[247] Zhong 16. See Zhao Gang, Chen Zhongyi, *Zhongguo mianye shi* (History of the cotton industry in China) (Taipei: Lianjing chuban shiye gongsi, 1977), 49: "According to He Qiaoyuan, *Min Shu*, *juan* 38, in the seventeenth century a large amount of cotton was still being produced in Fujian, at the county level. Afterwards, the production of sugarcane and tea became more profitable than cotton, and the peasants gradually gave up its cultivation. Peasant households in Fujian, however, continued to weave cotton. From the early Qing, merchants would transport sugarcane to Jiangnan and Zhejiang by boat, and would bring back cotton from Jiangnan to Fujian on the return trip, to supply the local cotton-weavers." See also Yang Guangfu, *Songnan yuefu* (Songs of Songnan), in *Shanghai zhanggu congshu*, ed. Shanghai tongshe, *juan* 8, 12 *xia*: "There is also high quality cotton. Shopkeepers along the *Yanghangjie* (Foreign traders street) act as agents for merchants from Fujian and Guangdong, and buy it at a cheap price." The *Yanghangjie*, known at the time as Rue de Whampoo, was not a street where there were foreign firms, but where there were Chinese merchants, mainly from Guangdong and Fujian, selling foreign goods. It is a small street running north-south from Berth 16 on the Bund. It is now known as Yangshuo Road. See Wu Guifang, *Shanghai fengwu zhi* (Scenery of Shanghai) (Shanghai: Wenhua chubanshe, 1982), 35, 38–41; Wang Tao, *Yingruan zazhi*, *juan* 1, 9 *shang* also noted, "The Cantonese (Yue) are from Shantou (Swatow), the Fujianese (Min) are from Taiwan; they transport sugar to Shanghai, and they sell it for millions (*shu baiwan jin*)."

[248] Hao Yen-p'ing, *The Commercial Revolution in Nineteenth Century China: The Rise of Sino-Western Mercantile Capitalism* (Berkeley: University of California Press, 1986), 275.

[249] Xu Run, *Xu Ruzhai zixu nianpu* (Chronological autobiography) (Xiangshan, 1927; reprinted Taiwan shihuo chuban youxian gongsi, 1978), 15; *Shenbao* July 18–24, 1885, January 30, 1888; February 24, 1888.

[250] Wu 4.

[251] The novel *The Human Tide*, written in the 1920s, devoted several pages to describing Chen's funeral, though the details were not necessarily accurate. See Wangzhusheng, *Renhaichao, shang ce*, 264–66.

[252] Zhen 46.

[253] Xing 88.

[254] Wu★ 48 *xia*.

[255] Li★ 49.

[256] Xing 32.

[257] Wu 51; Shu 24.

[258] Li★ 16.

[259] Shi 87.

[260] For details see *Shanghai difangshi ziliao*, vol. 6: *Lishi wenhua mingcheng—Shanghai* (Shanghai: Shehui kexue chubanshe, 1988), 261–62.

[261] Li★ 48 *xia*; Shi 87.

[262] Wen 80.

[263] Yin 6. On the Muslims of Nanjing in earlier times, see Susan Naquin and Evelyn S. Rawski, *Chinese Society in the Eighteenth Century* (New Haven: Yale University Press, 1987), 148.

[264] See Pott, *History of Shanghai*, 136; Xin 3, Mu 74, Li 72 *xia*, Jia 89 *xia*.

[265] Bing 17.

[266] Wu 24 *xia*.

[267] The Tongwen shuju was established by Xu Yuzi, from Guangdong, after the success of the Dianshizhai Publishing Company. The *Tongwen shuju*, the *Dianshizhai*, and the *Baishishanfang*, established by a man from Ningbo, were in competition. See Yao Gonghe, *Shanghai xianhua*, 16; Zheng Yimei, *Shu bao hua jiu*, 85.

[268] Yin 67.

[269] Chen 55.

[270] Shu★ 72, Li 43.

[271] Ren 42.

[272] Li 43, Chen 55, Ren 42.

[273] Xin 84. Guns could be purchased from various shops selling foreign goods, and advertisements for them appeared from time to time in the *Shenbao*. For example, the *Shenbao* of March 29, 1875, carried an

advertisement inserted by Augustine Heard and Co. for Remington rifles from the United States, together with a note that any "gentry or officials" who wished to purchase such guns should contact that firm.

[274] Ding 47.
[275] Wei 64 xia; Shu 72.
[276] Tan Yingke, Shenjiang shixia shengjing tushuo, juan shang, 20 xia.
[277] You 69. The Chinese term is taiji.
[278] Wu 22.
[279] Li 63.
[280] Chen 21.
[281] Wu 22.
[282] Chen 21.
[283] Li 63.
[284] Shu 86.
[285] Pao 47.
[286] Yin 1.
[287] Zhen 79.
[288] Zhong 87.
[289] Yi 32.
[290] Pott, History of Shanghai, 75.
[291] Yi★ 53.
[292] Xin 72 xia.
[293] Wu 94.
[294] Yao Gonghe, Shanghai xianhua, 143–44.
[295] Xin 15.
[296] Gui 23.
[297] Ren 64 xia.
[298] Yin 15; Yin 16.
[299] Zi 31.
[300] Xin 57.
[301] Heng 56
[302] Shen 13.
[303] Wen 24.
[304] Yu 40.
[305] Li★ 39; Wu 55.
[306] Li★ 39; Yi 43; Yi★2; You 12.
[307] Hai 74; Li★ 39.
[308] Ji 1; Jia 81 xia; Bing 8.
[309] Xing 24.
[310] Yi 48.
[311] Ren 18.
[312] Yi 5.
[313] Ji 53; Wu 96 xia; Wu 94.
[314] You 8; Li★ 60; Xu 49; Si 69.
[315] Bing 77 xia; Wu 37. The first of these examples was about an American who exhibited a bodiless head; the second about a foreigner who exhibited an Italian dwarf first in Shanghai, then in Hangzhou and other places. This dwarf was somewhat of a celebrity in Shanghai; he was also mentioned by Ge Yuanxu, Huyou zaji, juan 2, 33.
[316] Feetham, Report, vol. 1, 96.
[317] Pott, History of Shanghai, 67; Johnstone, The Shanghai Problem, 128–58; A. M. Kotenev, Shanghai: Its Mixed Court and Council (Shanghai: North-China Daily News & Herald Limited 1925; reprinted Taipei: Ch'eng-wen Publishing, 1968, 45–68; Hosea Ballou Morse, The International Relations of the Chinese Empire (London: Longmans, Green and Co, 1910–1918), vol. 2, 133–34; Ching-lin Hsia, The Status of Shanghai, 41–59; Feetham, Report, vol. 1, 99–100; 171–73. On the background of the Mixed Court, and particularly its role and function in the twentieth century, see also Thomas Blacket Stephens, Order and Discipline in China: The Shanghai Mixed Court, 1911–1927 (Seattle: University of Washington Press, 1992), 44–47.

[118] Haishang shushisheng, *Haishang fanhuameng*, vol. 2, 1127.

[119] Zhen 50; Wei 21; Hai 55; Wu 35; Bing 8; Li★ 59; Zhu 50; Ding 66.

[120] Cf. *Shenbao*, July 29, 1888, which reported that on the previous day the Western assessor had another engagement, and could not attend court. All cases scheduled for that day were heard by the Chinese deputy alone. None of the cases involved the interests of any foreigner.

[121] Kotenev, *Mixed Court*, 90–91.

[122] Mao 30; Ding 66; Ding 67; Heng 64; Wu 24 *xia*; Li★ 60; Wei 62; Geng 16 *xia*.

[123] Ding 66.

[124] Li★ 59.

[125] *Shenbao*, June 4, 1873.

[126] Shu★ 96; Ding 47.

[127] Wu★ 39.

[128] Kotenev, *Mixed Court*, 75.

[129] *Shenbao*, June 17, 1876.

[130] Shu★ 96. It was not much earlier, in fact, that torture was commonly used in Western countries. See Foucault, *Discipline and Punish*, and John H. Langbein, *Torture and the Law of Proof* (Chicago: University of Chicago Press, 1976).

[131] Shu★ 96.

[132] Zhu 50.

[133] Kotenev, *Mixed Court*, 66.

[134] *Shenbao*, June 21, 1887.

[135] *Shenbao*, June 23, 1887.

[136] Yi★ 62.

[137] John Henry Gray, *China: A History of the Laws, Manners and Customs of the People*, ed. William Gow Gregor (London: Macmillan and Co, 1878; reprinted Shannon: Irish University Press, 1972), vol. 1, 32–35 and 46–74 give a detailed description of Chinese prisons and methods of torture.

[138] *Shenbao*, June 11, 1874.

[139] Wu★ 86.

[140] Shu★ 96.

[141] Huang Shiquan, *Songnan mengyinglu*, 146.

[142] On this point, cf. Mark Elvin, "The Mixed Court of the International Settlement at Shanghai," in *Papers on China*, East Asian Research Center, Harvard University, vol. 17 (December 1963), 136.

[143] The Refuge for the Homeless was a Chinese charitable organization. According to the *Shanghai xian xuzhi* (Supplementary gazetteer of Shanghai County) ([Shanghai, 1918; reprinted Taipei: Ch'eng-wen Publishing, 1975], *juan* 2, 36–37), it was situated in the northern area of Shanghai, behind the Dawangmiao Temple in Xinzha. The number of homeless people from many districts in the International Settlement had grown to the point where, in 1879, the deputy magistrate of the Mixed Court, Chen Fuxun, and the magistrate, Mo Xiangzhi, contributed funds to purchase seven *mu* of land. To this was added six *mu* purchased with other contributions. Qu Kaitong was put in charge of the construction of ninety-six single-story houses on the land, which provided accommodation for more than two hundred unemployed and homeless people. In 1888 an additional fifteen houses were built to provide housing for female prisoners and other women whom the court had directed to stay in the refuge until they were appropriately married. In 1904 the managing directors, Lu Wenlu and Qu Qingshan, decided that it was necessary to teach the people in the refuge some practical skills and provided machinery for making leather handicrafts. The expenses for the Refuge for the Homeless were provided by the Mixed Court. According to Chen Dingshan (*Chunshen jiuwen*, 141) the expenses provided by the Mixed Court came from fines. In the essay contest held by the Shanghai Polytechnic Institute and Reading Room in the spring of 1893, one of the topics was, "In Shanghai, charitable halls stand as many as trees in a forest. Why is it that beggars can be seen everywhere in the streets, whereas in various European countries charitable institutions teach people handicrafts, which seems to be more effective. Discuss." The essay of the second prize winner mentioned the Refuge for the Homeless, pointing out many deficiencies in its management. Cf. *Gezhi Shuyuan keyi, 1893 nian chun-ji, di'er ming* (Essays of the Shanghai Polytechnic Institution and Reading Room, Spring 1983, Second Prize (Shanghai: Shanghai Polytechnic Institution and Reading Room, 1893), 5. Providing training in handicrafts is obviously an idea borrowed from the West. More information on the Refuge for the Homeless can be found in Chen Boxi, *Lao Shanghai, xia ce*, 11.

[144] Zhen 50.
[145] Bing 8.
[146] Shu 24.
[147] Jin 6. Elvin, "The Mixed Court," 137.
[148] Kotenev, *Mixed Court*, 91; Stephens, *Order and Discipline in China*, 47.
[149] Huayeliannong, *Haishang hua liezhuan*, mentions the "new yamen" on 232, 254, 515. On page 515 one of the functionaries of the yamen in the Chinese city says, "We are not like the policemen in the new yamen—things here are just so difficult!" Zhang Ailing, *Haishang hua* (page 515) provides a note: "the 'new yamen' refers to the Mixed Court in the International Settlement. They were able to disregard the views of the Chinese officials." As late as 1925, during the May 30 Movement, demonstrators shouted the slogan "To the New Yamen!" See Shanghai shehui kexueyuan lishi yanjiusuo, eds., *Wu Sanshi yundong shiliao* (Historical materials for the study of the May 30 Movement) (Shanghai: Shanghai renmin chubanshe, 1981), vol. 1, 670.
[150] Mao 23.
[151] Mao 8 *xia*. This story also appeared in the *Shenbao* on June 29, 1888. Cf. Qin Rongguang, *Shanghai xian zhuzhici* (Bamboo-branch rhymes of Shanghai County) (Shanghai, 1911; reprinted Shanghai: Shanghai guji shudian, 1989), 119: "None of the civil or military officials of the city died in battle; the dogs, however, lay down at the side of the coffin and died of hunger." The note to the poem adds: "When the Red Scarves (The Small Swords) occupied the city, apart from Magistrate Yuan Zude, not a single one of the civil or military officials was killed. The four dogs which the Magistrate kept stayed by his coffin, and all starved. The villagers painted this scene on the wall of Magistrate Yuan's temple." Cf. Wang Tao, *Yingruan zazhi*, *juan* 5, 104: "Magistrate Yuan kept four dogs; all of them refused to eat, and died. His subordinates made a record of these righteous dogs, and arranged appropriate funeral ceremonies for Magistrate Yuan."
[152] Yin 50 *xia*.
[153] Yin 50.
[154] Wei 91.
[155] Wu★ 87.
[156] Ding 8 *xia*.
[157] Hai 56 *xia*; Yi★ 49.
[158] Yuan 16.
[159] This sketch is in Cohn, *Vignettes from the Chinese*, 69. In his translation on page 68 Cohn translates the term *huishen xieyuan* as "an official from a local Buddhist association." *Huishen*, however, is an abbreviation of *huishen gongtang*, the Chinese term for the Mixed Court. *Xie* means "to decide judicially."
[160] Feetham, *Report*, vol. 1, 92.
[161] See Sun Guoda, *Gonggong zujie de xunbu* (Police in the International Settlement), in *Shanghai yishi*, ed. Tang Weikang, 44–50 (Shanghai: Wenhua chubanshe, 1987); Johnstone, *The Shanghai Problem*, 74–76.
[162] Hai 74.
[163] You 8.
[164] Mao 15.
[165] Si 66.
[166] Si 66.
[167] Cf. E.W. Peters, *Shanghai Policemen* (London: Rich and Cowan Ltd, 1937), 20: "The Indians, the Sikhs, generally act as traffic policemen. Big, impressive, simple men, they must be led. But with a man capable of leading them, they are hard nuts to crack. The Chinese usually complain that the Sikhs give them rougher treatment that the rest of the police during the riots."
[168] Philip C. C. Huang, "Between Informal Mediation and Formal Adjudication: the Third Realm of Qing Civil Justice," in *Modern China*, vol. 19, no. 3 (July 1993): 282.
[169] Li★ 58; Li★ 59; Li★ 60; Pao 44; Geng 39; Yin 1; Zhen 50; Zhen 60; Yuan 92; Xing 8; Ren 20.
[170] Sun Guoda, *Gonggong zujie de xunbu*, 47.
[171] Ge Yuanxu, *Huyou zaji*, *juan* 2, 21.
[172] Yin 1.
[173] Even in the twentieth century, many of the Chinese police in the settlements were from the criminal classes, or started their careers as hoodlums. The famous twentieth century gangsters Huang Jinrong and Gu Zhuxuan both started their careers as policemen and detectives in the settlement. See Si Yu, *Shanghai daheng Du Yuesheng* (The Shanghai arch-criminal Du Yuesheng) (Beijing: Zhongguo wenlian chubanshe, 1986),

28–29; Fan Songfu, *Banghui shili zhenwen* (Little known facts about secret societies) (Hong Kong: Zhongyuan chubanshe, 1987), 213; Frederic E. Wakeman, *Policing Shanghai, 1927–1937* (Berkeley: University of California Press, 1995), 28, 30–34; Brian Martin, "The Pact with the Devil: The Relations between the Green Gang and the French Concession Authority 1925–1935," in Wakeman and Yeh, *Shanghai Sojourners*, 266–304.

[374] Professionalization of the police force, whether under the settlement authorities or the Guomindang, did not begin until the twentieth century. See Wakeman, *Policing Shanghai*, 52–54.

[375] Li* 58–60.

[376] Pao 44.

[377] Yuan 92.

[378] Yin 1.

[379] Geng 39.

[380] Ren 20.

[381] Feetham, *Report*, vol. 1, 100–1.

[382] Chen 16.

[383] Yin 50.

[384] Zhu 50.

[385] Yuan 87. Zhao Xiaolian is mentioned in another story in the *Dianshizhai*. There he was having an affair with the concubine of a rich man from Suzhou, whom he had recently met at a theatrical performance. They were discovered and held up to public ridicule (Zhen 79). Zhao Xiaolian is also mentioned in Tiaoshui kuangsheng, *Shanghai liyuan xin lishi* (A new history of theaters in Shanghai) (Shanghai: Hongwen shuju, 1909), *juan* 1, 37–38.

[386] Shu* 24.

[387] His name appeared three times between June and August 1888: June 16; July 25; August 24.

[388] Ding 47.

[389] Xin 36.

[390] His name appeared four times in the period between July and September 1888: July 31; August 19; August 21; September 2.

PART THREE

A New Urban Culture

1. The Shanghai attitude towards things foreign

Few Chinese lived in the settlements before 1853, when the Small Swords Uprising in the Chinese city sent more than twenty thousand refugees (including many wealthy families) into that neighboring safe haven.[1] This alarmed both the Chinese and settlement authorities, but some Western merchants saw profit in building houses to rent to the Chinese. There were initially objections from both sides, but "the right of the Chinese to reside in the Settlement gradually became established by usage."[2] They were not restricted to any particular area, nor were Westerners. This was quite different from other treaty ports such as Hankou, where residents of the settlements, even Chinese working for foreigners, were "almost completely cut off from the rest of Hankow."[3]

In Shanghai, Chinese could not only reside in the settlements, Chinese merchants could invest there and even become partners in joint ventures.[4] According to Yen-p'ing Hao, the 250 compradors in Shanghai in 1870 had grown to 20,000 by 1900.[5] Yu Xingmin claims that 10,000 compradors and clerks worked in foreign enterprises as early as 1862.[6] Factory workers were more numerous, but their contact with foreign employers was probably much less than that of the middle-class clerks and employees in municipal offices.

Marriages or temporary liaisons between Chinese and foreigners did occur, but seem to have been limited in number. There are four cases mentioned in the *Dianshizhai*, whose commentaries are neutral and indicate no antagonism towards either the relationships or children of mixed race.[7]

Apart from certain missionaries or businessmen like Major, few foreigners made any serious attempt to gain an understanding of China.[8] The *Dianshizhai* occasionally mentioned foreigners who could speak a little Chinese: the Western prostitute who sang an indecent folk song in a teahouse on Fuzhou Road,[9] and two foreigners who visited a brothel in Hujiazhai.[10] In 1890 the *Dianshizhai* reported a concert held in a church, at which a famous *pipa* player, Zhou Yonggang, was asked to perform. Several hundred missionaries, diplomats, and businessmen sat in the audience, as well as a large group of Chinese. Zhou had been performing at the Yeshilou Teahouse when a Westerner heard him and was so delighted that he organized the church concert (Fig. 72).[11] These sorts of encounters were fairly unusual, but compared to earlier times, and elsewhere in China, they were significant.

Little anti-foreign feeling among migrants in the settlements

Clashes did occur between Chinese and foreigners in Shanghai during the nineteenth century. The first of these was the Qingpu Incident of 1848, in which Cantonese and Fujianese sailors and boatmen (not natives of Shanghai) attacked three foreign missionaries."[12] The Battle of Muddy Flat

72. A *pipa* concert held in a church (1890). Missionaries, members of foreign consulates, and businessmen, as well as a few Chinese make up the audience. The inscription at the side of the stage reads: "The True Path to the Heavenly City: The Trinity and the Ten Commandments." On the wall, the banner on the right reads: "Taking away our misery and our sins, and dying for us—this is the bounty of the Holy Son," and the one on the left, "Moved by Supreme Love, we do not distinguish between China and the West."

in 1854 was purely a military operation, involving clashes between Chinese imperial forces (sent to Shanghai to suppress the Small Swords rebels), and Western troops. No local Chinese were involved in these clashes.[13]

The *Dianshizhai* reported on the Ningbo Guild Incident and the Wheelbarrow Pullers' Anti-Tax Riot (Fig. 73).[14] These incidents arose from conflicts of interest rather than anti-foreignism as such. Hostilities in the Ningbo Guild Incident were directed specifically against the French, and did not involve, for instance, the British.[15] As Goodman has noted, "It would be problematic to assert that for the actors involved the riots involved a sense of nationalism."[16] Interestingly, the *Dianshizhai* titles of the two illustrations on this incident, "Seizing the *Gongsuo*" (Fig. 74) and "French Cruelty" (Fig. 75), do not accurately reflect the content of the commentaries. A careful reading of these reveals that, according to the *Dianshizhai*, most of the damage was caused by "scoundrels" (*wulai*). It is clear that the French did not open fire until demonstrators attacked the police station and refused to disperse.

The Wheelbarrow Pullers' Anti-Tax Riot, directed against the Municipal Council, was instigated by an increase in the wheelbarrow tax levy. It can be considered a type of tax revolt, similar to those discussed by Perry.[17]

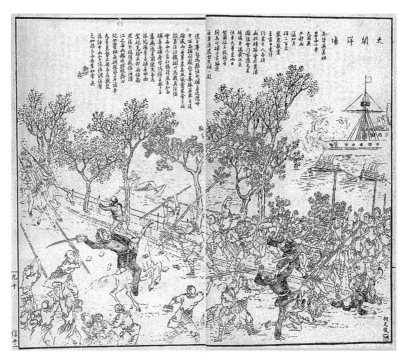

73. The Wheelbarrow Pullers' Revolt (1897). The Municipal Council decided to increase the tax on wheelbarrow pullers by 200 cents a month in 1897. The wheelbarrow pullers went on strike, and several thousand gathered at the Bund to protest. A non-striking wheelbarrow puller passed by, which infuriated the protesters. They surrounded him and he had to be protected by the police. The protesters then rioted and pulled down the fence of a foreign company to use the fence posts as weapons. Foreign employees got on the telephone (delüfeng) to notify the police in various stations, who hurried to the Bund and soon quelled the riot. As a result, the Municipal Council decided not to increase the tax for the time being.

During 1891 several anti-missionary incidents, including the destruction of churches and the killing of missionaries, occurred in Nanjing, Wuhu, Yangzhou, and other areas near Shanghai. Liu Kunyi, the governor-general of Liang-Jiang, ordered the daotai of Shanghai to protect foreign missionaries. The daotai duly posted armed troops near churches and missionary property. It was a tense time for foreigners in Shanghai, but no attack of any type was carried out against foreigners or their property. A few years later the Boxer Rebellion would spread throughout China, but there is no evidence of support for the Boxers in Shanghai. Despite the good deal of contact between Chinese and Westerners, large-scale clashes based on differences in race and culture did not erupt before the twentieth century. The experience of early Western residents in Shanghai is striking, especially compared to that of their counterparts in Canton.[18]

Lanning and Couling have tried to explain this difference in terms of racial and linguistic differences between the Chinese of Shanghai and Canton:

Where the Cantonese was aggressive, his Shanghai contemporary was peacefully complaisant. The southerner was a radical; the native of Wu a conservative. Shanghai had long since been reconciled to the *de facto* native government; Canton was ever ready to intrigue and rebel. As against the foreigner, the Cantonese was stand-offish at best, and had on many occasions shown active antipathy, particularly since the war, while the Shanghai man, though not impulsively pro-foreign, was at least willing to meet friendly advances half way. When, therefore, we find most of the early troubles with natives in or about the settlements in the early days arising from Fukien [Fujian] men or Cantonese.[19]

The probable reason is simple but significant: immigrants to Shanghai had gone there in search of opportunities lacking elsewhere. They harbored no strong anti-foreign feelings, otherwise they would not have gone to Shanghai at all. Those who fled natural disasters and did not wish to remain in Shanghai could always return to their native villages. By the twentieth century, of course, Shanghai had become a haven for nationalists and revolutionaries, but that is another matter.

Chinese traditionally referred to foreigners as *yi*, usually translated "barbarians." The use of the term *yi* to refer to Great Britain was formally banned in the Treaty of Tianjin of 1858.[20] As late as 1895, the Court had to reiterate that the word "barbarian" was not to be used in memorials.[21] In the 1860s, the Shanghai Chinese still referred to the International Settlement as the "barbarian quarter" (*yichang*).[22] But "in defense of the character *yi*,"[23] the *Shenbao* published an editorial in 1873, which argued that the term was not derogatory—at least Ernest Major was convinced that was the case. In 1874 he published a letter in the *North-China Herald*, arguing that *yi* was "a refined term for foreigner." He went on: "The Chinese have been the subject of much obloquy amongst Western nations for the supposed discourteous epithet of 'Ee'; and from fairness to them, it becomes a matter of at least some interest, if it can be proved that the favorite word 'Barbarian,' ironically applied by us to ourselves, turned out to be a myth of our own imagination."[24] Major's argument did not convince all readers of the *North-China Herald*, and the debate continued for several months. It is not clear when the term "barbarian quarter" gave way to "ten *li* of foreign settlement," but in the *Dianshizhai* of the 1880s, only the latter expression was used.[25] As Yao Gonghe noted, "At that time they called foreigners *yangguizi* or *yiren*. In the inner parts of China that was the case everywhere. Only in Shanghai did women, children, young and old, from ancient times to the present day, call foreigners *waiguoren*" (*nga-kok-nyung* in Shanghai dialect).[26] This was a neutral word with no derogatory overtones.

Generally, relations between Chinese and Westerners were harmonious. In 1873 the *Shenbao* reported the case of a drunken Westerner who had become involved in a fight with local residents. The first words state, "Chinese and foreigners have maintained harmonious relations for a long time. Rarely do we hear of disputes or disturbances."[27] In 1887 the *Dianshizhai*, commenting on a traffic accident, noted, "In this port, Chinese and Westerners have gotten along well together for a long time. Even in the middle of the night people can travel safely. There are no restrictions on their movements."[28] A story in the *Dianshizhai* dated 1888 suggests that Shanghai residents did not approve of aggressive behavior against foreigners. A mentally disturbed man from Jiangbei grabbed a knife and rushed into the streets, slashing at whomever he came by. In all, he wounded fifteen people. When he was arrested, "Liu laughed loudly and said, 'I wanted to kill foreigners.' Then everyone knew he was mad." The title of the sketch is "Madness is to be Feared."[29]

74. The Siming Gongsuo Riots (I) (1898). "Outside the West Gate of the city is the Siming Gongsuo. It was established in the second year of the Jiaqing period [1797], more than one hundred years ago. The number of corpses buried there is no less than ten thousand. It is extremely important as the lifeblood of the Ningbo *bang*.

In the thirteenth year of the Tongzhi period [1874], a baseless rumor stirred up trouble. The former French consul-general Godeaux was concerned about the situation of the merchants there and extended protection to them. He ordered that a wall be built to define the boundary of the Siming Gongsuo. This was agreed to by the consuls of eleven countries, permitting the Ningbo *bang* to conduct their business there in perpetuity. All this is in the official record, and the Chinese never expected that the French would not abide by this agreement.

The French later claimed to want to change the *gongsuo* into a school, a hospital, and a slaughterhouse. They tried to force the Ningbo *bang* to move out, but the people of Ningbo would not obey. Nor did local officials give their permission. The French knew that it would be hard for them to get their way, yet despite public opinion, in the early morning of the twenty eighth day of the fifth month, they flagrantly dispatched eighty soldiers, armed with rifles and carrying with them two huge cannons, to the Siming Gongsuo. They were led by the French consul-general and members of the Conseil Municipal.

After they had positioned themselves, the officers ordered the soldiers to demolish the wall surrounding the *gongsuo* on three sides. They blasted three holes, each about two *zhang* wide, in the walls, and the French soldiers entered the *gongsuo*. By this stage an enormous crowd of onlookers had gathered and worked itself into an uproar. All sorts of scoundrels flocked to the area in increasing numbers. Though completely unarmed, they urged each other to throw stones and hurl rocks, which poured down like rain. Given the strength of the French troops and large numbers of Chinese and Western detectives and policemen patrolling the area and making arrests, the local military and civilian officials eventually managed to suppress the rioters. Thanks only to these combined efforts did the French manage to avoid disaster. This cannot but be considered fortunate."

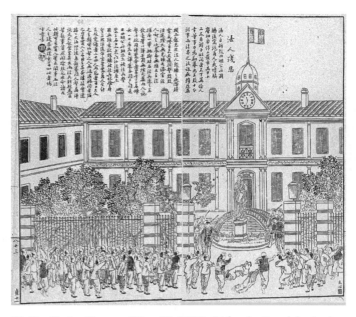

75. The Siming Gongsuo Riots (II) (1898). "After the French broke down the walls surrounding the Siming Gongsuo, righteous indignation filled the breasts of the Ningbo people resident in Shanghai. They urged each other to go on strike and close their shops. Among these were laborers, carpenters, and also vagrants with nothing to do, more than ten thousand in all. Fortunately, the directors [of the *gongsuo*] made every effort to dissuade them so the trouble did not spread.

Hoodlums and scoundrels in the French Concession, however, took advantage of the situation to cause trouble. First, on the night after the French broke down the wall, under cover of darkness, they broke all the electric lights and gas lamps. The streets went black as pitch, with the street lamps shedding no light. This angered the French. The next morning the scoundrels again gathered in front of the French police station and threw bricks and rocks. French soldiers tried to drive them away, but they did not disperse. In the end the French used bullets and other ammunition to attack them. This led to three men and one woman losing their lives. Local residents were panic-stricken, and closed their doors. On the same day French soldiers attacked and killed three people near the Siming Gongsuo.

The French police station outside the smaller East Gate was also attacked by scoundrels, who tried to break down the wall. The French soldiers opened fire and attacked them. Several bystanders were indiscriminately killed.

In all, as many as seventeen people were killed and twenty-four wounded in this conflict. They were all outsiders [not from Ningbo], and met with disaster for no reason. People who heard about it felt sorry for them.

Two men from Ningbo were playing dice for money in a certain teahouse when the oil lamps downstairs suddenly fell to the ground. In the confusion that followed, they mistakenly thought a fire had broken out and rushed outside in a panic. The French, who believed the Ningbo *bang* were about to revolt, recklessly opened fire, and more innocent people were killed. All this goes to show that the Ningbo people really did not cause the trouble. It was French cruelty and unreasonableness that led to this tragedy. Alas, alas."

The lack of political or nationalist consciousness in late nineteenth-century Shanghai showed pointedly in local residents' attitude towards the settlement's fiftieth anniversary jubilee. Chinese and Westerners cooperated to organize the anniversary celebrations; wealthy merchants, guilds and associations, as well as the general public, participated enthusiastically. Goodman has noted that Chinese guilds spent far more on these celebrations than the concession authorities—the Fire Brigade procession cost the Shanghai Municipal Council 500 taels, while the guild procession cost several thousand.[30] The harmonious atmosphere is commented on at length in no less than nine *Dianshizhai* sketches (see, for example, Fig. 76).[31] Similar scenes in *Dreams of Prosperity of Shanghai* give the same impression.[32]

These large-scale celebrations involved so many social groups and organizational details, it is likely the arrangements did not proceed so harmoniously as we might be led to believe from the reports. When questions such as Why did Chinese choose to be there? are raised, we may expect complex answers. Different people had different interests and purposes. Leaders of Chinese guilds found the celebrations an excellent occasion to show off their wealth and prestige, and thus gain face, as Goodman has argued. But most Chinese onlookers considered it simply another festival—if a rather spectacular one. In that sense, it was to them a "Chinese" occasion.

The sixtieth birthday of the Empress Dowager followed the next year, but the merchants and people of Shanghai on this occasion showed much less enthusiasm than the previous year. The *Dianshizhai* devoted only one sketch to it and commented that the scope of the celebrations could not be compared to that of the jubilee. An interesting aspect of the jubilee celebrations is that one lantern featured in a sketch carried the inscription "In Anticipation of Ten Thousand Years of Long Life," a reference to the Empress Dowager (Fig. 77).[33] The fiftieth anniversary celebrations and Cixi Taihou's birthday were not connected, but in the eyes of the people of Shanghai they were much the same sort of thing—at least there was no political distinction made between them.

The streets of Shanghai were typically packed with enthusiastic revelers on other similar occasions, such as the birthday of Queen Victoria and Bastille Day. This cooperative attitude does not imply political support for the settlement authorities, but it does demonstrate that in Shanghai a clearly defined national consciousness or collective antagonism towards foreigners had not developed at this point.[34]

"No Chinese or Dogs"—a different story in the nineteenth century

Shanghai's Public Garden has often been cited in twentieth-century nationalist literature for the notorious sign posted at its main gate: "No Chinese or Dogs." To twentieth-century Chinese, this sign justified Chinese hatred of foreign dominance and arrogance. If we look at contemporary sources, however, we see a very different picture.

Considerable research has been published on this topic in the past few years.[35] Here we will focus on certain historical details that help clarify the issue. There is no doubt that restrictions on Chinese entering the Public Garden were in force, but how did they develop? How did contemporary Chinese regard them, and what was the basis of their arguments?

The question of restrictions—and whether or not they were enforced—is not a simple one. There is clear evidence that restrictions, such as those as mentioned in the 1885 petition of Chinese merchants to the Municipal Council existed.[36] But in a Chinese guidebook to Shanghai (1883), we also read the following:

NEW URBAN CULTURE 123

The Public Park is situated on the southern bank of the Baida Bridge. Inside are many types of unusual flowers and trees, most of them from Europe. Reds and purples—I have never seen such fresh and bright colors; I had not even heard of them! As you enter, a large expanse of lawn greets you, and flowers nod everywhere. On Sundays many Westerners come here with their wives and children, some of them strolling hand in hand. Some just sit there chatting, and don't leave until the sun has set. The Public Garden is an oasis of serenity in a bustling city. The gates are strictly controlled and not many Chinese go there.[17]

The author clearly had been to the park himself. He comments that "not many Chinese go there," but the English language press at much the same time carried complaints from foreigners about the number of Chinese using the park,[38] and one might surmise that the restrictions were devised only after such complaints had been published. Even when the restrictions were applied, they seem to not have been absolute. In its reply to a Chinese complaint in 1881, the Municipal Council stated, "The police are authorized to allow entrance to well-dressed natives."[39]

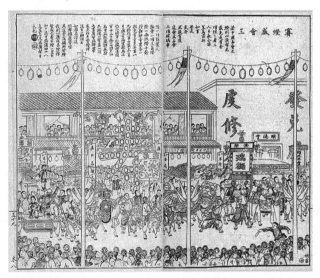

76. The fiftieth anniversary of the founding of the Foreign Settlements (1893). The Chinese characters on the lanterns read "Great Celebrations on the Founding of the Open Port." (See also Fig. 38, which depicts another view of the Jubilee).

Restrictions nevertheless existed. In 1881, in response to further complaints about the large number of Chinese using the park, the Municipal Council changed its previously selective restrictions in favor of more comprehensive ones. From 1881 to 1884 the rules were displayed at the gates of the Public Garden.[40] During this period, the matter was a constant topic of discussion between Chinese merchants and the Municipal Council. In 1885 the Chinese merchants submitted a petition to the Council with four suggestions: (a) that passes should be issued; (b) that certain times be restricted to Westerners, and certain times to Chinese; (c) that the area of the park might be extended towards the Bund; or (d) if that were not possible, that grass and flowers be grown in an area within the Racecourse, which could be used as a park, so long as it did not interfere with the races. Among the signatories to the petition of 1885 were Tang Jinxing, an influential merchant, and Yan Jiajing and Wu Hongyu, who had been educated overseas.

The Municipal Council discussed the petition two days after it was received and agreed to issue passes. It felt, however, that the matter needed to be discussed further with all concerned.[41] Couling asserts that the pass system was instituted in 1883,[42] but it may well have been that the number of Chinese issued passes was severely limited. In any case, the *Shenbao* published more complaints from Chinese in 1888.[43] According to Chinese sources, passes were not issued until 1889.[44] He Guisheng, the editor of the *Shenbao*, wrote of a Chinese friend who worked in a foreign company inviting him to the Public Garden. He asked if there were not restrictions, but his friend said that it didn't matter. He refused, saying that a walk in the park was supposed to be a pleasure, and he didn't want to break the rules. He also notes that after passes were issued, it became possible to visit the park freely. One evening he and a friend went to "drink flower wine" in the Public Garden and stayed from ten o'clock until midnight before returning home.[45]

But the pass system did not last very long. In 1890 the Municipal Council established a Chinese Public Garden, and Chinese were completely banned from the original park.[46]

The arguments put forth by the Chinese merchants in the 1880s were as follows: In their petition of 1885 they argued that the Public Garden should be for the general public, not for the exclusive use of one group. It had been constructed from revenue provided by taxpayers, which included many Chinese. This was a matter of equity. Interestingly, however, they agreed with the reasons Westerners did not want Chinese to have open access. They stated that the Chinese were "a mixed lot" (*liangyou buqi*), and it would not be appropriate to permit admittance to *all* Chinese, only to *certain* Chinese. Thus they suggested the issuance of passes.[47] The *Shenbao* pressed the Municipal

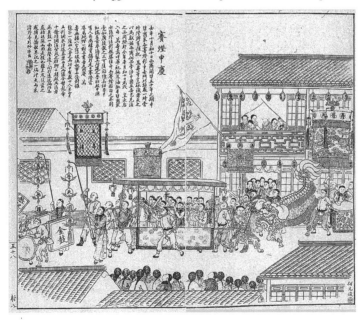

77. The sixtieth birthday of the Empress Dowager (1894). The commentary mentions that the founding of the Foreign Settlements had been celebrated the previous year, and the merchant groups had taken part with great enthusiasm. This year no merchant groups organize any celebration, but the Carpenters Guild in Hongkou organizes a small parade.

NEW URBAN CULTURE 125

Council to determine a quota on the basis of the size and capacity of the Public Garden. They did not suggest who should be counted in the quota, except to say that it should not be limited to rich merchants. The editors of the *Shenbao* for obvious reasons did not want settlement literati to be excluded. The last words of the editorial were: "We know the Westerners are by no means ill-disposed towards Chinese. Since there is a way to satisfy both sides, what need is there to continue excluding Chinese from the garden?" He Guisheng also took the view that it really was not feasible to allow access to all Chinese.[48]

The Chinese merchants and Chinese literati shared this view. If there were opposing views, we have no record of them in the most likely sources. The question of the pass was postponed. In 1888 the *Shenbao* published a letter from a reader pointing out that the Public Garden was not public, and this was unfair because Chinese taxpayers contributed to its construction and maintenance—as the 1885 petition had also argued. But this writer had another suggestion: Chinese could collect funds for the construction of a Chinese Public Garden, in which a rostrum could be built to proclaim imperial edicts on such virtues as loyalty, filial piety, frugality and so on. This letter was printed in the place usually occupied by the editorial, and the editor added a comment to the effect that the language of the letter was strong but not unreasonable. He went on to say that when Westerners came to China, Chinese did not dare interfere with their activities, but when Chinese went to the Old Gold Mountain [San Francisco] or the New Gold Mountain [Melbourne], they were discriminated against and even killed, but anger (like that expressed in the letter) was not going to help matters.[49]

No further letters appeared on this theme after the passes were issued in 1889. In 1890, however, a new argument was presented in an article in the *Shenbao*. The author once again argued that the Public Garden had been constructed with public money, thus the name. Chinese had repeatedly demanded permission to enter it, and the pass system was introduced. This in itself was a good thing, and many Chinese went there. However, especially on a summer's evening, some took prostitutes there; others would break branches or pick flowers, and then discard them on the ground. An incident of this type had happened in 1888 in the Xuyuan, a Chinese private garden open to the public. A dozen peonies, which the garden's owner had carefully cultivated, were about to bloom. Someone picked off eleven of them, destroying the whole effect. "So one cannot blame Westerners for not daring to allow [Chinese] to enter." The article went on to note that some Chinese were disorderly and caused trouble. He concluded that gardens should be divided into those for upper-class people, and those for the lower classes.[50]

In the 1880s the access question was based on the fact that taxpayers maintained the garden and so all taxpayers should have access to it. There was no suggestion that the Public Garden was on Chinese land and therefore Chinese should of course be admitted. The issue was clearly one of class, not race. The literati and merchants did not object to Westerners restricting lower-class Chinese so long as people like themselves were not also excluded.[51]

After the emergence of nationalism in the early twentieth century, the Shanghai Public Garden became the most well-known example of national humiliation; it has continued to serve as a an example of outrage for nationalist education by people of various political persuasions ever since.

Admiration for things foreign

Some people developed a sense of admiration towards the West, especially the Western humanitarian tradition. While the practice of "taking a bride by force" was common in Shanghai, and the *Dianshizhai* reported two such attempted kidnappings in the settlement, both cases were foiled by the intervention of a Westerner or the police (Fig. 78).[52] The treatment Western hospitals gave their patients also left a favorable impression, and led the *Dianshizhai* to comment, "Westerners value highly benevolence and righteousness."[53] In 1889 the *Dianshizhai* featured a missionary who had run a school for deaf, dumb, and blind children in Bombay and had come to Shanghai to establish a similar school. The sketch shows the doors and the windows of the school surrounded by curious onlookers.[54] In 1884 another report covered an incident in a silk filature. Women workers were queuing to receive their wages when one of them lost a decorative hairpin in the crush. She became so upset she began to sob loudly. When the foreign foreman heard about it, he paid her the cost of replacing the hairpin in addition to paying her wages, and he even arranged for someone to escort her home. "Westerners, it can be said, are good at practicing what they preach."[55] These instances of respect and helpfulness towards the weak or disabled made a strong impression on the Chinese.

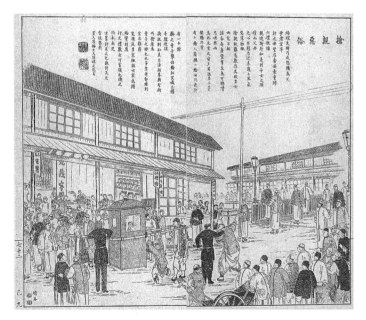

78. Stealing a bride by force (1885). About a dozen men are involved in carrying off a sedan chair with an unwilling bride. A child, the bride's brother, tries to stop them. This scene occurred in the French Concession, and the police were able to intervene.

Chinese employed by Westerners often praised them for their fairness and honesty. But in 1888 the *Dianshizhai* carried a report about a time bomb that had exploded on a steamship in mid-ocean, enroute from London to Australia. The man who had hidden the bomb had done so to claim 80,000 ounces of silver from an insurance company. This caused quite a sensation and horrified the Chinese: "Even someone with the slightest conscience would never think of doing such a thing. Now we know that there are treacherous and malicious people among Westerners, ten times worse than the Chinese. Those people who scamper around foreign firms are always saying that Westerners are upright and trustworthy, but what they say is based on only what they have seen."⁵⁶ This commentary shows fairly clearly how Westerners were seen by the Chinese working for them in Shanghai.

Most Chinese who had dealings with the foreigners—cooks, maidservants, rickshaw pullers and even compradors—had little in the way of Chinese education. As Liang Qichao put it, "The scholars cannot speak foreign languages, and those who can speak foreign languages are not scholars."⁵⁷ In 1897 the *Dianshizhai* carried a note on compradors: "Compradors for the foreign firms of Shanghai are generally illiterate. They have to ask other people to read and write their correspondence for them. They even have to ask other people to manage their family accounts. The reason is that when they were young they learned foreign languages and never gained familiarity with Chinese characters" (Fig. 79).⁵⁸ In fact, most compradors had only a bare smattering of English. Crash courses in English abounded in Shanghai, and advertisements for these are common enough in the pages of the *Shenbao*.⁵⁹ Compradors and some servants spoke "pidgin English," and foreigners in Shanghai needed some time to learn to understand it.⁶⁰

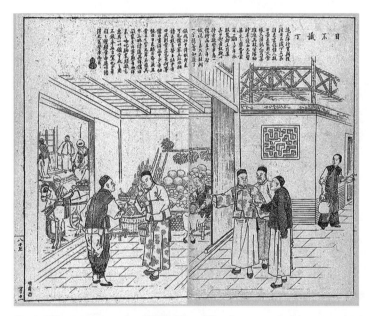

79. An illiterate comprador (1897). Pretending he can read, this comprador has mistaken a request for Western dogs for an invitation to dinner. The servant corrects him, to his great embarrassment.

Relations between Chinese and foreigners in Shanghai may have been harmonious, but there can be no doubt that the foreign authorities were "dominant." Some Chinese tried to ally themselves with this dominant group and relied on its power and prestige to lord it over other Chinese.

Employees in foreign firms, and even servants in foreign households, considered themselves a cut above the rest. The *Dianshizhai* reports of a steward in a certain foreign household who refused to pay the fare asked by a rickshaw driver,⁶¹ and of a young servant, impeccably dressed and smoking a cigarette, who bought a watermelon for his Western master. The peddler called him "Mister Boy" (*xizai xiangsheng*), whereupon he became very angry: "You just call me Mister, there's no need to add 'boy'!" After a few further exchanges, the young servant beat him for his insolence. This attitude on the part of servants was also mentioned in books written by Westerners. On occasion servants would go hunting with their masters in the countryside around Shanghai. They would refuse to pay fairly for supplies bought from the peasants, and threatened that, if they were not willing to accept the amount offered, the Western masters would shoot them.[62]

The arrogance and abusiveness of carriage drivers was especially notorious. This occupation appeared as a result of Western influence. Drivers' working conditions were vastly better than those of ordinary workers, and their sense of superiority led them to bully the weak and the poor. The carriage drivers of Shanghai quickly developed a bad reputation.[63] In the *Dianshizhai* their arrogance towards poor people and their insulting attitude towards women get critical notice:[64]

> Recently we have heard a lot of news about carriage drivers in the International Settlement causing trouble. Although they are strictly restrained by the police, alas, their perverse nature is already formed, and they are unwilling to reform. We often see carriage drivers, holding their reins high, come barreling through the ten *li* of foreign settlement. Whenever a rickshaw crosses their path, the rickshaw must give way. If there is the slightest hesitation, they urge their horses on, brandishing their whips, and even knocking over pedestrians. They then take their whips and viciously lash at them."[65] (Fig. 80)

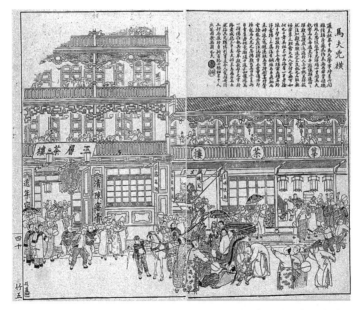

80. An accident in Nanjing Road (1892). A carriage driver has knocked over a middle-aged woman and a child. He screams at them and tries to beat them up but is restrained by onlookers. The sketch shows two teahouses—the one on the left is called the "Three-Story Teahouse."

In 1884 the *Dianshizhai* featured certain rickshaw-pullers, who were happy to have foreigners ride in their rickshaws. "Everyone is a customer. But when they carry Westerners, they really leap."⁶⁶ The rickshaw pullers were happy to have Western passengers, of course, because they could expect a larger fare from them—even though some Westerners refused to pay the fare requested.⁶⁷

To these people, the material culture of the West appeared very attractive. They happily accepted foreign culture, even if at a fairly superficial level. As we can see from the *Dianshizhai*, Shanghai residents quickly accepted horse racing, theaters, Western restaurants, and other forms of amusement, and developed a taste for keeping up with the fashions. Even the word "fashion" (*shimao*) evolved from a derogatory term to one of high praise. At the very beginning of this process of acculturation, even prostitutes shunned being seen as fashionable,⁶⁸ but it was not long before the dandies feared nothing more than to be thought unfashionable.

Tailors specializing in Western clothing, known as "*hong bang* tailors,"⁶⁹ worked in Shanghai at least as early as 1889. Generally speaking, people in Shanghai were conservative in their dress, preferring traditional Chinese clothing, even if the material they used was imported.⁷⁰ We can see from the *Dianshizhai* that even fashion-conscious types still wore long robes of silk and satin.⁷¹ Compradors also wore traditional Chinese clothing.⁷² As Yen-p'ing Hao noted, "Many of them liked the Chinese style, such as the long gown of blue silk and the closely fitting black cap on the shaven head."⁷³ Some Chinese who had returned to China from overseas, such as the interpreter for the Municipal Council, Yan Yongjing, soon changed their clothing to the Chinese style.⁷⁴ The main exceptions were some particularly daring prostitutes, who occasionally wore Western dresses (Fig. 81).⁷⁵ The only Chinese man in the *Dianshizhai* wearing a Western-style suit was Zhan Wu, the "Giant of Anhui" (Fig. 82). He had traveled in Europe and America as a sideshow attraction for three years, and his clothing must be considered atypical.⁷⁶ Despite their Chinese clothing, Shanghai dandies expressed their modernity by smoking cigarettes, wearing dark glasses, and carrying an umbrella (regardless of the weather). These affectations were satirized in the *Dianshizhai* commentaries, and are clearly visible in many of the illustrations.

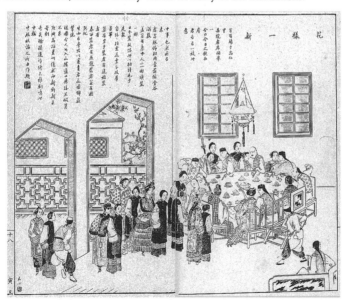

81. A banquet attended by courtesans (1888). The courtesan (*changsan tangzi*) in the middle of the sketch (eighth from the left) is wearing Western clothes; her bound feet can be seen beneath the skirt. The man fourth from the left is in typical playboy attire, even wearing his sunglasses indoors.

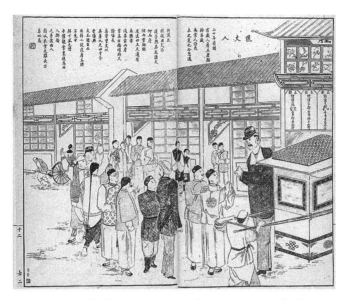

82. The Giant of Anhui (1886). This is the only example of a Chinese man wearing a Western suit in the *Dianshizhai*. The commentator disapproves of the way he earned a living: "What a pity! All he can really do was eat. He is no more than a source of amusement for Westerners, and he relies on them for his clothes and food. Although he is tall, what other use does he have?"

Western food, apart from any intrinsic appeal it may have had, was also seen as fashionable.[77] Western bands were also considered the height of fashion. The *Dianshizhai* ran a story in 1886 about a Cantonese merchant who hired a Western band to pave the way for a religious procession welcoming the spirits to the Temple of Tianhou, the Queen of Heaven. The writers of the *Dianshizhai* ridiculed him, noting that no man with any education would have conceived such a vulgarity (Fig. 83).[78] The custom caught on, however. Even well-off families, if they could afford it, hired Western-style bands on such occasions as weddings, whether or not the music played was suitable to the occasion.[79]

A new set of cultural values took shape in Shanghai, initially at the popular level, based on a desire to emulate the West. Some imported goods like dark glasses, cigarettes, and so on became status symbols. The national consciousness of the literati, even if not modern nationalism in the strict sense, was much stronger and more clearly defined than that of the general population. Some elites, such as those who opposed the Self-strengthening Movement completely rejected Western culture in all its forms. Others were anxious to "learn from the West," but their aims were to bolster the "wealth and power" of China. But this was quite different from the fairly uncritical embrace of things Western by the general population living in the foreign settlements of Shanghai.

83. Western music in a Chinese religious ceremony (1886). "Westerners use music to accompany everything. According to what I have seen, this includes military parades, funerals, the horse races held in the spring and autumn, and officials arriving at the quay to take up a new position. Yi-yi-ya-ya—it is quite pleasant to the ear. The tempo and the rhythm are like the movement of ten thousand feet, like beating time with clappers. Sometimes people with the means and curiosity in this commercial port hire such performers. This year, at the Double Nine Festival, Cantonese merchants resident in Shanghai participated in the procession to the Temple of the Queen of Heaven. Apart from the usual banners, gongs, fans, and umbrellas, they hired a Western band to accompany the procession. Anyone with any education would never have thought of anything so vulgar."

2. Concepts of health and the human body

Exposed to superior public facilities in the settlements, such as the improved drinking water, people grew to have higher expectations with regard to hygiene. The appearance of Western-style hospitals also encouraged such expectations, but in addition directly challenged certain basic philosophical and moral concepts.

Clinics and disease

The introduction of Western medicine into China gave rise to a reconceptualization of disease. This can be seen from an analysis of the types of illnesses for which Chinese patients sought treatment in Western hospitals.

The earliest and most popular Western hospitals in Shanghai were the Renji and Tongren hospitals. The first was established by William Lockhart in 1844 near the Chinese city, and moved to the International Settlement in 1847. In 1861, it again moved to Shandong Road, and in 1870 changed its name to "Chinese Hospital of Shandong Road."[80] Tongren Hospital, known in English as St. Luke's, was founded in 1866 under the auspices of the American Episcopal Church Mission.[81] Renji Hospital was particularly well thought of and is often mentioned in the writings of the literati. For example, in his *Miscellaneous Notes on Travels in Shanghai*, Ge Yuanxu comments, "In the International Settlement foreigners have established the Renji Hospital; they use foreign methods [there] to treat illness; they are particularly skilled at traumatology. Since this hospital was established, they have saved innumerable lives."[82] Wang Tao also mentioned Renji Hospital and the outstanding skill of its surgeon Dr. James Henderson.[83]

According to Renji Hospital statistics, the number of patients increased from 12,250 in 1869 to 14,241 in 1877, then to 17,252 in 1880–1881 and 76,000 in 1897–1898.[84] When compared to the population of the settlements at the time—76,713 in 1870, 110,009 in 1880, and 352,050 in 1900—these numbers are considerable.[85]

Emergencies, accidents and suicides

Emergencies were more often than not sent to Renji Hospital, located in the busiest area of Shanghai. The *Dianshizhai* tells of a woman servant in a brothel in the Beifuli area of the British Concession who got into a fight with a knife sharpener. She stabbed him with one of his own knives, and the wounded man was rushed directly to Renji.[86] Another case involved a brothel madam injured in a fire, the result of an exploded oil lamp; she, too, was sent to Renji Hospital for treatment.[87]

It was well known that a stomach pump could be used to save the lives of those who had swallowed opium. In 1885 the *Dianshizhai* provided a detailed description of the procedure, which concluded, "Western doctors who know this technique have spread it widely and saved many lives; they should be treated as living buddhas."[88] Another story concerned two merchants, Mr. Zhu from Yangzhou and Mr. Lü from Anhui. Their business had failed, and they resolved to commit suicide by swallowing opium in a brothel. They were discovered by a servant and sent to Renji Hospital. It was too late for Mr. Lü, but Mr. Zhu was saved.[89] Similar stories are to be found in the *Shenbao*.[90]

Emergency cases in the Hongkou area were sent to the Tongren Hospital. The *Dianshizhai* tells of two coolies robbed in a small inn on Tiantong Road in the American Concession. Each suspected the other, and a fight ensued, with one of them getting seriously wounded. The innkeeper sent the wounded man to Tongren Hospital.[91]

Eye disease

Sufferers from eye disease did not traditionally seek medical treatment, but this was another area in which Western surgery was noticeably effective, and attracted many patients (Fig. 84).[92] Dr. Henderson of Renji Hospital performed surgical procedures and relieved many cases of blindness.[93] Chinese doctors could not offer such treatment, and Henderson became famous for it.

Treatment in Western hospitals was provided free to the poor. In 1873 an advertisement placed in the *Shenbao* by Tiren Hospital mentioned this free treatment, and also that those with money could enjoy medical care in the hospital's clean wards. A Western specialist was available to treat eye disease, and Chinese interpreters were provided. The advertisement even invited Chinese doctors who wished to learn about Western medicine to visit the hospital.[94]

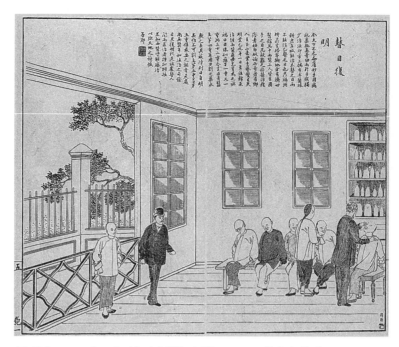

84. Sight restored to the blind (1892). A Western eye clinic in Fuzhou.

The Shanghai literati liked to compare Western doctors to the miracle workers of the Chinese tradition, Bian Que and Hua Tuo. The *Illustrated Guide to Shanghai* contained a few lines of verse in praise of Western hospitals: "Broken limbs can be repaired as if by magic. Using three fingers to restore to health can certainly not achieve this. Hua Tuo came under suspicion because he wanted to open Cao Cao's skull to cure his headache. Had Hua been alive today, his method would have been accepted."[95]

Traditional view of the human body

Surgery contravened one of the most fundamental principles of Chinese morality. One's body was bequeathed by one's parents, and its integrity had to be preserved. From a philosophical point of view, the human body was seen as an integral whole.[96] The idea of surgically removing part of the body could not be accepted within the framework of traditional Chinese medicine. To be sure, individual surgeons like Bian Que and Hua Tuo had been active in traditional China, but surgery remained so foreign to the Chinese worldview that as late as 1947–1948 a theory emerged that perhaps Bian Que had come from India.[97] Unschuld has also written about "the possibly legendary figure of Hua Tuo (110–207), whose successes in surgical practice are reminiscent of the reported achievements by the Indian physician Jivaka. He, too, had no successor to carry on his art; and frequent reference to Hua Tuo in Chinese and Western secondary literature as an early example of surgery and anesthesiology present a distorted picture of the actual significance of such practices in China."[98] Individual achievements in surgery were not accepted into the mainstream of Chinese medicine, and later generations were to remember these men as miracle workers rather than contributors to the corpus of medical science.

Whether the moral aspect or the philosophical view was more influential is immaterial; the paramount importance of the integrity of the human body was universally accepted. The cruelest capital punishment was the "death of a thousand cuts," in which the victim was put to death by the slow process of slicing the limbs and torso before decapitation.[99] The most common method of capital punishment was decapitation, but since preservation of the integrity of the body was a matter of major concern, strangulation, a slower and more painful death, was regarded as preferable.

Given the historical background and cultural differences, it was inevitable that conflict would occur between Chinese and Westerners in the area of medical treatment. As early as the 1860s, Dr. James Henderson, a surgeon resident in Shanghai, came up against a predictable Chinese reaction. "One man was unafraid of dying, and refused Henderson's advice that amputation alone would save him; the victim and his friends insisted that if he were left alive with just one leg he would be useless."[100]

The Chinese view on autopsy

Even by the late 1880s, the practice of postmortem examination was not accepted by the vast majority of people in Shanghai. In 1888 a foreigner died in the Astor Hotel in the Hongkou district. Doctors performed an autopsy to determine the cause of death. The *Dianshizhai* reported the matter with strong disapproval and incomprehension (Fig. 85):

> Western law does not allow physical mutilation. Even the most heinous criminals are not dismembered. However, the practice of dissection has not yet been forbidden. They say that after death, the body is not to be cherished, but may be abandoned. So they are not particular about the principle of the body and soul resting in peace. Moreover they claim that by investigating the disease of one particular person, they can deduce ways of treating other people with a similar disease. So the body of the dead person is made use of, from the crown to the heel, in the interests of others. Mo Zi was a heterodox philosopher, and he may have been willing to rub smooth his whole body from the crown to the head [so as to benefit the world]. But is this really in accordance with the wishes of the deceased? Moreover, some people die from a particular sickness while others with the same sickness do not, and many people die in much the same way, but the causes of their illness are in fact different. . . . But they use a cleaver to force someone already dead, and innocent of any crime, to undergo the cruel punishment of dismemberment. So it can be seen that for the main part their skills are vulgar and their hands are vicious."[101]

In 1891 the Mixed Court could not come to a conclusion in a similar case. A Chinese had been severely beaten by a French policeman in the French Concession. He was taken to hospital, where he died. The magistrate of Shanghai, Lu Yuanding, the English and French assessors from the Mixed Court, and the French consul went to the hospital to investigate the matter. Two Chinese eyewitnesses testified that they had seen the French policeman beat the man to death. The magistrate ordered Chinese coroners to make an examination of the body. They reported a wound to the left temple, and since according to the *Instructions to Coroners*[102] the temple was a vital point, the blow to the temple must have been the cause of death. The French doctor argued that this was insufficient evidence, and argued for a full autopsy. The Chinese magistrate absolutely refused. The victim was Chinese, and the cause of his death should be determined in the Chinese way. It was unthinkable to cut up his body. The investigation reached a stalemate, which was not resolved even after the magistrate had retired from his post. When he retired, the county gentry gave him farewell banquets, and merchants in shops along the route out of Shanghai offered cups of wine in his honor. The *Dianshizhai* applauded his refusal to compromise on this case, calling it a case of redressing the rights of the victim.[103]

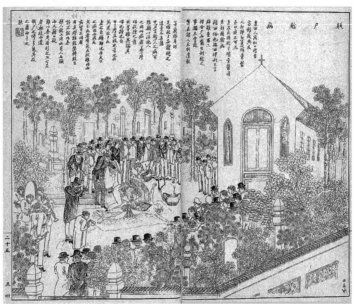

85. An autopsy (1888). After the sudden death of a foreigner, an autopsy was ordered to determine the cause of death. A Westerner is shown taking photographs of the scene with a camera. The sketch seems to be based on the author's imagination. The commentary stresses the writer's disgust and incomprehension at such an uncivilized practice.

Surgery

Despite cultural and philosophical reservations about surgery, its obvious effectiveness made it acceptable to many Chinese, especially those suffering from tumors, or women having difficulties in labor (Figs. 86, 87, 88). There are three stories in the *Dianshizhai* about people who came to Tongren Hospital in search of treatment, some of them from areas outside Shanghai. In 1885 a woman came from Anhui to have a tumor surgically removed (Fig. 89).

> There was a Western woman doctor by the name of Li Ying. Her original specialty was gynecology, but she also had some competence in general surgery. A woman from Anhui suffering from an immense tumor went to Tongren Hospital in Hongkou for treatment. The woman doctor palpated it, and said it could be cured. She took out a sharp knife and cut it off. Then the doctor applied medicine, and a few months later the patient was cured. When they weighed the tumor it was found to be a quarter of the woman's entire bodyweight. When the Chinese doctors heard about this, they could only click their tongues and bow their heads.[104]

86. A mother seeks treatment for her deformed child (1895). "This spring, a woman came to live in the Changfa Inn in the International Settlement. She spoke with a Shanzuo [Shandong] accent. Some time earlier she had given birth to a child of very strange appearance. . . . She had heard about the Tongren Hospital in the American Concession, where the Western doctors are skilled in the arts of Bian Lu and can cure strange ailments. So carrying her child, she went by sedan chair to seek treatment. The child was first examined by a female doctor, who determined that the five sense organs were normal, but on top of the head was yet another head; the two heads looking rather like a bottle gourd. The upper head, although it could not drink milk, had normal ears, eyes, mouth and nose. She reported this to the Director of the Hospital, Doctor Wen, who invited all the Chinese and Western doctors in Shanghai to come to the hospital to discuss this matter. The woman asked that the child's upper head be cut off, but the doctors felt that since the child was not yet a month old, its strength was insufficient. If they operated, there would be concern for the child's life. They asked her to wait a while longer, since at that time they could not treat the child by surgery. There was nothing the woman could do, and she sadly returned home."

In 1895 a similar operation was reported at the Simon Women's and Children's Hospital. After a description of the tumor, the report continues,

> She [a Western woman doctor] examined the tumor in great detail and found it was not incurable. Some days ago she asked all the Western doctors in Shanghai for their opinions; they then put the woman on a mechanical chair, and used medicine to make her drowsy. Then they cut the tumor out with sharp knives. Afterwards they sprayed water in her face, to wake her up again. They weighed her, and now she weighed only 70 to 80 lbs. So the tumor they cut out must have weighed 150 to 160 lbs. After it was removed, the woman could walk, sit, and get around. She had been relieved of a heavy burden, and was extremely happy. According to the Western doctors, a tumor of this size has never been seen before, so they preserved it in medicinal water and sent it to a major hospital in the West as material for investigation.[105]

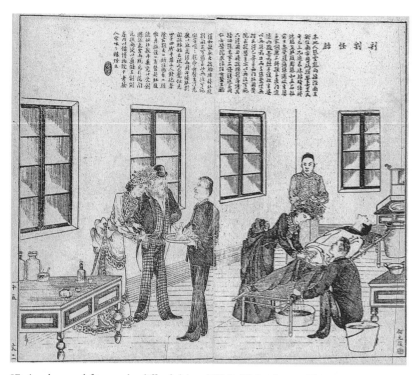

87. An abnormal fetus and a difficult labor (1896). "A local man, Zhang Yunbiao, was versed in the arts of the King of Huainan [the art of making bean curd]. He lived at Yanmatou, in the southern part of the city. His wife was nearly thirty when a 'pearl-fetus' began secretly to grow within her. When the time came for it to be born, her stomach was extremely swollen, like a five-picul melon. A few days ago she suddenly felt a great pain in her abdomen, and Zhang called the midwife. She could do nothing about it and left. Zhang was in a panic and had no choice but to go the Ximen Foreign Hospital for assistance. They also said that nothing could be done; all they could do was to cut off the baby's head with a knife. They then told them to go home. Zhang could see that the situation was serious, so he sent his wife to the Tongren Women's Hospital in search of a cure. A woman doctor examined her, and said that they would have to cut open her abdomen to remove the child's body. Zhang was desperate by this stage and had no choice but to follow their advice. The woman doctor first administered anesthesia, then cut open the woman's abdomen with a knife. It was obvious that the child was already dead, but it had four arms and four legs, like two people embracing. Apart from the head, which had already been cut off, there was yet another head, but only one body. The doctor sewed up her abdomen again and applied medicine, but her wounds had been too deep, and her vital energy had left her. She died in the hospital. We have heard that the dead child has been preserved in medicinal water, and kept inside the operation theatre. It will be placed in a museum for research."

88. A midwife in the Chinese city (1885). When the placenta remained in the womb after the birth of the child, the midwife removed it by hand, but ruptured the woman's intestines, resulting in her death. The sketch shows the woman's family beating the midwife.

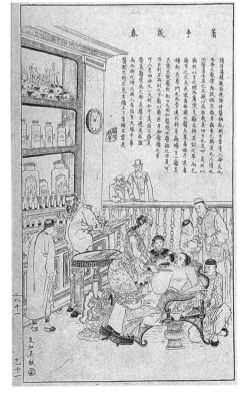

89. A surgical operation to remove a tumor (1885).

NEW URBAN CULTURE

Belief in the different nature of Chinese and Western bodies

Both the literati and the general populace believed that Chinese medicine was most effective in dealing with internal disorders. Many Chinese believed that Western bodies were different from those of the Chinese. As Wang Tao put it, "What is effective for Westerners may not be effective for Chinese. This is because their internal organs differ in thickness."[106] Ge Yuanxu also noted, "Foreign medicine is good for treating foreigners, but not for treating Chinese. The fact that people's bodies are different in nature has been recorded in traditional Chinese medical works as numerous as hairs on an ox. Medicine which can be used to treat people from the north cannot be used on those from the south. Dispositions may be strong or weak, and the nature of medicine can be gentle or violent. The natural disposition of Westerners is quite different. If medicine is not sufficiently violent, it cannot cure them. Chinese will seek treatment by Western methods only for various types of surgery. For internal ailments, they do not dare to try it."[107] An example of this thinking, on another level, was that many Chinese prostitutes (with the exception of the Cantonese salt water sisters, who serviced sailors) refused to accept Western customers (Fig. 90). This was not for moral reasons, but because they believed Western bodies were different.[108]

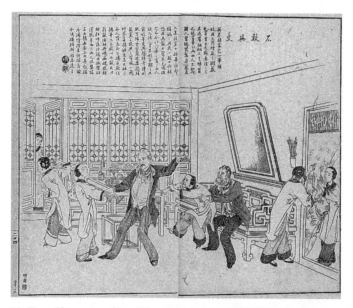

90. Two Chinese-speaking Westerners in a brothel (1897). The prostitutes are shown running away—one to a police station to seek protection.

Examples recorded in the *Dianshizhai* show people going to Western hospitals for surgical treatment, for childbirth, or emergencies. There is not a single case of Chinese going to a hospital for treatment of an internal disorder. One story relates how a Chinese went to a Western doctor for treatment of a disease that had proved difficult to diagnose, but this was only after all else had failed. A scholar-doctor from Anhui, Hu Xiaofeng, had a son about seventeen or eighteen years old. The boy had a morbid fear of noise and would sometimes even lose consciousness on being exposed to it. Hu, himself a doctor of some repute, could not diagnose the nature of his son's complaint. In 1891 he took him to a Western doctor, but he, too, had no success.[109]

There may well have been some Chinese in Shanghai who used Western medicine for internal ailments, but I have not found any mention of it in the press. The successes of pharmaceutical drugs were not so spectacular as surgery and perhaps were not newsworthy. Western drugs were not widely used, but that is not to say that they were not used at all. The first Western-style pharmacy in Shanghai was the Great Britain Pharmacy, which had opened already in the mid-nineteenth century. Several of its employees formed their own pharmacy in 1887, called the Chinese-Western Pharmacy, on one of the busiest roads in Shanghai, Fuzhou Road.[110] The *Dianshizhai* carried advertisements for this pharmacy and published congratulatory calligraphic messages from Li Hongzhang and Weng Tonghe, the Imperial Grand Tutor.[111] We have no material at our disposal to determine just what sort of people were customers of this shop. The fact that famous Chinese were asked to show their support, and that advertisements for the pharmacy contained such thoroughly traditional sentiments such as "Apricot Forest Blossoms in Spring" and "Hua Tuo and Bian Que Have Come Back to Life," show that a real attempt was made to attract Chinese customers.

Towards the end of the nineteenth century, Western pharmacies advertised their wares, giving Western medicines Chinese names, so as to make them more acceptable and understandable to the Chinese. They also hired Chinese shop assistants to explain the use of the medicines to customers. A *Shenbao* editorial of 1895, "On the Popularity of Western Medicine in China," noted that even then very few Chinese frequented Western pharmacies. But once books on Western pharmaceuticals had been translated into Chinese, and once pharmacies adopted the promotional methods mentioned above, Western medicine gradually became accepted.[112]

Introduction of Jennerian inoculation against smallpox

In broad terms, the theory of Chinese medicine was directed towards the preventing the development of disharmony and therefore illness. It stressed the interaction and organic unity of man and his environment, a holistic attitude towards the human body, the theory of the proper functioning of the five phases and the harmony of yin and yang. It followed that if one's diet was inadequate or lifestyle unhealthy, medicine should be taken before any illness developed.

The Chinese concept of strengthening the body against nonspecific diseases, or regulating the body as a preventive concept, is different in nature from Western immunization, which is also preventive. Immunization against smallpox had been experimented with in China, but did not become part of mainstream medicine and was generally ignored. Needham has pointed out that "the practice of smallpox inoculation begins to be documented in China in the Ming period, from the beginning of the sixteenth century A.D. onwards, that is, from a time much earlier than any accounts of it in other parts of the world. Moreover it was accompanied by a tenacious tradition that inoculation had first been introduced towards the end of the tenth century A.D. by wandering Taoist healers from Szechuan."[113]

Angela Leung argues, however, that this "tenacious tradition" is not reliable. "Although the technique of variolation was promoted in some Ming and Qing medical texts and practiced by private doctors, no known examples exist of Chinese public or private health clinics offering the procedure. Clinics offering Jennerian vaccination emerged only from the 1830s on."[114]

The degree to which traditional inoculation was actually practiced in late imperial China, or how effective it was, must remain unclear. It did not seem to be widespread; indeed, two Qing emperors died of smallpox.[115] In popular practice, people prayed to the "Goddess of Smallpox" to ward off the disease.[116] Macpherson notes that the Shanghai daotai Tu Zongying issued an order "forbidding the practice of [Chinese-style] inoculation . . . Henderson commented that 'the Taotai considers it of the greatest importance that this foreign method of vaccination be adopted in China.'" This suggests that Chinese-style inoculation was in fact practiced in Shanghai at the time, but was considered (by the daotai at least) inferior to Western-style vaccination. By this time Jennerian smallpox inoculation was regarded by the Chinese public (including the literati) as a practice of Western medicine that had been introduced to China.[117]

The first attempt to the introduce smallpox vaccination in modern times was undertaken in 1805 by the East India Company's senior surgeon Dr. Pearson. It was unsuccessful because the vaccine he had brought was too old and had lost its effectiveness.[118] By the 1870s, however, the effectiveness of the vaccine and its degree of acceptance by the Chinese is reflected in the numbers of Chinese being vaccinated: 1,200 at Gutzlaff Hospital and approximately the same number at the Municipal Depot.[119] The Chinese gentry and the charitable halls now also offered a free smallpox inoculation service.[120] Some public-minded Chinese with Western medical training also established free vaccination depots. The *Dianshizhai* gives an account of Cen Chunhua, who worked in a Western hospital. After having discussed the matter with foreign friends in medical circles, he established a smallpox clinic on Nanjing Road, where he administered vaccinations according to the latest methods, free of change. The sketch in the *Dianshizhai* shows his rooms full of women bringing their children to be vaccinated (Fig. 91).[121]

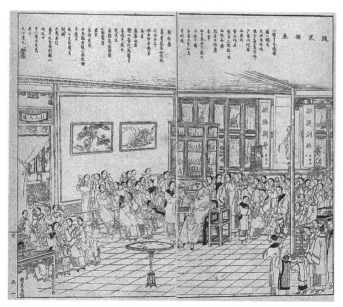

91. The Smallpox Inoculation Clinic established by Cen Chunhua on Nanjing Road. Despite its Chinese origins, smallpox inoculation was regarded as a practice of Western medicine.

The number of people seeking inoculation against smallpox in Shanghai continued to grow, but so did the number of deaths as a result of smallpox: 223 in 1891, 184 in 1893, 316 in 1896, 183 in 1899, 434 in 1904, 8063 in 1907.[122] The population growth over the same period went from 171,950 in 1890 to 501,541 in 1907.[123] These figures may be the result of more effective methods of keeping statistics, as Macpherson remarks, but the incomplete nature of such statistics must make any conclusions tentative. Macpherson also notes a lack of clarity as to who funded the service. Throughout the 1880s and 1890s advertisements and articles in the *Shenbao* continuously urged people to get vaccinated. For example, one *Shenbao* editorial in 1895 entitled "We Urge Families to have Their Children Inoculated against Smallpox—There Is No Need for Suspicion or Fear," explained the need for inoculation. If people still caught smallpox even after inoculation, this was due to technical reasons, not because there was any inherent danger in vaccination, and so on. Despite some reluctance, the number of people who came to accept the value of vaccination continued to grow.[124]

The crisis of Chinese medicine

The introduction and success of Western medicine seriously affected the confidence of Chinese regarding traditional Chinese medicine, and this was a cause of special concern among the literati. With the growing acceptance of Western medicine, practitioners of Chinese medicine faced new demands for professional accreditation. The Imperial Medical Academy, which conducted examinations, had been established in the first half of the seventh century. But this academy trained only doctors who served the imperial court or the government and did not have responsibility for standardizing medical knowledge or for exercising control over the medical profession.[125] Physicians trained by the Imperial Medical Academy made up only a tiny portion of the total number of practitioners who served the general population. For all intents and purposes there was no system of registration among medical practitioners. Lacking professional examinations and registration meant that many practicing physicians were in fact unqualified, a point noted by Dyer Ball.[126]

As Western medicine became better understood and accepted, complaints against traditional Chinese medicine increased. The *Dianshizhai* carried several reports about quacks.[127] Two of these refer to events in Shanghai. The first deals with a case of misdiagnosis which resulted in the death of the patient (Fig. 92).[128] The other concerns an apothecary in the International Settlement who misinterpreted a prescription, resulting in the near death of the man who took the medicine.[129] The sketches which accompany these stories show angry crowds storming the doctor's home or the chemist's shop, tearing down signboards, destroying furniture, and so on. The editorial comment is also scathing in its attack on the doctors or pharmacists who treated human life with such scant respect. Occasional misdiagnoses or other mistakes were to be expected, but each scandal further shook confidence in Chinese medicine, and this was a matter of some consequence.

Late nineteenth century Shanghai seemed to attract an inordinate number of charlatans. Some made a living by learning a few prescriptions by heart and thus giving the impression they had some medical knowledge.[130] In 1895 the *Dianshizhai* noted,

> In recent times medical practice degenerates by the day. All those who have read a few rhymed medical prescriptions go out into the world bragging and boasting. They are not able to cure even one in a hundred. Should they by chance have a success or two, they propagate this fact widely, enthusiastically claiming extraordinary skill. This is the reason we see so many commendatory signboards praising them. They do not realize that knowledgeable people look at them askance, and some even snigger behind their backs."[131]

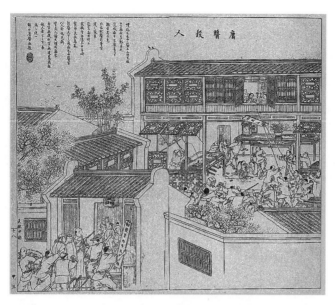

92. Angry crowds storm a Chinese clinic (1884). "These doctors treat human life like a child's game. This is intolerable to human feeling and the principles of Heaven. Military officials and executioners have no descendants—this is because they kill people. Now I want to add—neither should quack doctors have descendants."

There were reputable Chinese doctors in Shanghai, to be sure, such as Chen Duqing, whose fame was such that even the magistrate of Shanghai presented him with congratulatory scrolls and calligraphy engraved on wood, praising his skills.[132] Chinese doctors of only mediocre skill abounded, however, and their medical ethics were practically nonexistent. In 1890 the *Dianshizhai* recorded the following case:

> Doctors in Shanghai, should they be called to visit a patient in his home, are sure to postpone until evening before they go. They make a cursory examination, flick their sleeves and leave. The results of their bungling are indeed serious. . . . A certain doctor had rough knowledge of pulse diagnosis. He bragged that he was a famous physician, but often treated human life with scant respect. Patients feared him as if he were a tiger. They did not dare consult him. One day a wealthy family asked him to pay a home call, but he did not arrive until deep in the night. He had barely sat down before adopting an air of great busyness, taking off his hat and wiping away his sweat. In a great hurry he took the patient's pulse, wrote a prescription and left. He forgot, however, to take his hat. The patient realized he had cheated him, so he hid the hat. The doctor sent his sedan chair porter to collect the hat, but they said they didn't have it. The porter said that the doctor had left it near a red vase in the guestroom—how could they say they didn't have it? The patient said that seeing the doctor had been so busy the previous evening, perhaps he had left it at someone else's place. The porter went back and forth several times. The hat was embellished with green and pink jade; it was very valuable, and the doctor could not bear to lose it. So he told the truth, and admitted that he had not been anywhere else the previous evening. He could not have made a mistake about where he left it. The master of the house laughed, and returned it to him.[133]

Complaints about Chinese physicians were so common that even Western doctors were aware of them. The problem of lack of strict regulations, examinations, qualifications, registration, and so on for practitioners of traditional Chinese medicine was to continue throughout the Republican period.[134]

3. Changes in the pattern of human relations

Traditionally, families and clans exercised substantial control over their members, and the local gentry controlled the community at large. Members of a community were also linked through the *baojia* system—the mutual responsibility system. No matter how miserably the *baojia* system failed its purpose[135] or how much government policies concerning it were ignored in practice,[136] the *baojia* had managed to survive through the centuries as a neighborhood surveillance system.

As early as 1850 Chinese officials in Shanghai tried to institute a *baojia* system to control migrants,[137] but for a variety of reasons, it was not extended into the foreign concessions. In 1876 Ge Yuanxu noted that the quality of the *dibao* (local *baojia* constables) in the settlements was very poor,[138] but this in itself does not mean that a *baojia* organization was active there. In 1883 the Shanghai magistrate placed a proclamation in the *Shenbao*. "I have been ordered by my superiors to establish a *baojia* system [in the settlements]. I have ordered the managing director of the Bao'antang, Qu Kaitong, together with the other managers, to supervise local constables in an inspection of the residents and businesses in the settlements. If there are criminals or unemployed vagrants there, they must be reported to the sergeant of police. Anyone who hides them will be responsible for the consequences. They must first consult with the Western officials, then they must implement this order."[139] No further proclamations were issued on this matter, and there is no evidence that this one was ever acted on. It was not until the 1940s that a *baojia* system was instituted in Shanghai, under the Japanese.[140]

Of course, migrants still maintained links with their families, and sometimes family members followed them to Shanghai. With few exceptions, a clan did not migrate as a group, but migrants set up native-place associations and trade guilds, the *huiguan* and the *gongsuo*, respectively.[141] As seen from the material in the *Dianshizhai*, their activities mainly included organizing various celebrations, including religious festivals, and the providing financial aid for funerals (Figs. 93 and 94).[142] On occasion they organized public protests, such as those called for by the Ningbo native-place association, the Siming Gongsuo, in 1874 and 1898 on the issue of the use of land used for burials.

Migrants to Shanghai could choose whether to live in the same area with their fellow provincials, or have contact with their native-place association. They had alternatives. In this Shanghai differed from the rest of China. This freedom of choice provided new possibilities, which in turn led to new ideas about personal freedom. People migrated to Shanghai for various reasons. Some did not want others to know too much about them, others wanted to escape strict surveillance at home. A place in which the *baojia* system did not exist, in which they could freely choose where they lived and with whom they associated, offered a degree of protection.

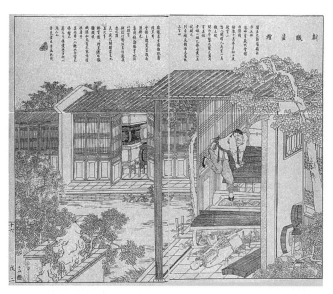

93. Coffins stored in the Huizhou Huiguan (1885). A thief pried open the coffins in the night in search of valuables. One of the corpses had been there for four years. Another illustration (Wu 40 *xia*) reported a similar incident in the Chaozhou Huiguan.

Neighborhoods without a sense of community

Changes in the structure of family and clan were also expressed in housing conditions. As the Chinese population of the settlements increased, foreign merchants built simple wooden houses for them to rent. Such houses were liable to catch fire easily, however, and during the 1860s a new architectural style known as *shikumen* (stone frame gate) developed. These were two-story brick dwellings, with wood for the doors, windows, and stairs. Each story had a parlor and an attached wing. This type of house could provide accommodation for more than one family, and in this it differed from the traditional Chinese house, in which various members of one extended family occupied various rooms of the same house. The "stone frame gates" became one of the most common types of dwelling in Shanghai. They were linked together in terraces, opening out onto a lane, as we can see in some *Dianshizhai* sketches.[143] In busy commercial areas, the ground floor was used as a shop and upstairs as accommodation, mainly for the shop employees.[144]

The size of the lanes varied. Some contained several dozen houses, some only a few. Each lane had a gate at its entrance, and the larger ones had a watchman. The street gates were opened early in the mornings and closed late at night. In some areas of the settlements neighbors barely knew each other. *Dreams of Prosperity in Shanghai* tells of a visitor from outside Shanghai looking for someone. He asks the neighbors, but a resident tells him, "Many people who live in the foreign settlements, even though they may be neighbors, do not talk to each other."[145] Of course, in the small lanes, some relationships did form, especially if residents had lived there many years. Since the settlements had no *baojia* system, however, neighborhoods had no institutional function. Hankou neighborhoods in contrast, were an important component in the local community, not only because of the *baojia* system, but because "every street had its own temple . . . [which]

served as the focus of neighborhood worship."[146] Residents of the settlements in Shanghai were usually separated from their workplaces (with the exception of certain shops in which the employees lived upstairs), which meant that neighbors did not share a communal life derived from the workplace. This psychological distance between neighbors also helped develop the concept and real possibility of privacy. It was strengthened by the new custom of meeting friends in teahouses, instead of visiting them at home.[147]

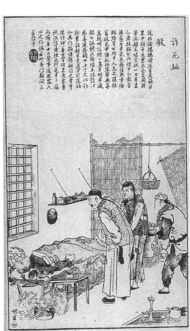

94. Funeral expenses gained by deception (1895). Shanghai guilds provided burial expenses for deceased members who could not afford a coffin. A tanner pretended to be dead to take advantage of this service, and the guild provided his family with 17,000 cash for funeral expenses. A few days later someone from the guild recognized the man in the street. The commentary notes that he should be punished, but does not say by whom. It also notes that Chen Zhuping (see Fig. 44) had seen similar attempts to defraud the guilds. Another *Dianshizhai* sketch (Wu 89) relates a similar incident involving the gold foil guild.

Resolution of disputes

Within the confines of the Chinese city, disputes between members of the same clan were resolved in the traditional manner, by clan elders. The *Dianshizhai* of 1885 tells of a property dispute between two brothers. Their uncle had tried to mediate many times, but eventually the dispute was brought before the clan elders.[148] In traditional China, these disputes were regarded as family scandals, which should not have happened in the first place. The conciliator would base his arguments on moral grounds and try to persuade the parties to the dispute to make concessions. The dispute was not seen as a private matter, but a moral issue. The elders of the clan had authority to pressure the disputants, and other members of the clan could also take part in the process. The sketch to this story shows an authoritative elder reprimanding and admonishing members of the younger generation. A large group of onlookers is gathered around.[149]

Most immigrants to Shanghai had already broken their links with the traditional family structures. No longer did respected elders mediate disputes, nor did gentry of high moral stature play this role. Disputes now often arose among people who were not members of the same clan or village.

Under these circumstances, many disputes in the settlements could not be resolved in the traditional manner and were referred to the Mixed Court. Even conflicts among family members, which would have been decided on the basis of "propriety" in traditional Chinese society, were referred to the court. One case in the *Dianshizhai* involved a man suing the wife and daughter of a man from Suzhou for allegedly inducing his wife to take up gambling—the parties to the dispute obviously knew each other well.[150] Another concerns a merchant who appealed to the Mixed Court to deal with his wife and her lover, who had eloped.[151] Another story tells of a man who demanded that his wife give up her employment, which she refused to do, and so he brought the matter to court.[152] Others involved mistreated wives appealing to the court for protection;[153] an even more remarkable case was that of a bride who fell out with her husband's family on her wedding day. In full bridal attire—phoenix coronet and embroidered robe—she took a rickshaw to the court to lay a formal complaint (Fig. 95).[154]

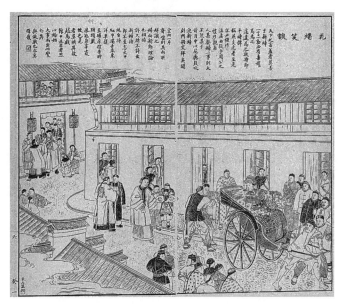

95. A Chinese bride complains to the Mixed Court (1887). A bride is carried in a rickshaw to lodge a complaint against her new in-laws.

Disputes between neighbors were also referred to the court. A twenty-six-year-old man had contracted syphilis, but continued to show physical affection toward the six-year-old daughter of a neighbor. The girl also became infected. Her mother felt the man should not have had any physical contact with her daughter knowing that he had contracted syphilis. She took the matter to the Mixed Court, which dismissed the case on the grounds of insufficient evidence.[155]

Acceptance of the legal process as a means of resolving disputes was also one reason private disputes between Chinese and Westerners did not develop into wider confrontations. All private conflicts between Chinese and foreigners recorded in the *Dianshizhai* were resolved through legal channels. This contrasts sharply with other areas in China, where a small incident could easily lead to a major conflict. The *Dianshizhai* records two incidents which occurred while Westerners were hunting in the environs of the city. One day in 1884 three Westerners from the Shanghai Paper Mills were hunting in the countryside and accidentally shot a fowl belonging to a peasant. When the peasant demanded compensation, they refused and instead assaulted him. They later threw a dollar at him and left, thinking that was the end of the matter. The villagers were not inclined to let them get away with this and tagged along behind them. The Westerners became so angry they then attacked the villagers, wounding five of them. The villagers reported the matter to the police.[156] In 1888 a peasant and his two sons were weeding a field when a Westerner, out hunting, accidentally shot the two boys. One was killed, and his brother was wounded.[157] Both of these cases were resolved before the Mixed Court, thus avoiding further complications.

From litigation trickster to lawyer

As the century progressed, the marked inclination of the Shanghai residents towards litigation was yet another measure of the decline of the constraints and customs of traditional society. Even an enlightened scholar like Wang Tao found cause for regret in this.[158] The acceptance of law however, led to another attitudinal change: among the Chinese of Shanghai the legal profession became respectable. The traditional Chinese view of lawyers (*songshi*) was that they were essentially deceitful, and the term is sometimes translated as "litigation trickster" or "pettifogger."[159] In *Bizarre Happenings Eyewitnessed Over Two Decades*, the fact that an official is discovered to have been a *songshi* in the past, and thus lacked respectability, touched off a scandal.[160] The general public loathed such operators, who were quick to provoke litigation between parties with a view to profiting themselves.[161]

Songshi are mentioned four times in the *Dianshizhai*, and on each occasion they are reviled in the strongest terms.[162] A sketch dating from 1885 entitled "Litigation Tricksters Should be Punished,"[163] prefaced its commentary with a searing attack: "These tricksters juggle black and white and act arbitrarily in their dealings with village folk." In another case two brothers fell out over an inheritance. The case was brought to Magistrate Pei, the same magistrate who had sentenced the unfilial son to wear the cangue, and who objected to a girl combing her hair in public. Pei decided that the argument had been instigated by a "litigation stick" (*songgun*), and sentenced the lawyer to one hundred strokes of the bamboo. The brothers were advised to sort the matter out between themselves (Fig. 96).[164]

When the Western legal system was first introduced, Chinese were amazed to find that the law was a highly respected profession.

> One of the aspects in which Western customs are very different from those of China concerns the position and reputations of lawyers. What are called lawyers in China, that is to say, the *songshi*, are the most liable to violate prohibitions. They play with words to manipulate the law and must be stopped from instigating trouble. They are harmful to the people's livelihood, and detrimental to society. Those who engage in this occupation are desperate to try to conceal themselves, since they fear that people will point at them and look at them, and there is nowhere they can take shelter. If people know them, they will certainly despise and loathe them, and spit at them. They are held in utter contempt. They have to be guarded against, warded off, avoided, and kept at a distance. In the West it is different. Lawyers are addressed respectfully and treated solemnly. In any legal case, the plaintiff and defendant themselves don't say a word themselves, but hire lawyers to argue on their behalf. The judge decides the rights and wrongs of the case according to the words of the two lawyers.[165]

The *Shenbao* made a similar comment:

> Originally we thought Western lawyers were like those Chinese scoundrels who provoke litigation. It is beyond comprehension how those guilty of such grievous crimes could dare to stand up in court and represent someone else. When we investigated this in detail, we realized that the system in other countries is beneficial to the people. To practice law, all must go

through a course of study, only then are they qualified to become lawyers; then they must submit to official examination, and only then can they practice this profession.[166]

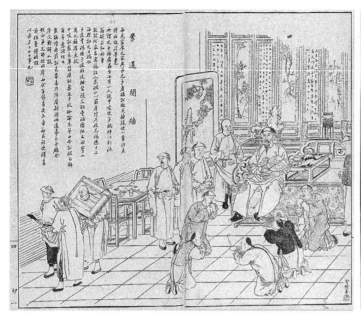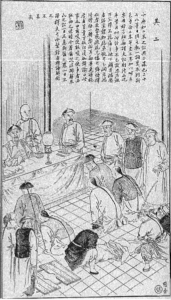

96. A Chinese magistrate solves a family dispute (1888). "A man from Shaoxing resident in Shanghai, Zhu Hongren, accused his elder brother Zhu Hongde of claiming all of the inheritance due to both of them. Magistrate Pei suspected that some troublemaker was instigating the two brothers to fight over their inheritance. On investigation, Zhu Hongde admitted that Shi Houfu had talked him into taking this action.

    The magistrate sent for Shi, who was beaten and sentenced to wear the wooden collar. The magistrate then explained to the brothers that the instigator had now been punished—and what did they plan to do? Under such pressure, the brothers decided to withdraw the case. The magistrate was delighted. He invited them to take a seat in the main hall of the yamen and ordered them to reconcile their differences. He then invited them to a meal. He was satisfied that the force of correct moral principles had resolved this dispute over inheritance.

    When five or six days later the brothers brought their case to the magistrate again, he was furious. They were too old to be punished physically, so all the magistrate could do was exhort them to think of how unhappy their deceased parents would be if they knew how relations between the brothers had deteriorated over this matter. The brothers expressed remorse at their behavior and resolved to reconcile yet again.

    The magistrate then ordered the unfortunate Shi Houfu, whom he regarded as the real culprit, to be whipped another hundred times. 'Since it was your fault the brothers fell out, you should now be responsible to see that they make up. For each day you fail to convince them to make up, you will fail to expiate your crime for yet another day.'"

Most Chinese finding themselves in a dispute would not, of course, hire a lawyer—but on occasion they did, and then they would hire a foreign lawyer. Ge Yuanxu noted, "In disputes between Chinese and foreigners, Chinese also invite foreign lawyers [to take their case]."[167] Several Western lawyers in Shanghai at the time enjoyed a high reputation among the Chinese. If a case were really serious, they would ask such lawyers to represent their interests, even in disputes with Westerners.[168] The *Dianshizhai* does not show a single example of a Western lawyer representing an individual Chinese, but for one case in 1887, when a Chinese steamer, the *Wannianqing*, was sunk by a foreign transport ship, both sides hired Western lawyers, and the Chinese side won. The reports suggest that this result was somewhat unexpected. The commentator surmised that the Chinese side had probably won because of a clash among the various Western interests, which meant that they could not present a united case.[169] A gradual education process, however, resulted in more Chinese relying on protection of the law as they became more accustomed to Western methods.[170]

"Drinking conciliatory tea"

Despite all this, the resilience of traditional practices drew the attention of Western observers, such as William Johnstone, who noted, "The Chinese have not been brought up to regard police protection in the same light as do foreigners. In most cases the foreigner in trouble calls the police. The Chinese in trouble will not call the police if he can help it; the Chinese citizen prefers to rely on established methods of acting through his trade guild or family."

One method of conciliation was commonly carried out in the teahouses, and in Shanghai the process was called "drinking conciliatory tea" (*chi jiang cha*). This practice was officially forbidden in both the Chinese city and the settlements.[171] As the *Shenbao* noted, "Those involved are mainly rough types, and incidents are bound to happen."[172] Chinese authorities, unwilling to delegate authority for the resolution of disputes to the non-elite, that is, those who were not officials, members of the gentry, or clan elders, frowned upon the practice, and all teahouses were required to display a notice: "Drinking Conciliatory Tea Forbidden by Order."[173] The practice persisted, however, in both the settlements and in the Chinese city. One 1873 news item in the *Shenbao* gives a general sense of its popularity:

> The practice of resolving disputes by reason, which is called drinking conciliatory tea, goes on in the innumerable teahouses of Shanghai every day. Whether in the Chinese city or outside it, not a day passes without it. It is also widespread in the settlements. If there is any dispute about weddings or funerals, or over money, these disputes can be resolved by this means. The teahouses are colloquially called "little courthouses." . . . Officials have repeatedly tried to ban them, but they have proved impossible to eradicate.[174]

As late as 1897 the *Dianshizhai* still noted that "small teahouses are places where villagers gather together to drink tea and negotiate."[175]

At least three *Dianshizhai* sketches are devoted to this practice. One from 1888 involves a case of long-term enmity between two men. One day one saw the other in front of a theater and threw mud in his face. The victim forced his attacker into the Shengpinglou Teahouse, where they asked someone to adjudicate. The result: the man who had thrown the mud agreed to buy the other incense and candles as an apology.[176] The second incident occurred in 1892 and involved a group of immigrants from Jiangbei living on a boat in the river near Hongkou. One night one of them returned home drunk and mistakenly boarded someone else's boat. The usual resident had been out all night gambling and had not returned, so the man decided to spend the night there (with the other man's wife). The next day the husband returned and was furious when he discovered what had happened. He forced the uninvited guest to a nearby teahouse, to negotiate a resolution. The first man admitted to being in the wrong and offered to buy incense and candles as compensation. Other people in the teahouse spoke on his behalf, and the matter was resolved.[177] The third story was from 1898. A young village woman lived in the suburbs of Shanghai; she was quite attractive and worked in a silk filature. One night on her way home, she passed the house of her future in-laws. Her betrothed suddenly came running out, grabbed her by the waist, and attempted to have sex with her. She resisted and screamed for help, and the man had to release her. The next day, when her father learned what had happened, he demanded that the young man go to a teahouse to resolve the matter. The argument was long and heated, and other people in the teahouse did their best to mediate. Eventually the future son-in-law agreed to give the girl's father incense and candles and to apologize. The father was in the end placated.[178]

Throwing filth into the face of one's enemy was another way of expressing one's desire for justice. Three such stories appeared in the *Dianshizhai*. One concerned a man from Anhui who ran a stocking shop in Lao Beimenwai Street. He was often late in paying his shop assistants. One assistant, after being dismissed, had tried to obtain his back pay for some time without success. One day he scraped out the flesh of a watermelon and filled it with dung. He threw it directly into the face of his former employer. He was later sentenced by the yamen to one day's imprisonment.[179] Another dispute arose between a private school teacher in the Chinese city and his landlord over rent. In the course of the ensuing fight, the teacher's wife threw filth at the landlord.[180]

These incidents took place in the Chinese city. In the settlements such money disputes would probably have been resolved according to law. For example, in the same year the *Dianshizhai* recorded a dispute between a settlement landlord and a tenant over arrears in rent, but it was resolved in the Mixed Court.[181]

Dispute resolution in a transitional period

Interpersonal relations changed gradually, and the transitional period produced interesting combinations of old and new. In 1906, after Li Boyuan died in Shanghai, a dispute over his estate occurred between his wife, concubine, and mother on the one hand, and his good friend and assistant Ouyang Juyuan[182] on the other. Li's family asked a famous opera singer, Sun Juxian,[183] to mediate. Sun, who was also a friend of Li's, called together more than a hundred notables of Shanghai (all of whom knew Li) to meet in a Western restaurant. He also invited the Chinese magistrate of the Mixed Court, Guan Jiongzhi,[184] as well as Ouyang Juyuan. Sun explained the situation, and asked everyone present to give his opinion. He also asked Guan Jiongzhi for advice as to how Western law would deal with this matter. Guan expressed an opinion, according to Western law as practiced in the Mixed Court. Ouyang Juyuan accepted these principles as a way to resolve the conflict. The resolution of this case was thus part-Chinese, part-Western. It followed the formula of "drinking conciliatory tea," but it was held in a Western restaurant. The Chinese representative to the Mixed Court took part in the deliberations and gave advice in Western legal terms. Such a combination of factors could only have happened in the settlements of Shanghai in the late transition period.

Long contact and familiarity with the Mixed Court also contributed to the particular mental outlook which distinguished Shanghai residents from other Chinese. After the 1911 Revolution, China established a new legal system with which the Chinese in the settlements were familiar:

At the beginning of the Republican period, China established formal law courts. If asked the difference between a civil case and a criminal case, eight or nine out of ten of ordinary citizens would just look vague and not know how to answer. But the residents in the settlements, even women and children, all knew that murder, robbery or assault were matters to be referred to the police station; disputes over money and other personal disputes were referred to the Mixed Court. They could clearly understand and distinguish between civil and criminal cases. This was not because the Chinese had any knowledge of the law, but because the Chinese [in the foreign settlements] had developed this habit.[185]

4. Relations between the sexes

Changes in relations between the sexes began with the change in women's status and behavior. The factories in the settlements attracted women from neighboring villages. The work was manual and the wages low, but nevertheless it meant they were no longer entirely economically dependent on their husbands, fathers, or brothers. Even the fact that they worked outside the home and were seen in public was unacceptable according to traditional morality. New economic factors gradually helped them change.

Women appear in public

Women who worked in the factories all day had no time to attend to their families or do traditional "women's work" such as sewing, spinning, and the like. The first customers of shops in the settlement selling such items as shoes and socks were factory women and prostitutes, since the provision of ready-made items freed them from having to make them themselves. Better-off women also started buying ready-made goods, and this led to their also abandoning their traditional tasks of spinning and sewing (Fig. 97).[186] Handicrafts traditionally had more than an economic function—among better-off families, the abilities to perform them were part of the concept of "feminine virtue." Even the new Western schools for girls in late nineteenth-century Shanghai included embroidery classes in the curriculum.[187]

This development was significant in changing the status of women. The fact that women from poor families appeared in public (i.e., worked in the factories) was regarded by the literati as one of the more pernicious consequences of the establishment of the foreign settlements. This could only lead to women becoming dissatisfied with their lot in life and losing their sense of modesty.[188] Better-off women could see no point in staying home and doing their embroidery.[189] This led to women turning up in places to which they were not traditionally supposed to go. Almost all the sketches of teahouses, opium dens, theaters, and restaurants show mixed company.[190]

It was not uncommon for women to visit opium dens. Sometimes men and women went together; sometimes women went by themselves. An 1889 story tells of a middle-aged and young woman who frequented an opium den. The young woman brought a child with her. When they had settled on the opium couch to enjoy their smoke, the child suddenly took ill. In reporting the case, the *Dianshizhai* offers no critique of the women but suggests that taking children there is not a good idea..[191] In 1890 the *Dianshizhai* told of a Ningbo man who took his lover to an opium den to share a pipe (Fig. 98). After they had settled on the couch, a thief stole the man's shoes. This left him in an embarrassing predicament, which was resolved when one of the hostesses lent him a pair.[192]

97. A shoe shop (1889). This shop is selling ready-made shoes and socks, which are displayed in boxes on the wall (left). The ready availability of such goods freed many women from the traditional task of making footwear for their family members.

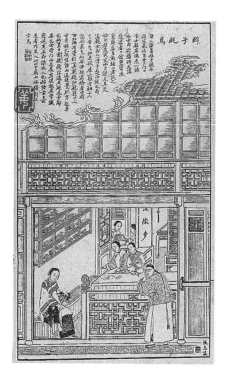

98. Lovers in an opium den (1890). The sketch shows a *liumang* (hoodlum) making off with the man's shoes.

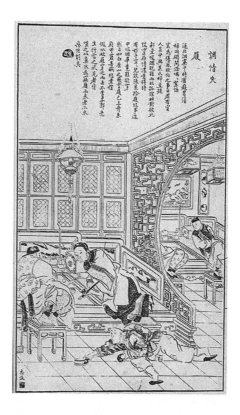

Protests against footbinding

Chinese men regarded bound feet as part of a woman's charm. One *Dianshizhai* story describes a wedding feast, at which one of the male guests wanted to fondle the bride's bound feet. It turned out that the foot wrappings were not clean, and the bride was so angry she knocked him to the floor with one kick. "They are said to be as sharp as bamboo shoots and as soft as silk floss. How could she allow anyone but her pillow partner to fondle them?"[193] The *Dianshizhai* also carried two news items about thieves stealing the foot wrappings or the tiny shoes of prostitutes.[194] In 1890 the *Dianshizhai* carried a story, "Western Women Bind Feet," in which they claimed that Cuban women also felt small feet were beautiful, and had started to bind their feet.[195] This commendation of small feet represents the taste of most educated men of the day.

Some Chinese scholars had raised objections to footbinding, but according to Pott, "The credit for starting a movement against the practice [of footbinding] belongs to the late Mrs. Archibald Little,[196] who, in the year 1895, started the T'ien Tsu Hui or Natural Foot Society (Fig. 99). Much was done in the way of rousing public opinion, and the reform was eventually taken up by the Chinese themselves."[197] As soon as Mrs. Little announced the anti-footbinding movement, the *Dianshizhai* published an immediate response. On April 24, 1895, Mrs. Little gave a public address in the Museum on Yuanmingyuan Road, in which she preached against the evils of footbinding. More than one hundred Chinese and Western women attended.[198] The *Dianshizhai* of May 5 reported this meeting as its first item.[199]

Two weeks later, the *Dianshizhai* featured a piece that pointed out the pain of footbinding, and again mentioned the anti-footbinding movement of Mrs. Little and her followers.

> The custom of footbinding is universal in China. It is not in accordance with nature; it is pain caused artificially. The flesh becomes putrid and the bones are broken. This goes on for several years before the small and delicate golden lotus is achieved. Anyone with the slightest conscience will feel compassion and take pity. For this reason several days ago Western ladies established the Natural Foot Society. They made speeches and showed drawings, exhorting Chinese to allow their feet to return to their natural shape, so as to avoid pain and suffering.[200]

It is not possible, from the material assembled above, to know how much the reform movement influenced ordinary Chinese women. But a news item in the *Dianshizhai* from 1897 gives us some insight into this aspect of the situation: People from Yangzhou in Jiangsu called women who had not bound their feet "yellow croakers" (*huangyu*), because natural feet had the shape of this species of fish. One old woman from Jiangbei who was manager of an opium den, had the nickname "Big-footed Yellow Croaker." One day she responded to sarcastic remarks about her feet with the comment, "Nowadays the Anti-Footbinding Society is everywhere. Soon you will see yellow croakers all over the place. So you had better stop laughing!" (Fig. 100).[201] If we believe this story, a movement which began in the upper strata of society in 1895 was clearly understood by an ordinary old woman in a not particularly respectable line of business only three years later.

99. The Natural Foot Society (1895). After first giving an outline of the origins of foot binding, the commentary goes on to say, "For hundreds and thousands of years innumerable women have suffered, but no one attempted to change this custom. So that is why Western women have established the Natural Foot Society, which more than one hundred people have joined. They pity the suffering of Chinese women with bound feet and try to do what they can to prohibit this, so their feet may return to the six-inch-long undamaged shape. This is an example of Westerners' sense of righteousness. But we fear this old custom will not be changed quickly, and their noble intentions will almost certainly be disappointed."

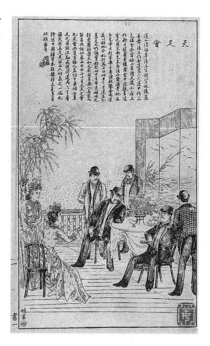

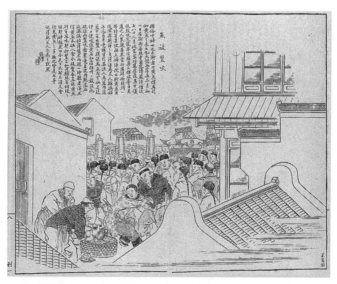

100. A yellow croaker (1897). Women with large feet were called *huangyu* "yellow croakers." The sketch shows such a woman who has been bitten on the backside by a turtle. The commentary notes dryly: "Yellow croakers are meant to be eaten; now one has been bitten by a turtle—perhaps it has a special taste?"

Relationships outside marriage

The ever-shifting, ever-changing population of Shanghai, together with a certain relaxation in moral standards, meant that a degree of "private life" was possible which would have been unthinkable in traditional society. Men and women whose relationships would not be tolerated under traditional concepts of morality could live in peace in Shanghai. As the *Dianshizhai* comments, "It is not easy to observe chaste widowhood. How much more difficult in Shanghai—how much more difficult in present-day Shanghai!"[202]

Similar comments can be found in other *Dianshizhai* commentaries. "The wind of lasciviousness in Shanghai is the strongest under Heaven, especially in the northern part of the city [i.e., the settlements]."[203] Several stories indicate that relations among men and women in Shanghai were fairly loose (Figs. 101 and 102). Five concern flirtation and seduction between neighbors.[204] Another tells of a man who arranged for his maid-servant/mistress to live in the settlements, out of sight of his wife.[205]

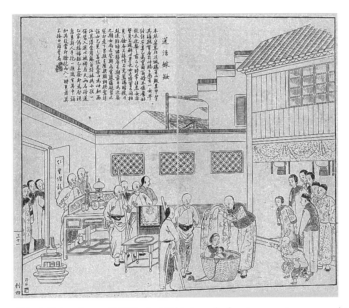

101. A living dowry (1898). A child is born before its parents marry and is included in the dowry, hidden in a basket.

The change in family structure and interpersonal relations resulted in relative freedom from clan or community pressure. The ease with which accommodations could be rented also made it easier for unmarried men and women to live together. In 1879 the *Shenbao* decried the situation: "The social situation in North Shanghai [the settlements] is such that men and women can take lovers. They decide the matter over a cup of tea. Then they rent a room and fly to and fro in pairs, like wild mandarin ducks. If they have a minor disagreement, or if the man's money runs out, they split up. It is as easy as that. This state of affairs is shockingly bad to begin with; but now they even go the court to resolve their disputes. This is even stranger."[206] Of course there were those who did not take their case to the Mixed Court, but sought private justice, often in a violent way. A woman over forty decided to live with her lover, but when the relationship turned unsatisfactory, she decided to move out. Her lover then hired ruffians to beat her up.[207] Another news item concerns a woman whose lover cut off her ear in a fit of anger.[208]

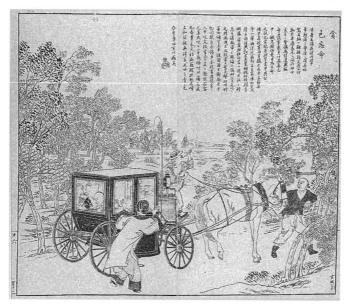

102. Sexual greed at the risk of life (1897). It was a popular pastime for Chinese dandies to take a *changsan* courtesan for a ride in a Hansom cab in the area of the Jing'an Temple. In this sketch a dandy faints after making love to the courtesan in the back seat of a cab.

Monks and nuns

Scandalous stories about relationships between Buddhist monks and nuns also circulated widely in Shanghai. Buddhist clergy were not immune from the general moral laxity around them. Of the nineteen *Dianshizhai* stories about monks and nuns,[209] only two are not critical.[210] Most tell of monks who had illicit sexual relations with respectable women. In the commentary to one of these stories, the writer sighs, "There are so many Buddha shops in Shanghai, far more than in any other place. Who knows how many women have entered them only to fall into a trap, lose their chastity, and destroy their good name." He then goes on to relate how a monk in the Longjing Temple in the International Settlement had forced a woman to spend the night with him in the temple. Chinese detectives investigated the matter, and he was arrested.[211] Another concerned a monk from Wutai Mountain who rented a storefront in Shanghai and set up a small Buddha shop.[212]

> He pretended to lead a pure and frugal life, but often broke his vows of chastity. Every day after sunset, he would don the fine robes and elegant hats of the secular and parade through the streets, seducing women of respectable households. One day the monk got into a fight in a brothel. His false queue was ripped off, and his shaven head revealed his true status. He begged, "Be lenient—think of my loss of face!" The other man laughed loudly and said, "I don't care about your face, monk, but I do care about the face of the Buddha! So I'll let you off."[213]

The *Dianshizhai* carried many stories about monks visiting brothels, or forming liaisons with prostitutes. In the Chinese city one monk persisted in carrying on with a "wandering prostitute." The monk's superior admonished him repeatedly, without result. Eventually he ordered him placed in a wooden cage and held up to the ridicule of the crowd.[214] Another story concerns a prostitute in a brothel on Fuzhou Road who particularly liked serving young Buddhist monks. She became the lover of a martial arts expert, who sent her a certain amount of money every month. Later she took up with an itinerant monk. When her previous lover heard of this, he came to beat the other man up. The monk was also proficient in the martial arts, and the former lover was no match for him. Some bystanders intervened and eventually the monk decided to take his leave.[215]

Generally speaking, monks would disguise their identity before visiting a brothel, but sometimes they were caught out. The *Dianshizhai* related the story of a young monk who was discovered because his disguise was inadequate. He was sent to the police in the French Concession, but the French police refused to deal with the matter (Fig. 103).[216] One itinerant monk liked to frequent a Japanese brothel. The Japanese prostitutes didn't mind, but a Chinese servant objected, on moral grounds. She reported the matter to the police, who tried to convince the monk to desist, but he refused. Eventually he was arrested.[217] Another monk was enjoying a theatrical performance at the Dangui Theater when he called over a prostitute to accompany him. Everyone in the theater stared at him, but he was not deterred—he even put on a show of attention to the prostitute (Fig. 104).[218]

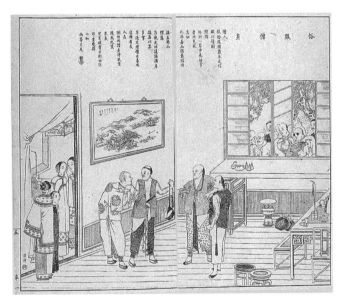

103. A monk in disguise visits a brothel (1886). He is discovered when his false queue falls off and is taken to the police station in the French Concession. The Frenchmen dismissed the case, to the monk's delight.

Certain Buddhist nuns of Jiangsu and Zhejiang had a reputation for being "nuns and at the same time prostitutes,"[219] but fewer scandals involving nuns are reported in the *Dianshizhai*. One nun kept a man overnight in the nunnery, and when discovered, loudly defended herself.[220]

Another story tells of a young nun who was brought before the police on the grounds that she did not observe the vows of chastity. The case was referred to the magistrate, and the local authorities permitted her to return to secular life.[221]

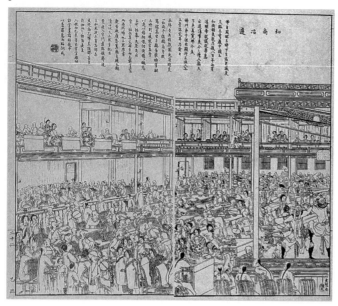

104. The Laodangui Theater (1884). The theatre is packed and the audience enthralled. The commentary tells of a monk who accompanied a prostitute to one of the performances.

Blackmail

Despite the lax moral atmosphere in Shanghai, people caught in illicit sexual relationships could still be subject to blackmail. In 1886 a monk from Wenchangge was found keeping two women in his temple; a Chinese detective made the discovery and blackmailed him.[222] Some people busied themselves "catching adulterers." In one sketch, the *Dianshizhai* describes such a woman and concludes that she envied women with lovers and their beautiful clothes; her enthusiasm for catching adulterers was born of jealousy.[223]

Two stories in the *Dianshizhai* describe people catching their lovers with other lovers. One story concerned a sexual deviant whose wife formed an illicit relationship with a carriage driver. She often went to the Tianxian Theater, where she met and had an affair with Zhao Xiaolian, a Peking opera actor who specialized in military roles. The carriage driver became jealous and joined forces with her husband to catch the woman and her new lover in the act of adultery.[224] Another story tells how a woman moved in with a man, but then took a new lover. The previous lover discovered them, and reported the matter. The woman claimed, however, that the new lover was in fact her original lover. The *Dianshizhai* writer sighed that women in the foreign territory had no sense of shame.[225]

Maisons de rendezvous

The Chinese authorities continuously issued orders against *maisons de rendezvous* (*taiji*), which provided secret meeting places for lovers.[226] According to a sketch dating from 1896, five or six such establishments operated along Zhongwang Street in the International Settlement. One day a guest died in one of them. When the police arrived, it happened that an off-duty policeman was caught in the company of an illicit lover. He was arrested, sentenced to be whipped four hundred strokes, locked up for a month, and escorted back to his native place. The commentator of the *Dianshizhai* sighed, "There are more *taiji* in Shanghai than just those in Zhongwang Street. Officer Wu is not the only man to visit them, either. Just take a look around the foreign settlement—they are everywhere. Alas, how can decency possibly return?"[227]

A story dating from 1890 concerns two friends, who made an appointment to meet at a *taiji*, each bringing his own lover. They did not realize that the police had the place under surveillance, and they were arrested. It was regarded as acceptable to visit brothels, because the women there were professional prostitutes; but it was not acceptable to arrange a rendezvous with a woman in a *taiji*, because this might damage her reputation.[228]

An article in the *Shenbao* in 1884 also noted, "Among all evil practices, the worst is the *taiji*. Recently an old woman from Ningbo made a livelihood of trapping women in the Hongkou area. Daughters of humble families, loitering in the narrow lanes and attracted by the lure of money, would be sure to lose their virginity and ruin their good names. The authorities had no choice but to prosecute."[229] Despite the arrests and punishments of *taiji* owners and their clients, the *taiji* continued to operate. A *Dianshizhai* commentary from 1897 hints that there might have been collusion between *taiji* owners and the police.[230]

5. Challenges to the traditional social order

As the newly commercialized society introduced new values, the traditional social order came under challenge. Clothing, food, dwellings—traditional symbols of class—underwent substantial changes. Money dominated in Shanghai, and traditional class concepts gave way to the concept of money as the criterion of class. The most common complaint among Shanghai literati was that class relations in Shanghai had become distorted. Wang Tao remarked that the clothes of people in Shanghai were becoming more and more resplendent by the day. There was no ostensible difference between people of different social classes. As soon as the nouveau riche merchants had made some money, they would don fox and raccoon furs and ostentatiously show off their wealth.[231]

Wealth, not family background or personal history, became the criterion of acceptability. The Shanghai residents would

> feel ashamed if their clothes were not elegant . . . judging people on the basis of the clothes they wear was not uncommon in the past, or nowadays, but people in Shanghai never cared to ask about someone's background, they only cared what clothes they wore. . . . They felt no shame in going to brothels; the shame was in going to a second-class one rather than a top-class one. It was shameful to go out in public in a two-wheeled carriage, or to go to the theater and not sit in the most expensive seats. . . . It was not shameful if their family was dishonest; it was not shameful if their behavior was improper; it was not shameful if they were illiterate or not

eloquent; the only things to be ashamed of are those mentioned above. Right and wrong are inverted, black and white are confused.[232]

Clothing and class

Privilege was open to all with the money to buy it. One 1895 *Shenbao* editorial commented:

More than ten years ago, only the rich could wear furs in winter and linen clothes in summer. Only children could wear delicate and colorful clothing. Nowadays, however, almost everyone wear furs and linen. When the season is appropriate for wearing silk, the streets are full of people in silk. When the season is appropriate for wearing satin, the streets are full of people in satin. The reason for this extravagance is the breakdown in class distinctions. There are no longer differences between noble and base; there is no distinction made as to status. What is the world coming to? A few days ago we noticed a sedan carriage, so elegant and neat. The carriage driver, a young man, was wearing a full-length mandarin silk robe. The woman in the carriage, looking very proper, was a certain famous prostitute. If the carriage driver had been wearing a short silk robe, that could be forgiven. People could still tell that he was a carriage driver. If the silk robe had a border, in the manner of carriage drivers who work for Westerners, people could tell that this was the costume of a carriage driver. This would also be acceptable. But nowadays they wear exactly the same clothes as the upper classes. It is only when they are actually driving a carriage that one can tell they are carriage drivers. When they put down the reins, and walk around in a free and easy manner, gathering their friends to frequent the brothels and taverns, as solemn and dignified as the heroes of Wuling, their clothing and footwear are so elegant and fine. Who could possibly know that every day they have to clean up horse dung and wash the wheels of the carriages. This extravagance has now gone to extremes. On observing this situation, we can but sigh thrice in despair.[233]

Prostitutes also liked to wear a particular style of long red skirt, previously worn only by legitimate wives. A common criticism ran "This practice could only be considered natural in Shanghai. People in other places would definitely not dare overstep the limits."[234] The early twentieth-century Shanghai writer Bao Tianxiao also mentioned the strict limitations on wearing this red skirt.[235] The *Shenbao* relates that at Chinese New Year prostitutes wore red skirts until the Lantern Festival, after which they would take them to pawnshops in the Shi Road area.[236] *Dissipation and Debauchery in Shanghai* also mentions prostitutes wearing these long red skirts at Chinese New Year.[237]

Prostitutes were generally forbidden to enter the Yuyuan Garden, the location of the Temple of the City God. If they did wish to go there, they would have to wear light makeup and plain, unadorned clothing, so that they could pass for respectable women. Upper-class women, on the other hand, had no compunction about wearing gaudy fashions, and sometimes looked more like prostitutes than the real prostitutes did.[238] In Shanghai, prostitutes set the fashion, and upper-class ladies followed.

Houses, transport, and courtesy titles

Inviting guests to a meal in a Western restaurant also became fashionable. This not only influenced eating habits, but also effected traditional Chinese etiquette: there was no longer any distinction between the "place of honor" and more humble positions.[239] Distinctions in appropriate dwellings and related nomenclature suffered the same fate. In 1890 the *Dianshizhai* noted how in earlier times only the official classes had the right to call their houses "residences" (*gongguan*). By the 1890s, however, anyone who had the money to build a fine house, whatever his class background, could hang up an engraved sign proclaiming his house a residence. The *Dianshizhai* poked fun at one uneducated carpenter, who had made a lot of money building houses for other people and was at last able to build one for himself. He asked a local scholar to write the characters for a large wooden placard indicating this was his "residence," but the scholar instead deliberately substituted the character 工 (*gong*) for 公 (*gong*)(Fig. 105). The carpenter, being barely literate, did not know the difference.[241]

105. The Zhang "Residence" becomes a source of local mirth (1890). An illiterate carpenter bought land and built a mansion on it. A local scholar, asked to write the calligraphy for an inscribed placard, wrote "workhouse" instead of "residence," knowing the carpenter could not read. The carpenter proudly hung the board over his front door, to onlookers' great amusement.

In his *History of Sordid Aspects of Society in Recent Times*, Wu Jianren tells a similar story. A certain Cantonese was employed by a foreigner as a cook. In front of his house he hung up a sign, calling it a "residence." A relative from Guangdong was surprised that the term "residence" could be used in this way, so asked the cook's nephew about it. The nephew replied: "Do you think Shanghai is the same as Guangzhou? There's nothing unusual about a sign proclaiming a residence here. Once they get rich living off the foreigners, they don't stop at the term 'residence'—they can even call their houses yamen!"[241]

The growing popularity of horse-drawn carriages also helped break down old class distinctions. Anyone with the money to hire a carriage could ride, prostitutes as well as officials. Upper-class young men taking prostitutes out for a ride liked to drive the carriages themselves, with the prostitutes and servants sitting behind them. If they were criticized for driving themselves, normally the task of a servant, and demeaning their own status, they would reply that this is what Westerners do.[242] *Dianshizhai* sketches show prostitutes being driven in horse-drawn carriages, or carried in sedan chairs, by their wealthy customers.[243] A particular type of dark blue sedan chair had been the special privilege of the magistrate, but Chinese New Year in Shanghai saw the streets full of dark blue sedan chairs. It was no longer possible even to tell the officials from the ordinary people.[244]

Courtesy titles also lost their old prestige. As the *Dianshizhai* points out, only the scions of the official class had been called "young master" (*shaoye*). Now any decent-looking young man was so addressed (Fig. 106).[245] The editors of the *Dianshizhai* were greatly troubled by these developments. Social mobility in traditional China was possible, but normally through the examination system. In late nineteenth-century Shanghai, however, money played the major role in social mobility. This encouraged the lower classes to emulate the aspirations, residences, titles, and clothing of the upper classes. The breakdown of old class distinctions followed in due course.

106. Young Master Dog (1891). A Manchu bannerman in Nanjing dressed his dog in fine clothing and had it carried in a sedan chair in a procession. The story is critical of the laxness in the use of titles in Shanghai, where even a dog can be addressed as Young Master.

Disintegration of the traditional class structure

At the same time, traditional privileges of the scholar in Chinese society had all but disappeared in the settlements of Shanghai. Settlement literati like Wang Tao were not of the same class as traditional scholar-officials, but they still resented rubbing shoulders with the lower classes. The brazen attitude of Shanghai prostitutes also resulted from the disintegration of the class system. In *Bizarre Happenings Eyewitnessed Over Two Decades*, Wu Jianren repeatedly sighs that "the rule of law no longer survives in Shanghai" and "Shanghai is a lawless place," because posthumous honorary titles were used in reference to some prostitutes and brothel madams who had once entertained a guest of high status.[246] A similar example given in the *Shenbao* describes prostitutes displaying a lantern, carried in front of their sedan chairs, with the inscription "Zhengtang gongwu" (magistrate on official duties). The term *zhengtang* traditionally referred only to prefects and magistrates, but by the late nineteenth century was being openly used by prostitutes.[247]

The *Dianshizhai* contains a record dating from 1897 of a meeting of Chinese and foreign officials' wives. The wife of the daotai, Cai Jun, called the meeting to discuss establishing the Shanghai Girls School. She organized a banquet in the Zhangyuan Garden, and invited the wives of all the elites of Shanghai, both Chinese and foreign. One hundred and twenty-two people took part. Most of the foreigners were wives of lawyers, of consuls, and nuns of various denominations. The Chinese included wives of local officials and gentry, among them the lover of the wealthy owner of the Tongdetang Medicine Shop, who had been a prostitute (Fig. 107).[248] Of course, the Zhangyuan was a favorite place of entertainment for all types of people in Shanghai; prostitutes often went there in their horse-drawn carriages, and the gentry liked to meet there as well. But for a prostitute to openly rub shoulders with upper-class ladies would have been unimaginable in traditional Chinese society.

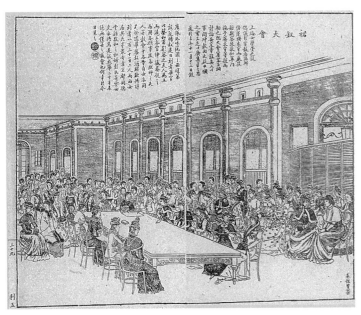

107. A meeting of women in the Zhangyuan (1898). Foreign officials' wives here discuss the foundation of the Shanghai Girls' School.

6. Vagrants and criminals

Shanghai began as a simple, unsophisticated place.[249] As it grew, migrants unable to find work, or who had lost their jobs became vagrants, tricksters, or hoodlums. This was reflected not only in the crime rate, but also in activities which, although not strictly illegal, were not in accordance with normal standards of morality. Vagrants and tricksters constituted a special element of Shanghai urban culture.

"Hollow grandees"

The development of the settlements led to the increasingly conspicuous enjoyment of material prosperity. Shanghai attracted the rich, of course, but it also attracted a large number of people who did not have the economic means to enjoy life there. The *Dianshizhai* relates how in 1884 a young man who took a prostitute out on the town in a horse-drawn carriage was discovered by his mother near the Nicheng Bridge. She caused a scene because the son had stolen the family's land title contracts and pawned them.[250] Somewhat earlier in the same year the *Dianshizhai* recounted the case of an apprentice in a bean-and-grain shop who had stolen two hundred *yuan* from his employer and fled into a brothel, from which he did not emerge for three days.[251]

Another type of trickster in Shanghai was known as the "hollow grandee" (*kongxin dalaoguan*). These men would dress up as dandies and frequent the brothels and theaters, accumulating debts until it was time to disappear. They were described thusly in Wu Jianren's *Bizarre Happenings Eyewitnessed Over Two Decades*: "Then there were the empty-handed types, who, although they had no money, wanted to play the grand official. They would go off in groups to the places of pleasure, as if they had nothing more serious things to do go on these expeditions. These so called 'hollow grandees' became a sort of local product of Shanghai."[252]

There are five more-or-less identical stories in the *Dianshizhai* about such people. Four of them involve not paying a brothel account; the other, not being able to pay the fee in a sing-song hall. The perpetrators were caught when one of the prostitutes, or sometimes one of the servants, recognized them in the street. The commentaries to four of these sketches are much the same:

> We don't know what sort of person a hollow grandee is, nor do we know what their names might be. They are barely out of their teens, handsome and charming, and good at ornamenting themselves . . . they are ostentatious and extravagant . . . their clothes are gorgeous. They swagger around the Halls of Qin and the Chambers of Chu. Sometimes they take a famous prostitute for a ride in a carriage, showing off all over town, completely without scruples. Sometimes they wear dark glasses, a cigarette drooping from their mouths. In the company of some spoilt young masters they eat, drink, and make merry. They ape each other and enjoy their romantic image. They consider themselves elegant young princes in a world of mud and mire.[253]

Two other stories use much the same language to describe their mien: impeccably dressed, smoking cigarettes and wearing foreign spectacles.[254] But these young men were in for a beating when they were discovered.[255] In the case of one, the prostitute who discovered him stole his clothes and valuables, including his foreign spectacles.[256] Another story tells of a fellow who went to the Pinyulou Sing-song Hall on Fuzhou Road, where he requested sixteen songs in a row. There were fifteen prostitutes on duty that day, and one of them sang twice. The owner was delighted, thinking that he had met one of the idle rich, until the time came to settle the bill, and he discovered the young man did not have any money. They detained him. The next day his mother came to entreat the owner, saying that his father used to run a hat shop, but that they had closed down. The family really could not afford to pay the debts accumulated by their son. She kowtowed repeatedly to the owner, who eventually took pity on her and let her son go (Fig. 108).[257]

108. Hollow grandees (1894). A well-dressed man requests sixteen songs in a row in the Pinyulou Sing-song Hall, but does not have the money to pay for them. He is detained, but eventually released after a tearful appeal from his mother.

Kidnappers

One of the most common crimes was kidnapping:

Chinese children, if they are healthy and attractive, need to be carefully guarded. Most of the kidnappers are women, and this nefarious business is so lucrative that many are engaged in it. Kidnappers grow bold as well as wily, picking up children who play on the street or go off on errands, even beguiling or snatching them away from their very doors. Both boys and girls are stolen, though boys are greater prizes, being always in demand as apprentices and adopted sons in families that have not been blessed with an heir, for the master of a house who has no son to burn incense before his ancestral tablet after his death and worship at his grave is the most miserable of all men. Still, pretty little girls are always easily disposed of, either in brothels or in private homes as slaves or future daughters-in-law.[258]

Kidnapped boys were usually sold in another part of the country.[259]

Seven kidnappings are recorded in the *Dianshizhai* (Fig. 109).[260] As the commentary to one of these stories notes, "Cases involving the kidnapping of young children pile up upon each other in the daily newspaper [*Shenbao*]. There are so many not all of them can be written about."[261] Among these cases only one kidnapper was caught, a swindler who disguised himself as an itinerant monk.[262] The commentary to a story dating from 1886 notes that the authorities had repeatedly prohibited the kidnapping and selling of children, but to no effect. Most such cases could not be solved, and even if they were, the kidnappers were imprisoned for only one month—hardly a deterrent.

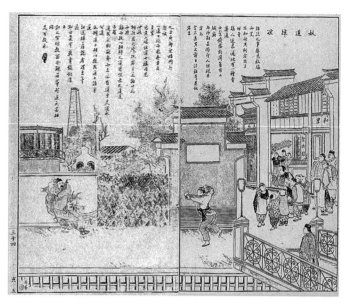

109. Daoist snatches a child (1888). "We often read about kidnappings in the newspapers, but we don't know what kind of people would do such a thing." The text goes on to tell of a Daoist in Shanghai who sold medicines in the streets. He snatched a child in the French Concession, was caught and sent to the police station. "In the last year many such Daoists have been arrested in various places in Jiangsu and Zhejiang. After interrogation it turns out they are all members of a bandit sect. Now it seems that the behavior of all such people is equally suspicious."

One middle-aged woman from Guangdong who lived in Baokang Lane bought five or six children to sell at a higher price later, either into brothels or as coolies. The matter only came to light because she mistreated them so badly that the neighbors heard their crying and reported the matter to the authorities.[263] Official crime statistics did not list kidnappings in a separate category because they were so difficult to solve.[264]

Thieves and robbers

The *Dianshizhai* features only two cases of premeditated murder,[265] which can also be found in official records. In 1884 the police station in the International Settlement arrested 5,365 Chinese criminals, of whom not even one was accused of murder. In 1885 two murderers out of 4,357 total criminals were arrested; in 1886 none at all; in 1898 four out of 25,763 and in 1900 five out of 25,221. In 1884, the most common crime among Chinese arrested was theft (1,169); creating a disturbance (usually setting off firecrackers) (943); disturbing public order (including drunkenness) (904). In 1898 creating a disturbance was the most common (15,874); followed by theft (3,128), and obstructing traffic (2,062).[266] The situation reflected in the *Dianshizhai* corresponds to these statistics. One can find every conceivable variety of theft cited in the *Dianshizhai*. One thief dressed smartly, and gained entry to people's houses on the pretext of asking after somebody's whereabouts, or inquiring about renting a room. Once inside, he would slip into his pocket whatever he could lay his hands on.[267] There were habitual petty thieves,[268] and thieves who visited brothels to steal the dark glasses and vest watches of fashionable brothel frequenters while their owners were otherwise occupied (Fig. 110).²⁶⁹ Other thieves specialized in stealing things from boat passengers (Fig. 111).²⁷⁰ One man dressed as a maid-servant to gain access to the valuables of guests at weddings and funerals.²⁷¹ In 1889 the *Dianshizhai* carried a story about the "Grand Thief of the Rivers and Lakes," Yang Hanqing. After he was arrested his wife and maid-servant came to visit him, both dressed in expensive silks and satins. Yang's career lasted five years, during which the loot he accumulated was substantial.²⁷²

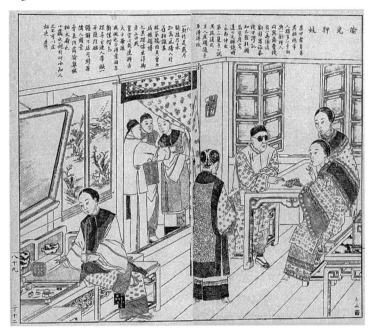

110. A dandy steals money to pay brothel debts (1887). He is dressed in the height of fashion: dark glasses and a vest pocket watch.

The crime rate in Shanghai continued to grow. "The coefficient of criminality in 1885 was 3.15, in 1890—3.45, in 1895—5.85. In 1900 it dropped for a while to 3.66 . . . in 1910 [it rose to] the enormous figure of 10.44."²⁷³

Robbery was also occasionally reported in the *Dianshizhai*. In 1885 it covered the case of a Hunanese robbing the Astor Hotel.²⁷⁴ In the same year the Runkang Native Bank was robbed, and in 1886 a fruit peddler from Xuzhou and nine others robbed the Chartered Mercantile Bank of India.²⁷⁵ The record suggests, however, that armed robbery was relatively uncommon. In 1885 there were 14 cases; in 1890, only 1; in 1895, four; and in 1897 and 1898, none at all.²⁷⁶

Swindlers

Few cases of swindlers survive in the official records, but they abound in the *Dianshizhai*. At least seventeen such cases were reported there.²⁷⁷ In 1885 the *Dianshizhai*, commenting on several remarkable cases, noted,

The world gets worse and worse, and men's hearts become more and more evil. Cases involving mendacious swindlers pile up on top of each other without end. A man from Guangdong called Li Renshan pretended to be the owner of a Guangdong shop, called the Ruishenghe, which opened for business on the left-hand side of the Sanyangjing Bridge. He had accumulated goods valued at several hundreds of thousands of dollars by the time he was discovered, and more than thirty businesses had been his victims. Recently there was also a man from Jiangxi called Xiao Jin who pretended to be the magistrate of Zhenze County....[278]

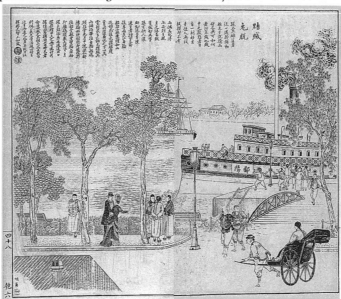

111. Cunning thief escapes like a rabbit (1892). Chen Liansheng was a notorious thief who specialized in robbing boats on the Yangtze River. He was arrested by a detective from the French Concession. He told the detective that he had many accomplices, and, if they went to the wharf, he could identify them. When they arrived, Chen leaped onto a departing boat, leaving the detective behind. The commentator notes, "The detective is not as smart as the thief."

In 1891 the *Dianshizhai* commented, "In recent times, men's hearts are not like in the old days. Deceit and fraud increase daily. Thieves, robbers, hoodlums—there is such confusion and turmoil. People find it difficult to take precautions."[279] And again in 1892, "Nowadays men's hearts are not like in the old days. Cases of fraud pile up one on the other. The most detestable, however, are those who, under the guise of charity, pursue private ends. In Shanghai alone, there are innumerable spurious charities."[280]

Petty swindlers abounded as well—like those selling bogus medicine,[281] failing to return borrowed clothes from a clothes-for-hire shop,[282] assuming a false identity to secure cash,[283] even cheating a peddler out of eggs.[284] Not all the swindlers were Chinese, however. An American on Fuzhou Road was able to cheat the curious into buying tickets to see "a newly arrived wild man from America (Fig. 112), with a head and no body."[285] Some swindlers became professionals, and special terms were applied to their particular trade. Hoodlums who specialized in extortion and blackmail were called "twig-breakers" (*chaishao*).[286] The situation of a woman entering into a false marriage or relationship and making off with the man's property a day or two afterwards was called "releasing a white pigeon" (Fig. 113).²⁸⁷ These terms were later to be found in both specialist works on the customs and attitudes of the people of Shanghai,²⁸⁸ and in more general glossaries of the Shanghai dialect.²⁸⁹ There are even specialist dictionaries of Shanghai's criminal argot.²⁹⁰

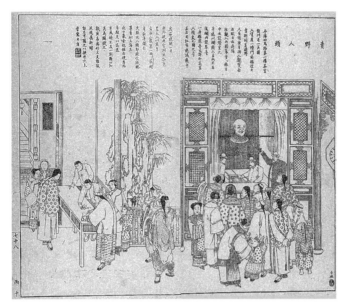

112. Head of a savage on display (1885). An American rented a house opposite the Diyilou Teahouse on Fuzhou Road and posted a billboard: "Recently Arrived: American Savage. A Head with No Body. On Display Now." This caused quite a sensation, and the expression "selling a savage's head" is still used in Shanghai, meaning to get money on false pretences.

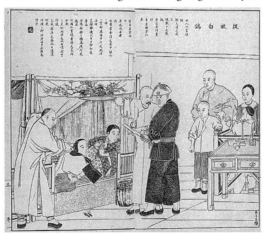

113. A "white pigeon" recaptured (1889). A man paid a large amount of money to a matchmaker to find a wife, but after one night together, the woman disappeared. Six or seven days later the man tracked her down in an inn in the French Concession and brought a policeman with him to arrest her. Twenty days later the *Dianshizhai* (Wu★ 35) reported that the innkeeper and the girl were accomplices, and this was not the first time they had cheated men in this way.

Perhaps because most swindlers did not really break the law, perhaps because their victims were reluctant to report the matter, or perhaps simply because these people were just too hard to catch, only a few accounts of them survive in the official record. In 1884 fifty such swindlers were convicted; in 1885, nineteen; in 1895, seventy-nine; and in 1900, also seventy-nine.[291]

Those convicted in the International Settlement were usually deported back to their place of origin and forbidden to return to Shanghai.[292] One such case appeared in the *Dianshizhai* in 1889. A man who styled himself "Managing Director of a Flower and Opium Den" was convicted of fraud, sentenced to jail by the Conseil Municipal of the French Concession, and deported to his place of origin.[293] Three Jiangbei men, who bought lettered paper to make a profit from what was supposed to be a moral duty, were ordered by the magistrate of Shanghai escorted back to their native villages.[294] As mentioned above, any policeman caught in a *taiji* was beaten and imprisoned, then sent back to his place of origin.[295]

Some of these people may well have returned to Shanghai. A monk expelled from the French Concession for fraudulent acquisition of goods returned the next year and was arrested again. A sketch of him and another criminal wearing the cangue in the streets appeared in the *Dianshizhai*. The commentator sighed, "There is no end to strange things in the ten *li* of foreign territory. The situation becomes worse and worse, and their tricks more and more amazing."[296] Such comments appeared elsewhere in the *Dianshizhai*[297] and can be seen in contemporary books as well.[298] For these and many other reasons, Shanghai became known as the "paradise of adventurers."[299]

Hoodlums

Many reports about such troublemakers were published in the *Dianshizhai*. Usually referred to as hoodlums (*liumang*), they were a relatively recent nuisance in late 1800s Shanghai, and even the term was unfamiliar at that time. As late as the 1870s and 1880s, the term *liumang* had to be explained, and even its pronunciation indicated. "Shanghai is a commercial entrepot, a mishmash from everywhere. Those who have no proper employment and roam the streets causing trouble when they get the chance are called *liumang*. The dictionary defines *mang* as 'a biting flying insect', and that is just what it means."[300] Another source gave a similar definition: "In the settlements, those who have no proper employment and who roam the streets and gather in groups to cause trouble are colloquially called *chaishao* 'twig-breakers.' They are also called *liumang*. The pronunciation of *mang* is the same as *mang* 'insect.'"[301] The *Dianshizhai* gives the following description. "There are more hoodlums in Shanghai than anywhere else. They group together in gangs of tens or hundreds and run wild through the streets. They bully the weak and insult the widowed."[302] They were indubitably a social nuisance, but from the descriptions above, their activities were fairly innocuous; they cannot be compared to the organized criminals of twentieth-century Shanghai. Most were born into the lower strata of society—the children of prostitutes in brothels or the illegitimate children of maid-servants.[303] Sometimes they were rough youngsters who had fallen under bad influence.[304]

> [They] form themselves into gangs and bands that cause trouble by going through the streets, creating a disturbance. Neither passers-by nor their own parents can restrain them. They are frivolous and skittish, and increase in number by the day and by the month. It is no wonder that their audacity increases and their arrogance continues to grow.[305] (Fig. 114)

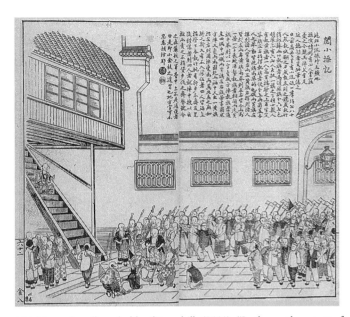

114. Young hoodlums hold military drills (1891). "In the northern part of Shanghai young hoodlums are practicing military drills in public. Concerned people have been worried about this for some time. It is on such a scale as to terrify people." The commentary goes on to say how disciplined the hoodlums were and urged "local officials to take preventive measures against possible trouble."

According to the records of the Municipal Council, the majority of criminals in the International Settlement were men between twenty and thirty years of age. Of these, most had no education.[306] In 1884 the *Dianshizhai* carried an account of a woman who worked in a silk filature being harassed by hoodlums on her way home.[307] This sketch was based on a report in the *Shenbao*:

> Recently, because of the war between China and France, many foreign firms have found business very light, and have had to lay off a number of workers. Those who have lost their jobs are youngsters and liable to cause trouble. Every evening they loiter on the street corners in the Hongkou area, waiting for the women workers at the Iveson and Company Silk Filature to leave work, so that they can harass them.[308] (Fig. 115)

The hoodlums wore a particular type of tightly buttoned jacket.[309] The *Dianshizhai* describes them in the following terms:

> They gather in groups of threes and fives. They wear tightly buttoned coats. They will occupy the entrance to a lane and have the gall to do anything. There is nothing they will stop at. If someone wearing expensive clothes happens to stroll by, they will either steal his watch or his money. They will fleece him unscrupulously. They are no different from thieves and robbers. They harass the maid-servants in the brothels, tease the prostitutes in their sedan chairs, and shout insults at the sedan chair bearers. They kick up an awful clamor whenever they want. It is not unusual for them to act as if there were no one else present.[310]

115. A group of *liumang* harrass women (1887). The women are on their way home from the Ewo Silk Filature. The ruffian in the middle, facing towards the front, is wearing the tightly buttoned jacket considered *de rigueur* for the well turned out *liumang*.

Liumang were so numerous that even the police were somewhat afraid of them. Once one of the editors of the *Dianshizhai*, Fu Genxin, witnessed a group of young hoodlums stealing something from a passer-by. At a distance a Chinese policeman looked on, but dared not intervene. When he noticed Fu, he simply stalked off. Fu realized that if even the police were afraid of the hoodlums, they would grow even more brazen and reckless.[311] This sort of behavior was what the official records called a "disturbance" or "disturbing public order."

Gamblers

The addiction to gambling in Shanghai is clear from the official records and from reports in the *Dianshizhai*. The number of Chinese convicted for gambling was also quite a large portion of the total number of convictions; in 1884 it occupied sixth place (415); in 1898, fourth place (1,202).[312] A commentary in the *Dianshizhai* dating from 1889 explains this phenomenon to a certain extent: "They have little capital and not much business. It is hard for them to earn money. So some people regard gambling as a way of making money."[313] According to the *Dianshizhai*, the Hongkou area was the most notorious for gambling. In 1891 the magistrate of Shanghai, Lu Chunjiang, and the International Settlement police launched a joint operation in the Hongkou area, but they arrested only a dozen or so people; most of the experienced gamblers had been warned of the raid and fled.[314] The *Dianshizhai* commented:

> The Shenjiawan area has six or seven gambling dens, and hundreds of thousands of people have been their victims. After the order prohibiting gambling was issued, more than seven hundred gamblers in that area gathered together to offer a sacrifice to the God of Gambling and swore that they would resist any policemen who might come to arrest them.[315]

Apart from these local clubs, some gamblers held their games in brothels, so as to avoid detection (Fig. 116).³¹⁶ Stories about fights, bankruptcy and even loss of life due to gambling can also be found in the *Dianshizhai*.³¹⁷ Not all gamblers were men. In the sketch accompanying the story about the man who accused another of luring his concubine into gambling, we can see beautifully dressed women and luxurious furnishings. These women are obviously rich, with plenty of leisure time (Fig. 117).³¹⁸

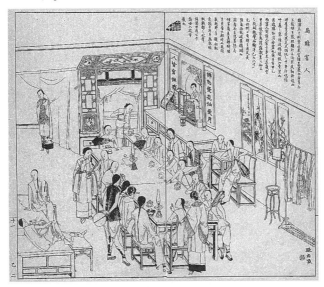

116. Gambling in a brothel (1884). Gambling was prohibited, but illegal gambling flourished. The scene shows a gambling party in a brothel in Qingyun Lane, organized by two men from Ningbo. The gamblers are all men, but there are many prostitutes among the onlookers. Some people are lying on couches smoking opium, others are sitting and chatting. The poem on the wall reads "Buddha loves flowers, Immortals love the moon. Men love sex, I love affection"—appropriate sentiments for an upper-class *changsan* brothel.

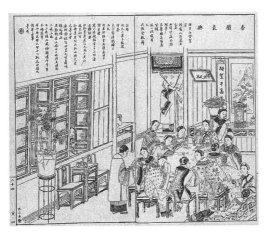

117. Women of leisure (1888). Concubines, prostitutes, and ladies of leisure are shown here gambling.

NEW URBAN CULTURE

While most of the reports in the *Dianshizhai* concerned Shanghai's material progress and social prosperity, the paper repeatedly commented in a reprimanding tone, "The foreign territory is a place which shelters evil people and countenances evil practices."[319] It went on, "[Life in the foreign territory] will destroy propriety, law, honor, and the sense of shame. If you want to see the most vile behavior in human existence, to see what you have never imagined, you must go to Fuzhou Road in the International Settlement. The practices there are so bad, one can but sigh."[320]

Sink of iniquity or model settlement?

The commentary to the 1884 *Dianshizhai* story of a young man who stole money from his employer then spent three days in a brothel reprimanded the boy's father for bringing him to a den of iniquity like Shanghai in the first place.[321] In 1889 a young man from Zhejiang went to Shanghai to buy things for his wedding. He soon found his way to the brothels and declined to return home. Eventually his parents sent someone to bring him back, but by that point he had contracted venereal disease.[322]

Such stories also appear in late Qing novels.[323] Suzhou is only one hundred or so kilometers from Shanghai, but "at that time Suzhou families would not allow their sons to go to Shanghai; they said Shanghai was not a good place, it was like a black dye pot—if you fell in, you would never be clean again."[324]

Western views of Shanghai were ambivalent. On the one hand it was a "sink of iniquity," on the other hand a "model settlement."[325] Shanghai's notoriety was such that those who regarded themselves as having high moral standards would refuse to go anywhere near it, like the scholar resident in the Chinese city who prided himself on the fact that he had never set foot inside the foreign settlements.[326]

Shanghai's reputation did not slow the growth of its population, however. It developed more and more into a playground to which people from surrounding districts would flock. Even Shanghai fashions soon became the standard for the fashion-conscious everywhere.[327]

Notes

[1] Pott, *Short History*, 37.

[2] Pott, *Short History*, 41.

[3] William T. Rowe, *Hankow: Commerce and Society in a Chinese City, 1796–1889* (Stanford: Stanford University Press, 1984), 47, 50.

[4] Hao, *Commercial Revolution*, 236–40.

[5] Yen-p'ing Hao, *The Comprador in Nineteenth Century China: Bridge Between East and West* (Cambridge, Mass.: Harvard University Press, 1962, reprinted 1970), 102.

[6] Yu Xingmin, *Shanghai 1862 nian*, 254.

[7] Pao 9; Zi 83 *xia*; Zhen 72 *xia*; Wei 83.

[8] Pott, *History of Shanghai*, 93. Rhoads Murphey, *The Outsiders: The Western Experience in India and China* (Ann Arbor: The University of Michigan Press, 1977), 103; C. P. Fitzgerald, *Why China? Recollections of China 1923–1950* (Melbourne: Melbourne University Press, 1985), 23–24; P. D. Coates, *The China Consuls: British Consular Officers 1843–1943* (Hong Kong: Oxford University Press, 1988), 83.

[9] Ren 90.

[10] Heng 24.

[11] You 12.

[12] Alexander Michie, *The Englishman in China* (London: William Blackwood and Sons, 1900; reprinted Taipei: Ch'eng-wen Publishing, 1966), 129. See also C. Lanning and S. Couling, *The History of Shanghai* (Shanghai: Kelly and Walsh Limited, 1921), 296–303; Pott, *History of Shanghai*, 22–23; J. K. Fairbank, *Trade and Diplomacy on the China Coast* (Cambridge, Mass.: Harvard University Press, 1969), 407.

[13] Montalto de Jesus, *Historic Shanghai* (Shanghai: The Shanghai Mercury Ltd., 1909), 42.

[14] Xin★ 90.

[15] *Shenbao*, May 4, 1874.

[16] Bryna Goodman, *Native Place, City and Nation: Regional Networks and Identities in Shanghai, 1853–1937* (University of California Press, 1995), 169.

[17] Elizabeth Perry, "Tax Revolt in Late Qing China: The Small Swords of Shanghai and Liu Depei of Shandong," in *Late Imperial China*, vol. 6, no. 1 (June 1985): 83. See also Pott, *History of Shanghai*, 95–98; 128–29; Montalto de Jesus, *Historic Shanghai*, 240–44; Ge Enyuan, ed., *Shanghai Siming gongsuo da shiji* (A record of major events relating to the Ningbo Guild Hall incident) (Shanghai: Juzhenfangsong yinshuju, 1920); *Minguo Shanghai xianzhi*, vol. 3, *juan* 14, 28–29; Kuai Shixun, *Shanghai gonggong zujie shigao*, 432–33; Sun Baoxuan, *Wangshanlu riji*, 86.

[18] Michie, *The Englishman in China*, 124; Pott, *History of Shanghai*, 21–22, Morse, *International Relations of the Chinese Empire*, vol. 1, 367–87.

[19] Lanning and Couling, *History of Shanghai*, 295–96. Hanchao Lu noted that a British Royal Naval Commander had made similar comments on the "nature" of Shanghai people being "soft," especially compared to the Cantonese. See Lu, *Beyond the Neon Lights*, 37–38.

[20] Wang Tieyan, ed., *Zhong-wai jiu yuezhang huibian* (Collection of treaties between China and foreign countries in former times) (Beijing: Sanlian shudian, 1957), vol. 1, 102.

[21] Guo Tingyi, *Jindai Zhongguo shishi rizhi* (Daily record of current events in modern Chinese history) (Taipei: Zhengzhong shuju, 1963), 927.

[22] Xianggang Xiandai chuban gongsi, ed., *Shi li yangchang hua Shanghai* (Ten *li* of foreign territory: Talks on Shanghai) (Hongkong, Xiandai chuban gongsi, 1970), 30–31; Huayeliannong, *Haishang hua liezhuan*, chap. 15, 10; ch. 27, 11; ch. 32, 6.

[23] *Shenbao*, November 21, 1873.

[24] *North-China Herald*, February 19, 1874.

[25] The term "barbarian quarter" was used only once in the *Dianshizhai*, and then purposefully, in the context of condemning the International Settlement authorities for using Chinese convict labor in building projects. Gui 8.

[26] Yao Gonghe, *Shanghai xianhua*, 5.

[27] *Shenbao*, April 12, 1873.

[28] Ren 96. See Li Pingshu, *Zixu*, 45.

[29] Mao 21.

[30] Goodman, "Improvisations on a Semicolonial Theme," 906.

[31] Mu 57–64 *xia*.

[32] Haishang shushisheng, *Haishang fanhuameng*, vol. 1, 377–79.

[33] She 58.

[34] The impression of Western residents of Shanghai of relatively harmonious relations with the Chinese was apparently shared by the Japanese. In his study of Japanese residents in Shanghai in the twentieth century, Fogel notes that "one of the great shocks of the early twentieth century to Japanese from many different walks of life was that Chinese nationalism should develop precisely as an anti-Japanese movement." See Joshua A. Fogel, "Shanghai-Japan: The Japanese Residents' Association of Shanghai," in *Journal of Asian Studies*, vol. 59, no. 4 (November 2000): 931.

[35] Wu Guifang, "Songgu mantan, san" (An informal discussion on old Shanghai, part 3), in *Dang'an yu lishi* (Archives and history), vol. 2, no. 1 (1986): 80–82; Ye Xiaoqing, "Shanghai Before Nationalism," in *East Asian History*, no. 3 (June 1992): 33–52; Robert A. Bickers and Jeffrey N. Wasserstrom, "Shanghai's 'Dogs and Chinese Not Admitted': Sign, Legend, History and Contemporary Symbol," in *China Quarterly* (1995): 444–66.

[36] *Shenbao*, December 8, 1885.

[37] Huang Shiquan, *Songnan mengyinglu*, 133.

[38] Bickers and Wasserstrom, "Dogs and Chinese Not Admitted," 445.

[39] S. Couling, *The History of Shanghai* (Shanghai: Kelly and Walsh, 1923), vol. 2, 204.

[40] Bickers and Wasserstrom, "Dogs and Chinese Not Admitted," 445–46.

[41] *Shenbao*, December 8, 1885.

[42] Couling, *History of Shanghai*, vol. 2, 205.

[43] *Shenbao*, September 21, 1888; November 7, 1888.

[44] Couling, *History of Shanghai*, vol. 2, 204.

[45] *Shenbao*, August 11, 1889.

[46] Bickers and Wasserstrom, "Dogs and Chinese Not Admitted," 446.

[47] *Shenbao*, December 8, 1885.

[48] *Shenbao*, August 11, 1889.

[49] *Shenbao*, September 21, 1888.

[50] *Shenbao*, July 8, 1890.

[51] As Bickers and Wasserstrom ("Dogs and Chinese Not Admitted," 464) point out, "Restrictions on entry to the parks was never merely a question of race, and focusing on the sign may lead one to forget how class and/or cultural prejudices were as much an element as racial or ethnic ones. Europeans in Shanghai themselves were far from homogeneous: there were strictly observed class divisions even within British society in the city."

[52] Wu 80; Ji 72.

[53] Yu 42.

[54] Yi★ 2.

[55] Jia 89 *xia*.

[56] Mao 14 *xia*.

[57] Liang Qichao, *Wushi nian lai Zhongguo jinhua gailun* (Outline of developments in China over fifty years) (Shanghai, 1923), 3.

[58] Heng 87. See also the comments of Feng Guifen quoted in Ssu-yu Teng and John K. Fairbank, *China's Response to the West: A Documentary Survey 1839–1923* (Cambridge, Mass.: Harvard University Press, 1975), 51.

[59] *Shenbao*, May 30, 1876, July 25, 1877.

[60] Yao Gonghe, *Shanghai xianhua*, 25. Pott, *History of Shanghai*, 93, Dyce, *Model Settlement*, 229–37.

[61] Jia 81 *xia*.

[62] Dyce, *Model Settlement*, 154. The *Dianshizhai* related the story of the Yongkang Rice Shop, which was not prospering, and had to close down. Some people had already paid for their rice but had not yet collected it, so the proprietor discussed the possibility of postponing the closure of the shop with the comprador, so that those people would be able to claim their rice. The comprador, however, was extremely vicious: he did not agree to this proposal, and confiscated the rice as well. (Xin★ 72).

[63] Zheng Yimei, *Shanghai hua jiu*, 8.

[64] Zhu 40; Shu 16; Ge 71; Xin★ 88. There is only one story about a decent carriage driver, who was able to help his former foreign employer, who had fallen onto difficult times (Shi 41).

[65] Zhu 40.

⁶⁶ Jia 81 *xia*.

⁶⁷ *Shenbao*, October 31, 1872.

⁶⁸ Zhimituren (The Man Who Points Out the Wrong Path), *Haishang yeyou beilan* (Complete guide to brothel visiting in Shanghai) (Shanghai, 1891), *juan* 3, 15.

⁶⁹ Wu★ 80. According to Wu Shenyuan, *Shanghai zuizao de zhongzhong*, 4–5, the term *hong bang*, literally 'red clique', derives from the fact that tailors who made Western clothing were 'in luck' (*zou hongyun*). Tailors who made Chinese clothing were called *ben bang*, literally 'local clique' tailors. Carpenters who repaired Western ships were known as *hongbang mugong*—red clique carpenters. See Shanghai shi gongshang xingzheng guanliju ji Shanghai diyi jidian gongyeju jiqi gongye shiliaozu, ed., *Shanghai minzu jiqi gongye* (The Shanghai national machinery industry) (Beijing: Zhonghua shuju, 1966), vol. 1, 59–60. According to *Shanghai cidian* (page 321), the Western tailors were originally called *feng bang*, because most of them had come from Fenghua, in Zhejiang. The term was later misinterpreted into *hongbang*.

⁷⁰ *Shenbao*, September 3, 1895.

⁷¹ Chen 49, Shu 48.

⁷² Heng 37.

⁷³ Hao, *The Comprador in Nineteenth Century China*, 181.

⁷⁴ Yi★ 48 *xia*. See Yu Xingmin, *Shanghai 1862 nian*, 465. Yu's evidence is a collection of photographs still kept by Yan's family in Shanghai.

⁷⁵ Yin 18, Wei 15.

⁷⁶ Ren 12, Chou 24. Zhan Wu was very well known at the time, and he is mentioned in several books on Shanghai. Cf. Liu Yanong, *Shanghai xianhua*, 82; Ge Yuanxu, *Huyou zaji*, *juan* 2, 36. Wang Tao met him in Scotland, and noted that he seemed to be quite rich. Zhan Wu married a woman from Australia, and died overseas in 1893. Cf. Wang Ermin, "Dianshizhai huabao li," 150. See also Robert Bogdan, *Freakshow: Presenting Human Oddities for Amusement and Profit* (Chicago: University of Chicago Press, 1988), 98–99.

⁷⁷ *Shenbao*, September 30, 1895.

⁷⁸ Xin 68.

⁷⁹ Wang Xiangqing, *Wang Xiangqing biji* (Miscellaneous jottings of Wang Xiangqing) (Shanghai: Shanghai shudian, 1926), *xia ce*, *juan* 6; Wu Jianren, *Guai xianzhuang*, chapter 78, *passim*.

⁸⁰ Macpherson, *Public Health*, 157; cf. Xu Run, *Zixu*, 303. After 1949, its name was again changed to "Annex to Shanghai Number Two Medical College." In 1972 it was changed to "Number Three Peoples Hospital." In 1984 its original name, the Renji Hospital, was restored. It specializes in cardiac surgery. It is still located at No. 145 Shandong Road. See *Shanghai cidian*, 371.

⁸¹ Pott, *History of Shanghai*, 92.

⁸² Ge Yuanxu, *Huyou zaji*, *juan* 1, 11.

⁸³ Wang Tao, *Yingruan zazhi*, *juan* 6, 12.

⁸⁴ Macpherson, *Public Health*, 157.

⁸⁵ Luo Zhiru, *Tongjibiao*, 21.

⁸⁶ Ji 40.

⁸⁷ You 72 *xia*.

⁸⁸ Bing 77.

⁸⁹ Shen 93.

⁹⁰ *Shenbao*, April 10, 1888; May 9, 1888.

⁹¹ Xin★ 32 *xia*.

⁹² Cataract surgery had been introduced into China from India during the Tang but never became a common practice in China. Unschuld, *Medicine in China: History of Ideas* (Berkeley: University of California Press, 1985), 238.

⁹³ Macpherson, *Public Health*, 152.

⁹⁴ *Shenbao*, February 14, 1873.

⁹⁵ Hushang youxi zhuren, *Haishang youxi tushuo, xia ce*, 31; Yao Wennan, ed., *Shanghai xian xuzhi* (Supplementary gazetteer of Shanghai County) (reprinted Taipei: Chengwen chubanshe, 1975), *juan* 2, 45–46.

⁹⁶ William C. Cooper and Nathan Sivin, "Man as a Medicine: Pharmacological and Ritual Aspects of Traditional Therapy Using Drugs Derived from the Human Body," in *Chinese Science: Explorations of an Ancient Tradition*, ed. Shigeru Nakayama and Nathan Sivin (Cambridge, Mass.: MIT Press, 1973), 203–72; Ye Xiaoqing, "Zhongguo chuantong ziranguan yu jindai kexue" (The Chinese traditional view of nature and modern science), in *Kexue yu wenhua* (Science and Culture) (Xi'an: Shaanxi kexue chubanshe, 1983), 158–60.

⁹⁷ Wei Juxian, "Bian Que de yishu lai zi Yindu" (Bian Que's medical skills came from India), in *Huaxi yixue zazhi* (Southwest China medical science journal), vol. 2, no. 1, (1947): 19–25; Lu Juefei, "Bian Que yishu lai zi Yindu zhiyi" (Questions on the validity of the theory that Bian Que's medicinal skills came from India), in *Hua-Xi yixue zazhi*, vol. 2, no. 8 (1947): 8–11; Wei Juxian, "Bian Que yishu lai zi Yindu de dabian" (Reply to questions on the validity of the theory that Bian Que's medical skills came from India), in *Hua-xi yixue zazhi*, vol. 3, nos. 4-6 (1948): 7–8.

⁹⁸ Paul Unschuld, *Medicine in China*, 151.

⁹⁹ Derk Bodde and Clarence Morris, *Law in Imperial China* (Cambridge, Mass.: Harvard University Press 1967), 91–92.

¹⁰⁰ Macpherson, *Public Health*, 152–53.

¹⁰¹ Chou 25.

¹⁰² The standard thirteenth century treatise on forensic medicine, by Song Ci (ca. 1250). Herbert Allen Giles, "The 'Hsi Yüan Lu' or Instructions to Coroners," in *China Review*, 1874–1875, 3:30–38, 92–99, 159–172; Brian E. McKnight, trans., *The Washing Away of Wrongs: Forensic Medicine in Thirteenth-Century China*, Center for Chinese Studies, The University of Michigan, 1981. Both translations reprinted Taipei, Southern Materials Center, Inc., 1982.

¹⁰³ Hai 74; Hai 82.

¹⁰⁴ Yi 81.

¹⁰⁵ Yu 6. The Ximen Hospital was established in 1884; it was also known as the Red House Hospital. In 1952, it was amalgamated with the gynecological departments of other hospitals into the Shanghai Municipal Gynecological Hospital attached to the Shanghai Medical University. See *Shanghai cidian*, 368.

¹⁰⁶ Wang Tao, *Yingruan zazhi*, *juan* 6, 120.

¹⁰⁷ Ge Yuanxu, *Huyou zaji*, *juan* 2, 41.

¹⁰⁸ *Shenbao* May 25, 1874; Heng 24.

¹⁰⁹ Shi 9.

¹¹⁰ Huang Kewu, "Cong *Shenbao* yiyao guanggao kan Minchu Shanghai de yiliao wenhua yu shehui shengshuo 1919–1926" (An analysis of the culture of medical treatment and social life in the early Republican period in Shanghai 1912–1926, based on advertisements for medicinal products in the *Shenbao*), in *Zhongyang yanjiuyuan jindaishi yanjiusuo jikan*, vol. 17, no. 2, (December 1988): 150.

¹¹¹ van Briessen, *Shanghai: Bildzeitung*, 17.

¹¹² *Shenbao*, October 2, 1895.

¹¹³ Joseph Needham, *China and the Origins of Immunology* (Hong Kong: Center of Asian Studies, University of Hong Kong, 1980), 6.

¹¹⁴ Angela Ki-che Leung, "Organized Medicine in Ming-Qing China: State and Private Medical Institutions in the Lower Yangtze Region," in *Late Imperial China*, vol. 8, no. 1 (June 1987): 143 n. 41.

¹¹⁵ Angela Ki-che Leung, "Diseases of the Premodern Period in China," in *The Cambridge World History of Human Disease*, ed. Kenneth F. Kiple (Cambridge: Cambridge University Press, 1993), 355

¹¹⁶ Maria Rudova, *Chinese Popular Prints* (Leningrad: Aurora Art Publishers, 1988), Plate 13.

¹¹⁷ *Shenbao*, June 14, 1875; March 24, 1895.

[118] J. A. Jewell, "Chinese and Western Medicine in China, 1800–1911," in S. M. Hillier and J. A. Jewell, *Health Care and Traditional Medicine in China, 1800–1982* (London: Routledge & Kegan Paul, 1983), 8–9.

[119] Macpherson, *Public Health*, 65.

[120] *Shenbao*, June 14, 1875.

[121] Bing 7.

[122] Macpherson, *Public Health*, 65.

[123] Luo Zhiru, *Tongjibiao*, 21.

[124] Zhao Hongjun, *Jindai Zhong-Xi yi lunzheng shi* (A history of the debates between Chinese and Western medicine) (Hefei, Anhui: Kexue jishu chubanshe, 1989), 54–56.

[125] Paul U. Unschuld, *Medical Ethics in Imperial China: A Study in Historical Anthropology* (Berkeley: University of California Press, 1979), 20–21; S. M. Hillier and J. A. Jewell, "Chinese Traditional Medicine and Modern Western Medicine: Integration and Separation in China," in Hillier and Jewell, *Health Care and Traditional Medicine*, 306–7; Leung, "Diseases of the Premodern Period of China," 360.

[126] J. Dyer Ball, *Things Chinese* (London: Murray, 1926; reprinted Detroit: Tower Books, 1971), 186–87.

[127] Jin 24; Li 55, Tu 80.

[128] Jia 18.

[129] Zhen 84.

[130] Paul U. Unschuld, *Medicine in China: A History of Pharmaceutics* (Berkeley: University of California Press, 1986), 4.

[131] Wen 6.

[132] You 84.

[133] You 63. The details of this incident were repeated in *Casual Talks About Past Events*, the only difference being that the novel transferred the incident to Guangzhou. See *Fubao xiantan*, in *Wan-Qing xiaoshuo da xi* (A compendium of late Qing novels) (reprinted Taiwan: Guangya chuban youxian gongsi, 1984), 123–28.

[134] Ye Xiaoqing, "Regulating the Medical Profession in China: Health Policies of the Nationalist Government," *Pacific Journal of Oriental Medicine*, no. 18 (June 2001): 68–76.

[135] Michael R. Dutton, *Policing and Punishment in China: From Patriarchy to "the People"* (Cambridge: Cambridge University Press, 1992), 55, 87–88.

[136] The government intended to bring both the gentry and scholars under *baojia* control, but local officials had to rely on the local gentry for support, and the gentry often adopted a policy of non-cooperation. See Kung-chuan Hsiao, *Rural China: Imperial Control in the Nineteenth Century* (Seattle: University of Washington Press, 1960), 45, 67–72.

[137] From the proclamation in the *North-China Herald* (August 10, 1850) it would seem that these regulations were mainly aimed at recent arrivals from Fujian and Guangdong. These were mainly sailors, and it was from this group that the Small Sword Society was to draw its members.

[138] Ge Yuanxu, *Huyou zaji*, juan 3, 59.

[139] *Shenbao*, September 10, 1883.

[140] When the Japanese occupied Shanghai, they immediately ordered a census and the establishment of *baojia* organizations. When the Kuomintang reoccupied the city, they too immediately ordered the reconstruction of the *baojia* system. Both regimes drew up very detailed regulations. See "1944 nian Shanghai tebie shi diyi qu bianzu baojia zanxing banfa" (Temporary regulations on the organization of the *baojia* system in the First District of the Shanghai Special City of 1944), in 1946 nian Shanghai shi zhengfu, *Shanghai shi biancha baojia xuzhi* (Notice on the organization of the *baojia* system in Shanghai city), held in the Shanghai Library. Hanchao Lu points out that the lack of a *baojia* system makes the "state-society relations" approach to Shanghai neighborhood research problematic. See Hanchao Lu, *Beyond the Neon Lights*, 19.

[141] On the *huiguan* and the *gongsuo*, see Bryna Goodman, *Native Place, City, and Nation*, passim.

[142] Wu 16; Wu 40 *xia*, Wu 89, Yu 64 *xia*.

[143] Xu 84; Yi 32, Gui 12.

[144] Chen Congzhou and Zhang Ming, eds., *Shanghai jindai jianzhu shigao* (A draft history of architecture in modern Shanghai) (Shanghai: Sanlian shudian 1990), 161–63; Luo Suwen, *Da Shanghai: Shikumen: xunchangren jia* (Great Shanghai and stone frame gate style houses: dwellings of ordinary families) (Shanghai: Shanghai renmin chubanshe, 1991), 14–18; Lu, *Beyond the Neon Lights*, 156–73; Leo Ou-fan Lee, *Shanghai Modern: The Flowering of a New Urban Culture in China, 1930–1945* (Cambridge, Mass.: Harvard University Press, 1999), 32.

[145] Haishang shushisheng, *Haishang fanhuameng*, vol. 1, 14.

[146] William T. Rowe, *Hankow: Conflict and Community in a Chinese City, 1796–1895* (Stanford University Press, 1989), 81–83.

[147] Wo Foshanren (Wu Jianren) *Zuijin shehui wochuo shi* (A history of sordid aspects of society in recent times) (Shanghai: Shiwu shuguan, 1910; reprinted Guangzhou: Huacheng chubanshe, 1988), 180.

[148] Bing 24.

[149] See Mao 4, 4 *xia*.

[150] Yin 24.

[151] Hai 55.

[152] Bing 8.

[153] Shu 24; Hai 91.

[154] Gui 6.

[155] You 71.

[156] Yi 1.

[157] Yin 66. For details on this case see *Shenbao*, June 13, 14, 16, 18, 19 and 28, and July 1, 1888.

[158] Wang Tao, *Yingruan zazhi*, *juan* 1, 10–11.

[159] Bodde and Morris, *Law in Imperial China*, 189. On page 584 *song gun* is glossed "litigation stick, trickster." See also Melissa Macauley, *Social Power and Legal Culture: Litigation Masters in Late Imperial China* (Stanford: Stanford University Press, 1999).

[160] Wu Jianren, *Guai xianzhuang*, ch. 73, 588.

[161] During the late Qing a rumor circulated that fellow villagers had plotted against Yang Naiwu because he had been, at some time in the past, a *songshi*. The case later became legendary as a miscarriage of justice. Cf. Chen Dingshan, *Chunshen jiuwen*, 112.

[162] Ding 93; Yi★ 19; Zi 46; Chou 38.

[163] Ding 93.

[164] Mao 4, Mao 4 *xia*; see also *Shenbao*, July 5, 1888.

[165] Tan Yingke, *Shenjiang shixia shengjing tushuo*, *juan shang*, 8 *xia*.

[166] *Shenbao* editorial, August 28, 1872.

[167] Ge Yuanxu, *Huyou zaji*, *juan* 2, 21.

[168] Tan Yingke, *Shenjiang shixia shengjing tushuo*, *juan shang*, 9.

[169] Ren 82.

[170] Johnstone, *The Shanghai Problem*, 77.

[171] Tan Yingke, *Shenjiangshixia shengjing tushuo*, *juan shang*, 12.

[172] *Shenbao*, October 16, 1873.

[173] *Shenbao*, June 19, 1872.

[174] *Shenbao*, October 16, 1873.

[175] Xin★ 13.

[176] Chen 22.

[177] Shi 23.

[178] Li★ 72 *xia*.

[179] Wu★ 48 *xia*.

[180] Wu★ 5.

[181] Wu 95.

[182] Ouyang Juyuan, who used the pen name Xiqiusheng (The Scholar Who Cherishes Autumn) is said to have written a number of novels ascribed to Li Boyuan. See Wei Shaochang, *Li Boyuan yanjiu ziliao*, 490–94.

[183] According to Tiaoshui kuangsheng, *Shanghai Liyuan xin lishi*, *juan* 1, 3, Sun Juxian was regarded as a just and sincere man, and was often asked to conciliate disputes. He also banned homosexual activity amongst the actors in the theaters, which was said to have added to their respectability.

[184] Guan Jiongzhi was the magistrate involved in the Mixed Court riots in 1905.

[185] Yao Gonghe, *Shanghai xianhua*, 63–64.

[186] Xu Ke, *Qing bai lei chao*, vol. 5, 2318.

[187] Tang Zhenchang, *Shanghai shi*, 332.

[188] Qin Rongguang, *Shanghai xian zhuzhici*, 54.

[189] Zhu Wenbing, *Haishang zhuzhici*, 27. For the later period see Shanghai xintuo gufen youxian gongsi (Shanghai Trust Co.), ed. *Shanghai fengtu zaji* (A survey of folklore from Shanghai) (Shanghai, 1932), 49–50.

[190] Yi 22; Hai 37; Yi★ 32; You 8 *xia*; Jin 30.

[191] Yi★ 32.

[192] You 8 *xia*.

[193] Chen 31.

[194] Gui 25; Yu 56 *xia*.

[195] Shen 73.

[196] Mrs. Little was a traveler and author, as well as a leader in the crusade against footbinding. She was the author of several books, including *Intimate China*, *The Land of the Blue Gown* and *Li Hung-chang: His Life and Times*, and *Guide to Peking* (New York: Brentano, 1902).

[197] Pott, *History of Shanghai*, 130–31; T. Richard, *Forty Five Years in China* (London: T. Fisher Union Ltd, 1916), 227–28.

[198] Shanghai tongzhiguan, ed., "Shanghai nianbiao." Manuscript; Shanghai Library; *Shenbao*, April 25, 1895.

[199] Shu 1.

[200] Shu 21. For more information on this movement, see Li Youning and Zhang Yufa, eds. *Jindai Zhongguo nüquan yundong shiliao* (Historical materials on the history of the women's movement in modern China) (Taipei: Chuanji wenxueshe, 1975); Howard S. Levy, *Chinese Footbinding, The History of a Curious Erotic Custom* (New York: Walton Rawls, 1966), 65–103. Mrs Little's anti-footbinding activities can be read in her own account in *The Land of the Blue Gown*, 305–31.

[201] Li★ 8.

[202] Xin 15.

[203] Wu 8.

[204] Ren 63; Xing 24; Geng 53; Heng 48; Zhong 95.

[205] Wu★ 88.

[206] *Shenbao*, June 16, 1879.

[207] Wu★ 55.

[208] Geng 53.

[209] Ding 46; Ding 60; Ji 24; Ji 70; Wei 38; Wei 62; Bing 16; Bing 65; Xing 28; Yi★ 22; Yin 50 *shang-xia*; She 80 *xia*; Wen 40, Gui 13; Xin★ 96; Yi 22; Shu★ 55; Ren 6.

[210] Xing 28, Bing 65.

[211] She 80 *xia*.

[212] Buddha shops (*Fo dian*) were one of the peculiarities of Shanghai. A group of Buddhist monks and nuns would rent a shop, install a few statues, and invite believers to offer incense there.

[213] Wen 40.

[214] Gui 13.

[215] Xin★ 96.

[216] Xin 5.

[217] Ding 46.

[218] Yi 22.

[219] Xin 76.

[220] Yi★ 22.

[221] Bing 16.

[222] Ren 60.

[223] Wu★ 88.

[224] Zhen 79.

[225] Wu★ 70.

[226] Xing 8; You 69; Wu 24 *xia*.

[227] Xing 8.

[228] You 69.

[229] *Shenbao*, February 13, 1884.

[230] Heng 64.

[231] Wang Tao, *Yingruan zazhi*, juan 1, 10. The breakdown in the distinctions in dress between various social classes was apparent as early as the Kangxi period. See the diary of Yao Tinglin in *Qingdai riji huichao* (Collected diaries of the Qing period), ed. Shanghai renmin chubanshe, (Shanghai: Shanghai renmin chubanshe, 1982), 165. The traditional system went into a stage of rapid disintegration, however, only in the last decades of the Qing dynasty.

[232] Tan Yingke, *Shenjiang shixia shengjing tushuo*, juan *shang*, 4–5. Similar sentiments can be found in "Shen Jiang louxi" (Degeneration of customs in Shanghai), a commentary published in the *Shenbao* on April 7, 1873.

[233] *Shenbao*, September 8, 1895.

[234] Zhimituren, *Haishang yeyou beilan*, juan 4, 6–7.

[235] Bao Tianxiao, *Yi, shi, zhu, xing de bainian bianqian* (Changes over a hundred years in clothing, food, dwellings, and travelling) (Hongkong: Dahua chubanshe, 1974), 38.

[236] *Shenbao*, February 28, 1874.

[237] Xiaoxiangguan shizhe, *Haishang huatianjiudi zhuan*, juan 1, 24.

[238] Xiaoxiangguan shizhe, *Haishang huatianjiudi zhuan*, juan 1, 27–28.

[239] Zhu Wenbing, *Haishang zhuzhici*, 19. Traditional Chinese seating arrangements were very complicated. Zheng Jiuping et al. eds., *Zhongguo chuantong liyi liwen* (Traditional Chinese rites and protocols) (Hunan: Sanhuan chubanshe, 1990), 31–37 lists sixteen possible patterns.

[240] Xu 30.

[241] Wo Foshanren (Wu Jianren), *Zuijin shehui wochuo shi*, 264.

[242] Xiaoxiangguan shizhe, *Haishang huatianjiudi zhuan*, juan 1, 7.

[243] Geng 84, Zi 24.

[244] Qin Rongguang, *Shanghai xian zhuzhici*, 44; Xiaoxiangguan shizhe, *Haishang huatianjiudi zhuan*, juan 1, 24; Xia Lin'gen, *Jiu Shanghai sanbai liushi hang*, 91–94.

[245] Jin 22.

[246] Wu Jianren, *Guai xianzhuang*, 636–37.

[247] *Shenbao*, August 25, 1895.

[248] Li★ 39. This conference is also discussed in Tang Zhenchang, *Shanghai shi*, 332, where it is incorrectly stated that this meeting was called by Jing Yuanshan, and that more than more than fifty foreign ladies attended. Two schools were established, but were closed down in 1899 and 1900. The reason, according to Tang Zhiyun (*Jindai Shanghai da shiji* [Record of major events in modern Shanghai] [Shanghai: Cishi chubanshe, 1989], 525), was lack of funds. If we take into account the personal fate of Jing Yuanshan himself, however, it would seem that more than economic factors were involved. Jing Yuanshan had been deeply involved in the reform movement. When the Empress Dowager deposed the Guangxu Emperor in January 1900, Jing Yuanshan, together with the gentry and reformers in Shanghai, including Cai Yuanpei, Huang Yan, and others, submitted a memorial to the Zongli Yamen, stating their opposition. On January 29 Sheng Xuanhuai secretly told Jing Yuanshan that the Qing Court had ordered his arrest, and urged him to flee to Macao where Jing was put under house arrest by the Portuguese authorities. It was not until after the Boxer Rebellion that Jing was able to return to Shanghai. In the turmoil of the years 1899 and 1900, Jing was obviously not in a position to deal with the affairs of a girls' school. More information of the Jing Yuanshan affair can be found in Tang Zhenchang, *Shanghai shi*, 331–33; Tang Zhijun, *Jindai Shanghai da shiji*, 517, 525, 547; and Chen Xulu, Fang Shiming and Wei Jianyou, eds., *Zhongguo jindaishi cidian* (A dictionary of modern Chinese history) (Shanghai: Cishu chubanshe, 1982), 484–85. Wang Shuhuai, *Wairen yu wuxu bianfa* (Foreigners and the Hundred Days Reform) (Taiwan: Jinghua yinshuguan), 1965, 221–23 notes that Jing fled to Macao after his opposition to the deposition of the Guangxu Emperor, and that friends amongst the foreign missionaries there devised a scheme to save him.

[249] Many books describe the nature of Shanghai before it became an open port. See *Minguo Shanghai xianzhi* (Gazetteer of Shanghai County during the Republic) (Taipei: Chengwen chubanshe, 1975) under "Customs." "Shanghai is in an out of the way area on the coast. The people live simply, and are mostly law abiding." Lu Binsheng, *Zhongguo heimu daguan* (A panorama of sinister events in China) (Shanghai: Zhonghua tushu jicheng gongsi, 1918), *juan shang*, 4: "The people in my home town have always been honest and kind. Recently it has come into communication (with the outside world), and the atmosphere has greatly changed." Mao Xiangling, *Sanlüe huibian*, quoted in *Shanghai Xiaodaohui qiyi shiliao huibian* (Documents on the Small Sword Uprising in Shanghai), ed. Shanghai lishi yanjiusuo (Shanghai: Shanghai renmin chubanshe, 1958), 808: "Migrants came to reside there, and the customs gradually changed." Wu Jianren, in the preface to *Guai xianzhuang* complained: "A place in which, sixty years ago, people lived honest and simple lives, has become a refuge for the frivolous and the deceitful." See also *Shenbao* editorial of February 12, 1874, of which the first words are, "Before Shanghai became an open port, the people were frugal and honest, and their lifestyle was not luxurious."

[250] Yi 9.

[251] Jia 16–17.

[252] Wu Jianren, *Guai xianzhuang*, 1.

[253] Xu 11.

[254] Ge 32; Xing 64.

[255] Gui 41.

[256] Xing 64.

[257] Li 48.

[258] Gamewell, *Gateway to China*, 210.

[259] Yi★ 56, Ji 96 *xia*, Ji 36.

[260] Yin 34; Yi★ 56; Yi★ 57; Ji 96 *xia*; Ji 36; Xin 57; Li 54.

[261] Ji 96 *xia*.

[262] Yin 34.

[263] Xin 57.

264 Luo Zhiru, *Tongjibiao*, 238.

265 Ge 15; Zhong 96.

266 Luo Zhiru, *Tongjibiao*, 238.

267 She 72 *xia*.

268 Wu★ 41.

269 Zi 89.

270 Pao 48; Zhu 39.

271 Ren 51.

272 Wu 39. *Shenbao*, August 21, 1873.

273 Kotenev, *Mixed Court*, 93.

274 Ding 47.

275 Xin 84.

276 Luo Zhiru, *Tongjibiao*, 238.

277 Bing 9; Bing 64; Bing 78; Geng 5; Geng 16 *xia*; Hai 95; Gui 49; Gui 72; Wei 21; Wei 62; She 72 *xia*; Pao 77; Chou 35 *xia*; Xin★ 63; Wu★ 2, Wu★ 35; Ding 23.

278 Wu 28.

279 Hai 95.

280 Pao 77.

281 Pao 77.

282 Xin★ 63.

283 Geng 16 *xia*.

284 Gui 72.

285 Bing 78.

286 Ji 17. *Shenbao*, January 26, 1888, gives five explanations as to the origin of this term (*chaishao*); none of them is particularly convincing.

287 Wu★ 3; Wu★ 35. This practice was usually a combined effort—a man and a woman acting in collusion. The expression *fang bai ge* refers to a woman's returning to her old home after marriage being like a pigeon returning to its nest. See also Wang Zhongxian and Xu Xiaoxia, *Shanghai suyu tushuo* (Shanghai colloquialisms with illustrations) (Shanghai: Shehui chubanshe 1935; reprinted Shanghai: Shanghai shudian 1999), 9–10.

288 E.g. Ge Yuanxu, *Huyou zaji, juan* 2, 8–10.

289 Yan Fusun, ed., *Shanghai suyu da cidian*, (Dictionary of Shanghai colloquialisms) (Shanghai: Yunxuan chubanshe, 1924), 27, 56, 65.

290 Dian Gong, ed., *Shanghai pianshu shijie* (The world of swindlers in Shanghai) (Shanghai: Saoye shufang, 1914); Qian Shengke, *Shanghai heimu huibian* (A collection of stories about evil in Shanghai) (Shanghai: Shishi Xinbao fusongpin, 1917–1918 [2 vols.]); Lu Binsheng, *Zhongguo heimu daguan*.

291 Luo Zhiru, *Tongjibiao*, 238.

292 A similar story can be found in Haishang shushisheng, *Haishang fanhuameng*, vol. 2, 1127.

293 Xing 8.

294 Xing 6.

295 Xing 8.

296 Wei 62.

297 Zhong 93.

298 Xu Ke, *Qing bai lei chao*, vol. 4, 1749.

299 G. E. Miller, *Shanghai: The Paradise of Adventurers* (New York: Orsay Publishing House, 1937).

[300] Ge Yuanxu, *Huyou zaji, juan* 2, 22.

[301] Huang Shiquan, *Songnan mengyinglu*, 101.

[302] Tu 78; *Shenbao*, September 5, 1888.

[303] Wu 84.

[304] Ji 17.

[305] Yuan 31.

[306] Luo Zhiru, *Tongjibiao*, 130.

[307] Yi 19.

[308] *Shenbao*, August 30, 1884.

[309] Qin Rongguang, *Shanghai xian zhuzhici*, 53; Haishang shushisheng, *Haishang fanhuameng*, vol. 1, 50, 386.

[310] Xu 84.

[311] Xu 84.

[312] Luo Zhiru, *Tongjibiao*, 238.

[313] Wu 69.

[314] Hai 50.

[315] Zhen 7.

[316] Yi 11.

[317] Yi 11; Xu 61.

[318] Yin 24.

[319] Wu★ 70.

[320] Gui 29.

[321] Jia 16–17.

[322] Yi★ 43.

[323] Such as Li Boyuan, *Wenming xiaoshi*, passim.

[324] Bao Tianxiao, *Chuanyinglou huiyilu, shang ce*, 180. Ouyang Juyuan, the assistant and friend of Li Boyuan, died from syphilis at the age of 25. In commenting on this, Bao Tianxiao noted, "Such a talented young man, had he not come to this filthy settlement, would not have fallen victim to this." See Wei Shaochang, *Li Boyuan yanjiu ziliao*, 498.

[325] Pott, *History of Shanghai*, 92.

[326] Yao Gonghe, *Shanghai xianhua*, 143.

[327] Yao Gonghe, *Shanghai xianhua*, 70–71; Xu Ke, *Qing bai lei chao*, vol. 4, 1699.

PART FOUR

Religious Practices

Religious practice in Shanghai, although in many ways much the same as in other parts of China, also demonstrated certain characteristics peculiar to Shanghai. The commercialization and urbanization of the city did not diminish participation in traditional popular religion, but the mixed nature of the Shanghai population meant that religious practices deriving from many provinces of China were practiced there. Wealth and a concentrated population made Shanghai celebrations more extravagant than elsewhere, and the vast size of the gatherings often alarmed the Chinese authorities. Religious festivals relating to agricultural cycles all but disappeared, while commercial influences encouraged a level of vulgarization distasteful to the literati.

Since there was no unifying Shanghai identity, no one organized citywide religious celebrations. Some people participated in activities arranged by their native associations or guilds, while others were content to be onlookers. There does not seem to have been any confrontation between various types of religious practice from different traditions.

On the whole, the settlement authorities did not concern themselves with the religious beliefs of the Chinese and did not interfere with Chinese religious activities, except insofar as large processions or ceremonies might occasionally impinge on public order.[1] Chinese officials, however, tried to exert a degree of control over popular religion in the settlements, and their interventions inevitably had an effect on people in the Chinese city.

1. Official attitudes

Official (or state) religion is generally distinguished from popular religion by virtue of Chinese officials providing funds and taking part in its ceremonies.[2] But in Shanghai the official classes and the general population participated in the same religious ceremonies to a considerable extent. The city magistrates would offer incense and perform sacrifices to Guanyin, the City God, Tianmu, Guan Gong and the Dragon King.[3] Other local officials and the gentry would also participate in certain parts of "popular" religious ceremonies.

With no clear demarcation between official religion and popular practices, it is not easy to define exactly what might be considered orthodox popular religion, and unorthodox popular religion.[4] Some practices were permitted or encouraged by the government, while others were banned. Some were banned, not because they were heterodox, but because their constituency had become too large, or because they were overly secularized or vulgarized. Other practices were criticized by individual officials or individual scholars on the grounds that they contravened Confucian principles. Such practices, however, were relatively small-scale, and the government did not react to them.

Heterodoxy

Worship of idols of no particular recognized religious affiliation was a typical aspect of heterodox religion. In 1891 the *Dianshizhai* reported the case of the magistrate in Yangzhou discovering local people worshipping a nameless idol, apparently neither Daoist nor Buddhist in origin. The idol was immediately burned. In reporting this news, the *Dianshizhai* commentator noted that this sort of occurrence was by no means limited to Yangzhou. "The spread of heterodoxy in China has been going on for quite some time. Some stupid women do not even ask what god it is they are supposed to be worshipping."[5]

Such practices were not uncommon in Shanghai: "At every pile of mud or gravel, along every road or waterway, one is sure to see people attired in their best clothes and hats offering up incense and candles, paper money and silk, and praying. They do not care that sensible people laugh at them. These customs have persisted for a long time, and they are difficult to correct immediately."[6]

> To the north of the railway bridge, abandoned graves piled up on each other, and exposed coffins were also quite numerous. Exposed to the sun and rain for many years, the lids of the coffins split, and if it should rain continuously for a period of ten days, it was quite natural that water seeped in. Evil witches and devilish sorceresses spread all sorts of rumors, saying that if one burned incense and prayed, then drank this water, chronic illnesses would be immediately cured. Stupid people were deceived by this and vied with each other to spread this story. . . . Some time later a charitable hall hired laborers to bury the coffins and ordered local constables to keep guard. After a few days, these practices disappeared.[7]

Another story concerns a merchant who transported goods between Fujian and Shanghai. On one occasion, after reaching Shanghai, he discovered a hole in his boat, which happened to be blocked by a dead snake. He immediately lit incense and candles and prostrated himself before the snake. The *Dianshizhai* commented on his stupidity and ignorance (Fig. 118).[8]

Such occurrences can be found in many contemporary books on Shanghai. In the early twentieth century two stone figures stood to the west of the racecourse. These had once flanked the entrance to a grave some ten *li* from the city, but had been bought by a Westerner for forty-two *yuan*, and brought to Shanghai as a sort of decorative statuary. Some Shanghai people believed the statues to be bodhisattvas and began to burn incense in front of them. The number of worshippers swelled to a flood, and the lower halves of the statues became blackened with the accumulated soot from the candles and incense. Settlement authorities issued an official notice emphasizing that the statues were not gods, but to no avail. Eventually in the interests of efficient traffic and public order, the statues were moved elsewhere.[9]

The Procession of the City God

The City God was an important deity in every locality, and the first duty of a new magistrate was to offer incense at the local Temple of the City God. Reverence towards the City God was of equal importance to officials and to the local people.[10] The Shanghai City God was a deification of Qin Yubo, who had lived towards the end of the Yuan and into the first few years of the Ming dynasty.[11]

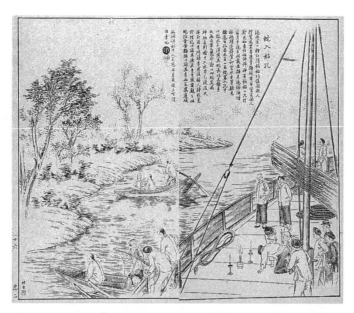

118. A merchant offers incense to a snake (1896). A merchant specializing in transporting goods between Fujian and Shanghai discovered that a snake had blocked a hole in his boat, thus preventing it from sinking. The sketch shows the merchant offering incense to the snake spirit for saving his life. He later gave the serpent a proper burial.

The *Dianshizhai* provides a description of a ceremony in the Temple of the City God. The occasion was the acceptance of a tablet presented by the Qing Court on the suggestion of the governor of Jiangsu, Kui Jun.

> The Court gave permission, and a tablet inscribed "Protection and Blessing to Heaven and Earth" in the Emperor's calligraphy was presented to the temple. On the day of the presentation, the Daoist priest in charge of the temple prepared the vestments and other instruments of worship for the ceremony, and organized the celebrants. Before dawn, they came to the Hall of Longevity and waited until the local officials and gentry arrived. After the presentation ceremony, they respectfully placed the tablet on a palanquin. It was then lifted high and carried from the Hall of Longevity. Preceded by incense and strewn flowers, the procession moved along to the accompaniment of drumming and music. When they reached the door of the temple, seal-holding officials and the gentry knelt by the side of the path, in order of precedence, to show their respectful reception [of the tablet]. . . . Afterward the tablet was suspended in the Temple with great decorum. The gentry and officials, again in order of precedence, paid obeisance and expressed their congratulations. Then they all made their own ways home. Onlookers were so numerous they blocked the roads.[12] (Fig. 119)

The Procession of the City God was held on the Qingming Festival, the Feast of the Hungry Ghosts, and the First Day of the Tenth Month. The colloquial name for this series of processions was the "Three Circuits." From contemporary descriptions, we know that officials, the gentry, and the general populace participated in different stages of the ceremonies. At the sound of the fifth watch, just before dawn, local officials and gentry would offer incense at the temple and make obeisance to the City God, after which they would withdraw. Then the Master of Religious Ceremonies would lead the people in worship. The procession, the main event in the ceremony, followed. By seven o'clock, the participants would form into groups, such as artisans, carpenters, butchers, yamen runners, local constables and so on. They wore costumes related to their trades—for example, butchers dressed as executioners. Some of the participants in the procession were costumed as criminals, with red clothes and white trousers, with handcuffs and fetters or wearing the wooden collar, or carrying a long wooden strip on their backs indicating they were to be beheaded. Male criminals walked; children were carried on shoulders, while women were carried in uncovered sedan chairs.[13] Many marchers dressed as various heroes and villains in popular dramas; the female characters and clowns often acted out flirtatious scenes. This was also an occasion for a bit of gentle fun at the expense of the officials. One character in the procession was the "Plague Official." He rode in a sedan chair, his face made up like a clown in a local opera, wearing a black-gauze officials' hat. In his right hand he held a white paper fan, and in his left a chamber pot, from which he pretended to drink.

119. A tablet from the Imperial Court for the Temple of the City God (1896). The sketch shows the officials and gentry of Shanghai turning out to welcome it. The tablet reads: "Protection and Blessing to Heaven and Earth."

Wang Tao described the Procession of the City God this way:

Every year at the Qingming Festival, the Fifteenth Day of the Seventh Month [The Feast of the Hungry Ghosts], and the First Day of the Tenth Month, the people of Shanghai carry the City God to the Northern Altar, to the accompaniment of drums and music, where they offer sacrifices to Heaven and the spirits. The celebrants, together with their paraphernalia, sedan chairs, and the like, block the streets and lanes. There are at least several hundred horses there. Prostitutes, their hair pinned in a bun and wearing the reddish-brown clothing worn by convicts in ancient times, chained and shackled like prisoners, are carried in sedan chairs, following the horses. This is known as 'the fulfillment of their wishes.' Frivolous young men in the marketplace get mixed up in this ceremony; they point at [the prostitutes], gawk at them, follow them, and think it is a source of great amusement. Respect for the spirits has degenerated to bawdiness.[14]

It is not clear when the Procession of the City God finally died out. Some authors think that it had faded by the late Qing.[15] Others claim that a modified procession was held during the early years of the Republican period, but only once or twice.[16] A third view is that it survived until the outbreak of war with Japan.[17] This ceremony was held in 1924, during which the burning incense and candles started a fire, and the Temple of the City God was destroyed. The gangster boss Huang Jinrong contributed the funds to rebuild, and thus gained control over it.[18]

Limits on behavior at processions

Officials were generally prepared to tolerate such displays, even if they regarded them as being in bad taste.[19] After the 1870s, however, they began to worry that processions and festivals might spin out of control, and they placed limits on the sorts of behavior allowed at them.[20]

In 1872 the magistrate of Shanghai banned women from playing the role of criminals in processions.

Women who dress up as criminals, painting their faces with powder and dressing in reddish-brown costumes, ride in uncovered bamboo sedan chairs [as criminals on the way to the execution ground] and follow the ceremony. This leads to frivolous young men following the procession and flirting with them. This is especially damaging to local custom and the hearts of the people. There are prohibitions against this in the statutes. Another festival is due soon, and we greatly fear that ignorant women will revert to their previous practices. We will send officials to stop such practices when the time comes and are giving forward notice of this prohibition now.[21]

In 1873 the magistrate banned all "spirit-welcoming ceremonies,"[22] but the Procession of the City God seems to have been an exception. One sketch indirectly refers to this procession with the comment, "Those with ailments believe if they make a vow to dress as criminals and follow the procession, they will be able to eliminate their affliction and dispel their ill luck." The story concerns a boat-dweller who participated in the Procession of the City God dressed as a criminal. After the ceremony, he staggered through the French Concession intoxicated, blowing a whistle. The police tried to stop him, but he started beating them with his handcuffs. This scene was witnessed by a foreigner who helped the police escort him to the court. He was sentenced to seven days imprisonment. The *Dianshizhai* commented dryly, "A make-believe criminal has become a real criminal—this can hardly be considered eliminating an affliction" (Fig. 120).[23]

In the settlements no Procession of the City God took place on Qingming, but on the fifteenth day of the seventh month, the Feast of the Hungry Ghosts, the City God was taken from his temple and led through the settlements in procession. The Feast of the Hungry Ghosts was one of the major Buddhist festivals and was celebrated throughout the whole country.[24]

As far as the settlement authorities were concerned, they had no reason to interfere in such activities as long as they presented no threat to public order. If arrangements were made with the police beforehand, the ceremonies would proceed without incident. In 1888 the Silk Guild in the International Settlement organized a theatrical performance as a gesture of gratitude towards their patron spirits. The guild hall managers were dressed in great style as they solemnly moved forward to offer incense. The crowd of onlookers was large; the police station had been advised in advance and had sent a number of officers to ensure that law and order were maintained.[25]

120. A boatman dressed as a criminal lands in trouble (1888). On his way home after the Procession of the City God, this boatman got into a fight with police in the French Concession.

The attitude of officials to the religious activities of the Chinese population was, to a certain degree, related to the personality of the magistrate. It is not surprising to learn that a magistrate such as Ye Tingjuan, renowned for his seriousness, issued orders banning flower drum songs and women from attending the local theaters; he also issued orders banning women's dressing as criminals in religious ceremonies.[26] Sometimes a prohibition was based on practical reasons, for example, this order from the Shanghai magistrate in 1873:

> This is the busiest period in the tax-collecting season, but some activities are interfering with people paying taxes. I have heard that in Districts 22 and 24 people are collecting money for "welcoming-the-spirit" ceremonies. These people should go about their everyday business in a law-abiding way, and not pay any attention to those who want to collect money for these ceremonies. At the same time, they should hurry to pay arrears on last year's taxes. If anyone dares to resist this order, the local sergeants are authorized to report their names to the county, and they will be punished. If the local constables know about this but cover it up, they will be punished too. Everyone must respect this order. Do not disobey![27]

In times of desperate difficulties, however, officials might participate in certain popular rituals that they would avoid under normal circumstances. A particularly hot and dry summer had left the area around Shanghai in a serious drought, and the price of rice rose from 3,000 to 5,000 cash a load. Ye Tingjuan was extremely worried and heard that a man living behind the Temple of the City God had asked three Daoist priests from Jiangxi to come to his house to exorcise demons. Ye Tingjuan engaged them to perform a ceremony to pray for rain. The ceremony started on the sixth day of the seventh month, and peasants from eighty-seven villages took part—each household sending one member. Ten dragons performed the dragon dance to the accompaniment of gongs and drums. Some people wore palm-bark rain capes and bamboo-leaf hats, as if it were raining. Some even burned their flesh in acts of self-mortification. The officials announced that the proceedings would go on continuously for three days, and if there were no rain, they would continue indefinitely until it finally rained. The officials also demanded that even greater numbers of people take part in the rain ceremonies.[28] Under these circumstances, neither the usual Confucian disdain for spirits nor the requirements of filial piety in protecting one's body were of any consideration.

2. Attitudes of the literati

The literati were more critical of popular religious practices than were local officials. This group was not only concerned about social order; principles also had to be considered. The practice of self-mutilation associated with the Feast of the Hungry Ghosts had its origins in the Buddhism and expressed a form of filial piety.[29] From the scholar's perspective, self-mutilation was the very opposite of filial piety (Fig. 121).[30]

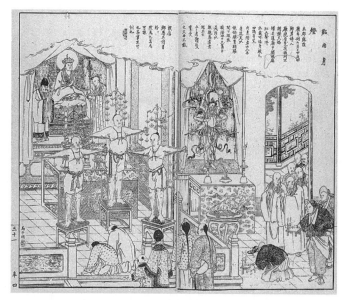

121. A human lamp stand (1886). On the evening of the fourteenth day of the seventh month, some people participated in a ritual in the Temple of the City God known as "lighting a human lamp stand." The upper parts of the body were uncovered, and forty-nine oil lamps were attached to iron hooks hanging from the arms. This was said to be a form of expression of gratitude to their parents. The *Dianshizhai* disagrees: "'Our body, head, and skin are from our parents. We should not dare injure them.' Is this not in the *Classic of Filial Piety*? Stupid villagers who cannot read imitate each other in doing this. Their intention can be understood, but their example must not be followed."

Other popular religious practices were not unacceptable to the elite in principle, but rather in the way they were practiced. The literati stressed purity of heart and the fundamental meaning of religious activities. The *Dianshizhai* often featured derogatory comments about popular religious practices (see Fig. 122), but no comments to the effect that belief in spirits itself was unreasonable. In fact, some stories in the *Dianshizhai* demonstrate that disbelief in the spirits, or blasphemy, would not go unpunished.[31]

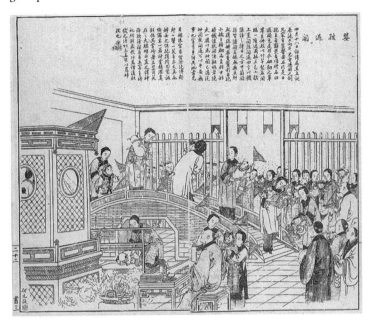

122. Carrying babies across the bridge (1895). On the eighteenth day of the fourth month, the custom in Shanghai was for mothers to take their babies to a temple to be carried across a bamboo bridge specially built for the occasion. This symbolized their passing from one year to another without mishap. But the *Dianshizhai* disapproves: "Intelligent and upright people know spirits bring good fortune or disaster according to their own plans. Surely this cannot be achieved by prayers and worship. This is just a case of Buddhist monks and Daoist priests concocting various pretexts to make money by cheating women and children."

Spiritual sycophancy

Excessive stress on the external, formalistic practice of religion was referred to as spiritual sycophancy, or "fawning on the spirits." In 1886 the *Dianshizhai* expressed its disapproval of a certain temple in which a Buddhist reliquary was installed, with pearl lamps decorating the altar; the sparkle of the lamps was meant to attract passers-by. "Buddhism is based on the fundamental principle of purity and quietness. The organization of noisy celebrations is not in accordance with its lofty purpose. The display of baubles and playthings to dazzle the eyes and ears has nothing to do with Buddhism and brings no good to people; it is no more than a means to extract money from the vulgar and stupid."[32]

RELIGIOUS PRACTICES   195

In 1891 a temple in Xiamen installed three huge candles, each more than one *zhang* and seven *chi* in length (approximately 6.6 meters). The *Dianshizhai* commented, "The way of serving the spirits lies in sincerity, not in the size of candles."³³

The praise extended to a certain nun clearly shows the attitude of the scholar-official class: "There is an itinerant Buddhist nun from Cangzhou who cares only for purity and self-cultivation. She visits people's houses to talk about Buddhism and does not seek alms. Her only aim is to urge people to preserve a pure mind and to do good deeds. One day she visited a rich family. The maid-servant presented her with a piece of cloth. The nun brought her hands together in an expression of thanks, then placed the cloth on a table for a short time. She then returned it to the woman. She said: 'Lord Buddha already knows about your meritorious deed. Since you have given this cloth to me, it is mine to dispose of. I just noticed that your mother-in-law's clothes are tattered. Could we not use this cloth to make her some clothing?' The maid-servant was ashamed, and left." The commentary added, "This nun deeply understands the true spirit of the Buddha."³⁴

In 1896 the *Dianshizhai* published an allegorical story entitled *The City God Travels in Disguise* in which the City God expresses his views on the secularization and vulgarization of religion. "If men do not cultivate their inner selves, though they might burn incense all day and all night, it will be of no use" (Fig. 123).³⁵ Occasionally the literati made their distaste of certain popular practices quite explicit. Commenting on a Cantonese merchant's hiring a Western band to take part in the "welcoming-the-spirit" ceremonies, the *Dianshizhai* noted, "Those who have studied books or who understand [moral] principles would not have done this."³⁶

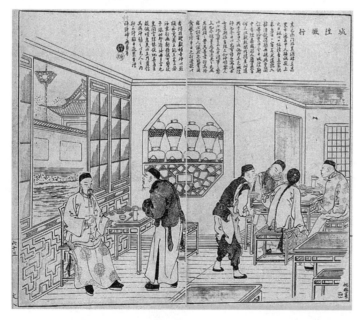

123. Complaint of the City God (1896). "Outside the South Gate of a certain locality, the proprietor of an inn—an old man over sixty—was very sincere and honest. On the day of the Lantern Festival, he lit a single stick of incense in his house as an act of worship. Suddenly a guest of solemn appearance came into the inn and bought some wine. He was drinking by himself, without any companions, and started chatting with the old man. They got on very well. The old man said, 'There are a lot of people burning incense in the Temple of

the City God today. A huge crowd—it will be very lively. Why don't you go and have a look? Why just stay here by yourself feeling grumpy?'

The guest said, 'I am none other than the City God of Shanghai. Today is the Lantern Festival, so the men and women of the city crowd into the temple to burn incense. But they don't realize that spirits judge people on the basis of what is in their hearts and don't care about meaningless rituals. Some of these people are like dogs following a smell; some are prostitutes spending money earned plying their trade. Even worse, some of them are really evil and think only of harming other people. Their clothes and hats are so solemn and dignified, but they are no different than wild animals. They do not practice even everyday decency. Then they fawn on the spirits with incense and candles, and sacrifices of meat and wine, as if that will drive away their filthy smell. I couldn't stand it any more. It would be better for them not to do anything disgraceful in the course of their everyday lives, then their sincerity would be recognized by the spirits. So I ran away and took refuge here for the time being. Do not tell anyone about this.'"

3. Organizers of religious activities

Religious festivals were important occasions for expressing community solidarity and for friendly competition among various civic groups.

The Procession of the City God was an indigenous Shanghai religious practice, and despite its grand scale and the large numbers of occupational groups participating, it involved only locals in the Chinese city, not Chinese in the settlements.

Large-scale religious ceremonies in the settlements were organized by the guild halls and native-place organizations;[37] some were organized by the temples. A few of the temples were associated with a particular trade.

Rice-transporters' guild and temple

The Daoist Temple at Xinzha, also known as the Temple of the Four Kings of the Golden Dragon,[38] was the temple at which Shanghai rice-transporters, particularly the boat dwellers from Jiangbei, worshipped. Activities there are mentioned twice in the *Dianshizhai*. The first was on the occasion of the Lantern Festival in 1897:

> After a theatrical performance by the rice transporters guild in the Xinzha Temple, on the sixteenth day [of the first lunar month] the board of managers of the temple hired the Tianfu Theater to put on two additional performances. After the lamps had been extinguished, all the members of the board gathered at the temple to burn incense . . . suddenly a villager fell prostrate to the ground. He then stood up and said that a spirit was issuing instructions through him. He said that the Temple God was manifesting his presence and that all should respectfully listen. An epidemic was going to occur during the spring of the current year. All present must perform good deeds. On the sixteenth day of the fourth month they must carry the Temple God in procession, so as to dispel the epidemic and protect the people. The procession was limited to a distance of twenty *li*, and could not go beyond this boundary. He also complained that the money contributed by people in the rice trade during the Tongzhi period had not yet been acquitted. Only Mr. Qu and Mr. Lu of the Board of Directors were honest in their

dealings, and deserved commendation. And so on. After he finished speaking, he ordered that the Temple Boat should be made ready, because that evening he wanted to go to the Yellow River on a tour of inspection. Then the peasant suddenly awoke from his trance. All those who had heard him were terrified.[39]

That same year the *Dianshizhai* gave a vivid description of a procession in the same temple:

> During the procession at the Xinzha Temple a few days ago, the ceremony was brilliant and the celebrants lustrous. There were people walking on stilts and theatrical performances on raised stages. All the performances were so fresh and dazzling, the audience gasped in amazement. There is no need to go into detail. What follows was the most amazing: After the six ranks of scholars and officials came the tax collector (Fig. 124), wearing a gauze hat on his head and a red robe, carrying a wine-pot; he pretended to sprinkle wine along the road and acted like a muddle-headed official. He was preceded by several tablets, showing his various official positions; they indicated in large characters that he was a mandarin of the Thirteenth Degree; that he had been appointed to the position of magistrate of Tangshui County in Tengzhou Prefecture, and that he was entitled to wear the caltrop decoration[40] and a straw raincoat. He acted the part to the full, without any self-respect. He was followed by several bodyguards, carrying paper foreign guns on their shoulders, protecting a tax collection cart, swaggering to and fro. It was remarkably true-to-life. This particular act had not been witnessed in earlier processions. Raucous laughter, furious cursing—they completely exhausted all the possibilities, even to the smallest detail. We wonder if those people [the officials] could see it, would they also burst out laughing? Some people say that since purchasing an official title became possible, the quality of officials has degenerated. They are like fish drawn from the water, dragging their tails. The funds they spend on prostitutes are also used to acquire the privileges of office. We are inundated with such people; they are just everywhere.[41]

Interestingly enough, the commentary does not reprimand the participants in the procession for these irreverent attitudes, but stresses the degeneration of the official class.

Southern immigrants and the worship of Tianhou

Immigrants brought their local customs to Shanghai. Their influence on customs in Shanghai was proportionate to their numbers and their wealth. Tianhou, the Queen of Heaven, Protectress of Seafarers, had been worshipped by people from the coastal provinces of Guangdong and Fujian since at least the Song dynasty.[42] In the late nineteenth century, Cantonese and Fujianese merchants monopolized a lucrative trade transporting sugar from Shantou and Taiwan to Shanghai, and cotton from Shanghai back to Shantou and Taiwan.[43]

Shanghai's traditional sand-junk merchants had also been worshippers of Tianhou. The Small Sword Society destroyed the Tianhou Temple in 1853, and two years later Yu Songnian, whose family had made its money as sand-junk merchants, raised funds to reconstruct it.[44] These merchants, however, were a very small cohort among the residents of Shanghai. After the development of steam-powered boats, sand junks went into decline, and the merchants who transported goods on them gradually dwindled. They were replaced by the merchants from Guangdong and Fujian who continued the worship of Tianhou, even after the demise of her traditional worshippers in Shanghai. The construction of a new temple was financed by these Guangdong and Fujian merchants.

124. A procession organized by the Xinzha Temple (1897). The figure in the center of the sketch is a caricature of a tax collector. He has a gauze hat on his head, a wine pot in his hand, and is pretending to sprinkle wine along the road. The signs carried in front of him read: "Mandarin of the Thirteenth Rank" and "Wearer of the Caltrop Collar."

The twenty-third day of the third lunar month was designated Tianhou's birthday. On that day, the Cantonese, Fujianese, and other seafarers put on theatrical performances to express their respect.[45] Wang Tao recalled,

> The twenty-third day of the third month is the birthday of the Queen of Heaven. Colorful lanterns shine brightly. There is playing of flutes and singing. The area around the Eastern Gate is particularly lively. I have heard that not one of the rich merchants fails to exhaust his funds on this particular celebration. Along the streets, the shops and stores vie with each other to attract attention. They exhibit their bronze bells and tripods, and unprecedented displays of the most elegant calligraphy and painting. The light from precious candles soars into the air. Incense from golden burners wafts upwards. They burn heavy sandalwood from Kannada, the powerful fragrance expressing the harmony between Heaven and Earth. The fragrance pervades the air for several *li*. At that boats from far and near gather together, forming a wall of sails. Along the banks of the Huangpu River, cymbals and drums assail the ear throughout the whole night.[46]

In 1884, the new Temple of the Queen of Heaven was completed. Two sketches (Fig. 125) show details of the dedication ceremony. The commentary to them runs as follows:

> The new Temple of the Queen of Heaven has been built on the site of the previous Hongkou Railway Station.[47] On the twenty-fourth day of the fifth month, the statue was carried in procession from the Imperial Quarters at the East Gate to the new temple. As it passed through the International Settlement and the French Concession, crowds lined the streets, standing still in rapt attention. The whole town turned out the witness the event. All the participants in the procession behaved with the utmost decorum. Chinese and Western policemen, under the

direction of the Inspector of Police, took care of every detail and controlled every aspect. The procession was heralded by the usual cymbals and gongs to clear the way, followed by the Carriage of the Queen of Heaven and the Master of Ceremonies on horseback. Then came the Presentation Umbrella [with the names of the donors] inscribed in silver characters—a blaze of gorgeous color. Music played continuously. The next group in the procession rode on horseback: people dressed up as characters in traditional operas; young girls approaching the age of fastening the hairpin [marriageable age], in bright feminine attire, their hands on the reins, gracious and well poised. Then there were celestial boys and jade maidens on white horses, and children dressed up as the Eight Immortals, their horses prancing with quick, light steps—a vivid image indeed. Then came three horses neighing in the wind, with silk saddlecloths and jadelike reins—truly dazzling. Their riders were wearing brand new costumes and boots. Then we saw three portable stages, on which young children enacted scenes from traditional opera. It was remarkably true-to-life. This was followed by a group of Cantonese dressed up in official garb—hat, robe, and trousers—with golden bracelets on their wrists, beating gongs and carrying flags. Others were wearing straw hats and dark glasses, their full-length robes of lotus-colored snow-blue satins and processed silk. Some were holding flags or banners—there must have been thousands of them. Then the sound of gongs and drums, reed wind-pipes continuously playing—this was the hired band. A portable pavilion was then carried by, the sound of drums and gongs could be heard within it. Those hired for the occasion beat gongs as they carried it. Twenty-some men then passed by, carrying ten or so incense burners on their shoulders. The smoke from the incense wafts upwards, assailing the nostrils. Then several pairs of men on horseback passed, each holding high the personal banner of a high military official. The Cantonese and Fujianese cliques burned incense and made offerings of whole pigs and goats, cakes and fruits. They also went by, column after column. Then villagers dressed up as guards rode in chariots, holding up high the imperial edict, and other people just walked past with sticks of plain incense in their hands. All were serious and solemn, with no idle chatter. The Carriage of the Queen of Heaven was ornamented with yellow satin and red pedestals. On its roof stood five cranes reaching towards Heaven. About forty people followed, carrying incense. People crowded into the streets and lanes along the route. It was really a most magnificent procession, a vast panorama of Great Peace.[48]

In 1886 the *Dianshizhai* gave further details of the Procession to the Temple of the Queen of Heaven, this time on the occasion of the Double Ninth Festival, held on the ninth day of the ninth month.[49]

The Feast of the Hungry Ghosts

The Feast of the Hungry Ghosts was another important celebration organized mainly by the Guangdong and Fujian native associations, though other native-place associations also played a minor part. Every year, the Guangzhao Shanzhuang invited large numbers of Buddhist monks and Daoist priests to celebrate this feast, and so it became the major center for this celebration in Shanghai. Even coolies and workers in the silk filatures and factories would contribute funds every year towards the cost of this celebration.[50]

In 1877, the daotai of Shanghai, Liu Ruifen, approved a petition from the deputy of the Shanghai magistrate in the International Settlement that the event should be banned. In his order he stated, "Every year between the seventh and eighth month, people from Fujian, Guangdong, Ningbo, Shaoxing, and other places hold a festival known as the Feast of the Hungry Ghosts. It is very disorderly, and various undesirable elements take advantage of the situation to mix with the

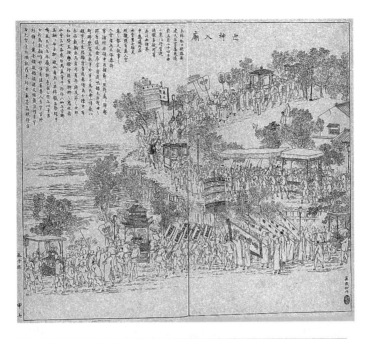

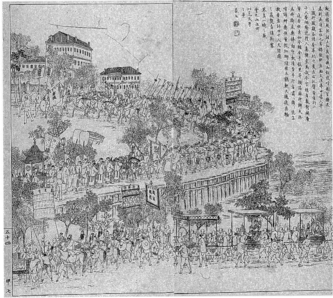

125. Welcoming ceremonies for a statue of the Queen of Heaven (1884).

crowd and cause trouble. They use the occasion to loot and steal, and engage in all sorts of iniquities. This order is to advise the consuls of all countries and to issue strict instructions to the managers of the guild halls of Fujian, Guangzhou, Chaozhou, Hui'an, Ningbo, and Shaoxing."[51]

These prohibitions had no effect. In 1887 and 1894 the *Dianshizhai* reported clashes between participants in this festival and the police. In 1887 it reported,

The Feast of the Hungry Ghosts is particularly extravagant in Shanghai. Toward the end of last month, a group of Daoist priests and laity held a procession and burned incense. As they were passing along Nanjing Road in the British Settlement, burning paper money along the way, a Sikh policeman tried to stop them, but they took no notice. So he arrested two of them, and took them to the police station. The other participants were furious. They gathered a group of their ox-headed and horse-faced fanatics, with long protruding teeth and flashing angry eyes, and swarmed in front of the police station, brandishing weapons to provoke a fight.[52] (Fig. 126)

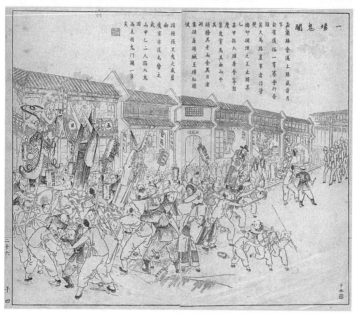

126. Feast of the Hungry Ghosts (1887). A group of Daoist priests and laity holds a procession during the Feast of the Hungry Ghosts and gets into a fight with police as they pass through the British Settlement.

The sketches in the *Dianshizhai* show people in the crowd carrying paper lanterns with the words "Salvation of Lonely Ghosts" inscribed on them. There are also paper effigies, ghosts in human form in various sizes, fighting with the police. In 1894 the *Dianshizhai* mentioned this festival again:

> The Feast of the Hungry Ghosts always occurs at mid-year. This festival is based on the words of the Buddha, offering universal salvation. Afterwards, however, people misunderstood its significance, and would fill bowls with grain and fruits as sacrificial offering to the spirits. It has lost its original meaning, and its latter-day followers have expanded it. It has reached a peak nowadays. The Cantonese believe in ghosts—to an inappropriate degree. This in itself is enough to attract disaster. This year in the Hongkou area a Mr. Lu and Mr. Lin organized the Feast of the Hungry Ghosts. The embellishments and ornamentation for the occasion were extremely luxurious and extravagant. They made a papier-mâché effigy of a Chinese policeman, and even gave him a number, 152, which was written in foreign numerals on his arm. It was carried in the procession. It just so happened that a Chinese policeman with the number 152 was passing by. When he saw this he was furious. He accused them of deliberately insulting him. He arrested Lu and Lin, and, together with the paper effigy, brought them to the Mixed Court. Lin was fined five *yuan* and Lu two *yuan,* as a warning to those who might offend the police.[53]

Other deities

The guild halls of Shanghai also organized the worship of the patron deities of various crafts. The carpenters of Ningbo built a small temple to Lu Ban in the Hongkou district, and they held a ceremony there once a year, on Lu Ban's birthday, the twentieth day of the third lunar month.[54] Lu Ban was also the patron deity of bricklayers, tilers, and plasterers.[55] The shoemakers of Shanghai worshipped Sun Bin as their patron-ancestor, and celebrated his birthday on the fifteenth day of the third lunar month; the tinsmiths and coppersmiths worshipped the Daoist deity Taishang Laojun as their patron-ancestor, and celebrated his birthday on the fifteenth of the second month.[56]

The *Dianshizhai* mentioned the God of Gambling in the Shenjiawan area immediately after an order had been issued prohibiting gambling.

> A few days ago, eight bosses of both large and small gambling dens gathered together more than seven hundred gamblers. They offered up a sacrifice of meat and wine to express their gratitude to the God of Gambling [Fig. 127]. When the ceremony was over, they held a banquet—at least one hundred tables—at which they drank freely and shouted with joy. The eight bosses announced to the crowd that if in the future policemen from either the settlements or the Chinese city came to arrest them or threaten them, they should courageously resist the enemy. Those who were first to join the fray would be rewarded, and those who ran away would be punished. If anyone disobeyed this order, they should not think it strange if they were not treated sympathetically, but were instead beaten until they were half dead. When the gamblers heard these words they all stood up and said to the bosses, "We will certainly obey your orders!" After this the meeting broke up, with great exuberance.[57]

127. The Gamblers' Alliance (1898). After gambling was formally prohibited, more than seven hundred gamblers gathered to offer sacrifice to the God of Gambling and swear that they would resist any policeman who might come to arrest them.

In 1897 the *Dianshizhai* reported a fight that had broken out between a group of beggars and members of a theatrical troupe outside the city walls, in which the beggars called on the help of the Beggar Ancestor (*Gaizu*).[58] There is no further information on the God of Gambling or the Beggar Ancestor in these news items.

Temple fairs

The major religious festival organized by the temples occurred on the eighth day of the fourth lunar month every year, the birthday of Śakyamuni.[59] On that day statues of the Buddha would be dusted and cleaned, and sutras chanted. The Jing'an Temple, one of the major Buddhist temples in Shanghai, had been destroyed during the Taiping Rebellion and was rebuilt in 1880. It was dedicated on Śakyamuni's birthday in 1881. This was an occasion of a great celebration, and the peddlers of Shanghai were not slow to set up their stalls in its vicinity. From then on, every year at this time, a temple fair of three days' duration would be held at the Jing'an Temple.

In 1885 the *Dianshizhai* gave a detailed description of a temple fair in Xujiahui:

> The area to the northwest of Shanghai is called Xujiahui. Every year on the eighth day of the fourth month they perform the Ceremonial Ablution of the Buddha. The altars are all opened [to the public], and innumerable men and women come to take part in this ritual. This year, on the day of the incense offering, the sky was clear, the air fresh, and the visitors were thick as a woven mat. Carved wheels and embroidered hubs vied with each other in an endless stream.[60]

As far as individual religious devotion was concerned, the two most popular temples in Shanghai included the Temple of the City God and the Hongmiao (Red Temple).[61] The latter was also known as the Temple of the Protector of the Peace. Dating from the Ming dynasty, it was originally a Buddhist temple, but a Daoist priest converted it into a Daoist temple during the Kangxi period.[62] The "Protector of the Peace" is said to refer to Yuan Shao of the Three Kingdoms, or alternatively, to Yuan Shansong of the Eastern Jin period.[63]

The Hongmiao was nominally Daoist, but Daoist deities and Buddhist bodhisattvas were not clearly differentiated. The major deity in the main hall was Guanyin, and in the eastern hall Guan Gong. There were images of the God of Wealth, the Three Great Emperors (the Ruler of Heaven, Ruler of Earth and Ruler of Water), the King of the Underworld, and other various deities in the Hall of the Constellations of Heaven.[64] The Hongmiao was located inside the International Settlement, and, although a humble collection of just a few rooms, it attracted an incessant stream of supplicants praying for children, for wealth, for long life, or seeking divine guidance by drawing lots.[65]

The Hongmiao's popularity can be seen in the pages of the *Dianshizhai*. Situated on one of Shanghai's main streets, its entrance was quite narrow, and its buildings no different from those of ordinary houses or shops in the area. A tablet inscribed "Temple of the Protector of the Peace" hangs over the front entrance. The Huarongchang Candle Shop stands to its left; the Dechang Rainwear Shop to its right (Fig. 128).[66] The commentary to this sketch gives us an insight as to how people believed in the efficacy of worship and prayer, and the way they responded if their prayers were answered: by offering up incense, donating inscribed tablets or decorating the statue of the deity to whom they had been praying.

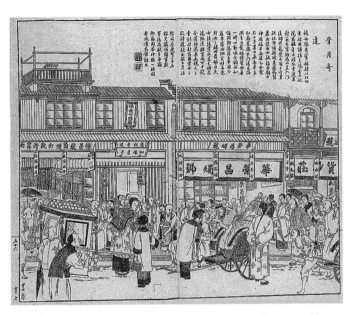

128. The Hongmiao (1897). This temple was very small, squeezed between two shops. The text tells of a woman from Jiangbei who encountered her long-lost mother there.

The Hongmiao flourished into the twentieth century. In later life, Mao Dun recalled the Spring Festival in Shanghai in 1933: The rest of the city was depressed and bleak that year, but "the tiny Hongmiao on Nanjing Road was so packed one could not get inside. Families of rich businessmen went there to offer incense, as did high-class prostitutes."[67]

4. Social environment and its effects

Religious practices connected with agricultural society were no longer practiced in the settlements, except for, of course, the Spring Festival, which was celebrated in a secular fashion as the Chinese New Year. Nonetheless, ceremonies of thanksgiving to the local God of the Earth after a successful harvest were still being practiced in towns only a few miles away.[68] Sometimes the magistrate of Shanghai would hold an agriculture-related ceremony, such as that praying for rain, but the participants almost invariably came from the villages. Residents of the settlements and the Chinese city showed little interest in taking part. This is in contrast to other cities, Beijing for example, where most festivals reflected their agricultural origins well into the Republican period.

There was a strong trend towards vulgarization in popular religion, such as the admixture of all sorts of monsters and clowns in processions.[69] Sometimes Buddhist sutras were sung to the tunes of brothel songs.[70] The temple fairs and the Ceremony of Ablution of the Buddha were more like marketplaces or spring outings. Important traditional religious beliefs and practices such as the "reverence for written paper" and abstinence from beef became unsustainable and irrelevant in the settlements.

RELIGIOUS PRACTICES

Excursions to "offer incense"

In the springtime, Shanghai women customarily traveled to some temple located in scenic surroundings outside the city to "offer incense." These occasions were a favorite opportunity to get together for an outing. In 1896 the *Dianshizhai* reported that a group of seventy brothel madams and prostitutes from the city had visited Putuoshan, ostensibly for the purpose of offering incense in the temples there (Fig. 129). We read in a contemporary source that it was often said that Shanghai women used to have a sense of dignity and decorum, and would never have thought of climbing mountains and touring temples. But since large numbers of peasant women from the villages had flocked to Shanghai to work in the foreign settlements, the standards of the population had declined.[71]

129. Brothel madams visit a holy mountain (1896). Seventeen madams travel to the holy Buddhist mountain Putuoshan to offer incense. Along the way one of them becomes possessed by a spirit. Beating her face, she says: "You people have been polluting Buddhist holy ground year after year. The Buddha has witnessed this with growing anger for a long time. You destroy young flowers (girls) and abuse good families. Now you dare to use the money you have acquired in this way to offer incense to flatter and beg the spirits, but you are begging for good fortune in vain. Do you think Buddha is like a corrupt official in your secular world?" The commentary suggests the madams should mend their ways.

In 1887 the *Dianshizhai* carried a commentary critical of women offering incense or attending theatrical performances in honor of some deity as being no more than an excuse to go out and appear in public.

Some women go to the temples to burn incense or go to watch performances in honor of the spirits, but those who are quiet and shy by nature do not like to take part, and those who are concerned with modesty and a sense of shame are not happy to join in. There are always one or two, however, who like to show off their charms. Should they hear of some lively event, they call together their girlfriends, gather up their skirts and off they go together. They attract frivolous attention. In fact they bring this upon themselves. . . . On the occasion of the renovation of a temple, local people hold a theatrical performance in honor of the spirits. To the left and the right are wooden poles supporting the stage, which is mounted on wooden planks. For a few cash [locals] can climb onto the benches and watch an opera."[72] (Fig. 130)

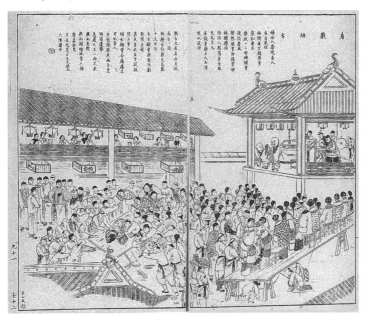

130. Women at a theatrical performance (1887). This performance was held in honor of a local deity. The stage has collapsed, making this occasion newsworthy.

This item used the occasion of the stage collapsing (*tan tai*) to poke fun at the women concerned, since that expression means "to lose face" in Shanghai dialect. Shanghai local officials had banned women from going to temples to offer incense as early as 1872.[73] This, like other such prohibitions, was quite widely ignored.

"Buddha shops"

Shanghai attracted many people in search of opportunities, including a considerable number of Buddhist monks, nuns, and Daoist priests. However, the city did not have sufficient temples to absorb them. This led to yet another Shanghai novelty—certain monks or nuns would hire a room, install a few statues and try to attract customers to buy and burn incense there. These were the so-called "Buddha shops" (Fig. 131). By 1876, there were nearly two hundred such establishments in the settlements. In 1874 an article in the *Shenbao* wrote of them:

A friend came from the villages to Shanghai. He has been sojourning here for more than half a month. We were chatting over a cup of wine and [I] asked him, 'What do you think of Shanghai?' My friend reeled off a number of impressions: the streets in the settlements were broad and

RELIGIOUS PRACTICES 207

clean, the foreign buildings impressive, the theaters huge, the restaurants and the teahouses magnificent, the horse-drawn carriages novel, and so on. But then he shook his head and said, "There is a very strange thing here which I can't understand. Can it be that the people of Shanghai have all taken to going to Western churches?" I was very surprised, and responded, "Why do you say that?" He said, "As soon as I arrived in Shanghai, I noticed that Western churches were everywhere. There are some Buddhist temples around, but these are no more than a few rooms rented by the people in the settlements, barely enough for the purposes of worship."[74]

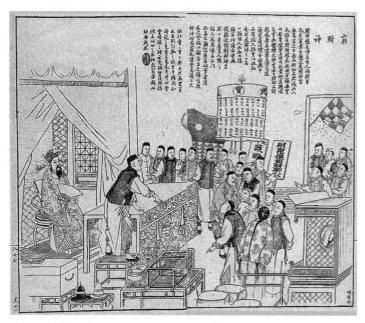

131. A Buddha shop (1896). The story relates how a shop whose major deity was the God of Wealth lost so much money that everything, including the God of Wealth statue, had to be sold at auction.

Buddha shops were officially banned, and in 1876 the *Shenbao* carried an editorial on the topic: "The private construction of temples has always been forbidden. Recently, certain Buddhist monks and nuns, and Daoist priests who have come to these settlements from elsewhere, rent rooms, which they call a sort of monastery or temple. They install a statue of the Buddha and organize various Buddhist activities. They entice stupid men and foolish women to go there to burn incense. Ignorant women acknowledge them as their teachers, to learn more about Buddhism. They then use this title to scrounge money and fish for profit. Some women claim to submit to Buddhist discipline, while declining to have their hair cut and their heads shaved. There are more and more such women every day. There must be one or two hundred Buddha shops in the tiny area of the settlements. The Daoist superior of Shanghai County, Zhu Jintao, made an application that they be banned. The magistrate of Shanghai County ordered the Bureau of Buddhist and Daoist Affairs to investigate the matter. The bureau found they had not engaged in any illegal activities, but they had privately established temples and ordained monks and nuns—these were prohibited activities. In addition, the origin of the Buddhist monks and Daoist priests was unclear; men and women mixed together [in the Buddha shops], and this was harmful to public morality. The county yamen and the Mixed Court jointly issued an order banning all of them. If any of them dared to stay, they would be immediately arrested and punished.[75]

Such prohibitions had no effect. Later sketches and stories in the *Dianshizhai* show that nothing had changed.

The God of Wealth

In the commercially oriented city of Shanghai the birthday of the God of Wealth was a special occasion. Traditionally this was held on the fifth day of the first lunar month. The eve of this birthday was set aside for various welcoming ceremonies. All shops and businesses in Shanghai honored the God of Wealth. The original deity was said to have been Zhao Gongming of the early Zhou, or another Zhao Gongming of the Three Kingdoms period. Another wealth god was He Wulu of the Yuan dynasty; who was later canonized as the God of Riches of the Five Roads.[76] It would seem that both these figures lay behind the wealth god Lutoushen, who was worshipped by the people of Shanghai.[77]

In 1895, on the fourth day of the Spring Festival, a drunken foreigner staggered into a Chinese restaurant in which a religious ceremony in honor of the God of Wealth was in process. The owner of the shop offered him a libation as if he were the God of Wealth personified. The *Dianshizhai* reported:

> The God of Wealth is known colloquially as the God of the Crossroads. There is a tradition that on the evening of the fourth day of the first month sacrifices of meat and wine are offered in welcome. People light candles and incense, and pray for prosperity in the coming year. All the shops and stores in Shanghai follow this custom. The Tongxing Restaurant in Hanbury Road in the American settlement is no exception. On the evening of the fourth day of the first month this year, just as they were in the process of displaying the sacrificial food and offering up money, a Westerner in a state of intoxication suddenly staggered in and brazenly sat himself down at the table on which the sacrifices had been placed, swallowing like a tiger and gulping like a wolf, using knives and chopsticks simultaneously. The proprietor of the shop decided to treat him as if he were the God of Wealth, so he just let him eat his fill and let him go. Someone said that this was a false God of Wealth, and even though he had enjoyed a feast, it was not going to do any good. The shop owner was surprised. Someone else explained, 'There are so many feasts for the God of Wealth going on at the moment—how could there be so many spirits to enjoy the smoke and fire of cooked food? It is not really the God of Wealth who accepts most of these offerings. A false God of Wealth is not as good as a living God of Wealth. A Westerner suddenly appeared in this shop just now. How are we to know that a real spirit was not mysteriously present in his enjoyment of our food? This restaurant might really make a lot of money!' Those who heard him all grinned broadly.[78]

The God of Wealth was worshipped in Shanghai, and business in Shanghai continued to prosper, which in turn led to an even greater devotion to the God of Wealth. Worship of this deity was not limited to once a year, and temples in his honor proliferated.[79] Some people even rented private houses to turn them into temples in his honor. But in 1896 the *Dianshizhai* told the story of a God of Wealth who had fallen on hard times:

> The God of Wealth, the bodhisattva of the North Terrace,[80] controls the wealth of the people. All those in search of wealth are constantly visiting him, so there is no reason for him to fear

poverty. This, however, is not always the case. There is a Temple to the God of Wealth on Beihai Road in the northern part of Shanghai. Supplications to this particular god, however, were not efficacious, so the amount of incense offered up there became negligible. The man who ran the temple could only raise his eyes to the ceiling and sigh. He owed quite a lot of money on rent, and the God of Wealth could not help. The landlord was making things difficult for him. He had no choice but to sell his property in order to compensate the landlord. So he arranged for all the goods in the temple to be auctioned, to pay the rent. Everything belonging to the God of Wealth was carried away. Only the statue of the God of Wealth remained, all alone. The landlord took pity on him and arranged for the statue to be installed in the Yangong Temple outside the West Gate. Some busybodies even placed advertisements in the newspapers to express their thanks to the landlord for his virtuous behavior. Alas! That God of Wealth was just so poor. We have seen cases in Shanghai of people having to auction their goods to pay the rent, but these were mainly poor and unemployed people, or swindlers building castles in the air, who appeared like the head of the Dragon King and disappeared like his tail. People who pray for wealth must surely be at a loss to explain how such a dignified and imposing spirit as the God of Wealth could have gotten into this predicament.[81]

Sorcerers

Many Chinese believed that disease was caused by demons or "evil pneumas," and in Shanghai it was very common to enlist the aid of a sorceress if they fell sick. The *Dianshizhai* looked askance at such practices: The [relatives of the sick person] prepare candles and incense, and they ask her [the sorceress] to inspect the house. This is called 'looking for immortals.' The sorceress claims that she herself is an immortal—this is mere nonsense."[82] Most stories of sorceresses in the *Dianshizhai* are meant to expose them and ridicule the stupidity of those who believed in them, such as the following account:

> Since ancient times, sorcerers and doctors have been considered similar, since they both use their skill to benefit people's lives. However, if doctors do something wrong, it is because of a mistake, it is not deliberate. If sorcerers do something wrong, it is based on fraud, and it is deliberate. So sorcerers should be prohibited, but not doctors. In the Lujiabang area to the south of Shanghai there is a sorceress by the name of Old Woman Yang. She was from Jinling [Nanjing] and claimed she could tell the future by observing incense smoke. The village people believed in her and said that she had the eyes of an immortal. Some time ago she fell victim to a sudden illness and died. A shroud and coffin were prepared. The body was placed in the coffin, and, as the lid was about to be put into place, suddenly she sat up, and demanded something to eat. This was strange indeed. Some people said, however, that this was merely an act, to make her skill appear more convincing. From that time on she could discuss the affairs of the netherworld with confidence, deliberately exaggerating to create a sensation to extract even more money [from those who believed in her].[83]

If the family of a person who had fallen ill believed that the illness was due to malignant spiritual influences, they might also call in one or more Daoist priest. There are two such stories in the *Dianshizhai*. One concerns a woman who believed her sickness was the result of hexing by a chthonic snake. She had tried innumerable methods to cure herself without success. The family asked a Daoist priest to exorcise the snake, but his magic was insufficient, and he himself became its victim.[84] The other story concerns a Daoist priest from Hubei who pasted up advertisements in the streets and alleys, praising himself as an exponent of the spiritual way who could cure sickness by magic.[85]

There were also occasions when people sought the aid of a sorceress to find out information. Here is one account:

> It is a common failing of women to believe in the powers of sorcery. There is a woman in Hongkou whose husband makes a living on a steamship. Recently he went to another port, he did not come back on time, and his wife was worried about him. She made inquiries from a sorceress. The sorceress said that he had died and his wife must immediately establish his merits, so that he could escape the sea of bitterness. The woman was pained that his soul was lost and could not return, and she arranged for a 'calling back of the soul' ceremony, and she invited the sorceress to hold a repentance ceremony. Someone told her not to be in a hurry to do this; it would be better to wait until reliable information was available. The woman said that the information had been confirmed by the sorceress, and it was not possible that she would want to deceive her. So they poured libations of wine as offerings to the spirit of the dead and cried to Heaven. At this point, her husband turned up without a care in the world. They thought they had seen a ghost, so they rushed to hide themselves. The husband was amazed and asked what was going on. His wife told him what the sorceress had told her, but by this time the old woman had gathered up her ritual implements and run away. The wife, laughing through her tears, asked him why he had come back so late. He explained that the ship had been stranded in shallow waters, and this had delayed his return.[86]

Some people started their careers as doctors and ended up as sorcerers. In 1891 the *Dianshizhai* reported the case of a man from Jiangbei who had practiced acupuncture and moxibustion for some time. He could not support himself, however, so he rented a room in the French Concession, and installed statues of Guanyin, Zhong Kui, Hua Tuo and others. He claimed to be the reincarnation of Zhong Kui and said he could cure disease by exorcising evil spirits. He wore a mantle draped over his shoulders and would dance and gesticulate with his eyes half-closed, mumbling incantations. For those who sought his help, he would prescribe incense ash, or acupuncture and moxibustion. He then told them to go home, and offer incense, candles and the three sacrifices to the spirits to express their gratitude, and then take the medicine (Fig. 132).[87]

There were also a few people in Shanghai who claimed they were Daoists with a special affinity with the world of spirits and demons (Fig. 133). As far as we can see from the *Dianshizhai*, most of them had not been in Shanghai very long, and people did not know much about their backgrounds. If a local person were to suddenly pretend to be in communion with the netherworld, he would not be particularly convincing. In 1897 the *Dianshizhai* mentioned that a local man in the Chinese city had announced that he had achieved the way of the immortals, but his neighbors just made fun of him.[88] The *Dianshizhai* was generally critical about such matters. "Belief in ghosts and spirits has been an entrenched custom in the Wu region for a long time. So the cunning take advantage, and the stupid are deceived."[89]

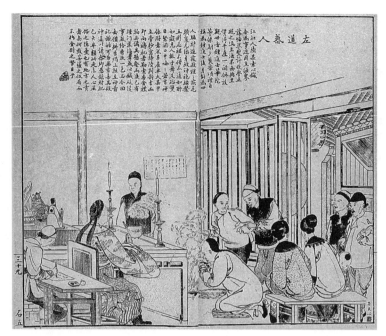

132. An acupuncturist adds sorcery to his skills (1891).

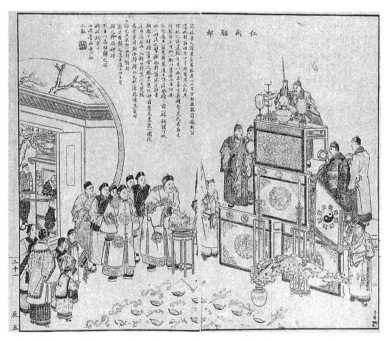

133. A Daoist priest exorcises a haunted house (1888). The Daoist told the owner to perform good deeds, so he donated two hundred *yuan* to disaster relief. The receipt was ceremoniously burned, and the house was successfully exorcised.

"Reverence for lettered paper"

Among the gentry in Qing China, one of the important aspects of personal moral cultivation was the custom of "reverence for lettered paper." Many charitable halls in Shanghai County organized "Lettered Paper Societies" whose task it was to collect paper on which characters had been written for appropriate disposal, and at the same time to exert supervision and control over the users of paper and thus the written word—both among individuals and shops.[90]

Details of this custom are also to be found in the *Dianshizhai*. In 1890 a description of ceremonies in Taiwan tells how the ashes of lettered paper were solemnly scattered into the ocean (Fig. 134).[91] Even small details are recorded in the *Dianshizhai* sketches, such as the special receptacles for lettered paper (usually a bamboo basket). One sketch dated 1889 shows an old man carrying such a receptacle, on which is inscribed "Wenchang Pavilion—Show Reverence for Lettered Paper."[92]

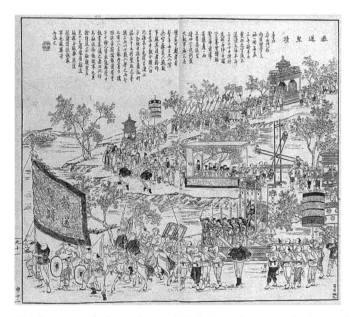

134. Reverence for lettered paper (1890). Every three years the Society for Reverence for Lettered Paper in Taipei collected the ashes of lettered paper which had been burnt during the previous three years and ceremoniously deposited them in the ocean. The sketch shows the parade held on the twentieth day of the third month, and includes people dressed in costumes from traditional drama. At the end of the parade can be seen the large urns containing the ashes. The banner at the front of the procession reads: "Respectfully Escorting Sacred Remains."

In praising local gentry or influential people, reverence for lettered paper was listed with other types of virtuous behavior.[93] We read in the *Shanghai County Gazetteer Supplement* that

> the Yishan Charitable Hall stands outside the Great South Gate. In the tenth year of the Tongzhi period the pediatrician Gu Mingzhao established a Bureau of Reverence for Lettered Paper and provided funds to buy land and build a Temple to Cang Jie [the mythical inventor of

writing]. The area of the land was one *mu* and 1.5 *li*. In conjunction with the gentry of Shanghai and Nanhui, they reported to the daotai and the magistrate in the twelfth year [of the Tongzhi period]. Then they started to collect and ceremonially burn lettered paper and printed tracts, promoting reverence for lettered paper and filial piety. They also collected ashes [of burned lettered paper] from Chuansha and Nanhui, so as to dispose of them in the ocean."[94]

This custom was also observed by illiterate villagers, although the reason for their respect was different from those of the literati. They were more concerned about reward and retribution.[95] Treatises on reward and retribution devoted much space to "reverence for lettered paper." In *The Infallibly Efficacious Divination Rods of the Holy Emperor Guan Gong* we read, "During the Kangxi period, a man died of a very minor ailment. This was because he himself would burn the paper on which he had written, and then casually throw the ashes away. For this reason his life was shortened by five years."[96] Another case from the same book relates: "A scholar achieved the title of Presented Scholar. A spirit appeared to him in a dream and said, 'Your ancestors paid reverence to lettered paper. This has brought illustriousness to their children and grandchildren.'"

There are occasional stories about showing reverence for lettered paper in the *Dianshizhai*. One concerns an old man from Suzhou who was accepted into the Bureau of Reverence for Lettered Paper because of his exceptionally virtuous life. One night he was returning to his home carrying a load of lettered paper, when he encountered a ghost. The ghost was repelled by the luminescence of the lettered paper and so the man was saved.[97] Another story made the point that, if one did not show reverence for lettered paper, virtuous behavior in other areas was of no use:

> A rich man in Liyang took a wife. She was also from a rich family, and her dowry was very large. She was also good-looking. Before ten days had passed after her marriage, everyone in the family was full of praise for her virtue. One day she was struck by lightning and died. Nobody knew the reason for this. The lightning continued to encircle her bedroom. Suddenly, with a crash of thunder, a bolt of lightning split open her clothes chest. On investigation, it was discovered that the soles of her shoes had been padded with lettered paper. This shows that blatant irreverence for lettered paper cannot be forgiven. Using lettered paper to pad the soles of her shoes was a deliberate act of disrespect. Her contempt for principles was excessive and Heaven wanted to make clear its punishment. Alas, alas! Should we not pay attention to this?"[98] (Fig. 135)

But it became more and more difficult to sustain this custom in Shanghai of the late nineteenth century. Printed materials, including newspapers, were more and more common, and paperwork associated with the every increasing numbers of firms and factories made "lettered paper" virtually ubiquitous in matters of commerce. The Shanghai gentry and other upholders of traditional values did not let up in their efforts to keep such customs alive, however. They constantly published articles in the *Shenbao* exhorting people to continue showing proper reverence."[99] One item reported the gentry-managers of the Shanghai charitable halls suggesting that official announcements, which were usually pasted on the walls along the streets, and so eventually became ragged and damaged, should be pasted onto wooden boards. The magistrate of Shanghai agreed with this suggestion and ordered that appropriate wooden boards be made, and that old announcements should be carefully removed and delivered to the Hall of Assistance and Benevolence (Jishantang) in the southern part of the Chinese city. The last sentence in his order read: "This method is in accordance with the principles of reverence for lettered paper. All people acting in this way will certainly achieve unlimited good fortune."[100]

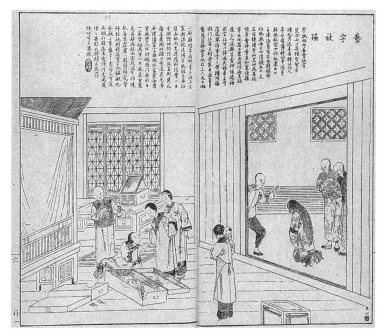

135. Irreverence for the written word results in sudden death (1896). A woman who seemed to have led a blameless life is struck dead by lightning (right panel). After her death it was discovered she had used paper with writing on it as padding in her shoes (left panel).

In the same year, 1873, the *Shenbao* carried an "Official notice from the Magistrate of Shanghai on the Implementation of Reverence for Lettered Paper," and ten days later published "Regulations on Showing Reverence for the Written Word," which listed very detailed regulations, including rules to the effect that women were not allowed to embroider characters onto silk or cotton cloth, that shops were not permitted to have the name of their establishment printed on their wrapping paper, that it was forbidden to print the size of shoes and stockings on them, that laundries were not permitted to dye material on which there was any writing, and so on. According to convention, such an official announcement should have been delivered to all the shops by local constables, but there was some concern that the constables would take advantage of the opportunity to pick fights, so the clerks of the charitable halls were entrusted with this task. This meant that the magistrate had lent his authority to the charitable halls in this matter, and if any shop or individual infringed on the regulations, or did not submit to the authority of the charitable halls, they would have to answer to the court.[101]

Some individuals also wrote articles in the newspapers suggesting that people should not only respect paper that had been written on, but should also respect paper that was going to be written on; that one should not write anything indecent on paper, including articles which were not truthful, and so on.[102] Another article criticized women who hid money in their stockings, because coins had characters on them, and such a hiding place was deemed disrespectful.[103]

Despite this campaign, respect for lettered paper continued fade most seriously. In 1877 the *Shenbao* published an article "On the Charitable Halls Collecting Lettered Paper,"[104] in which the author complains that despite the fact that "charitable halls in Shanghai are as numerous as trees in a forest, and people collecting lettered paper were also as numerous as trees in a forest," the result still left much to be desired. He blamed what he regarded as the irresponsible attitude of the officials charged with this task. The gentry also felt uneasy about the letterhead paper and other printed material produced and used by foreign firms and factories.[105] People often placed exhortations relating to the reverence for the written word in the advertisement columns of the *Shenbao*. Spending money on such advertisements was considered a good deed. In 1876, someone writing under the name "Master of the Hall of Eight Chants" published an advertisement: "An Appeal to Gentlemen in Foreign Firms and Silk Filatures to Show Reverence for Lettered Paper." The author mentioned that one day he had noticed wrapping paper on which there was writing in the foreign firm Iveson and Company. After the package had been opened the paper was thrown away, and the quality-control docket had been thrown away as well. He felt very uneasy about this, so he decided to place an advertisement in the newspaper to exhort people to do the right thing, because, as the last line in the advertisement put it, "reverence for lettered paper prolongs life and ensures a just reward."[106]

At this stage, "lettered paper" meant paper with Chinese characters written on it. Two years later, however, the *Shenbao* published an article "On Showing Reverence for Lettered Paper of All Countries," in which foreign writing was also included. "The form of writing of different countries is different, but its function is the same. So we urge all countries—south, north, west and east—to respect all types of lettered paper, be they foreign or Chinese, for the honor and glory of all."[107] Respecting foreign paper was then extended to concern for the lack of this practice in areas outside China. In 1885 the *Shenbao* published an announcement under the name of Ye Qunying, of Tong'an County, Fujian, in which he said that he had lived in Luzón for many years. He had seen the grass mats made and sold by the Chinese there, who used Chinese characters as trademarks. The people who bought these mats, however, used them for wrapping corpses or for women in childbirth. This was an offence against the sages, and the writer suggested that animals or other objects be used as trademarks instead of characters.[108] This man was clearly not a member of the gentry, but a supporter of tradition nonetheless.

The authorities in the Chinese city had the power to punish those who violated these regulations, as was recorded by the *Dianshizhai* in 1896:

> Lettered paper has always been collected by charitable halls and ceremoniously burned by them; this is to show respect for the written words of the sages. Recently, some people from Jiangbei made it their business to collect old account books and old copies of newspapers such as the *Shenbao* and the *Hu Bao*, and sold them at ten times their cost by smuggling them out of Shanghai to Tianjin and Tanggu. They sold them in shoe shops as padding for soles. They could get about fifty cash per catty. Betraying principles in search of private profit—nothing is worse than this. The gentry-manager of the Association for the Reverence for Lettered Paper found out and requested that the magistrate prohibit this trade. Three people were arrested by the Baojia Bureau and sent to the county yamen, where they were sentenced to be beaten with a bamboo cane and ordered back to their home districts.[109]

Settlements authorities did not even give nominal support to this practice. As Shanghai was grew more and more prosperous, the vast increase of printed materials meant that the maintenance of this ancient tradition had become impossible.[110]

The decline of agriculture-based traditions and beliefs

The slaughter of oxen was forbidden by Chinese authorities. In the settlements, however, the increases in the foreign population led to local Chinese becoming more accustomed to Western food, and eating beef became increasingly common. Abattoirs set up near the Nicheng Bridge are featured in a *Dianshizhai* sketch dated 1895.[111] Even as beef became a common ingredient in the diet of the Shanghai people, admonitions supporting traditional prohibitions continued to be published. Wang Tao noted, "People in Shanghai have no inhibitions about eating beef. There are shameless butchers everywhere. No one can stop them. Since the arrival of the Westerners, people who eat beef have increased in number. They are brazenly open about it, and they even display beef in the marketplace. They do not see anything wrong in this."[112] In 1886 the *Dianshizhai* commented, "Westerners eat beef as if it were pork or mutton. Despite its strength in plowing, they do not treasure [the ox] in the least. Since this port was opened, we do not know how many hundreds, thousands, millions have been slaughtered. This is a great catastrophe. Recently they have even begun slaughtering calves—this is even more cruel." It went on to relate the following story:

> A few days ago, at a tea stall to the left of the Eight Immortals Bridge, a young villager was found with a plough ox, wanting to sell it. There are slaughterhouses in that area, so the intention of the villager was quite obvious. An officer from the police station in the Chinese city, Mr. Deng, happened to be strolling by when the ox fell to its knees before him. Its tears flowed as it wept, as if begging him to save its life. Mr. Deng felt great compassion when he saw this, and he took out ten Mexican silver dollars and took the ox home with him. Two days later, the ox died. Alas! The ox knew it was going to be killed. It implored someone to save it and was indeed saved. The ox's intelligence proved to be its good fortune. The difference between dying of natural causes and being slaughtered is the difference between Heaven and Earth. If only all people under Heaven were so solicitous as Mr. Deng![113]

Articles commenting on this matter appeared constantly in the *Shenbao* as well.[114] Abstinence from beef was a major virtue in the traditional conception of reward and retribution. Tracts on proper moral behavior are full of such examples—sudden death after eating beef, abstinence from beef as a guarantee of success in the imperial examinations, if not for oneself then for one's grandsons and so on.[115]

The *Dianshizhai* contains a story dated 1885 with the title "Retribution for a Killer": "Oxen also have their own constellation in the firmament. So the killing of an ox is strictly prohibited. But some people kill the ox secretly to make a large profit. After relying on its strength, they kill it. The unrequited spirit of the ox cannot speak, but can it be that it will not seek justice?" The *Dianshizhai* went on to tell the story of a man who died when, for no apparent reason, he slipped and fell into a pot in which he had been cooking beef (Fig. 136).[116]

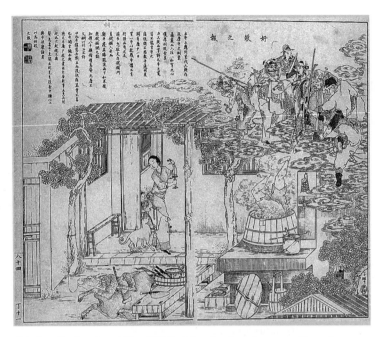

136. Retribution for a killer (1885). A butcher bought an ox. Along the way home they passed by a native bank (*qianzhuang*), and the ox knelt down, tears falling from its eyes, and begged to be spared. Someone offered eight thousand cash, but the butcher would not agree. The next morning his wife discovered that he had fallen into the cauldron and was cooked together with the ox. The sketch shows the stars in the ox constellation ordering the punishment.

Although Shanghai people did not strictly observe the prohibition against eating beef, the prohibition existed nonetheless; slaughtering oxen was illegal, and there was an awareness that the eating of beef was immoral. In a list of crimes the expression "he secretly slaughtered an ox, boiled the meat, cut it up when it was cooked, then displayed it in a market stall" was not uncommon.[117] In 1885 an epidemic of cattle plague hit Shanghai, and the *Dianshizhai* told the story of a scholar who had saved his ox—and at the same time provided a good advertisement for cattle plague medicine (Fig. 137):

> A certain scholar, who despite the fact that he had studied books, did not abandon cultivation of the earth. During an epidemic of cattle plague, his ox fell victim to it, and he clearly knew that it would be difficult to cure. However, he still acquired all sorts of fantastic cures, and mixed them with boiling water, and poured the mixture into the ox's mouth. The night passed and the next day the ox could eat again. That miraculous cure was none other than the cholera cure, available from the Xinchang Jewelry Shop on Jiujiang Road.[118]

No matter that eating beef had become widespread, the traditional gentry still tried to maintain traditional prohibitions—and even some of the progressive settlement literati still regarded abstinence from beef to be meritorious. The editors of the *Dianshizhai* were among them, including Wang Tao. The issue of eating beef became a hotly debated subject among reformers in the late Qing. In one conversation among a group of friends at a meal in a Western restaurant in Li Boyuan's novel *A Brief History of Enlightenment* we read the following exchange:

> Yao Wentong said, "Over the many generations since our founding ancestor, we have never eaten beef. So please don't insist."
> Hu Zhongli laughed loudly. "You are supposed to be an advocate of new learning, but you won't even eat beef. This is sure to make your reformist friends laugh at you!"
> Yao still refused.
> Kang Botu said, "The oxen of Shanghai are different from those in China proper. There, the oxen plough the fields and exert themselves for the good of man, and so people cannot bear to kill them and eat them. The foreigners in Shanghai, however, rear cattle and make them fat, so that they can kill them for their meat. So they are called edible oxen, and eating them cannot be considered wrong."[119]

137. An ox begs to be spared (1885). "Not long ago a peasant leading a young ox passed by the Baida Bridge. A policeman stopped him, saying that according to the regulations of the settlements one could not lead an ox across the bridge [into the settlements]. He asked him where he had come from and where he was going. The villager said that he had come from Eight Immortals Bridge and was bringing the ox to the slaughterhouse in the settlements. Just as they were speaking, the ox groaned several times and knelt in front of the policeman, as if it were begging him to save its life. This was strange indeed. It must be that it loved life and feared death, the same as human beings. Oxen have their own star in the firmament and plough the fields for man. Their contribution is not inconsiderable. There is no reason to kill an ox. The ox had no control over the situation but surely understood what was happening. If one has sympathy with victims of injustice, one should also consider the ox and put down one's butcher knife."

RELIGIOUS PRACTICES 219

These debates, hesitations, and especially the protests from the traditionalists, appeared as part of the disengagement from this aspect of traditional Chinese culture. Once the process was complete, debates on the issue faded into silence. Views either for or against became equally meaningless. By the late nineteenth century, eating beef was accepted as if it had always been so.

Notes

[1] One might compare this with the strict control of the Japanese authorities over temple organization in Taiwan after 1895. Cf. Stephan Feuchtwang, "City Temples in Taipei under Three Régimes," in Elvin and Skinner, *The Chinese City between Two Worlds*, 263.

[2] Stephan Feuchtwang, "School-Temple and City God," in G. William Skinner, ed., *The City in Late Imperial China*, (Stanford: Stanford University Press, 1977), 581–608. Cf. Marcel Granet, *The Religion of the Chinese People*, (Oxford: Blackwell, 1975), 97, who divides Chinese religion into three categories: peasant religion, feudal religion and official religion. On the latter, he notes "It was not reserved to one social class; it was, in a sense, a national religion; in the first place because it was instituted for the benefit of the whole nation, but also because the influence of its principles permeated the religious life of all its members."

[3] Shanghai tongshe, *Shanghai yanjiu ziliao*, 528–48, "Liushi nian qian Shanghai: jiu zhangbu zhong de zhanggu" (Shanghai sixty years ago: Anecdotes from an old account book) in which the author discusses two old Shanghai County account books he found in a second-hand book stall, with records from 1872 to 1875 recording in detail the religious ceremonies and sacrifices in which the magistrate participated during the year.

[4] Susan Naquin, "Transmission of White Lotus Sectarianism," in David Johnson, Andrew Nathan, and Evelyn S. Rawski, *Popular Culture in Late Imperial China* (Berkeley: University of California Press, 1985), 255–91, regards the White Lotus sects as being heterodox at some times, and orthodox at others.

[5] Hai 10.

[6] Geng 48.

[7] Ding 48.

[8] Zhong 16.

[9] Zheng Yimei, *Shanghai xianhua*, 41; Yao Gonghe, *Shanghai xianhua*, 3; Chen Dingshan, *Chunshen jiuwen*, 9.

[10] Feuchtwang, "City Temples," 280–81.

[11] Shanghai tongshe, *Shanghai yanjiu ziliao*, 501–7; Cao Yishi, *Shanghai xian Chenghuang shen song* (In praise of the city god of Shanghai County), 1847, copy held in the Shanghai Library. Qin attained the degree of *jinshi* in 1344, and served under the Yuan as a magistrate in Shandong, and as a departmental director of the provincial government of Fujian. Zhu Yuanzhang approached him several times, but he was reluctant to serve the new dynasty. Eventually he accepted a position in the Hanlin Academy. When the Emperor heard of Qin Yubo's death, he is said to have declared, "Yubo was reluctant to serve me in life. Now let his spirit serve me after death." Thus Qin Yubo was appointed the city god of Shanghai. See Frank Ching, *Ancestors: 900 Years in the Life of a Chinese Family* (London: Harrap Limited, 1988), 77–90.

[12] Xing 2.

[13] Liu Yanong, *Shanghai xianhua*, 90–93; Zhang Chunhua, *Hucheng suishi quge* (Street songs of yearly events in Shanghai) (Shanghai, 1839; reprinted in *Shanghai zhanggu congshu*, 1936), 4 xia.

[14] Wang Tao, *Yingruan zazhi*, juan 1, 12–13.

[15] Chen Liansheng and Chen Yaoting, "Shanghai Daojiao yu zhuyao daoguan" (Daoism in Shanghai and its major temples), in *Lishi wenhua mingcheng: Shanghai*, 250.

[16] Liu Yanong, *Shanghai xianhua*, 93.

[17] Wu Guifang, *Shanghai fengwu zhi*, 292.

[18] Fu Xiangyuan, *Qingbang daheng: Huang Jinrong, Du Yuesheng, Zhang Shaolin zhuan* (Green Gang Bosses: Biographies of Huang Jinrong, Du Yuesheng and Zhang Shaolin) (Beijing: Zhongguo wenshi chubanshe, 1987), 205–8.

[19] One might compare the role of carnivals in Europe, which were considered a "controlled escape of steam." See Peter B. Burke, *Popular Culture in Early Modern Europe* (London: Temple Smith, 1978), 197–98.

[20] Liu Yanong, *Shanghai xianhua*, 91–92.

[21] *Shenbao*, October 30, 1872.

[22] *Shenbao*, March 31, 1873.

[23] Chen 5.

[24] Xin 42–43; Xin 32; Zhu 94.

[25] *Shenbao*, February 21, 1888.

[26] Shanghai tongshe, *Shanghai yanjiu ziliao*, 530.

[27] *Shenbao*, March 31, 1873.

[28] *Shenbao*, July 1, 1873.

[29] Derk Bodde, trans. and annot., *Annual Customs and Festivals in Peking*, by Tun Li-ch'en (Hong Kong: Hong Kong University Press, 1965), 61–62; Victor H. Mair, *T'ang Transformation Texts* (Cambridge, Mass.: Harvard University Press, 1989), 17–18.

[30] Cohn, *Vignettes from the Chinese*, 38–39.

[31] Si 43.

[32] Geng 4.

[33] Hai 34; Wu 67, Wu 48, Hai 77, Pao 21, Heng 54.

[34] Zhong 25.

[35] Wen 63.

[36] Xin 68. Similar disapproval of such practices can be seen in Shu 22, Hai 90.

[37] See Peter J. Golas, "Early Ch'ing Guilds," in Skinner, ed., *The City in Late Imperial China*, 555–80, on page 577.

[38] The golden dragon refers to Liu Yi, a character in a Tang dynasty story *The Biography of Liu Yi*, later rewritten as a Yuan *zaju* under the title *Liu Yi Transmits a Message*. Liu Yi was later transformed into a water spirit, and was worshipped by those who traveled on rivers and lakes. See Zong Li and Liu Qun, *Zhongguo minjian zhushen* (Popular deities of China) (Shijiazhuang: Hebei renmin chubanshe, 1986), 338, 368; V. R. Burkhardt, *Chinese Creeds and Customs* (Hong Kong: South China Morning Post, Ltd, 1955), vol. 2, 165–66.

[39] Xin* 58.

[40] The place names are presumably fictitious. The lowest official grade was the Ninth Degree, so the Thirteenth Degree was even lower. The term *ling* in *shajiaoling* refers to the peacock feather decoration worn on the hats of high officials. The word for water caltrop in Shanghaiese is *sa-kauh-ling*, homophonous with *shajiaoling*.

[41] Yuan 39.

[42] Tianhou, also known as Tianfei, is known as Mazu in Guangdong, Fujian and Taiwan. See Zong Li and Liu Qun, *Zhongguo minjian zhushen*, 389–402; Wu Huanchu, *Tianfei niangma zhuan* (Biography of Tianhou, Queen of Heaven) (Ming (Wanli period); reprinted Shanghai: Shanghai guji chubanshe, 1990).

[43] Wang Tao, *Yingruan zazhi*, juan 1, 8.

[44] For the background to the Tianhou Temple in Shanghai, see Shanghai tongshe, *Shanghai yanjiu ziliao*, 517–23.

[45] Ge Yuanxu, *Huyou zaji*, juan 1, 3.

[46] Wang Tao, *Yingruan zazhi*, juan 1, 13.

[47] The abandoned railway station for the Wusong-Shanghai line.

⁴⁸ Jia 53–54.

⁴⁹ Xin 68. See also Wu Guifang, *Shanghai fengwu zhi*, 293.

⁵⁰ *Shenbao*, September 13, 1873; Chen Boxi, *Lao Shanghai, xia ce* 71, Hushang youxi zhuren, *Haishang youxi tushuo, juan* 3, 26; Goodman, *Native Place, City and Nation*, 91–103.

⁵¹ *Shenbao*, August 20, 1877.

⁵² Zi 26.

⁵³ She 15.

⁵⁴ You 27; Shanghai shi gongshang guanliju, ed., *Shanghai minzu jiqi gongye*, 60; Golas, "Early Ch'ing Guilds," 577–78; Quan Hansheng, *Zhongguo hanghui zhidu shi* (A history of the guild hall system in China) (Shanghai: Xin shengming shudian, 1934), 57–62; Gu Chengfu, *Hushang suishi fengsu* (Annual festivals in Shanghai) (Shanghai: Huadong shifan daxue chubanshe, 1989), 64.

⁵⁵ Li Qiao, *Zhongguo hangyeshen chongbai* (The worship of Chinese occupation deities) (Beijing: Zhongguo huaqiao chubanshe, 1990), 83–84.

⁵⁶ Gu Chengfu, *Hushang suishi fengsu*, 49 and 63.

⁵⁷ Zhen 7.

⁵⁸ Yuan 77.

⁵⁹ Peter Gregory and Patricia Ebrey, *Religion and Society in T'ang and Sung China* (Honolulu: University of Hawaii Press, 1993), 13.

⁶⁰ Ding 55. This area has of course traditionally been predominantly Catholic, but the commentary makes no mention of this.

⁶¹ Liu Yanong, *Shanghai xianhua*, 93.

⁶² Shanghai wenshiguan, ed. *Lishi wenhua mingcheng: Shanghai*, 251.

⁶³ Tang Weikang, *Shanghai yishi*, 225.

⁶⁴ Tang Weikang, *Shanghai yishi*, 226.

⁶⁵ Hushang youxi zhuren, *Hushang youxi tushuo, juan* 3, 14 *xia*; 25 *xia*; Chen Boxi, *Lao Shanghai, xia ce*, 65.

⁶⁶ Heng 56.

⁶⁷ Mao Dun, "Duoshi er huoyue de suiyue" (Busy and eventful months and years), *Xinhua wenzhai* (October 1982): 198.

⁶⁸ She 59.

⁶⁹ Zi 26, Xin 42–43.

⁷⁰ Xin 32.

⁷¹ Qin Rongguang, *Shanghai xian zhuzhici*, 54 .

⁷² Ren 91.

⁷³ *Shenbao*, July 5, 1872.

⁷⁴ *Shenbao*, December 11, 1974.

⁷⁵ *Shenbao*, August 17, 1876. Similar news items or articles in the *Shenbao* are on August 19, 1876; October 31, 1877; November 5, 1877; and April 10, 1876.

⁷⁶ Zong Li and Liu Qun, *Zhongguo minjian zhushen*, 625–35; Bodde, *Annual Customs and Festivals in Peking*, 2.

⁷⁷ E.T.C. Werner, *A Dictionary of Chinese Mythology* (Shanghai: Kelly and Walsh, 1932; reprinted New York: Julian Press, 1961), 514–17. Wen 87; Li* 52, Yu 34.

⁷⁸ Yu 34. The expression *fa yang cai* is still used in Shanghai dialect, and implies an unexpected, large windfall. Apparently even in the nineteenth century, Chinese thought doing business with foreigners was a shortcut to instant wealth. According to Qin Rongguang, Shanghai residents would offer up a sheep's head and a carp to the God of Wealth. Zhao Xuantan originated as a God of Wealth among the Muslims, thus the sheep's head. The carp is a traditional symbol of wealth. See Qin Rongguang, *Shanghai xian zhuzhici*, 44.

[79] Clarence Burton Day, "Shanghai Welcomes the God of Wealth," in *The China Journal*, vol. 8, no. 6 (June 1928): 289–94; reprinted in *Popular Religion in Pre-Communist China*, (California: Chinese Materials Center, Inc., 1975), 39–46.

[80] This term refers yet another wealth god, Xuantan (Yuantan) Pusa, the Bodhisattva of the North Terrace. Werner (*Chinese Mythology*, 515), describes him as "the Mohammedan Hsüan (Yüan)-t'an P'u-sa," the term *pusa* apparently not being incompatible with his supposed origin.

[81] Wen 87.

[82] *Shenbao*, June 16, 1879; see also Liu Yanong, *Shanghai xianhua*, 66–67.

[83] Wu 22.

[84] Shi 22.

[85] Li 63.

[86] Mao 22.

[87] Shi 39.

[88] Heng 33.

[89] Jia 89.

[90] See Rev. Justus Doolittle, *Social Life of the Chinese*, vol. 2 (New York: Harder and Brothers, 1865), 167–69; J.J.M. de Groot, *The Religious System of China*, vol. 6 (Leiden: E. J. Brill, 1892–1910; reprinted Taipei: Literature House Ltd, 1964), 1010–1023.

[91] Shen 91.

[92] Chen 44 *xia*.

[93] For example, "In the third year of the Guangxu period, Sheng Xuanhuai, a powerful member of the gentry of Wujin, single-handedly managed distribution of medicine, medical treatment, provision of coffins, care of the aged, care of unwanted children, reverence for lettered paper and so on." *Shanghai xian xuzhi, juan* 2, 39.

[94] *Shanghai xian xuzhi, juan* 2, 36.

[95] Doolittle, *Social Life*, vol. 2, 170; George Ernest Morrison, *An Australian in China* (London: Horace Cox, 1895; reprinted Hong Kong: Oxford University Press, 1985), 170. This custom was still strong in the villages of twentieth century China. Cf. Mao Tun, "Spring Silkworms," in *Spring Silkworms and Other Stories*, translated by Sidney Shapiro (Beijing: Foreign Languages Press, 1956), 20.

[96] *Guan sheng dijun wanying lingqian* (Infallibly efficacious divination rods of the sage Guandi) (Beijing: Liulichang Dongmenwai Longwenzhai, 1846), *juan xia*, 3, 46.

[97] Chen 44 *xia*.

[98] Xing 6.

[99] Articles in the *Shenbao* included "A brief description of showing reverence for the written word" (October 3, 1872); "Lightning strikes those who neglect to show respect for the written word or grain" (March 4, 1873).

[100] *Shenbao*, March 14, 1873.

[101] *Shenbao*, December 31, 1873.

[102] *Shenbao*, January 10, 1874.

[103] *Shenbao*, April 18, 1876. Cf. *Shenbao*, March 9, 1876 and March 11, 1876.

[104] *Shenbao*, October 1, 1877.

[105] Doolittle, *Social Life*, vol. 2, 170.

[106] *Shenbao*, July 10, 1876.

[107] *Shenbao*, November 28, 1879.

[108] *Shenbao*, July 17–25, 1885; July 28–29, 1885, August 1–2, 1885.

[109] Xing 6.

[110] In the new-style Chinese schools, however, this practice was continued well into the twentieth century. The Jiangnan Technical School in which Lu Xun studied as a young man, was so "modern" that the practice there was to study in Chinese and English on alternate days. Nevertheless, a small temple to the Guan Gong was built, at the side of which was a brick stove for the incineration of lettered paper. The four characters *Jing xi zi zhi* (Show reverence for lettered paper) were inscribed on the stove. Cf. Lu Xun, *Dawn Blossoms Plucked at Dusk*, 74. Wolfram Eberhard, *Guilt and Sin in Traditional China* (Berkeley: University of California Press, 1967), 48 reproduces a print from Shanghai, undated but probably circa 1920. The sketch depicts the first of the eighteen hells, and proclaims a warning: *Jing xi zi zhi*—Show reverence for lettered paper.

[111] Shu* 64.

[112] Wang Tao, *Yingruan zazhi*, juan 2, 23.

[113] Geng 72 *xia*.

[114] *Shenbao* editorials of September 28, 1877 and October 3, 1877.

[115] *Guan sheng dijun wanying lingqian*, juan xia, 4, 45. Wolfram Eberhard, *A Dictionary of Chinese Symbols: Hidden Symbols in Chinese Life and Thought*, trans. G. L. Campbell (London: Routledge & Kegan Paul, 1986), 223, reproduces a sketch of an ox; the lines of the drawing are made up of various exhortations not to eat beef. The sketch has the title "Song of exhortation against killing oxen or eating beef" (*Quan jie sha shi niu ge*).

[116] Ding 84. This story is copied directly, without mentioning its source, from Ji Yun, *Yuewei caotang biji* (Notes from the thatched hut of the man who sees details) (Chongqing: Chongqing chubanshe, 1996), 324.

[117] *Shenbao*, September 28, 1879.

[118] Wu 12.

[119] Li Boyuan, *Wenming xiaoshi*, 113. Bao Tianxiao, *Chuanyinglou huiyilu, shang ce*, 31, recalls that when he was a child he was taken to Shanghai for the first time by his mother and grandmother, and experienced the novelties of Shanghai had to offer, like strolling along Fuzhou Road, going to a teahouse, riding in a horse-drawn carriage and so on. His mother and grandmother, however, maintained the prohibition against the eating of beef, and so would not allow him to take a meal in a Western restaurant. One might also speculate as to whether the eating of beef was in some way symbolic of progressiveness, as was apparently the case in Japan at much the same time. See Seidensticker, *Low City, High City*, 102.

Afterword

The basic characteristics of Shanghai culture took shape during the second half of the nineteenth century. Many factors contributed to the formation of this new urban culture: the rapid commercialization of Shanghai; the ability of Shanghai residents to absorb Western influences; the degree to which they understood the West, and their own attitudes to the rapidly changing world around them.

One can legitimately ask how much of this change was rooted in traditional society, that is, a result of internal change, and how much change was brought about by external factors, the new environment of the Shanghai settlements. Some trends were already in evidence before the period under consideration. Evidence for the breakdown in clothing distinctions can be found as early as the Kangxi period; indecent theatrical performances, illegal killing of cattle and the selling of beef, all took place to a certain extent in areas around Shanghai prior to the establishment of the settlements. The difference was in the theoretical prohibition or the open acceptance of such practices. Some breakdown in class and status symbolism might have occurred before the nineteenth century, but the environment of the settlements dramatically exacerbated this process. What was previously unacceptable became common practice. Occasional criticism by certain scholars of footbinding in traditional China did not influence social practice. The impact of their objections was not comparable with the anti-footbinding movement of the late nineteenth century. Variolation against smallpox and time-measuring machines existed in traditional China, but the fact that such things existed cannot be compared to the widespread use of inoculation or the social impact of clocks and watches in the settlements. Causes for the rapid changes in late nineteenth century Shanghai have to be sought primarily in the new environment of Shanghai itself.

A number of literati resident in Shanghai—Wang Tao, Li Shanlan, Qian Xinbo, He Guisheng, Han Ziyun, to mention just a few—were friends, and came from similar backgrounds. Some spent their lives translating and introducing Western science, literature, and philosophy into China, and in many ways they can be considered the forerunners of the Chinese intellectual elite of the twentieth century. Their scholarly interests, and their influence, had nothing to do with the daily life in the settlements, which only provided a base for their activities. Others, like the literati associated with the *Shenbao* and the *Dianshizhai,* were closely involved with the emerging values of the foreign settlements, and contributed to the formation of a new literary culture based on the rapidly developing urban culture.

Other commercial cities in China also developed their own urban culture and identity. In Shanghai, however, that culture was so distinct and confident that by the twentieth century it could stand in opposition to the center of traditional Chinese culture itself. One of the basic underlying causes for the literary battles between the Beijing School and the Shanghai School in the 1930s was the tension between the tastes of the intellectual elite of Beijing and the urban popular culture of

Shanghai. Some writers, such as Lu Xun, lived in Shanghai, but never identified with the Shanghai School. Others, such as Zhang Ailing, came to typify it.

In hindsight, it is clear that the people of Shanghai in the nineteenth century lacked a strongly developed sense of political consciousness. Most of them did not seem to mind that they were excluded from certain activities in the settlements; on the contrary, they were quite happy with many aspects of foreign jurisdiction, such as the protection offered by the Mixed Court. Such a conclusion may seem untenable given the virulent nationalism of Shanghai in the twentieth century, but that is what the contemporary evidence tells us. In twentieth-century Shanghai large numbers of people participated in various anti-foreign demonstrations, such as the Mixed Court Riots and the May 30th Movement. Such was simply not the case in the nineteenth century. The contrast can be seen clearly in the role of the Zhangyuan: in the nineteenth century, it was an entertainment center. In the twentieth it became a public space for intellectuals and revolutionaries to hold meetings, make speeches, and carry out other political activities.

Despite different political attitudes in the nineteenth and the twentieth centuries, the basic characteristics of Shanghai culture were clearly formed during the nineteenth century. Since the early twentieth century, various descriptions of Shanghai culture, whether critical or laudatory, have been fairly uniform in defining its general characteristics—tolerant, open-minded, efficient, and innovative on the one hand, but superficial, materialistic, insincere, and decadent on the other. The establishment of the Peoples Republic put an end to the particular environment which gave birth to the Shanghai style, but the its unmistakeable characteristics are still very evident in contemporary Shanghai.

Key to Illustrations

Part One

1. A Chinese military map used during the Sino-French War 7
2. The treaty-signing ceremony at the conclusion of the Sino-French War 7
3. A British steamship collides with a Chinese boat 8
4. Major's editorial statement on the Kapsin coup in Korea 10
5. Shanghai literati at the grave of courtesan Hua Xiangyun 17
6. A scholar is assaulted by a prostitute's servant 19
7. A hot air balloon 21
8. A submarine 21
9. Westerners transform corpses into fertilizer 23
10. An editorial correction 23
11. A drunk encounters a walking corpse 26
12. The filial daughter of a *Shenbao* editor 27
13. A chaste widow becomes pregnant 28
14. Provincial examination candidates present a petition in the capital 30
15. The "Republic of Taiwan" in 1895 31
16. Eight-legged ghosts 32

Part Two

17. Chinese convicts employed in road building 43
18. Horse-drawn carriages cause traffic accidents 45
19. Sanitary regulations in the settlements 46
20. The public fountain in the jubilee celebrations 50
21. The Diyilou Teahouse 50
22. Free water supply in the French Concession 51
23. A water tower on the Huangpu River 55
24. Death caused by an electric shock 56
25. The Gengshangyicenglou Teahouse 58
26. Fuzhou Road at night 59
27. Street prostitutes in the teahouse 59
28. A Western prostitute on stage in a sing-song hall 60
29. Chinese in a Western restaurant 62
30. Display of a leopard in front of a restaurant 62
31. The Zhangyuan Garden 64
32. Li Hongzhang in the Zhangyuan 64
33. An outing on a summer evening 65
34. Horse racing 66
35. Paper hunting 67
36. Cricket in Shanghai 68
37. Lanterns displayed for the anniversary celebrations 70
38. French National Day celebrations 70
39. The circus 71
40. A roller coaster 72
41. "The Sun at Noon" 73

42. The newly installed chiming clock at the Chinese Customs House   74
43. A shop specializing in imported goods   75
44. The funeral of Chen Zhuping   78
45. Village girls drown in a boating accident   79
46. Girl performing on a tightrope   79
47. Circus bear kills a child   80
48. Armed bank robbery   80
49. Robbery by Jiangbei women   81
50. A "flower and opium" den   82
51. Three foreign sailors arrested   83
52. Women flee to Shanghai to be with their lovers   84
53. Female opium den attendants punished   87
54. A thief on trial in the Shanghai yamen   87
55. Torture instruments on display for foreign visitors   89
56. The Inspector of Police assesses jail conditions   91
57. A husband is beaten by his wife's employer   91
58. A runaway wife is put in the stocks   92
59. A girl combing her hair in public is rebuked by the magistrate   94
60. Magistrate punishes an unfilial grandson   95
61. Unfilial sons sentenced to stand in a wooden cage   95
62. A son beats his father   96
63. Women lying drunk in the streets of Shanghai   97
64. Selling aphrodisiacs   97
65. Sikh policemen steal a silver watch   99
66. Chinese detectives beat a suspect   100
67. Detectives on trial   101
68. Detectives sentenced   101
69. Chinese detective beaten up by an angry crowd   103
70. Transvestites arrested by Chinese detective   105
71. A transvestite prostitute arrested   105

Part Three

72. A *pipa* concert held in a church   118
73. The Wheelbarrow Pullers' Revolt   119
74. The Siming Gongsuo Riots (I)   121
75. The Siming Gongsuo Riots (II)   122
76. Fiftieth anniversary celebration of the founding of the Foreign Settlements   124
77. The sixtieth birthday of the Empress Dowager   125
78. Stealing a bride by force   127
79. An illiterate comprador   128
80. An accident in Nanjing Road   129
81. A banquet attended by courtesans   130
82. The Giant of Anhui   131
83. Western music in a Chinese religious ceremony   132
84. Sight restored to the blind   134
85. An autopsy   136
86. A mother seeks treatment for her deformed child   137
87. An abnormal fetus and a difficult labor   138
88. A midwife in the Chinese city   139
89. A surgical operation to remove a tumor   139
90. Two Chinese-speaking Westerners in a brothel   140

91. The Smallpox Inoculation Clinic   142
92. Angry crowds storming a Chinese clinic   144
93. Coffins stored in the Huizhou Huiguan   146
94. Funeral expenses by deception   147
95. A Chinese bride complains to the Mixed Court   148
96. A Chinese magistrate solves a family dispute   150
97. A shoe shop   154
98. Lovers in an opium den   154
99. The Natural Foot Society   156
100. A yellow croaker   156
101. A living dowry   157
102. Sexual greed at the risk of life   158
103. A monk in disguise visits a brothel   159
104. The Laodangui Theater   160
105. The Zhang 'Residence' become a source of local mirth   163
106. Young Master Dog   164
107. A meeting of women in the Zhangyuan   165
108. Hollow grandees   167
109. Daoist snatches a child   168
110. A dandy steals money to pay brothel debts   169
111. Cunning thief escapes like a rabbit   170
112. Head of a savage on display   171
113. A 'white pigeon' recaptured   171
114. Young hoodlums hold military drills   173
115. A group of *liumang* harass women   174
116. Gambling in a brothel   175
117. Women of leisure   175

Part Four

118. A merchant offers incense to a snake   190
119. A tablet from the Imperial Court for the Temple of the City God   191
120. A boatman dresses as a criminal in a procession   193
121. A human lamp stand   194
122. Carrying babies across the bridge   195
123. Complaint of the City God   196
124. A procession organized by the Xinzha Temple   199
125. Welcoming ceremonies for a statue of the Queen of Heaven   201
126. Feast of the Hungry Ghosts   202
127. The Gamblers' Alliance   203
128. The Hongmiao   205
129. Brothel madams visit a holy mountain   206
130. Women at a theatrical performance   207
131. A Buddha shop   208
132. An acupuncturist adds sorcery to his skills   212
133. A Daoist priest exorcises a haunted house   212
134. Reverence for lettered paper   213
135. Irreverence for the written word results in sudden death   215
136. Retribution for a killer   218
137. An ox begs to be spared   219

Bibliography

Works in Chinese

"1944 nian Shanghai tebie shi diyi qu bianzu baojia zanxing banfa"1944年上海特別市第一區編組保甲暫行辦法 (Temporary regulations on the organization of the baojia system in the First District of the Shanghai Special City of 1944). In *Shanghai shi biancha baojia xuzhi* 1946 年上海市政府, 上海市編查保甲須知 (Notice on the organization of the *baojia* system in Shanghai city), edited by 1946 nian Shanghai shi zhengfu. Held in the Shanghai Library.

A Ying 阿英. "Mantan chuqi baokan de nianhua he rili" 漫談初期報刊的年畫和日歷 (On new year pictures and calendars in the early period of newspapers and magazines). In *A Ying sanwen xuan* 阿英散文選 (Collected essays of A Ying), edited by Qian Xiaoyun 錢小雲 and Wu Taichang 吳泰昌, 280–81. Tianjin: Baihua wenyi chubanshe, 1981.

Bao Tianxiao 包天笑. *Shanghai chunqiu* 上海春秋 (Annals of Shanghai). Vol. 1 (1924); vol. 2 (1926). Reprinted Shanghai: Shanghai guji chubanshe, 1991.

———. *Chuanyinglou huiyilu* 釧影樓回憶錄 (Memoirs of the Bracelet Shadow Chamber). Reprinted Hong Kong: Dahua chubanshe, 1971.

———. *Yi, shi, zhu, xing de bainian bianqian* 衣食住行的百年變遷 (Changes over a hundred years in clothing, food, dwellings, and travel). Hong Kong: Dahua chubanshe, 1974.

Cao Yishi 曹一士. *Shanghai xian Chenghuang shen song* 上海縣隍城神頌 (In praise of the city god of Shanghai County). 1847. Copy held in Shanghai Library.

Chen Boxi 陳伯熙. *Lao Shanghai* 老上海 (Old Shanghai), Shanghai: Taidong shuju 泰東書局, 1919.

Chen Congzhou 陳從周, and Zhang Ming 張明, eds. *Shanghai jindai jianzhu shigao* 上海近代建築史料 (A draft history of architecture in modern Shanghai). Shanghai: Sanlian shudian, 1990.

Chen Dingshan 陳定山. *Chunshen jiuwen* 春申舊聞 (Old tales of Shanghai). Taipei: Chenguang yuekanshe, 1964.

Chen Gaoyong 陳高傭 et al. *Zhongguo tianzai renhuo biao* 中國天災人禍表 (Tables of natural and man-made disasters in China). Reprinted Shanghai: Shanghai shudian, 1986.

Chen Liansheng 陳蓮笙, and Chen Yaoting 陳耀庭. "Shanghai Daojiao yu zhuyao daoguan" 上海道教與主要道觀 (Daoism in Shanghai and its major temples). In *Lishi wenhua mingcheng—Shanghai* 歷史名城—上海, edited by Shanghai wenshiguan 上海文史館, 243–59. Shanghai: Shehui kexue chubanshe, 1988.

Chen Xulu 陳旭麓, Fang Shiming 方詩銘, and Wei Jianyou 魏建猷, eds. *Zhongguo jindaishi cidian* 中國近代史辭典 (A dictionary of modern Chinese history), Shanghai: Cishu chubanshe, 1982.

Chi Zhizheng 池志徵. *Huyou mengying* 滬游夢影 (Dream shadows of travels in Shanghai). Shanghai, 1893. Reprinted Shanghai: Shanghai guji chubanshe, 1989.

Di Pingzi, ed. 狄平子. *Qingdai huashi* 清代畫史 (History of painting in the Qing dynasty). Shanghai: Youzheng shuju 有正書局, 1927.

Dian Gong 顛公, ed. *Shanghai pianshu shijie* 上海騙術世界 (The world of swindlers in Shanghai). Shanghai: Saoye shufang 掃葉書房, 1914.

Fan Songfu 樊崧甫. *Banghui shili zhenwen* 幫會勢力珍聞 (Little known facts about secret societies). Hong Kong: Zhongyuan chubanshe, 1987.

Fang Hanqi 方漢奇. *Zhongguo jindai baokan shi* 中國近代報刊史 (A history of the press in modern China). Taiyuan: Shanxi renmin chubanshe, 1981.

Fu Xiangyuan 傅湘源. *Qingbang daheng: Huang Jinrong, Du Yuesheng, Zhang Xiaolin waizhuan* 青幫大亨－黃金榮, 杜月笙, 張嘯林外傳 (Green Gang bosses: Biographies of Huang Jinrong, Du Yuesheng and Zhang Shaolin). Beijing: Zhongguo wenshi chubanshe 中國文史出版社, 1987.

Ge Enyuan 葛恩元, ed. *Shanghai Siming gongsuo da shiji* 上海四明公所大事記 (A record of major events relating to the Ningbo Guild Hall incident). Shanghai: Juzhen fangsong yinshuju 聚珍仿宋印書局, 1920.

Ge Gongzhen 戈公振. *Zhongguo baoxue shi* 中國報學史 (A history of the press in China). Taipei: Xuesheng shuju, 1982.

Ge Yuanxu 葛元煦. *Huyou zaji* 滬游雜記 (Miscellaneous notes on travels in Shanghai). Shanghai, 1876. Reprinted Shanghai: Shanghai guji chubanshe, 1989.

Gezhi Shuyuan keyi, 1893 nian chunji, di'er ming 格致書院課藝1893年春季第二名 (Essays of the Shanghai Polytechnic Institution and Reading Room, Spring 1983, second prize). Shanghai: Shanghai Polytechnic Institution and Reading Room, 1893.

Gong Chanxiang 龔產興. "Wu Youru jianlüe" 吳有如簡略 (Wu Youru: A brief introduction). *Meishu yanjiu* 美術研究, 1990, no. 3: 31–38.

Gu Chengfu 顧承甫. *Hushang suishi fengsu* 滬上歲時風俗 (Annual festivals in Shanghai). Shanghai: Huadong shifan daxue chubanshe, 1989.

Guan sheng dijun wanying lingqian 關聖帝君萬應靈籤 (Infallibly efficacious divination rods of the sage Guandi). Beijing: Liulichang Dongmenwai Longwenzhai 琉璃廠東門外龍文齋, 1846.

Guo Tingyi 郭廷以. *Jindai Zhongguo shishi rizhi* 近代中國時事日志 (Daily record of current events in modern Chinese history). Taipei: Zhengzhong shuju 正中書局, 1963.

Guwu yueshike 古吳閱世客 (Observer of the old world of the Wu area). *Haishang fanhua tu* 海上繁華圖 (Illustrations of the prosperity of Shanghai). Shanghai, 1884.

Haishang chuanzhusheng 海上穿珠生 (The Pearl-Attired Scholar of Shanghai). *Shanghai funü huo xianxing* 上海婦女活現形 (True-to-life descriptions of Shanghai women). 4 volumes. Shanghai: Xinxing shuju 新興書局, 1928.

Haishang shuomengren 海上說夢人. *Xiepuchao* 歇浦潮 (Quiet tides on the Huangpu River). 3 volumes. Shanghai: Shanghai guji chubanshe, 1991.

Haishang shushisheng 海上漱石生 (The scholar who washes his mouth with rocks), *Haishang fanhuameng* 海上繁華夢 (Dreams of prosperity in Shanghai). 4 volumes. Shanghai, 1895. Reprinted Shanghai: Shanghai guji chubanshe, 1991.

He Ma 赫馬. *Shanghai xianhua* 上海閑話 (1) (Chats on Shanghai). Shanghai: Wenhua chubanshe, 1956.

Hu Daojing 胡道靜. "Shanghai xinwen shiye zhi shi de fazhan" 上海新聞事業之史的發展 (The development of the history of the press in Shanghai). *Shanghai tongzhiguan qikan* 上海通志館期刊, December 1934. Reprinted Hong Kong: Longmen shudian, 1965, no. 3, *juan* 2, 947–1034.

———. "Shen Bao liushiliu nian shi" 申報六十六年史 (A history of sixty-six years of the Shen Bao). In *Xinwen shi shang de xin shidai* 新聞史上的新時代 (A new era in the history of journalism), 81–104. Shanghai: Shijie shuju, 1946.

Hu Shi 胡適. "*Haishanghua liezhuan* xu" 海上花列傳序 (Preface to *Flowers on the Sea*). In *Haishanghua* 海上花, translated by Zhang Ailing 張愛玲, 9. Taipei: Huangguan zazhi chubanshe 皇冠雜誌出版社, 1983.

Hu Xianghan 胡祥翰. *Shanghai xiao zhi* 上海小誌 (Concise gazetteer of Shanghai). Shanghai: Chuanjingtang shudian 傳經堂書店, 1930. Reprinted, Shanghai: Shanghai guji chubanshe, 1989.

Hua Rende 華人德. Preface to *Wu Youru shinü baitu* 吳友如仕女百圖 (One hundred classical beauties of Wu Youru). Shanghai: Shuhua chubanshe, 1988.

Huang Kewu 黃克武. "Cong Shenbao yiyao guanggao kan Minchu Shanghai de yiliao wenhua yu shehui shengshuo 1919–1926" 從申報醫藥廣告看民初上海的醫療文化與社會生活 (An analysis of the culture of medical treatment and social life in the early Republican period in Shanghai 1912–1926, based on advertisements for medicinal products in the Shenbao). *Zhongyang yanjiuyuan jindaishi yanjiusuo jikan* 中央研究院近代研究所季刊, vol. 17, no. 2 (December 1988): 141–94.

Huang Mengtian 黃蒙田. *Tan yi lu* 談藝錄 (A record of discussions on art). Hong Kong: Shanghai shuju, 1973.

Huang Shiquan 黃式權. *Songnan mengyinglu* 淞南夢影錄 (Record of dream shadows of Songnan). Shanghai, 1883. Reprinted Shanghai: Shanghai guji chubanshe, 1989.

Huang Xiexun 黃協塤. "Ben bao zuichu shidai zhi jingguo" 本報最初時代之經過 (Development of this newspaper in its earliest period). In *Zuijin ershi nian, di erbian* 最近二十年－第二編 (The most recent twenty years, volume 2), edited by Shenbao guan. Shanghai: Shenbao guan, 1922.

Huayeliannong 花也憐儂 (Han Ziyun 韓子雲). *Haishang hua liezhuan* 海上花列傳 (Life stories of flowers on the sea). Shanghai, 1894. Reprinted in 4 volumes. Taipei: Tianyi chubanshe 天一出版社, 1974.

Hushang youxi zhuren 滬上游戲主人 (Master of Entertainment in Shanghai). *Haishang youxi tushuo* 海上游戲圖說 (Illustrated guide to entertainment in Shanghai). Shanghai, 1898.

Jia You 賈攸. "Zhangyuan yu Xinhai Geming" 張園與辛亥革命 (The Zhangyuan and the 1911 Revolution). In *Shanghai yishi* 上海軼事, edited by Tang Weikang et al., 166–68. Shanghai: Wenhua chubanshe, 1987.

Jiaochuan zizhu shanfang zhuren 絞川紫竹山房主人 (Master of the Purple Bamboo Mountain Hut on Dragon River). *Hua Xiangyun zhuan* 花湘雲傳 (Biography of Hua Xiangyun). In *Xinji Haishang qinglou tushuo* 新輯海上青樓圖說 (New illustrated edition of green bowers in Shanghai). Shanghai, 1895.

Ji Yun 紀昀. *Yuewei caotang biji* 閱微草堂筆記 (Notes from the thatched hut of the man who sees details). Chongqing: Chongqing chubanshe, 1996.

Kuai Shixun 蒯世勛. *Shanghai gonggong zujie shi gao* 上海公共租界史稿 (A draft history of the Shanghai settlements). Nanjing : Zhongyang Yanjiuyuan, 1933. Reprinted Shanghai: Shanghai renmin chubanshe, 1980

Lai Guanglin 賴光臨. *Zhongguo jindai baoren yu baoye* 中國近代報人與報業 (Newspapermen and the press in modern China). Taiwan: Shangwu yinshuguan, 1980

Li Bizhang 李必樟, ed. and trans. *Shanghai jindai maoyi jingji fazhan gaikuang 1854–1898: Yingguo zhu Shanghai lingshi maoyi baogao huibian* 上海近代貿易經濟發展概況 1854–1898: 英國駐上海領事貿易報告匯編 (General outline of the development of trade and economics in modern Shanghai, 1854–1898: The trade report of the British Consulate in Shanghai). Shanghai: Shanghai shehui kexueyuan, 1993.

Li Boyuan 李伯元. *Wenming xiaoshi* 文明小史 (A short history of civilization). Reprinted Shanghai: Shanghai guji shudian, 1982.

———. *Nanting si hua* 南亭四話 (Four talks from the South Pavilion). Reprinted Shanghai: Shanghai shudian, 1985.

Li Pingshu 李平書. *Qiewan laoren qishi zixu* 且頑老人七十自敘 (Autobiography of Old Man Stubborn at Seventy). Shanghai, 1923. Reprinted Shanghai: Shanghai guji chubanshe, 1989.

Li Qiao 李喬. *Zhongguo hangyeshen chongbai* 中國行業神崇拜 (The worship of Chinese occupation deities). Beijing: Zhongguo huaqiao chubanshe, 1990

Li Youning 李又寧, and Zhang Yufa 張玉法, eds. *Jindai Zhongguo nüquan yundong shiliao* 近代中國女權運動史話 (Historical materials on the history of the women's movement in modern China). Taipei: Chuanyi wenxueshe 傳藝文學社, 1975.

Liang Jialu 梁家祿. *Zhongguo xinwenye shi* 中國新聞業史 (A history of the press in China). Nanning: Guangxi renmin chubanshe, 1984.

Liang Qichao 梁啓超. *Wushi nian lai Zhongguo jinhua gailun* 五十年來中國進化概論 (Outline of developments in China over fifty years). Shanghai, 1923.

Liu Yanong 劉雅農. *Shanghai xianhua* 上海閑話 (Chats on Shanghai). Taipei: Shijie shuju, 1960.

Liu Yazi 柳亞子. *Nanshe jilüe* 南社紀略 (An outline record of the Southern Society). In *Liu Yazi wenji* 柳亞子文集 (Collected Works of Liu Yazi), edited by Liu Wuji 柳無忌. Shanghai: Shanghai renmin chubanshe, 1983.

Lu Binsheng 路濱生, ed. *Zhongguo heimu daguan* 中國黑幕大觀 (A panorama of sinister events in China). Shanghai: Zhonghua tushu jicheng gongsi 中華圖書集成公司, 1918.

Lu Dafang 盧大方. *Shanghaitan yijiulu* 上海灘憶舊錄 (Memories of the Shanghai Bund). Taipei: Shijie shuju, 1980.

Lu Juefei 盧覺非. "Bian Que yishu lai zi Yindu zhiyi" 扁鵲醫術來自印度質疑 (Questions on the validity of the theory that Bian Que's medicinal skills came from India). *Hua-Xi yixue zazhi* 華西醫學雜誌, no. 8, vol. 2 (1947): 8–11.

Luo Suwen 羅素文. *Da Shanghai—Shikumen: xunchangren jia* 大上海—石庫門: 尋常人家 (Great Shanghai and stone frame-gate-style houses: dwellings of ordinary families). Shanghai: Shanghai renmin chubanshe 上海人民出版社, 1991.

Luo Zhiru 羅志如. *Tongjibiao zhong zhi Shanghai* 統計表中之上海 (Shanghai in statistical tables). Nanjing: Guoli zhongyang yanjiusuo 國立中央研究院社會科學研究所, 1932.

Ma Guangren 馬光仁, ed. *Shanghai xinwen shi 1850–1949* 上海新聞史 1850–1949 (A history of the press in Shanghai, 1859–1949). Shanghai: Fudan Daxue chubanshe, 1996.

Mao Dun 茅盾. "Duoshi er huoyue de suiyue" 多事而活躍的歲月 (Busy and eventful months and years). *Xinhua wenzhai* 新華文摘, no. 10 (October 1982): 184–96.

Mao Xianglin 毛祥麟. *Sanlüe huibian* 三略匯編. Quoted in *Shanghai Xiaodaohui qiyi shiliao huibian* 上海小刀會起義史料匯編 (Documents on the Small Sword Uprising in Shanghai), edited by Shanghai lishi yanjiusuo, 808. Shanghai: Shanghai renmin chubanshe, 1958.

Minguo Shanghai xianzhi 民國上海縣志 (Gazetteer of Shanghai County during the Republic). Reprinted Taipei: Chengwen chubanshe, 1975.

Nakano Miyoko 中野美代子, and Takeda Masaya 武田雅哉. *Seikimatsu Chūgoku no Kawara-ban: E-iri Shimbun Tensekisai Gahō no Sekai* 世紀末中國のかわら版—繪入新聞"點石齋畫報"の世界. Tokyo: Fukutake Books, 1989.

Qi Rushan 齊如山. *Jingju zhi bianqian* 京劇之變遷 (Changes in Peking opera). Beiping: Guoju xuehui 國劇學會, 1935.

Qian Shengke 錢生可. *Shanghai heimu huibian* 上海黑幕匯編 (A collection of stories about evil in Shanghai). Shanghai: Shishi Xinbao fusongpin 時事新報附送品, 1917–1918.

Qian Xiaoyun 錢小雲, and Wu Taichang 吳泰昌, eds. *A Ying sanwen xuan* 阿英散文選 (Collected essays of A Ying). Tianjin: Baihua wenyi chubanshe, 1981.

Qin Rongguang 秦榮廣. *Shanghai xian zhuzhici* 上海縣竹枝詞 (Bamboo-branch rhymes of Shanghai County). Shanghai, 1911. Reprinted Shanghai: Shanghai guji shudian, 1989.

Qingdai riji huichao 清代日記匯抄 (Collected diaries of the Qing period). Edited by Shanghai renmin chubanshe. Shanghai: Shanghai renmin chubanshe, 1982.

Qu Yuan 蘧園. *Fubao xiantan* 負曝閒談 (Casual talks about past events). Shanghai: Shishi Xinbao, 1933. In *Wan-Qing xiaoshuo da xi* (晚清小說大系) (A compendium of late Qing novels) Reprinted Taiwan: Guangya chuban youxian gongsi, 1984.

Quan Hansheng 全漢生. *Zhongguo hanghui zhidu shi* 中國行會制度史 (A history of the guild hall system in China). Shanghai: Xin shengming shudian 新生命書店, 1934.

Ranli laoren 燃藜老人. "Shanghai yangchang" 上海洋場 (Shanghai's foreign territory). Manuscript. Shanghai Library.

Shanghai cidian 上海辭典 (Dictionary of Shanghai). Edited by Shanghai shi difangzhi bangongshi 上海市地方志辦公室. Shanghai: Shanghai shehui kexueyuan chubanshe, 1989.

Shanghai shehui kexueyuan lishi yanjiusuo 上海社會科學院歷史研究所, ed. *Wu Sanshi yundong shiliao* 五卅運動史料 (Historical materials for the study of the May 30 Movement). Shanghai: Shanghai rennin chubanshe, 1981.

Shanghai shi gongshang xingzheng guanliju ji Shanghai diyi jidian gongyeju jiqi gongye shiliaozu 上海市工商行政管理 局及上海第一機電工業局機器工業史料組, ed. *Shanghai minzu jiqi gongye* 上海民族機器工業 (The Shanghai national machinery industry). Beijing: Zhonghua shuju, 1966.

Shanghai shi shizhengfu gongcheng guanliju 上海市市政工程管理局. *Shanghai gonglu shi* 上海公路史 (A history of public roads in Shanghai). Beijing: Renmin jiaotong chubanshe, 1989

Shanghai shi wenxian weiyuanhui 上海市文獻委員會. *Shanghai renkou zhi lüe* 上海人口志略 (Outline of the population of Shanghai). Shanghai, 1948.

Shanghai tongshe 上海通社. *Shanghai yanjiu ziliao* 上海研究資料 (Historical materials for research on Shanghai). Shanghai: Zhonghua shuju, 1936. Reprinted Shanghai: Shanghai shudian, 1984.

——— ed. *Shanghai yanjiu ziliao xuji* 上海研究資料續集 (Continued collection of historical materials for research on Shanghai). Shanghai: Zhonghua shuju, 1939. Reprinted Shanghai: Shanghai shudian, 1984.

Shanghai tongzhiguan 上海通志館, ed. "Shanghai nianbiao" 上海年表. Manuscript. Shanghai Library.

Shanghai wenshiguan 上海文史館, comp. *Lishi wenhua mingcheng—Shanghai* 歷史文化名城—上海 (A historically and culturally famous city: Shanghai). Volume 6 in *Shanghai difangshi ziliao*. Shanghai: Shanghai shehui kexueyuan chubanshe, 1988.

Shanghai xian xuzhi 上海縣續志 (Shanghai County gazetteer supplement). Shanghai, 1918. Reprinted Taipei: Chengwen chubanshe, 1975.

Shanghai xintuo gufen youxian gongsi 上海信托股份公司 (Shanghai Trust Co.), ed. *Shanghai fengtu zaji* 上海風土雜記 (A survey of folklore from Shanghai). Shanghai, 1932.

Shenbao guan, ed. *Zuijin wushi nian, di erbian* 最近五十年第二編 (The most recent fifty years: second volume). Shanghai: Shenbao guan, 1922.

Shenbao shiliao bianxiezu 申報史料編寫組. "Chuangban chuqi de *Shenbao*" 創辦初期的申報. In *Xinwen yanjiu ziliao* 新聞研究資料, vol. 1. Beijing: Xinhua chubanshe, 1979.

Si Yu 斯余. *Shanghai daheng Du Yuesheng* 上海大亨杜月笙 (Shanghai's arch-criminal Du Yuesheng). Beijing: Zhongguo wenlian chubanshe, 1986

Songbei yushensheng 淞北玉魷生 (Wang Tao 王韜). *Haizou yeyoulu* 海陬冶游錄 (A guide to the brothels of Shanghai). Shanghai, 1879.

Sun Baoxuan 孫寶瑄. *Wangshanlu riji* 忘山盧日記 (Diary of the Master of Wangshan Studio). Shanghai: Shanghai guji chubanshe, 1983.

Sun Guoda 孫果達. *Gonggong zujie de xunbu* 公共租界的巡捕 (Police in the International Settlement). In *Shanghai yishi* 上海軼事, edited by Tang Weikang et al., 44–50. Shanghai: Wenhua chubanshe, 1987.

Sun Yutang 孫毓棠. *Zhongguo jindai gongye shi ziliao diyi bian* 中國近代工業史資料第一編 (Materials on the history of modern industry in Shanghai, vol. 1). Beijing: Kexue chubanshe, 1957.

Tan Yingke 談瀛客. *Shenjiang shixia shengjing tushuo* 申江時下胜景圖說 (Illustrated guide to beautiful scenery in contemporary Shanghai, vol. 1). Shanghai, 1894.

Tang Weikang 湯偉康, Zhu Dalu 朱大路, and Du Li 杜黎 eds. *Shanghai yishi* 上海軼事 (Anecdotes about Shanghai). Shanghai: Wenhua chubanshe, 1987.

Tang Zhenchang 唐振常. *Shanghai shi* 上海史 (History of Shanghai). Shanghai: Shanghai renmin chubanshe, 1989.

Tang Zhijun 湯志鈞. *Jindai Shanghai da shiji* 近代上海大事記 (Record of major events in modern Shanghai). Shanghai: Cishu chubanshe, 1989.

Tiaoshui kuangsheng 笤水狂生. *Shanghai liyuan xin lishi* 上海梨園新歷史 (A new history of theatres in Shanghai). Shanghai: Hongwen shuju 鴻文書局, 1909.

Wang Ermin 王爾敏. "Zhongguo jindai zhishi pujihua chuanbo zhi tushuo xingshi—*Dianshizhai huabao li*" 中國近代知識普及化傳播之圖說形式—點石齋報例 (Pictorial representations of the dissemination and popularization of knowledge in nineteenth century China: Examples from the Dianshizhai Pictorial). *Zhongyang yanjiuyuan jindaishi yanjiusuo jikan* 中央研究院近代史研究所集刊, no. 19 (June 1990): 135–72.

Wang Kangnian 汪康年. *Wang rangqing biji* 汪穰卿筆記 (Miscellaneous jottings of Wang Xiangqing). Shanghai: Shanghai shudian, 1926.

Wang Shuhuai 王樹槐. *Wairen yu wuxu bianfa* 外人與戊戌變法 (Foreigners and the Hundred Days' Reform). Taiwan: Jinghua yinshuguan 精華印書館, 1965.

Wang Tao 王韜. *Songyin manlu* 淞隱漫錄 (Random jottings of a Wusong recluse). Shanghai, 1887. Reprinted Beijing: Renmin wenxue chubanshe, 1983.

———. *Songbin suohua* 淞濱瑣話 (Tales of trivia from the banks of the Wusong). Shanghai, 1893. Reprinted Hunan: Yuelu chubanshe 岳麓出版社, 1987.

———. *Yingruan zazhi* 瀛壖雜志 (Maritime and littoral miscellany). Shanghai, 1875. Reprinted Shanghai: Shanghai guji chubanshe, 1989.

Wang Tieyan 王鐵崖, ed. *Zhong-wai jiu yuezhang huibian* 中外舊約章匯編 (Collection of treaties between China and foreign countries in former times). Beijing: Sanlian shudian, 1957.

Wang Zhongxian 汪仲賢, and Xu Xiaoxia 許曉霞. *Shanghai suyu tushuo* 上海俗語圖說 (Shanghai colloquialisms with illustrations). Shanghai: Shehui chubanshe, 1935. Reprinted Shanghai: Shanghai shudian, 1999.

Wangzhusheng 网蛛生 (The Spiderweb Scholar). *Renhaichao* 人海潮 (The human tide). Shanghai: Zhongyang shudian, 1926. Reprinted Shanghai: Shanghai guji chubanshe, 1991.

Wei Juxian 衛聚賢. "Bian Que de yishu lai zi Yindu" 扁鵲的醫術來自印度 (Bian Que's medical skills came from India) *Hua-Xi yixue zazhi* 華西醫學雜誌, no. 1, vol. 2 (1947): 19–25.

———. "Bian Que de yishu lai zi Yindu de dabian" 扁鵲的醫術來自印度的答辯 (Reply to questions on the validity of the theory that Bian Que's medical skills came from India). *Hua-Xi yixue zazhi* 華西醫學雜誌, no. 4/6, vol. 3 (1948): 7–8.

Wei Shaochang 魏紹昌. *Li Boyuan yanjiu ziliao* 李伯元研究資料 (Research material on Li Boyuan). Shanghai: Shanghai guji shudian, 1980.

Wo Foshanren 我佛山人 (Wu Jianren 吳趼人). *Zuijin shehui wochuo shi* 最近社會齷齪史 (A history of sordid aspects of society in recent times). Shanghai: Shiwu shuguan 時務書館, 1910. Reprinted Guangzhou: Huacheng chubanshe, 1988.

Wu Guifang 吳貴芳. *Shanghai fengwu zhi* 上海風物志 (Scenery of Shanghai). Shanghai: Wenhua chubanshe, 1982.

———. "Songgu mantan, san" 淞古漫談 (三) (An informal discussion on old Shanghai, part 3). *Dang'an yu lishi* 檔案與歷史 (Archives and history), vol. 2, no. 1 (1986): 80–82.

Wu Huanchu 吳還初. *Tianfei-niangma zhuan* 天妃娘媽傳 (Biography of Tianhou, Queen of Heaven). Ming (Wanli period). Reprinted Shanghai: Shanghai guji chubanshe, 1990.

Wu Jianren 吳趼人 (Wu Woyao 吳沃堯). *Ershi nian mudu zhi guai xianzhuang* 二十年目睹之怪現狀 (Bizarre happenings eyewitnessed over two decades). Reprinted Taipei: Guangya youxian gongsi, 1984.

Wu Micha 吳密察. *Taiwan jindaishi yanjiu* 台灣近代史研究 (Research on modern Taiwan history). Taipei: Daoxiang chubanshe 稻鄉出版社, 1990.

Wu Shenyuan 吳申元. *Shanghai zuizao de zhongzhong* 上海最早的種種 (First appearance of various things in Shanghai). Shanghai: Huadong shifan daxue chubanshe, 1989.

Xia Lin'gen 夏林根. *Jiu Shanghai sanbai liushi hang* 舊上海三百六十行 (Three hundred and sixty trades in Old Shanghai). Shanghai: Huadong shifan daxue chubanshe, 1989.

Xiang Dicong 向迪琮. "Shanghai *Dianshizhai* shiyin shu bao ji qi jiqizhe" 上海點石齋石印書報及其繼起者 (Lithographic printing of books and newspapers at the Dianshizhai in Shanghai, and their successors). In *Shanghai difangzhi ziliao* 上海地方志資料, vol. 4. Shanghai: Shanghai shehui kexue chubanshe, 1986.

Xiang Hua 向華. *Shanghai shi hua* 上海史話 (Talks on the history of Shanghai). Hong Kong: Muwen shuju 牧文書局, 1971.

Xianggang Xiandai chuban gongsi 香港現代出版公司, ed. *Shi li yangchang, hua Shanghai* 十里洋場, 話上海 (Ten *li* of foreign territory, talks on Shanghai). Hong Kong: Xiandai chuban gongsi, 1970.

Xiaoxiangguan shizhe 瀟湘館侍者. *Haishang huatianjiudi zhuan* 海上花天酒地傳 (Dissipation and debauchery in Shanghai). Shanghai, 1884.

Xu Ke 徐珂. *Qing bai lei chao* 清稗類鈔 (A collection of Qing anecdotal material). Shanghai: Shangwu yinshuguan, 1920. Reprinted Beijing: Zhonghua shuju, 1984.

Xu Renhan 徐忍寒. "*Shenbao* qishiqi nian da shiji" 申報七十年大事記 (Major events over seventy-seven years of the Shenbao). In *Shanghai difang shi ziliao* 上海地方史資料, vol. 5, 22–35. Shanghai: Shanghai shehui kexue chubanshe, 1986.

Xu Run 徐潤. *Xu Ruzhai zixu nianpu* 徐愚齋自敘年譜 (Chronological autobiography). Xiangshan, 1927. Reprinted Taiwan: Shihuo chuban youxian gongsi 食貨出版有限公司, 1978.

Xu Xuejun 徐雪筠 et al., trans. "Haiguan shinian baogao" 海關十年報告 (Decennial Reports on Open Ports). In *Shanghai jindai shehui jingji fazhan gaikuang* 上海近代社會經濟發展概況 1882–1931 (A general survey of Shanghai's contemporary social and economic development, 1882–1931). Shanghai: Shanghai shehui kexueyuan chubanshe, 1985.

Xu Zaiping 徐載平. "*Shenbao* shi ruhe jikua *Shanghai Xinbao* de?" 申報是如何擠垮"上海新報"的? (How did the Shenbao gain ascendancy over the Shanghai Xinbao). In *Xinwen yanjiu ziliao* 新聞研究資料, vol. 15. Beijing: Zhongguo zhanwang chubanshe 中國展望出版社, 1982.

Yan Fusun 嚴芙孫, ed. *Shanghai suyu da cidian* 上海俗語大辭典 (Dictionary of Shanghai colloquialisms). Shanghai: Yunxuan chubanshe 雲軒出版社, 1924.

Yang Guangfu 楊光輔. *Songnan yuefu* 淞南樂府 (Songs of Songnan). In *Shanghai zhanggu congshu* 上海掌故叢書, edited by Shanghai tongshe 上海通社, vol. 8. Shanghai: Shanghai tongshe, 1935.

Yang Yi 楊逸. *Haishang molin* 海上墨林 (Painting and calligraphy in Shanghai). Shanghai, 1920. Reprinted Shanghai: Shanghai guji chubanshe, 1989.

Yao Gonghe 姚公鶴. *Shanghai xianhua* 上海閑話 (Chats on Shanghai). Shanghai: Shangwu yinshuguan 商務印書館, 1917.

Yao Jiguang 姚吉光, and Yu Yifen 俞逸芬. "Shanghai de xiaobao" 上海的小報 (Tabloid newspapers in Shanghai). In *Xinwen yanjiu ziliao* 新聞研究資料, vol. 3, 232–36. Beijing: Xinhua chubanshe, 1981.

Yao Tinglin 姚廷麟. *Yao Tinglin riji* 姚廷麟日記 (The diary of Yao Tinglin). In *Qingdai riji huichao* 清代日記匯抄 (Collected diaries of the Qing period), edited by Shanghai renmin chubanshe. Shanghai: Shanghai renmin chubanshe, 1982.

Yao Wennan 姚文楠, ed. *Shanghai xiangtu zhi* 上海鄉土志 (History of the Shanghai region). Reprinted Taipei: Chengwen chubanshe, 1975.

Ye Xiaoqing 葉曉青. "Jindai Xifang keji de yinjin ji qi yingxiang" 近代西方科技的引進及其影響 (The introduction of Western science and technology and its influence). *Lishi yanjiu* 歷史研究, no. 1 (1982): 3–17.

———. "Zhongguo chuantong ziranguan yu jindai kexue" 中國傳統自然觀與近代科學 (The Chinese traditional view of nature and modern science). In *Kexue yu wenhua* 科學與文化 (Science and culture), 158–60. Xian: Shaanxi kexue chubanshe, 1983.

———. "Shanghai yangchang wenren de gediao" 上海洋場文人的格調 (Lifestyles of the literati in the Shanghai foreign settlements). *Ershiyi shiji* 二十一世紀, (February 1992): 134–36.

Yu Xingmin 于醒民, and Tang Jiwu 唐繼無. *Shanghai 1862 nian* 上海 1862 年 (Shanghai in the year 1862). Shanghai: Shanghai renmin chubanshe, 1991.

———. *Jindaihua de zaochan er: Shanghai* 近代化的早產兒: 上海 (Shanghai: A premature child of early modernization). Taipei: Taiwan Jiuda wenhua gufen youxian gongsi 久大文化股份有限司, 1992.

Yu Yueting 俞月亭. *Woguo huabao de shizu* 我國畫報的始祖 (The ancestor of the pictorial in China). Beijing: Xinhua chubanshe, 1981.

Zeng Pu 曾樸. *Niehaihua* 孽海花 (Flowers on a sinful sea). Reprinted Shanghai: Shanghai guji chubanshe, 1985.

Zhang Ailing 張愛鈴, trans. and annot. *Haishanghua* 海上花. Taipei: Huangguan zazhi chubanshe 皇冠雜誌出版社, 1983.

Zhang Chunhua 張春華. *Hucheng suishi quge* 滬上歲事衢歌 (Street songs of yearly events in Shanghai). Shanghai, 1839. Reprinted in *Shanghai zhanggu congshu*, edited by Shanghai tongshe, vol. 8. Shanghai: Shanghai tongshe, 1936.

Zhang Hailin 張海林. *Wang Tao pingzhuan* 王韜評傳 (A critical biography of Wang Tao). Nanjing: Nanjing Daxue chubanshe, 1993.

Zhang Jinglu 張靜廬. *Zhongguo jindai chuban shiliao, chubian* 中國近代出版社史料初編 (Historical sources on publishing in modern China, part 1). Shanghai: Qunyi chubanshe 群誼出版社, 1953.

———. *Zhongguo jindai chuban shiliao, erbian* 中國現代出版史料二編 (Historical sources on publishing in modern China, part 2). Shanghai: Qunyi chubanshe, 1954.

———. *Zhongguo xiandai chuban shiliao, yibian* 中國現代出版史料乙編 (Historical sources on publishing in contemporary China, part B). Beijing: Zhonghua shuju, 1959

Zhang Junliang 張君良. "Haishang xiaobao fanlun" 海上小報泛論 (A general discussion on the mosquito press of Shanghai). In *Shinian* 十年 (The decade). Shanghai: Shenshi dianxunshe, 1934.

Zhao Gang 趙崗, and Chen Zhongyi 陳鐘毅. *Zhongguo mianye shi* 中國棉業史 (History of the cotton industry in China). Taipei: Lianjing chuban shiye gongsi 聯營出版事業公司, 1977.

Zhao Hongjun 趙洪鈞. *Jindai Zhong-Xi yi lunzheng shi* 近代中西醫論爭史 (A history of the debates between Chinese and Western medicine). Hefei, Anhui: Kexue jishu chubanshe, 1989.

Zhao Wenlin 趙文林, and Xie Shujun 謝淑君. *Zhongguo renkou shi* 中國人口史 (History of China's population). Beijing: Renmin chubanshe, 1988.

Zheng Jiuping 鄭久平, Jian She 簡舍, Ouyang Nan 歐陽楠, Ji Feng 紀豐 eds. *Zhongguo chuantong liyi liwen* 中國傳統禮儀禮文 (Traditional Chinese rites and protocols). Hunan: Sanhuan chubanshe 三環出版社, 1990.

Zheng Yimei 鄭逸梅. *Shu bao hua jiu* 書報話舊 (Talks about the old days of books and newspapers). Shanghai: Xuelin chubanshe, 1983.

———. *Zheng Yimei xuanji* 鄭逸梅選集 (Selected works of Zheng Yimei). Haerbin: Heilongjiang renmin chubanshe, 1991.

Zhimituren 指迷途人 (The Man Who Points Out the Wrong Path). *Haishang yeyou beilan* 海上冶游備覽 (Complete guide to brothel visiting in Shanghai). Shanghai, 1891.

Zhiwuyashi zhuren 知無涯室主人 (Master of the Hall of Knowledge Without Boundaries). *Ru ci Shanghai* 如此上海 (Such is Shanghai), vol. 1. Shanghai: Dadong shuju, n.d.

Zhu Hongjun 朱鴻鈞, ed. *Gujin huashi* 古今畫史 (History of ancient and modern painting). Shanghai: Guangyi shuju 廣藝書局, 1917.

Zhu Wenbing 朱文柄. *Haishang zhuzhici* 海上竹枝詞 (Bamboo branch rhymes of Shanghai). Shanghai: Zhongguo jicheng tushu gongsi 集成圖書公司, 1908.

Zong Li 宗力, and Liu Qun 劉全. *Zhongguo minjian zhushen* 中國民間諸神 (Popular deities of China). Shijiazhuang: Hebei renmin chubanshe, 1986.

Works in English

Beers, Burton F. *China in Old Photographs 1860–1910*. New York: Charles Scribener's Sons, 1978.

Bickers, Robert A., and Jeffrey N. Wasserstrom. "Shanghai's 'Dogs and Chinese Not Admitted'—Sign, Legend, History and Contemporary Symbol." *China Quarterly* 142 (June 1995): 444–66.

Bodde, Derk, and Clarence Morris. *Law in Imperial China*. Cambridge, Mass.: Harvard University Press, 1967.

Bodde, Derk. trans. and annot. *Annual Customs and Festivals in Peking*, by Tun Li-ch'en. Hong Kong: Hong Kong University Press, 1965.

Bogdan, Robert. *Freakshow: Presenting Human Oddities for Amusement and Profit*. Chicago: University of Chicago Press, 1988.

Britton, Roswell S. *The Chinese Periodical Press 1800–1912*. Shanghai, 1933. Reprinted Taipei: Ch'eng-wen Publishing, 1966.

Burke, Peter B. *Popular Culture in Early Modern Europe*. London: Temple Smith, 1978.

Burkhardt, V. R. *Chinese Creeds and Customs*. Hong Kong: South China Morning Post, Ltd., 1955.

Ch'en, Jerome. *China and the West*. London: Hutchinson and Co., 1979.

Ching, Frank. *Ancestors: 900 Years in the Life of a Chinese Family*. London: Harrap Limited, 1988.

Coates, P. D. *The China Consuls—British Consular Officers, 1843–1943*. Hong Kong: Oxford University Press, 1988.

Cohn, Don J. ed. and trans. *Vignettes from the Chinese: Lithographs from Shanghai in the Late Nineteenth Century*. Hong Kong: The Chinese University of Hong Kong, 1987.

Cohen, Paul A. *Between Tradition and Modernity: Wang T'ao and Reform in Late Ch'ing China*. Cambridge, Mass.: Harvard University Press, 1974.

Cook, Christopher. *The Lion and the Dragon: British Voices from the China Coast*. London: Elm Tree Books/Hamish Hamilton Ltd., 1985.

Cooper, William C., and Nathan Sivin. "Man as a Medicine: Pharmacological and Ritual Aspects of Traditional Therapy Using Drugs Derived from the Human Body." In *Chinese Science: Explorations of an Ancient Tradition*, edited by Nakayama and Sivin, 203–72. Cambridge, Mass.: MIT Press, 1973.

Couling, S. *The History of Shanghai*, volume 2. Shanghai: Kelly and Walsh, 1923.

Davidson-Houston, J. V. *Yellow Creek, the Story of Shanghai*. London: Pitnam and Company Limited, 1962.

Day, Clarence Burton. "Shanghai Welcomes the God of Wealth." *China Journal*, vol. 8, no. 6 (June 1928): 289–94. Reprinted in *Popular Religion in Pre-Communist China*, 39–46. California: Chinese Materials Center, Inc., 1975.

de Groot, J. J. M. *The Religious System of China*. Leiden: Brill, 1892–1910. Reprinted, Taipei: Literature House Ltd, 1964.

Doolittle, Rev. Justus. *Social Life of the Chinese*. New York: Harder and Brothers, 1865.

Dutton, Michael R. *Policing and Punishment in China: From Patriarchy to "the People."* Cambridge: Cambridge University Press, 1992.

Dyce, Charles M. *The Model Settlement: Shanghai 1870–1900*. London: Chapman & Hall Ltd., 1906.

Dyer Ball, J. *Things Chinese*. London: Murray, 1926. Reprinted, Detroit: Tower Books, 1971.

Eberhard, Wolfram. *A Dictionary of Chinese Symbol: Hidden Symbols in Chinese Life and Thought*. Translated by G. L. Campbell. London: Routledge & Kegan Paul, 1986.

Eberhard, Wolfram. *Guilt and Sin in Traditional China*. Berkeley: University of California Press, 1967.

Elman, Benjamin A. *From Philosophy to Philology,* Cambridge, Mass.: Harvard University Press, 1984.

Elvin, Mark. "The Mixed Court of the International Settlement at Shanghai." *Papers on China*, East Asian Research Center, Harvard University, vol. 17 (December 1963): 131–59.

———. "The Administration of Shanghai, 1905–1914." In *The Chinese City between Two Worlds*, edited by Mark Elvin and G. William Skinner, 239–62. Stanford: Stanford University Press, 1974.

Elvin, Mark, and Skinner, G. William, eds. *The Chinese City between Two Worlds*. Stanford: Stanford University Press, 1974.

Fairbank, J. K. *Trade and Diplomacy on the China Coast*. Cambridge, Mass.: Harvard University Press, 1969.

Feetham, Richard (The Hon. Mr. Justice Feetham, C.M.G.). *Report to the Shanghai Municipal Council*. Shanghai: North China Daily News and Herald Ltd., 1931–1932.

Feuchtwang, Stephan. "City Temples in Taipei under Three Régimes." In *The Chinese City between Two Worlds*, edited by Mark Elvin and G. William Skinner, 263–301. Stanford: Stanford University Press, 1974.

———. "School-Temple and City God." In *The City in Late Imperial China*, edited by G. William Skinner, 581–608. Stanford: Stanford University Press, 1977.

Fitzgerald, C. P. *Why China? Recollections of China 1923–1950*. Melbourne: Melbourne University Press, 1985.

Fogel, Joshua A. "Shanghai-Japan: The Japanese Residents' Association of Shanghai." *Journal of Asian Studies*, vol. 59, no. 4 (November 2000): 927–50.

Foucault, Michel. *Discipline and Punish: The Birth of the Prison*. London: Peregrine Books, 1979.

Gamewell, Mary Ninde. *The Gateway to China: Pictures of Shanghai*. Fleming H. Revell & Company, 1916. Reprinted, Taipei: Ch'eng-wen Publishing, 1972.

Giles, Herbert Allen. "The 'Hsi Yüan Lu' or Instructions to Coroners." *China Review* 3 (1874–1875): 30–38, 92–99, 159–172. Reprinted Taipei: Southern Materials Center, Inc., 1982.

Golas, Peter J. "Early Ch'ing Guilds." In *The City in Late Imperial China*, edited by G. William Skinner, 555–80. Stanford: Stanford University Press, 1977.

Goodman, Bryna. *Native Place, City and Nation: Regional Networks and Identities in Shanghai, 1853–1937*. Berkeley: University of California Press, 1995.

———. "Improvisations on a Semi-Colonial Theme, or, How to Read a Celebration of Transnational Urban Community." *Journal of Asian Studies*, vol. 54, no. 4 (November 2000): 889–926.

Granet, Marcel. *The Religion of the Chinese People*. Oxford: Blackwell, 1975.

Gray, John Henry. *China: A History of the Laws, Manners and Customs of the People*. Edited by William Gow Gregor. London: Macmillan and Co, 1878. Reprinted, Shannon: Irish University Press, 1972.

Gregory, Peter, and Patricia Ebrey. *Religion and Society in T'ang and Sung China*. Honolulu: University of Hawaii Press, 1993.

Hao, Yen-p'ing. *The Comprador in Nineteenth Century China: Bridge Between East and West.* Cambridge, Mass.: Harvard University Press, 1962. Reprinted 1970.

———. *The Commercial Revolution in Nineteenth Century China: The Rise of Sino-Western Mercantile Capitalism.* Berkeley: University of California Press, 1986.

Henriot, Christian. "Chinese Courtesans in the Late Qing and Early Republican Shanghai (1849–1925)." *East Asian History*, no. 8 (December 1994): 33–52.

———. *Prostitution and Sexuality in Shanghai: A Social History, 1849–1949.* Cambridge: Cambridge University Press, 2001.

Hershatter, Gail. *Dangerous Pleasures: Prostitution and Modernity in Twentieth Century Shanghai.* Berkeley: University of California Press, 1997.

Hillier, S. M., and J. A. Jewell. *Health Care and Traditional Medicine in China, 1800–1982.* London: Routledge & Kegan Paul, 1983.

———. "Chinese Traditional Medicine and Modern Western Medicine: Integration and Separation in China," in *Health Care and Traditional Medicine in China, 1800–1982*, edited by S. M. Hillier and J. A. Jewell, 306–35. London: Routledge & Kegan Paul, 1983.

Hsia, Ching-lin. *The Status of Shanghai.* Shanghai: Kelly and Walsh Limited, 1929.

Hsiao, Kung-chuan. *Rural China: Imperial Control in the Nineteenth Century.* Seattle: University of Washington Press, 1960.

Huang, Philip C. C. "Between Informal Mediation and Formal Adjudication: the Third Realm of Qing Civil Justice." *Modern China*, vol. 19, no. 3 (July 1993): 251–98.

Hummel, Arthur W. ed. *Eminent Chinese of the Ch'ing Period.* Reprinted Taipei: Ch'eng-wen Publishing, 1970.

Jewell, J. A. "Chinese and Western Medicine in China, 1800–1911," in *Health Care and Traditional Medicine in China, 1800–1982*, edited by Hillier and Jewell, 3–17. London: Routledge & Kegan Paul, 1983.

Johnson, David, Andrew Nathan, and Evelyn S. Rawski. *Popular Culture in Late Imperial China.* Berkeley: University of California Press, 1985.

Johnstone, William Crane. *The Shanghai Problem.* Stanford: Stanford University Press, 1937. Reprinted Connecticut: Hyperion Press, 1973.

King, F.H.H., and Prescott Clarke, eds. *A Research Guide to China-Coast Newspapers 1822–1911.* Cambridge, Mass.: East Asian Research Center, Harvard University, 1965.

Kiple, Kenneth F., ed. *The Cambridge World History of Human Disease.* Cambridge: Cambridge University Press, 1993.

Kotenev, A. M. *Shanghai: Its Mixed Court and Council.* Shanghai North China Daily News & Herald Limited, 1925. Reprinted Taipei: Ch'eng-wen Publishing, 1968.

Kuhn, Philip A. *Soulstealers: The Chinese Sorcery Scare of 1768.* Cambridge, Mass.: Harvard University Press, 1990.

Lamley, Harry J. "The 1895 Taiwan Republic: A Significant Episode in Modern Chinese History." *Journal of Asian Studies*, vol. 27, no. 4 (1968): 739–62.

Langbein, John H. *Torture and the Law of Proof*. Chicago: University of Chicago Press, 1976.

Lanning, C., and S. Couling. *The History of Shanghai*. Shanghai: Kelly and Walsh Limited, 1921.

Lee, Leo Ou-fan. Shanghai Modern: *The Flowering of a New Urban Culture in China, 1930–1945*. Cambridge, Mass.: Harvard University Press, 1999.

Leung, Angela Ki-che. "Organized Medicine in Ming-Qing China: State and Private Medical Institutions in the Lower Yangtze Region." *Late Imperial China*, vol. 8, no. 1 (June 1987): 134–66.

———. "Diseases of the Premodern Period in China." In *Cambridge World History of Human Disease*, edited by Kenneth F. Kiple, 354–62. Cambridge: Cambridge University Press, 1993.

Levy, Howard S. *Chinese Footbinding: The History of a Curious Erotic Custom*. New York: Walton Rawls, 1966.

Little, Mrs. Archibald. *The Land of the Blue Gown*. New York: Brentano's, 1902.

Liu Ts'un-yan, ed. *Chinese Middlebrow Fiction: From the Ch'ing and the Early Republican Eras*. Hong Kong: Chinese University of Hong Kong Press, 1984.

Lu, Hanchao. *Beyond the Neon Lights: Everyday Shanghai in the Early Twentieth Century*. Berkeley: University of California Press, 1999.

Lu Xun. "A Glance at Shanghai Literature." In *Selected Works of Lu Hsun*, vol. 3, 114–28. Peking: Foreign Languages Press, 1959.

Lu Xun. *Dawn Blossoms Plucked at Dusk*. Peking: Foreign Languages Press, 1976.

Macauley, Melissa. *Social Power and Legal Culture: Litigation Masters in Late Imperial China*. Stanford: Stanford University Press, 1999.

Macpherson, Kerrie L. *A Wilderness of Marshes: The Origins of Public Health in Shanghai, 1843–1893*. Oxford: Oxford University Press, 1987

Mair, Victor H. *T'ang Transformation Texts*. Cambridge, Mass.: Harvard University Press, 1989.

Mao Tun. "Spring Silkworms." In *Spring Silkworms and Other Stories*, translated by Sidney Shapiro, 9–38. Peking, Foreign Languages Press, 1956.

Martin, Brian. "The Pact with the Devil: The Relations between the Green Gang and the French Concession Authority 1925–1935." In *Shanghai Sojourners*, by Frederic Wakeman and Wen-hsin Yeh, 266–304. Berkeley: University of California Press, 1992.

Mather, Richard B. trans. Shih-shuo Hsin-yü: A New Account of Tales of the World, by Liu I-ch'ing, with commentary by Liu Chün. Minneapolis: University of Minnesota Press, 1976.

McKnight, Brian E. *The Washing Away of Wrongs: Forensic Medicine in Thirteenth-Century China*. Ann Arbor: Center for Chinese Studies, University of Michigan, 1981.

Meskill, John. *Gentlemanly Interests and Wealth on the Yangtze Delta*. Ann Arbor: Association for Asian Studies, 1994.

Michie, Alexander. *The Englishman in China*. London: William Blackwood and Sons, 1900. Reprinted Taipei: Ch'eng-wen Publishing, 1966.

Miller, G. E. *Shanghai: The Paradise of Adventurers*. New York: Orsay Publishing House, 1937.

Montalto de Jesus. *Historic Shanghai*. Shanghai: The Shanghai Mercury Ltd, 1909.

Morrison, George Ernest. *An Australian in China*. London: Horace Cox, 1895. Reprinted Hong Kong: Oxford University Press, 1985.

Morse, Hosea Ballou. *The International Relations of the Chinese Empire*. London: Longmans, Green and Co, 1910–1918.

Murphey, Rhoads. *The Outsiders: The Western Experience in India and China*. Ann Arbor: The University of Michigan Press, 1977.

Murphey, Rhoads. *Shanghai, Key to Modern China*. Cambridge, Mass.: Harvard University Press, 1953.

Nakayama, Shigeru, and Nathan Sivin, eds. *Chinese Science: Explorations of an Ancient Tradition*. Cambridge, Mass.: MIT Press, 1973.

Naquin, Susan, and Evelyn S. Rawski. *Chinese Society in the Eighteenth Century*. New Haven: Yale University Press, 1987.

Naquin, Susan. "Transmission of White Lotus Sectarianism." In *Popular Culture in Late Imperial China*, edited by David Johnson et al., 255–91. Berkeley: University of California Press, 1985.

Needham, Joseph. *China and the Origins of Immunology*. Hong Kong: Centre of Asian Studies, University of Hong Kong, 1980.

Perry, Elizabeth J. "Strikes among Shanghai Silk-weavers." In *Shanghai Sojourners*, edited by Frederic Wakeman and Wen-hsin Yeh, 305–41. Berkeley: University of California Press, 1992.

Perry, Elizabeth. "Tax Revolt in Late Qing China: The Small Swords of Shanghai and Liu Depei of Shandong." *Late Imperial China*, vol. 6, no. 1 (June 1985): 83–111.

Peters, E. W. *Shanghai Policemen*. London: Rich and Cowan Ltd., 1937.

Pott, F. L. Hawks. *A Short History of Shanghai*. Hong Kong and Singapore: Kelly and Walsh, 1928.

Rankin, Mary Backus. *Elite Activism and Political Transformation in China: Zhejiang Province, 1895–1911*. Stanford: Stanford University Press, 1986.

Richard, T. *Forty Five Years in China*. London: T. Fisher Union Ltd, 1916.

Rowe, William T. *Hankow: Commerce and Society in a Chinese City, 1796–1889*. Stanford: Stanford University Press, 1984.

———. *Hankow: Conflict and Community in a Chinese City, 1796–1895*. Stanford: Stanford University Press, 1989.

Rudova, Maria. *Chinese Popular Prints*. Leningrad: Aurora Art Publishers, 1988.

Seidensticker, Edward. *Low City, High City—Tokyo from Edo to the Earthquake: How the Shogun's Ancient Capital Became a Great Modern City, 1867–1923*. San Francisco: Donald S. Ellis, 1983.

Skinner, G. William, ed. *The City in Late Imperial China.* Stanford: Stanford University Press, 1977.

Stephens, Thomas Blacket. *Order and Discipline in China: The Shanghai Mixed Court, 1911–1927.* Seattle: University of Washington Press, 1992

Teng, Ssu-yu, and John K. Fairbank. *China's Response to the West: A Documentary Survey 1839–1923.* Cambridge, Mass.: Harvard University Press, 1975.

Unschuld, Paul U. *Medical Ethics in Imperial China: A Study in Historical Anthropology.* Berkeley: University of California Press, 1979.

———. *Medicine in China: A History of Ideas.* Berkeley: University of California Press, 1985.

———. *Medicine in China: A History of Pharmaceutics.* Berkeley: University of California Press, 1986.

van Briessen, Fritz. *Shanghai-Bildzeitung 1884-1898, Eine Illustrierte aus dem China des ausgehenden 19. Jahrhunderts.* Zürich: Atlantis Verlag AG, 1977.

van Gulik, R. H. *Sexual Life in Ancient China.* Leiden, 1974.

Wagner, Rudolf G. "The Shanghai Illustrated Newspapers *Dianshizhai huabao* and *Feiyingge huabao*: an Introductory Survey." Paper presented at the Association for Asian Studies Annual Convention, April 1991.

———. "The Role of the Foreign Community in the Chinese Public Sphere." *China Quarterly* 142 (June 1995): 423–43.

———. "The *Shenbao* in Crisis: The International Environment and the Conflict Between Guo Songtao and the *Shenbao*." *Late Imperial China*, vol. 20, no. 1 (June 1999): 107–43.

Wakeman, Frederic. *Policing Shanghai, 1927–1937.* Berkeley: University of California Press, 1995.

Wakeman, Frederic, and Wen-hsin Yeh. *Shanghai Sojourners.* Berkeley: University of California Press, 1992.

Werner, E.T.C. *A Dictionary of Chinese Mythology.* Shanghai: Kelly and Walsh, 1932. Reprinted New York: Julian Press, 1961.

Ye Xiaoqing. "Shanghai Before Nationalism." *East Asian History*, no. 3 (June 1992): 33–52.

———. "Unacceptable marriage and the Qing Code: the Case of Yang Yuelou." *Journal of the Oriental Society of Australia*, vol. 27–28 (1995–1996): 195–212.

———. "Commercialisation and Prostitution in Nineteenth Century Shanghai." In *Dress, Sex and Text in Chinese Culture*, edited by Antonia Finnane and Anne McLaren, 37–57. Melbourne: Monash Asia Institute, 1999.

———. "Regulating the Medical Profession in China: Health Policies of the Nationalist Government," *Pacific Journal of Oriental Medicine*, no. 18 (June 2001): 68–76.

INDEX

aphrodisiacs, selling of, 96, 97–98
auctions, 208, 210
autopsies, 1, 135–36. *See also* human body
Bao Tianxiao, 11, 35n32, 162, 224n119

baojia (mutual responsibility) system, 145–46, 181n141, 216
barbarian quarter (*yichang*), 120
beauty contests, 15
beef, eating of, 1, 61, 205, 217, 218–20, 224n119
bicycle races, 22, 69. *See also* three-man bicycle team
billiard rooms, 57
blackmail. *See* "twig-breakers"
boat racing, 66–67
Boxer Rebellion, 119
Buddha shops, 158, 207–8

Cai Erkang, 5, 9, 14
Cao Xiang, 43–44, 106n4
Cen Chunhua, 142
Chen Zhuping, 77, 78, 147
Chinese authorities, 117; *Dianshizhai* differs from, 2; modern roads controlled by, 47; joint investigation with the Mixed Court, 88; jurisdiction of, 98; orders issued by, 1, 161; representation in the Mixed Court, 92; warrants issued by, 104
Chinese city, 117, 139, 159; and "drinking conciliatory tea," 151; lifestyles in, 56–57; midwives in, 139; residents of, 205; and running water, 52; and Small Swords Uprising, 117; streets, 46–47, 93
Chinese medicine, 140, 141, 143–45
Chinese police, 93, 98, 100–6, 174, 199; afraid of *liumang*, 174; criminal backgrounds of, 116n374; in the French Concession, 88; and maintenance of public order, 199; as moral guardians, 104–6; notoriety of, 99–102; public anger towards, 103. *See also* detectives
Chinese yamen 86–90, 92, 93, 94, 96
cholera, 48, 53. *See also* epidemics, running water
churches, 117, 118, 119, 208
cigarettes, 129, 130, 131, 166
circus, 55, 71, 78, 80
clocks, 72–74, 75. *See also* watches
compradors, 33n1, 117, 128, 130, 178n62
courtesans (*changsan tangzi*): in public conveyances, 59, 158; and beauty contests, 15; *changsan* brothel, 175; hired as companions, 58, 130; and literati complaints, 19; "talented courtesans," 16, 18
cricket, 67, 68

dandies (*huahuagongzi*): attitudes of, 19; fashions of, 57, 59, 130; making love to a courtesan, 158; stealing money to pay brothel debts, 169
detectives, 99–100; cases investigated by, 158; as moral guardians, 104–6; patrolling and making arrests, 121, 170; public anger towards, 103; on trial, 101. *See also* Chinese police
Dianshizhai Pictorial: attitudes toward, 8; as a commercial enterprise, 28; contributing artists, 12–13; distribution, 9–10; editorial policy of, 6, 25, 26; nature of, 20–33; original sketches of, 36n66; readership, 11; during the Sino-French War, 5–6; as source for social history, 1–2
Dianshzhai Printing Company, 4, 5, 12
dispute resolution, 147–48, 150, 153;"drinking conciliatory tea" (*chi jiang cha*), 151–52
Diyilou Teahouse, 18, 19, 50, 55, 57, 171

electricity, 54–56, 69
Empress Dowager, 30, 75, 123, 125, 185n249
epidemics, 48. *See also* cholera, running water

fashion, 57, 130, 131, 162, 169, 176
Feiyingge Pictorial, 12
Feng Zicai, 29
Festival of the Hungry Ghosts, 2, 190–92, 194, 200, 202
Fiftieth Anniversary of the Accession of Queen Victoria, 49–50, 54–55, 69
Fiftieth Anniversary of the Founding of the Foreign Settlement (Jubilee celebration), 68–70, 123–24
filial piety: and daughter of *Shenbao* editor, 26–27; unfilial sons punished, 89, 94–95; imperial edicts on, 126; self-mutilation and, 194
fire brigade, 49, 69, 72, 123. *See also* running water
"flower and opium dens" (*huayanjian*), 82, 172
footbinding, 155–56, 225. *See also* Natural Foot Society
Forbidden City, 51
Fu Genxin (Fu Jie), 12, 174
Fuzhou Road: entertainment and night life along, 57–59; as major Shanghai attraction, 224n119; Western-style restaurants on, 60–61; sing-song

halls on, 56, 141; and street lighting, 54; 166; teahouses on, 117, 171

gambling: in brothels, 175; —dens, 90; men guilty of, 102; prohibitions against, 203; women take up, 148, 175
gaslight (*dihuo*), 53, 69
Ge Yuanxu: as author of guidebook, 100; on *baojia* system, 145; on resolution of disputes, 150; on Shanghai drinking water, 48; on Western hospitals and medicine 133, 140
gentry: banquets arranged by, 64, 136; lack of power in settlements, 106; leading members of, 52; role in religious ceremonies, 190–91; resolution of disputes, 151; role in maintaining customs, 213–16; wives of, 165
God of Gambling, 203. *See also* gambling
God of Wealth, 208, 209–10, 222n78
Gong Xiaogong (Gong Cheng, Gong Banlun), 14, 16, 18
gongsuo, 118, 121, 122, 145. *See also* guilds, native-place associations, *huiguan*
Guan Jiongzhi, 152
Guangxu emperor, 30, 32, 185n249
guilds: carpenters, 125; and celebrations, 69, 123; functions of, 145–47; leaders of, 123; Ningbo incident, 118; as organizers of religious activities, 188, 192, 197, 201, 203; and riots, 118; and theatrical performances, 72. *See also gongsuo*, *huiguan*, native-place associations

Han Ziyun (Huayeliannong), 18, 225
He Yuanjun (He Mingfu), 12
hollow grandees (*kongxin dalaoguan*), 166–67
Hongmiao (Temple of the Protector of the Peace), 204, 205
hoodlums (*liumang*), 82, 154, 165, 170, 172–74
horse racing, 65–67, 69, 130, 132
hospitals, Western, 1, 2. *See also* Renji, Tongren
Hua Xiangyun, 16–18
Huang Chengyi, 48–49
Huang Shiquan, 15, 90
Hu Bao, 6, 216
huiguan, 145, 146, 200. *See also* guilds
human body, 1, 22, 132, 135, 141. *See also* autopsies
Hundred Days Reform, 32, 34n16
hygiene: basic principles of, 45; concept of, 1, 52, 132; and drinking water in Shanghai, 48–49; regulations, 46, 90. *See also* sanitary regulations, running water, public health

immigrants, 76–85, 120, 145, 165, 181n138, 198, 205

Jiang Jianren, 39n114

Jiangbei people: boat dwellers, 81, 197; and "lettered paper," 172; a madman, 120; monkey trainer, 78; prostitutes, 82; as refugees, 77, 94; sorcerer, 211–12
Jiang Zhixiang, 4
Jin Chanxiang (Jin Gui), 12
Jing'an Temple, 53, 158, 204
Jing Yuanshan, 185n249

Kapsin Coup, 10
Kidnapping, 84, 127, 167–68
"kitten plays" (*mao'erxi*), 63. *See also* Peking opera

lawyers, 85, 90, 91, 149, 150, 151. *See also* "litigation trickster"
Li Boyuan: as author, 219; dispute over his estate, 152; as Shanghai literatus, 14–16
Li Guangdan, 49
Li Hongzhang, 5, 22, 29, 30, 41n190, 45, 64, 141
Li Pingshu, 13–14, 52
Li Shanlan, 14, 15, 225
Lin Daiyu, 18, 104
literati: ambivalence of, 18; associated with the *Shenbao* and the *Dianshizhai*, 9, 12, 37n66, 225; attitude towards Chinese officials, 29; disappearing privileges of, 164; as educated Confucians, 26; national consciousness of, 131; new careers of, 13–14, 20; open to "new learning," 2; on popular religious practices, 194, 195, 196; Public Garden and, 126; on running water, 49; self-indulgence and self-destruction, 14–16; social circles of, 225; views on medicine, 134, 143
"litigation trickster" (*songshi, songgun*), 149–51, 182n162. *See also* lawyers
Little, Mrs. Archibald, 155. *See also* Natural Foot Society
Liu Ruifen, 200
Liu Yongfu, 5, 8, 31, 42n1, 99
Lu Yuanding, 135–36

Ma Ziming, 12, 103
maisons de rendezvous (*taiji*), 81, 86, 161, 172
Major, Ernest: aims of, 1, 11; and book-theft scandal, 5; Chinese image of, 9–10; editorial policy of, 2, 6, 8, 20, 25–26, 28–29; establishment of Dianshizhai Printing Company, 4–5; knowledge of Chinese, 9, 117; influence on artistic style, 24; reprinting of the *Tushu jicheng*, 34n10; obituary of, 35n47; and Wu Youru, 13
"middle brow" taste, 11
medicine, Western, 132, 134, 141–143. *See also* Chinese medicine
missionaries, 69, 85, 117, 119, 127, 133, 185n249
Mixed Court: abolition of severe torture, 86–88; cases referred to, 82, 147; cases resolved at, 149, 153; and conflicting views on autopsies, 135; dealing with Chinese police, 100, 102;

establishment of, 85, 98; and hard labor, 44; as "New Yamen," 93; protection offered by, 226. *See also* New Yamen, *Shenbao*

Municipal Council: and anti-tax riots, 118–19; ban on "wandering prostitutes," 59; dealing with Chinese police, 100; hygiene regulations, 46; petition to, 123; records of, 1, 173; street lighting, 53–54, 56; traffic regulations, 44. *See also* settlement authorities

Muslims, 77–78

Nanjing Road, 49–50, 54, 56, 57, 69

nationalism: lack of in early Shanghai, 118; and modern nationalism, 131; and "No Chinese or Dogs," 123–26; in twentieth-century Shanghai, 226

native-place associations, 197, 200. *See also* guilds, *huiguan*, *gongsuo*

Natural Foot Society, 155–56. *See also* footbinding

New Learning, 2, 20, 25

New Yamen, 86, 90–93, 115n350. *See also* Mixed Court

"Nightless City," 1, 50, 53, 54, 56, 57

"No Chinese or Dogs," 123–26. *See also* Public Garden

Norwegian explorers, 22

official seats (*guanzuo*), 71

opium dens: Cantonese and, 78, 81; gas lighting in, 53; illegal hostesses, 86, 87; as major Shanghai attractions, 57–58; women in, 153, 154. *See also* "flower and opium dens"

Ouyang Juyuan (Xiqiusheng), 16, 152, 183n183, 187n325

paper hunting, 67

Pei Dazhong, 89, 93, 94

Peking opera: actors, 29, 104, 105, 152, 160; characters in, 200; female audiences of, 207; "indecent operas," 60, 88; performed by prostitutes, 63; performed for Li Hongzhang, 64; *Visiting Shanghai in a Dream*, 75–76. *See also* "kitten plays," theatrical performances

Pidgin English, 128

prostitutes, 45; and bound feet, 155; as companions, 57, 65, 126; escaping hometown, 82, 83; Japanese, 159; participation in religious activities, 197, 205, 206; in Peking opera, 63; role in breaking down traditional hierarchies, 162–165; transvestites, 105; Western, 60, 117; and Western customers, 140. *See also* "wandering prostitutes," "wild chickens"

Public Garden, 63, 123–26. *See also* "No Chinese or Dogs"

public health, 1, 45, 48. *See also* hygiene

Qian Xinbo, 4, 9, 14, 15, 18, 33n2, 225

Refuge for the Homeless, 90, 114n344

regulation on dogs, 102

"releasing a white pigeon" (*fang bai ge*), 170, 171, 186n288. *See also* swindlers

Renji Hospital, 88, 132, 133

Republic of Taiwan, 30, 31–32, 42n201. *See also* Sino-Japanese War

restaurants, Chinese, 208; Western, 1, 57, 130, Haitianchun, 55, 61; Wanjiachun, 56; Yijiachun, 61; Yipinxiang, 56, 60–61, 62; and dispute resolution, 152

"reverence for lettered paper," 1, 172, 205, 213–16

roller coaster, 71–72

running water, 1, 47–49, 51–52. *See also* hygiene

sanitary regulations, 45–46. *See also* hygiene

self multilation, 27, 194. *See also* human body

"selling a savage's head" (*mai yeren tou*), 171. *See also* swindlers

settlement authorities: conflicts with Chinese officials, 85, 92; concerns for public order, 189, 192; hygiene regulations of, 46; initial attitude towards Chinese migrants, 117; lack of interest in moral and religious issues, 90, 188; orders issued by, 1; use of Chinese convicts in construction projects, 43–44. *See also* Municipal Council

Shanghai Girls School, 165, 185n249

Shanghai Polytechnic Institute, 55, 114n343

Shanghai Xinbao, 4, 33n4

Shenbao, 1; and advertisements for *Dianshizhai*, 5; as commercial enterprise, 28–29; and editorial on *Dianshizhai*, 11; exhortations on "lettered paper," 216; first issue of, 4; and Hundred Days Reform, 32–33; literati associated with, 14; "News from the Mixed Court," 104; on Sino-French War, 6, 9

Sikh policemen, 72, 85, 98, 99, 104, 202

Siming Gongsuo Riots (Ningbo Guild Incident), 118, 121–22, 145. *See also gongsuo* and *huiguan*

sing-song halls, 56, 57, 60, 166, 167

Sino-French War (1884–1885), 5, 6–7, 9, 173

Sino-Japanese War (1894–1895), 28, 30, 84. *See also* Republic of Taiwan

Small Sword Society, 76, 93, 117, 118, 181n138

smallpox, 141–43, 225

stealing a bride by force (*qiangqin*), 127

stone frame gates (*shikumen*), 146

Subei people. *See* Jiangbei people

sunglasses, 59, 130, 131, 166, 169

Sun Juxian, 152

Sun Yusheng, 14

surgery, 1, 133–134, 136–39, 140, 141

swindlers, 186n288; disguised as monk, 167; foreign, 85, 170, 171; in official records, 172; recorded in *Dianshizhai*, 86, 169. *See also* "releasing a white pigeon," "selling a savage's head," "twig-breakers"

Taiping Rebellion, 13, 76, 85
Tang Jingsong, 30–32
Tang Jinxing, 124
teahouses: "Crystal Palace," 57–58; and "drinking conciliatory tea," 152; illustrations of, 99, 101, 129; lighting in, 53, 55; as major attractions of Shanghai, 224n119; as meeting places, 147; new style, 1, 208; performances in, 117. *See also* Diyilou Teahouse
telegraph, 69, 75
telephone, 55, 69, 75, 119
Temple of the City God: festivals associated with, 72; magistrate offering sacrifices in, 188, 189; official ceremonies in, 190, 191; popularity of, 204; and praying for rain, 193; and processions, 192; and Yuyuan Garden, 162
Temple of Tianhou (Queen of Heaven), 131–32, 188, 198–201, 221n42
"Ten *li* of foreign territory," 1, 3n1, 75, 120, 172, 176
The Bund: celebrations along, 49, 50, 54, 68, 69; public clock on, 73, 74; riot at, 119; street lighting along, 56
theaters: Dangui Theater, 104, 159, 160; gas lamps in, 53; size of, 208; as popular places, 55, 57, 130. *See also* Peking opera
theatrical performances: "indecent operas," 225; as occasions for illicit meetings, 116n386, 159–60; organized by guilds, 72, 197–98; punctuality for, 73; women attending, 206–7. *See also* Peking opera
three-man bicycling team, 74
Tian Zilin (Tian Ying), 12
tiger stove (*laohu zao*), 49
Tongren Hospital, 132–33, 136, 137, 138
torture, 86–90
traffic regulations, 44, 45
transvestities, 104, 105
Tushanwan Printing Company, 4
"Visiting Shanghai in a Dream" (*Mengyou Shanghai*), 75–76
"twig-breakers" (*chaishao*), 170, 172. *See also* swindlers

vagrants, 48, 166

"wandering prostitutes" (*liuji*), 58, 59, 159, 160. *See also* prostitutes
Wang Tao: association with Major, 9; association with courtesans, 15–18; as author, 25; contributions to the *Dianshizhai*, 30; disapproval of "litigation tricksters," 149; in Hong Kong, 4, 35n49; lack of traditional privileges, 164; Major's praise for, 26; and Qian Xinbo, 33n2; praise for Western hospitals, 133; remarks on clothes as symbols of class, 161; views on eating beef, 218; views on Western medicine, 140; social circle of, 225; on Tianhou's birthday, 199

watches, 73, 98, 99, 169. *See also* clocks
welcoming-the-spirit ceremonies, 192–93, 196
Western (musical) bands, 131–32, 196
Western-style tailors (*hong bang*), 130, 179n69. *See also* Zhan Wu
Wheelbarrow Puller's Anti-Tax Riot, 118–119
"wild chickens" (*yeji*), 60. *See also* prostitutes
women workers, 78–79, 127, 152, 153, 173, 174, 206
World's Fair in Paris (1890), 22
Wu Jianren, 11, 163, 164
Wu Youru: artistic style of, 40n152; association with Major, 9, 29, 35n45; criticized for new style, 24–25; family background of, 37n73; influence of, 40n154; misinformation about, 40n165; as principal artist for the *Dianshizhai*, 5–6, 12–13

Xinzha Temple (Temple of the Four Dragons), 197–198, 221n38

Yang Yuelou, 29, 41n186
Yangshupu Garden, 53, 63. *See also* Public Garden
Yao Gonghe, 13, 83, 120
Yao Zirang, 52
Ye Tingjuan, 29, 193
Yinghuan Pictorial, 5, 11
Yuan Xiangpu, 14

Zeng Guofan, 30
Zeng Guoquan, 12, 13, 29
Zhan Wu ("The Giant of Anhui"), 130, 131, 179n76
Zhang Chunfan, 14
Zhang Zhidong, 29–30
Zhang Zhiying (Zhang Qi), 6, 12, 13
Zhangyuan Garden, 61, 63, 64, 165, 226
Zhao Xiaolian, 104, 116n385, 160
Zhou Muqiao (Zhou Quan), 12, 13
Zhu Ruxian, 12
zoos, 61, 62
Zuo Zongtang, 14, 29, 30